HUNGARIAN
CLASSICAL BALLADS
AND THEIR FOLKLORE

HUNGARIAN CLASSICAL BALLADS
AND THEIR FOLKLORE

NINON A.M.LEADER, Ph.D.

Fellow, Clare Hall, Cambridge
formerly Lecturer in Hungarian
Department of Slavic Languages and Literature
University of California, Berkeley

CAMBRIDGE

AT THE UNIVERSITY PRESS

1967

Published by the Syndics of the Cambridge University Press
Bentley House, 200 Euston Road, London, N.W. 1
American Branch: 32 East 57th Street, New York, N.Y, 10022

Library of Congress Catalogue Card Number: 67–11526

86386

Printed in Great Britain
at the University Printing House, Cambridge
(Brooke Crutchley, University Printer)

To HELENA M. SHIRE

PREFACE

This work has a twofold aim. (1) It seeks to provide for the non-Hungarian specialist an accurate analytical description of the main Hungarian classical ballads in their several versions. In order to clarify the issues in this connection I have given a general account of Hungarian ballad scholarship, of the geographical distribution of these ballads, and some particulars of the historical circumstances of their formation. (2) It seeks to examine the characteristics, recurrent themes, motifs, underlying folk-beliefs of Hungarian classical ballads and to relate them to their international parallels, with particular reference to English and Scottish balladry.

Although the individual studies by Hungarian folklorists such as S. Solymossy, Gy. Ortutay and L. Vargyas have justly earned a reputation for their authors, the Hungarian ballad material itself has remained, on the whole, *terra incognita* in Western studies. In motif-indexes and general accounts of international balladry, Hungarian material is barely mentioned, the references are only too often inaccurate, drawn from arid second-hand sources and are in most cases confined to single versions. I therefore hope that this work will help somewhat to fill the gap which exists in international ballad scholarship in so far as Hungarian material is concerned. I also hope that it will sharpen an awareness of some of the special characteristics of both the Hungarian and the English-Scottish material.

I want in a conspicuous place to thank Mrs Helena M. Shire, without whose advice and help this book could not have come into being, and Dr R. R. Bolgár, who most kindly advised me over difficulties of translation and presentation. So many of their comments and suggestions are incorporated in this work that I have made no attempt to indicate them by special reference. I should like to thank Professor D. Sinor, who offered me free access to his excellent library and drew my attention to several interesting articles, particularly in the ethnographical field, my friend István Kemény, who enlightened me on several points and Professor Linda Dégh for her patience in reading my

MS and for her many excellent comments. Chapter 2 relies on D. Pais's rediscovery and interpretation of the data concerning the Hungarian bards ('Reg' and 'Árpád és Anjou-kori mulattatóink', *A Magyar Nyelvtudományi Társaság Kiadványai*, nos. 75, 81, Budapest, 1948, 1953).

I should also like to express my heartfelt gratitude to Dr and Mrs H. Youngman, whose great generosity made possible my first three years of study at Cambridge University, to my tutor Miss Alison Duke, for her constant kindness and helpfulness, and to the Council of Girton College, Cambridge, for a travelling grant to Helsinki which enabled me to include in my book ballad material which was inaccessible in England. I am also indebted to the Department of Slavic Languages and Literatures at the University of California for its kind hospitality, and to its Chairman, Professor F. J. Whitfield, whose interest and stimulating personality I enjoyed during the last years of completing this book. Finally, I should like to express my appreciation to Mrs Grace O'Connell for her efficient help in preparing the final form of the manuscript.

N.A.M.L.

CONTENTS

Preface *page* vii

Map of Hungary xii

1 A General Introduction to Hungarian Balladry 1

2 The Bards 8

THE DISCUSSION OF THE MAIN HUNGARIAN
CLASSICAL BALLADS—PART I

3 Magic Ballads
   'Clement Mason' 19
   'The Miraculous Dead' 44

4 Christian Legendary Ballads
   'The Fair Maid Julia' 55
   'The Three Orphans' 82

5 Ballads of Love and Intrigue
   'The Two Royal Children' 98
   'Anna Molnár' 107
   'Kate Kádár' 125
   'The Daughter of the Cruel King' 142
   'The Maid who was Sold' 148
   'The Dishonoured Maiden' 179
   'Anna Betlen' 223
   'Barcsai' 230
   'Balthasar Bátori' 239

★

THE DISCUSSION OF THE MAIN HUNGARIAN
CLASSICAL BALLADS—PART II

6 Ballads of Love and Intrigue (*cont.*)
   'The Asp' 251

'The Maid and her Goose'   *page* 255
'Szilágyi and Hagymási'   255
'The Maid who was Cursed'   258
'Thomas Magyarósi'   263
'The Girl who was Ravished by the Turks' (I)   266
'The Girl who was Ravished by the Turks' (II)   270
'The Great Mountain Robber'   272
'Little Sophie Kálnoki'   281
'Fair Anna Bíró'   284
'Ladislav Fehér'   288
'The Prince and the Princess'   291
'The Girl who was Danced to Death'   292

7   Ballads of Family Conflict

'Ilona Budai' *or* 'The Cruel Mother'   296
'Beautiful Kate Bán'   300
'Lady Albert Nagy-Bihal' *or* 'The Mother of the Rich
    Woman'   303
'The Brother and the Sister who had been Imprisoned by
    the Turks'   307
'Merika' *or* 'The Daughter-in-law who was Burned to
    Death'   313
'Poisoned John'   317

★

8   Considerations by Way of Conclusion   319

Appendix I

(*a*) Magic ballads
    'The Dead Bridegroom'   326

(*b*) Christian legendary ballads
    'The Virgin Mary Sets Out'   328
    'When the Virgin Mary was Walking'   330
    'Good Evening, you Rich Innkeeper'   331

(c) Ballads of love and intrigue

    'The Maid Under the Apple-Tree'   *page* 332
    'The Turtle-dove that has Lost its Mate'   333
    Supplements to 'The Maid who was Sold'   336
    1 'Bey, Pasha of Buda'   336
    2 'Anna'   337
    3 'Gabriel Bátori and Clara Bátori'   338

    Supplements to 'Fair Anna Bíró' (Robbery and Murder)   340
    1 'The Three Robber-lads'   340
    2 'The Bonny White Shepherd'   341

(d) Ballads of family conflict

    'The Little Maple-Tree'   342

(e) Two ballads from Moldavia

    'The Soldier-girl'   344
    'Young King Matthias'   346

Appendix II   348

Selected Bibliography   350

Motif Index   353

Index of Ballad Titles   363

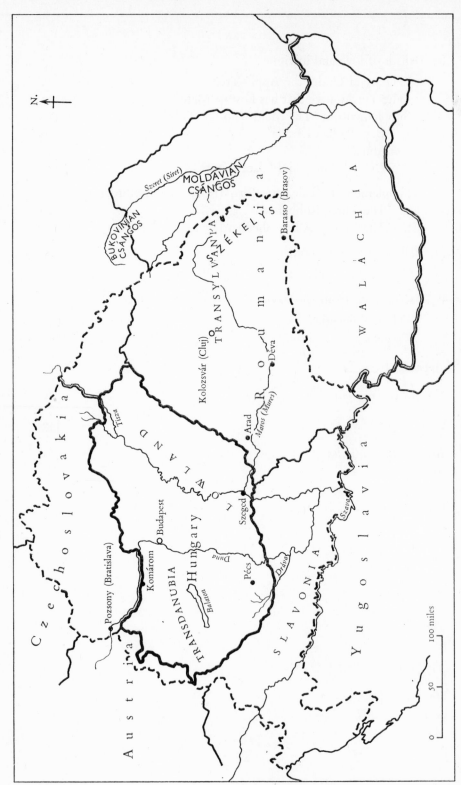

N

MOLDAVIAN
CSÁNGOS

Szeret (Siret)

BUKOVINIAN
CSÁNGOS

T R A N S Y L V A N I A

S Z É K E L Y S

Barasso (Brasov)

R o u m a n y a

Kolozsvár (Cluj)

W A L A C H I A

Deva

Czechoslovakia

Tisza

L O W L A N D

Arad

Maros (Mures)

Szeged

Pozsony (Bratislava)

Komarom

Budapest

Duna

Pécs

Dráva

Szava

Austria

TRANSDANUBIA

Hungary

Balaton

S L A V O N I A

Y u g o s l a v i a

0   50   100 miles

HUNGARY. THE OLD BOUNDARY IS SHOWN BY THE BROKEN LINE.

1

A GENERAL INTRODUCTION TO
HUNGARIAN BALLADRY

The Hungarian ballads were collected much later than their Western counterparts. Hungary had no Vedel, no Percy, and no Ritson. Struggling with the after-effects of the Turkish occupation on the one hand and with Habsburg oppression on the other, she had no time for the eighteenth-century cult of the naïve element in poetry or (until a relatively late date) for the Romantic glorification of the folk as artist.

The first signs of an interest in folksong were shown at the very end of the eighteenth century by a few enthusiasts, but it was not until the middle of the nineteenth century that public interest was properly aroused. This was the time of that upsurge of patriotic feeling which prepared and accompanied the war of Independence (1848–9).

The first collection of folksongs and tales was published in 1846–8 by John Erdélyi, *Népdalok és mondák* (Folksongs and Tales). The material in it was collected during the years following 1830, as a result of an appeal by the Hungarian Academy. But the work contained all sorts of fabrications written by village notaries, priests, students and other amateur poets, and Erdélyi had edited the various pieces arbitrarily, changed the order of the stanzas in certain pieces and even put together stanzas which were collected in different parts of Hungary. Nevertheless, he did include several genuine ballads, mostly those which we shall describe as ballads of the new style, and some which may date back to earlier times, although their style and tune suggest an eighteenth-century origin (examples: 'Ladislav Fehér'; 'The Girl who was Danced to Death').

Fifteen years later there appeared a more workmanlike collection. This was *Vadrózsák* (Wild Roses) (1863), produced by the Unitarian pastor John Kriza. His material had been assembled for more than twenty years before he found the money to publish it, and the fact that Erdélyi had preceded him in publication was the great tragedy of his life. He, and the friends who helped him to gather his texts, had worked in Transylvania, and *Vadrózsák* contains most of the classical ballads ('Clement Mason', 'Anna Molnár', 'Barcsai' version B, 'Ilona Budai', and 'The Fair Maid Julia', to mention only the most outstanding). Kriza moreover was careful to record his pieces just as he received them, and although some of his collectors did not apply an equally high standard but inserted lines and rhymes here and there, on the whole the texts he furnished were of great value. His volume was widely admired and evoked a lively feeling of patriotic pride.

It also caused a considerable stir in literary and academic circles, since it provoked an immediate attack by the Rumanian Julian Grozescu. At this early stage in the development of ballad scholarship, the wildest claims could be made to appear plausible, and Grozescu accused Kriza of having borrowed his material from Rumanian sources, stating that 'Anna Molnár', 'Clement Mason', and 'Barcsai' were mere fabrications translated from the Rumanian. His arguments were based on the fact that these ballads have indeed their Rumanian counterparts, but he went beyond his evidence. Kriza and the Hungarians felt that their honour had been attacked, and the exchanges between the two parties became increasingly acrimonious.

The poet John Arany, who translated several Scottish ballads (including 'Sir Patrick Spens') and whose own modern ballads are among the treasures of Hungarian literature, nicknamed this controversy between Grozescu and Kriza, or rather between Grozescu and the Hungarian nation, the Vadrózsa (or Wild Rose) Trial, and it has been referred to by that title ever since. In the end, the controversy, the conduct of which did not reflect much credit on the manners of either side, had a beneficial result, since it was followed by a nation-wide search for classical ballads in order to prove that they existed in more than one version. This resulted in the recording of much new material, and eventually the points at issue were settled many years later by S. Solymossy, who showed in his extensive analysis of 'Anna Molnár' and 'Clement Mason' that they could not have been borrowed from Rumanian sources.[1]

In the meantime, Kriza planned a second volume, but died before he could publish it, and the next important advance came with the publication of the *Magyar Népköltési Gyüjtemény* which the Kisfaludy Society began in 1872, and which made use of Kriza's new material. This great

---

[1] See the discussion on 'Clement Mason'. In the case of 'Anna Molnár', Solymossy proved merely that it reached Hungary 'from the West'. This is the Hungarian representative of the Halewijn ballad, and Solymossy had contented himself with pointing out that the multiple murder motif did not occur in the Rumanian versions. The *Vadrózsa* controversy also prompted Lajos Abafi to examine the international connections of Hungarian ballads, but unfortunately his work has remained unpublished.

collection of Hungarian folk poetry and folk tales was to run to fourteen volumes, the last of which did not appear until 1924. The first, however, published in 1872, contained new versions of the ballads which had appeared in *Vadrózsák*. The second presented a collection of texts preserved in County Csongrád together with a number of new-style ballads, while the third (1882) contained Kriza's unpublished material, further collections by E. Benedek and J. Sebesi and the folk tales of B. Orbán. Unfortunately, however, some of these pieces were of questionable authenticity, a few by Sebesi were downright fabrications.

A great number of such fabrications were composed during the 1870s and 1880s, and it is a relief to find such an excellent collector as Lajos Kálmány giving us trustworthy, authentic ballad material. His volumes (*Koszorúk az Alföld vadvirágaiból*, 'Garlands from the Wild Flowers of the Lowland', I–II, Arad, 1877–8; *Szeged Népe*, 'The People of Szeged', I–III, Arad, 1881–2, 1891) provide us with our first important evidence that the classical ballads were known outside of the Transylvanian region (a view widely held in Hungary as a result of the romantic theory that ballads are composed in mountainous areas only, such as Scotland and Transylvania. This is voiced also by A. Greguss, *A balladáról*, 'About Ballads', Budapest, 1863–4), and by the early edition of *Vadrózsák*.

A. Bartalus also deserves mention. He was the first to attempt to record the tunes as well as the texts of traditional pieces. He lacked, however, expert musical knowledge, and his seven-volume work (*Magyar Népdalok*, 'Hungarian Folk-songs', Budapest, 1873–96) is not reliable where the music is concerned.

By the beginning of the present century, ballads were being collected from all parts of Hungary. Here the pioneer was Béla Vikár, who toured the country using the phonograph for his recordings. Most of his collection has remained in manuscript, but in 1905 the material he recorded from County Somogy was published as the sixth volume of the *Magyar Népköltési Gyüjtemény*. With him we arrive at a period when merely to list the important collections would require several pages. Their names will be found in the Bibliography, and only the best known need perhaps be mentioned here. Zoltán Kodály and Béla Bartók started their tour of Hungary in 1905. L. Lajtha and L. Vargyas followed in their footsteps, and the latter has made a notable collection of ballad material together with tunes, though his recordings are for the most part still unpublished. More recently P. P. Domokos, B. Rajeczky as well as J. Jagmas and J. Faragó have collected Hungarian material from

Moldavia. P. Balla, G. Lükö, S. Veress, and Z. Kallós have also collected from the *Csángós*.

Gy. Ortutay and L. Vargyas have published the most significant articles concerning modern Hungarian ballad scholarship. Gy. Ortutay's recent studies deal with the history of folklore research in Hungary and with problems relating to narrative techniques in folk tales and traditional ballads. L. Vargyas has been investigating the French and Hungarian ballad connections and the traces of a possible Hungarian heroic epic tradition from the Conquest and pre-Conquest period in old style Hungarian ballads. The results of their latest investigations are available in English, French and German in *Acta Ethnographica*.

THE BALLAD MATERIAL

From these collections there emerges a ballad material in which we can distinguish two main groups: ballads of old style and ballads of new style.

(1) The ballads of old style are distinguished by the circumstance that most of them have their international counterpart. Most of their tunes belong to the old pentatonic group of Hungarian folksongs (cf. Bartók, *Das Ungarische Volkslied*, Berlin, 1925). They are astrophic, rhymeless, and the lines are irregular dodecasyllables, octosyllables (and sometimes, from the dodecasyllable: six-syllable lines). The oldest ones make frequent use of alliteration, parallelism, and the repetition of half-lines, and international ballad devices (formulae, incremental repetition, sharp questions-evasive answers) are employed in the narrative. Their metric and musical tradition can be traced back to the Ugric community in the pre-Christian era (see Z. Kodály, *Folk Music in Hungary*, London, Barrie and Rockliff, 1960).

(2) The ballads of new style. This group consists of material which we may divide roughly into three types:

(*a*) '*Betyár*-ballads.' This is the most important and valuable body of new-style ballads and the peculiar circumstances of their origin deserve attention. The *betyárs* were 'outlaws' of the Robin Hood type. There were usually peasant lads who did not want to join the Austro-Hungarian imperial army, or who had committed some crime, often only a minor crime, and so had to flee from the law. They robbed the rich, and although they did not really help the poor the people's sympathy was with them, the general attitude being one of a strong resentment against the 'authorities'. The *betyár* songs and ballads were

4

composed in the nineteenth century and recount the adventures of these peasant lads who became popular heroes. Often composed by the *betyárs* themselves, they are told in the first person. They relate the sad moment when the *betyár* is captured, tell stories of horse-stealing, contain laments in the prison, relate the sorrow of the *betyárs'* loves, or their drinking and merry-making.

The significance of these *betyár* songs lies not so much in their text as in the new style of the tunes which accompanied them. Bartók gives a detailed account of the characteristic features of these new-style songs. Such a large-scale renaissance as took place in Hungarian folk music and folk balladry in the middle of the nineteenth century is not, to my knowledge, found elsewhere in Europe. The new style spread rapidly over the whole of Hungary proper. It gradually displaced the old style and has remained popular up to the present time. (In Transylvania, however, the new style gained ground mostly in music.)

(*b*) The second type is inferior to the *betyár* songs: it contains horror stories, violent murders and tragedies related in the 'Bänkelsänger' style, with very little literary merit. Occasionally, however, we find among them pieces which were influenced by the stylistic devices of old-style ballads.

(*c*) The third type consists of ballads created in our own time, which relate local tragedies. These have some fine traits, but have not yet acquired the traditional ballad stamp, and it is questionable whether they ever will.

GEOGRAPHICAL DISTRIBUTION

Most of the classical ballads were recorded in Transylvania, among the *Székely* population. The *Székelys* are a Hungarian-speaking clan of uncertain origin who, probably because of their relative isolation, have preserved archaic traditions.

Some classical ballads were recorded also in Moldavia and Bukovina among the *Csángós* in the 1930s and more recently in the 1950s. The name *Csángó* serves to describe all the members of the Hungarian minority living in Moldavia and Bukovina. Some *Csángós* settled in Moldavia in the fifteenth–sixteenth century as Hussite refugees from Hungary proper, but most of them are *Székelys* who emigrated to these regions in the eighteenth century. The ballads recorded among the *Csángós* belong thus to the Transylvanian tradition representing most purely the old Ugric type meter and music.

5

The *Alföld* (Lowland) is the homeland of the new-style balladry, although some of the classical ballads have been preserved there in more complete versions than in Transylvania (examples: 'The Maid who was Sold'; 'The Dishonoured Maiden'). 'The Girl who was Ravished by a Turk I'; 'Beautiful Kate Bán', 'Ladislav Fehér', and 'The Girl who was Danced to Death' also come from the Lowland. Presumably there were many more classical ballads known in the Lowland at an earlier time, but the rate of loss was rapid. One must bear in mind that this region was almost completely depopulated during the Turkish occupation of Hungary, and so the normal continuity of oral transmission was irrevocably severed. To make matters worse, the early collectors worked on the Transylvanian material, and by the time interest shifted to the Lowland (i.e. by the late nineteenth century) many of the texts and tunes could no longer be recovered.

Some versions of the classical ballads were discovered in Transdanubia (in the western part of Hungary) and also here and there in other parts of the country, but the most important geographical units are the three regions we have mentioned before. We shall not, at this stage, go into further detail on the geographical distribution, since the discussion of every ballad will contain references to the regions in which the ballad was recorded.

SOME REMARKS CONCERNING THE
ORGANISATION OF BALLAD MATERIAL
IN THIS BOOK

We shall be dealing in this present work primarily with the older material.[1] This has been divided according to its subject-matter: magic ballads; Christian legendary ballads; ballads of love and intrigue, and ballads of family conflict. Thirteen ballads are discussed in part I (chapters 3, 4 and 5), according to the following system:

1. Introductory notes.
2. Translation of the main version.
3. Bibliography to the other versions.
4. Description of the ballad, taking all versions into account.
5. Discussion of the relation of the Hungarian ballad to international balladry.

---

[1] The new-style ballads, since they require somewhat different comparative treatment, will be discussed—it is hoped—in a future volume.

6. Discussion of motifs.
7. The relation of the ballad to the beliefs and superstitions current at the time it was composed.
8. The date of the ballad.
9. Special Hungarian characteristics of the ballad.

Ballads which are of less importance are simply accompanied by notes following the translation of the main version, and are discussed in part II (chapters 6 and 7). Sometimes when I have felt it necessary I have included the full translation of more than one version of a certain ballad to illustrate the extent of divergency between the different tellings. Included in part II are ballads (1) which are known to, and have been discussed by, Western scholars; (2) which may be considered as 'secondary' ballads, i.e. which seem to have taken their material from the confluence of different Hungarian ballads; (3) which seem to have preserved old traits but whose style and tune belong to the new ballads; and (4) ballads of family conflict, which appear in a separate chapter in part II. The two more important ballads which belong to this group, 'Lady Albert Nagy-Bihal' and 'Ilona Budai', have no close international parallels. Ballads which have been recorded in fragmentary versions or are embedded in folk tales are given in the Appendix. I have also found it advisable to include in the Appendix two ballads which were found only recently in Moldavia in one fragment and in a single version.

In discussing the ballads I have confined myself to the examination of published ballad text material. The disentanglement of the intricate and involved problems of the ballad tunes, their origin and interrelationship lies outside my competence and will be, I have no doubt, admirably dealt with in one of the announced forthcoming volumes of *A Magyar Népzene Tára*, edited by Z. Kodály *et al.*, which will have the ballad music as its exclusive subject-matter.

In translating the ballads I have tried to follow the original narrative as faithfully as possible and have therefore kept the tense changes of the Hungarian even though this sometimes creates an odd impression in English.

Owing to the nature of the material in the bibliography to the various ballad versions, I have not followed the usual practice of giving first reference to the earliest recorded versions. These are very difficult to obtain, some of them are almost inaccessible. I have therefore referred first to versions printed in the two most recent collections: Csanádi-Vargyas, *Röpülj*; and Ortutay, *Magyar Népköltészet*, II. I have painstakingly collated the original versions, i.e. the first published versions to the material published in the two above-mentioned works, in each case.

2

THE BARDS

This chapter is in the nature of an historical excursus whose purpose is to shed light on the composition of the old-style ballads; and it may help to explain why these ballads contain so many motifs which derive from the medieval and pre-medieval Hungarian culture. We shall be considering a body of evidence which suggests that there were professional minstrels and therefore traditional songs and tales recounted by these minstrels at a date earlier than the composition of the first ballads. This material is now lost, but if it existed, then the chances of it having formed the soil out of which the ballads grew are indeed considerable.

We have no texts written in Hungarian previous to the thirteenth century, but we have indirect evidence that a vernacular orally transmitted literature did exist at an earlier date. When The Anonymous or rather Master Peter—as recent research has identified him after long years of discussion—chief secretary to Béla III and later Provost of Esztergom, wrote his twelfth-century *Gesta Hungarorum*, the first work of Hungarian history whose text has been preserved in full, he announced that:

It would not be proper, but indeed quite unseemly, if the noble Hungarian nation were to learn the story of its past and its heroic deeds, like some dream, from the tales of peasants and the garrulous songs of minstrels. Let it rather now hear the truth about these matters in a manner worthy of its nobility from the sure testimony of documents and the clear interpretation of history.

If Master Peter is not deliberately misleading us, it follows that well-established legends about the national past were circulating in his day, and that there existed professional minstrels who were regarded as pre-eminently the guardians and transmittors of these legends. His statement plainly deserves investigation, and when we look into it we find a good deal of evidence that these *ioculatores* did exist and not only in the twelfth century. This evidence is admittedly fragmentary. The terms we find—*regös, igric, ioculator*—have not always the same meanings, and their relation to each other is not clear. But in spite of these uncertainties, we are left in no doubt that a class of professional minstrels did flourish in medieval Hungary, whose activities included singing and story telling.

8

First of all, we hear of the *regüs* or *regös*. He has been identified with the shamans or magician-priests of the pre-Christian era who became the target of persecution when the nation was officially christianised under S. Stephen I. Lays, known as *regös* songs were preserved among country people in Hungary until recent times, and have been recorded. They are spells, plainly medieval in origin, and they were chanted by men wearing masks reminiscent of the Sun-Stag of pagan legend. Some of them though magical in character include statements that the singer is a loyal servant of S. Stephen, which appear to have been intended as safeguards against ecclesiastical disapproval.[1]

Taken in themselves, the *regös* songs merely indicate the survival of a primitive magic tradition, but we have further a certain Regös who is a chamberlain of Andrew II (1219), and in a sixteenth-century deed the mutilated transcript of a grant made by Lajos I in 1346 which mentions a certain property called 'Regtelük' and says that the name describes the property of those who are bound to the service of royal table companions and are known in the vulgar tongue as *regüs*. The Latin phrase *combibatores regales condicionarii* does not lend itself to easy interpretation. *Condicionarius*, according to du Cange, is used initially of freedmen to whose freedom some condition of service was attached. It is possible therefore that the *regüs* were royal serfs liberated on condi-

---

[1] The *Regüs* question is very complicated. It is generally accepted that there were in the eleventh century: (*a*) *regüs* songs of the spell type; (*b*) historical songs celebrating the deeds of the Árpád kings; (*c*) (probably) historical songs celebrating the deeds of Hungarian pre-Christian heroes. It is also established that the Hun legends are taken from Germanic and other chronicles by the Hungarian chroniclers (Simon Kézai, *Gesta Hungarorum* (C 13), and Master Peter (C 12)).

The two extreme theories are:

(1) That the primitive Hungarians had no poetic tradition, the pagan *regüs* being priests (shamans), and that the custom of singing about heroes was taken over from the Slovene peoples in the Danube basin whom they conquered.

(2) That the primitive Hungarians had a strong poetic tradition probably similar in type to the Ostiaks whose heroic songs were collected by Reguly in C 19 (A. Reguly and S. Pápay, *Osztják Hősénekek*, Budapest, 1944), and to the heroic songs of the Turkic tribes with whom they formed coalitions for a considerable period before the conquest, the *regüs* being the transmitters of this tradition. That their heroic songs about more or less contemporary kings and also about the early Magyar heroes (Álmos, etc.) were naïve forms of the epic.

To my mind the main fact in support of (1) is that none of the Magyar legends go back before the conquest period, for the Hun legends have to be dismissed as external in origin anyway, while the main fact in support of (2) is that the other Finno-Ugrian peoples all have a marked poetic tradition—heroic in the case of the Ostiaks, shamanesque with the Finns, Voguls, Cheremiss. One could perhaps reconcile (1) and (2) by suggesting that the Magyars when they arrived in the Danube basin had a shamanesque poetic tradition and probably possessed heroic songs similar to the Ostjaks and to the Turkic tribes with whom they associated, that the Slavic influence promoted their singing about national heroes, and that the shamanesque songs were finally pushed out by Christian persecution. None of this is, however, very relevant to the present work which can rest quite happily on the fact that there was by C 12 certainly a poetic tradition of heroic songs and singers called *ioculatores*.

tion that they entertained the king. But the word might have been loosely employed to indicate that the *regüs* had to render this particular service for their lands being in all further respects the equals of other royal tenants. It is evident, however, that by the fourteenth century the word *regüs* was being used to denote an entertainer. But what was the entertainment they provided?

Light comes from a collection of texts which refer not to *regüs* but to *igrec*, a term which they render in Latin as *ioculator*. These texts, taken from legal documents, run from 1165 to 1329 and originate from the environs of modern Pozsony. They contain references to a vill Igrickarcha (Igrecfolva, Igrechfolva) described in one instance as Igrech, *villa ioculatorum* (1244). Persons connected with this place figure as ioculatores: 'Cheme ioculatori, de villa Igrechfolva, Thomas ioculator, de villa igrechfolva (1329).' A deed of 1253 gives a list of men from the vill Karcha who are *ioculatores* and whose names—Grimace, Glittering, Fat, Honey, Tart—are certainly appropriate to professional entertainers. Finally, in 1255, the king Béla IV (similarly to Andrew III in 1292) talks of *ioculatores nostri*, which suggests that the *igrec* had a status similar to the *regüs* who were *combibatores regales*, and that the names *igrec* and *regüs* may have been interchangeable.

In later (fourteenth- and fifteenth-century) documents from the same area, the references are no longer to *ioculatores* in general, but more specifically to pipers and actors. We hear also of *lantos* (flute-players) and *hegedüs* (violinists). By 1447 Igrickarcha has become Siposkarcha, *sipos* being the word for piper. One is tempted to assume that the *igrec* or *ioculatores* had perhaps been throughout their history musicians and dancers rather than minstrels, and this assumption finds support in their very name; for *igrec* is a Slavonic word. If the Magyars learned to call their entertainers by a foreign name, this could have been only because the entertainers themselves were foreign. But non-Magyar-speaking Slavs would naturally have relied on non-verbal means for amusing their audience. They would not have had the fluency or the access to the national legends which a minstrel would find indispensable.

However, the evidence of Master Peter points the other way. His *ioculatores* are certainly minstrels in the proper sense of the word and they are, we must remember, the contemporaries of the *igrec-ioculatores* of the earlier Pozsony documents. He refers to them on several occasions and always because, in spite of his advertised contempt for popular legend, he is compelled to use them as a source of information. In particular, he mentions them as the only ones to preserve the story about the early Magyar leader, Botond, staving in the gates of Constantinople. And the minstrels did not die out. The historian of Matthias Corvinus, the fifteenth-century Italian Humanist Marzio Galeotto, describes how minstrels used to sing in the king's court. They extolled the deeds of past and present heroes, used the vernacular and accompanied their songs on the harp. And one of Galeotto's colleagues, Antonio Bonfini, has left us in his *Res Hungaricae* a startling description of the feasting after the battle of Kenyérmező (the *Kossovo* of Serbo-Croatian heroic epics, 1479) which reveals how great a taste the Hungarians had for heroic songs. The victorious soldiers could not return to their camp since night was falling, and the rich food and drink that they had captured inspired them to celebrate their success by a grand feast. They laid tables among the piles of corpses; and when they had eaten and drunk they sang the praises of their leaders and chieftains in improvised songs. Finally, they began to dance, fully armed, to the sound of their own rhythmic shouting. And one of the leaders, Paul Kinizsi, when encouraged to join them, lifted a dead Turk from the ground in his teeth and leaping into the middle of the ring danced there for a long time with this macabre burden.

Thus, we have evidence of magic incantations and legends surviving from a pre-Christian period. Their transmission would seem to have been in part at least the work of minstrels who along with other entertainers formed a recognised professional class. The members of this class may have been not only minstrels, but dancers, musicians, and even acrobats as well in so far as their personal skill permitted. Or there may have been a distinction between those who composed and sang and those who made music or danced, a distinction expressed in the use of two words, *regüs* and *igrec*, but obliterated in the Latin *ioculator*.[1]

These entertainers were socially in an ambiguous position. They were persecuted by the Church. The reason for the persecution may have been the existence of a connection between the medieval minstrels and the shamans of the old pagan religion, or it may have been due to a general ascetic disapproval of worldly frivolity. Councils passed decrees against *ioculatores* and those who listened to their art. Priests were specifically warned as at the Synod of Buda (1279) to keep away from them. On the other hand, we have seen that they received royal support. We hear, for example, of Andrew sending a female *ioculator* to

---

[1] Pais, working on the legal documents which mention the *igrec*, has put forward the theory that the *igrec* were not only a recognised professional class, but also the members of a community living in special villages, and exercising their art by hereditary right.

accompany his daughter to keep her gay.[1] They sang at the royal court, in the castles of the nobles, but also at village festivities. Galeotto informs us that all classes, noble and peasant, enjoyed vernacular poetry and puts this down to the fact that the same form of the language was spoken by everybody, and that poetry was the storehouse of the ancient legends and traditions of the people. It was an important vehicle of popular education.

By the fifteenth century, however, and perhaps even earlier, another category of entertainers began to take its place alongside the traditional minstrels. The spread of Latin schools produced in Hungary as elsewhere the unemployed clerk or, to use a more romantic description, the wandering scholar. Poor men's sons whom charity had supported through grammar school or university, but who lacked the influence to procure a living and were too restless for a monastery, wandered from place to place to find employment for their talents. Such men would act as clerks to town or parish councils. They tried their hand at teaching, tutoring, fortune-telling, witchcraft, weather-forecasting, divination, magic and even doctoring. But many just took their place in rich households as hangers-on, doing odd jobs, telling stories, writing verses to amuse their patrons, making music if they could, clowning if music failed. Their activities overlapped with those of the old-fashioned minstrel. The clerk, if his gifts lay in that direction, would certainly try to compose vernacular poetry, and in such compositions the traditional style would blend with borrowings from literary sources.

When we come to the sixteenth century, after the Turkish victories of 1526, we find that the breaking up of the old order leads to a substantial increase in the number of these educated vagabonds. Monks are driven from their monasteries, and trained laymen from the households and cities where they would normally have found employment. And by this time the two groups—the minstrels of the traditional sort and the wandering scholars—are much more closely intermingled. The pleasure the people took in listening to heroic songs was as great as ever. We have the testimony of Sidney that in 1576: 'In Hungarie I have seene it the manner at all Feastes, and other such like meetings, to have songs of their ancestors valure, which that right souldierlike nation, think one of the chiefest kindlers of brave courage.'[2] But now, alongside the oral tradition a written literature was developing in the vernacular. The work of the literate and educated, this literature transplants

---

[1] E. Faral, *Les jongleurs en France au moyen âge* (Paris, 1910), p. 63.
[2] *Defence of Poesie*, ed. A. Feuillerat (Cambridge, 1923), p. 24.

into Hungarian the accepted literary forms. The clerks wrote satirical songs. They wrote songs to sing at weddings and suchlike celebrations and complaints on their own miserable and unsettled life. Their texts were rough, their rhymes monotonous; but their rhythms were light and varied, being composed so as to be set to tunes.

Some of their works, however, contain elements which cannot be ascribed to the usual Humanist literary tradition. The written, like the oral, production of the age drew on the popular heritage of motifs and legends. What is more it drew not on one but on a number of cultures. Slovene and Croat refugees fought side by side with the Hungarians in the border fortresses and served with them in the castles of the nobility. Transylvania, the main centre of resistance, had its indigenous Wallach population. Turkish prisoners contributed their own strange beliefs and songs. All these groups learned each other's tunes, rhythms and stories. The resulting amalgam found some expression even in the written literature, tied though that was to conventional models. Such works as the description of the capture of Szabács in 1476 (which, if genuine, was composed in the same year) or the Franciscan Dömötör Csáth's *Conquest of Pannonia*, which dealt largely with the legend of the White Horse, are obviously indebted to the type of song that Sidney heard, while an even greater wealth of popular material crept into the novels, into stories like that of *Szilágyi and Hagymási*. In that tale the two heroes are prisoners in Constantinople. The sultan's daughter falls in love with Szilágyi and the three escape together. But when they reach safety Hagymási, also enamoured of the girl, challenges his friend to a duel.

Szilágyi and Hagymási presents us with a tale which we should not be surprised to find in a ballad, and the same is true of some of the other sixteenth-century stories such as *Telamon* or *Gismunda and Giscardus*. We have arrived at the beginnings of Hungarian balladry.

It is generally agreed that the oldest of the existing Hungarian ballads date back to the seventeenth century or perhaps the end of the sixteenth. Their language, imagery and rhythms all make this probable.[1] They had their roots in the oral tradition we have been describing. It is perhaps relevant that Sidney mentions his Hungarian experiences

---

[1] L. Vargyas (*Ethnographia*, **71**, 163–276) dates the earliest Hungarian ballads in the fourteenth century or before. His suggestion is based on certain French parallels to Hungarian ballads, from which he concludes that most of the old Hungarian ballads are of French origin. On the basis of these conclusions he dates the Hungarian ballads as belonging to a period for which there are data for the presence of French settlers in Hungary, i.e. the fourteenth century and before. For a recent summary of his theory, see L. Vargyas, 'Rapports internationaux de la ballade populaire hongroise', *Littérature Hongroise—Littérature Européenne*, ed. I. Sőtér (Budapest, 1964), pp. 69–104, p. 100.

immediately after he has been talking about the 'old song of Percy and Duglas' that is 'sung but by some blinde Crowder, with no rougher voyce, then rude stile'. But even if the 'songs of heroes' which were sung in Matthias's court or in the camps that Sidney visited were not ballads themselves, they almost certainly contained episodes which were appropriate for treatment in ballad form. Homeric and Scandinavian parallels make it overwhelmingly likely that the lays produced by the medieval Magyar bards were epic in character. The memorizing of an epic, the ready mastery of the tags which complete lines, fill gaps and hold the story together is possible only for professionals. We have seen that after the Turkish invasion the breakdown of the older order involved among other changes the replacement of the medieval professional bards by amateurs: clerks who sang to amuse their patrons, soldiers who sang to cheer their comrades, itinerant entertainers, many of whom had no links with any tradition. It is easy to see that epic would have been beyond the powers of such men. The change to a shorter and simpler form, treating individual episodes, would appear to be a very natural one in the circumstances. Moreover, the new material which was flooding into the country—the Humanist tales, the romances with their love interest, the foreign legends—wedded for the most part to concise prose forms, was not suited to epic treatment. It demanded brevity. We can see that the general conditions existed for the development of a genre possessing some of the qualities of epic— its objectivity, its reliance upon narrative, its avoidance of overfull description—but altogether smaller in its compass; the times demanded a sort of pocket epic, and it seems likely that some crude form of the ballad came into being as an answer to this need.

It seems worth noting that few of the ballads, as we have them, seem particularly suited to amusing soldiers in the field. Nor do they really seem the sort of stuff one would sing to rich nobles at a feast or to their wives in the bower. They do not glorify the great. They do not praise courtly love. They are not military in tone. They reflect the life of the peasants and the lesser gentry, but at the same time they do not strike one as well fitted for performance at village feasts. There surely something more like a dance and less like a story would be appropriate. One may consider the possibility of the ballad having been primarily a spinner's or weaver's song. In that setting a certain rhythmic repetitiveness as well as the narrative quality would be well in place. And in England at least the great age of ballad production does seem to coincide with the great age of domestic cloth manufacture. It is interesting too that some of the earliest French love songs (which tell a little story, use a refrain, etc.) represent the singer as seated at the loom and are commonly referred to as *chansons de toile* (K. Bartsch, *Altfranzösische Romancen und Pastourellen*, Leipzig, 1870, for texts). Courts, camps, and village festivals had existed from the Middle Ages—forms of poetry associated with them could well have come into being earlier. If the ballad was one of those forms, one would expect to find a long ancestry for it. But this ancestry is lacking. Our theory connecting the ballads with the cloth industry would explain why they became widely popular at the time they did and it is supported by the fact that even at the present time ballads are often sung in spinning rooms. In the absence of definite historical evidence, this theory must remain, however, a speculation.

THE DISCUSSION OF
THE MAIN HUNGARIAN
CLASSICAL BALLADS

PART I

3

MAGIC BALLADS

Introduction

Themes which make substantial reference to magic practices are very popular in English, Scottish, and Scandinavian balladry. By comparison, these themes appear only rarely in our Hungarian material.

Although quite a number of these ballads mention events incapable of natural explanation, we find only four which could be properly called ballads of magic where definite reference is made to magical rites.

These are 'Clement Mason' and the ghost-ballad 'The Dead Bridegroom', in which magic rites are performed; 'The Miraculous Dead', in which a human being produces an action that has a magic result; and 'The Three Orphans', where again we have reference to magic practices. The latter, however, has such marked Christian overtones that it seemed necessary to include it in the next section among the Christian legendary ballads (see chapter 4).

In all of these ballads the principal motifs have their parallels in the international stock of traditional ballads.

'CLEMENT MASON'

This ballad was first published by J. Kriza at the end of the first volume of his ballad collection *Vadrózsák*. He wrote: '"Clement Mason" and "Ilona Budai" have arrived just in time to get a seat at the very end of the first table. But they can say with the host in the anecdote: "The head of the table is here, where I am sitting."'

Version **A**

1 Twelve masons took counsel together
   That they would build the tall castle of Déva,

2 That they would build it for half a bushel of silver,
   For half a bushel of silver, for half a bushel of gold.

3 They set about building the tall castle of Déva,
   What they piled up by noon fell down by nightfall,
   What they piled up by nightfall fell down by morning.

4 Again the twelve masons took counsel together,
   How it would be possible to make strong the wall.

5 Between them they made a solemn compact:
  'Whichever of our wives comes here the first of all

6 Her let us take gently, throw into the fire,
  Her tender ashes let us mix with the lime,

7 Only so can we make strong the tall castle of Déva,
  Only so can we win the rich price for it.'

8 'My coachman, my coachman, my big coachman,
  It would be my wish to go to my husband!

9 Place the horses between the shafts, let us take to the road,
  Let us take to the road, to the tall castle of Déva!'

10 It was rough weather, the rain poured down,
   'Let us turn back, my Mistress, my star!

11 I dreamt a dream last night, that was not good,
   Let us turn back, my Mistress, my star!'

12 'It is not your coach, they are not your horses,
   Drive on the horses, let us go on forward!'

13 'I dreamt a dream last night, that was not good:
   I was walking in Clement Mason's courtyard,

14 Behold, his courtyard was covered in mourning,
   In his courtyard a deep well had opened,

15 His little son drowned in it.
   Let us turn back, my Mistress, my star!'

16 'It is not your coach, they are not your horses,
   Drive on the horses, let us go on forward!'

17 On they went, on they went towards the castle of Déva,
   Clement Mason caught sight of them.

18 He became terribly frightened, he prayed:
   'My God, my God, take her away somewhere!

19 May all my four bay horses break their legs,
   May all the four wheels of my coach break into pieces,

20 May the burning arrow of God [thunderbolt] fall on the road,
   May my horses snort and turn home!'

21 On they went, on they went towards the castle of Déva,
   No harm came to the coach or to the horses.

22 'Good morning, good morning to you twelve masons,
   And among you twelve masons, to Clement Mason!'

23 'Good morning, good morning, my woman-wife,
   Why have you but why have you come here, for your undoing?

24 Now we are going to take you gently, throw you into the fire,
   We are going to mix your tender ashes with the lime,

20

25 Only so can we make strong the tall castle of Déva,
Only so can we win the rich price for it.'

26 'Wait, wait you twelve murderers
That I might say good-bye to my women-friends,
To my women-friends, to my little son!'

27 The wife of Clement Mason, when she had been home,
They took her gently, threw her into the fire...

28 When Clement Mason went home,
His little son came to meet him:

29 'Father, father, tell me truly,
Where is she, where is my mother, where has she gone?'

30 'Do not cry my son, do not cry, she will be back by nightfall,
If she will not come back by nightfall, she will come by morning.'

31 'My God, my God, the morning too has come,
My mother has not yet come home!'

32 'Go away, my son, to the tall castle of Déva,
There is your mother, she is built into the stone-wall.'

33 His little son set out crying,
He set out crying to the tall castle of Déva.

34 Three times he shouted at the tall castle of Déva:
'Mother, sweet mother, speak but one word to me!'

35 'I cannot speak my son, for the stone wall presses me,
I am built in between high stones here.'

36 Her heart broke, so did the ground under her,
Her little son fell in and died.

Versions

'Clement Mason' is very popular in Transylvania and Moldavia, from where some seventeen versions and several fragments have been published. L. Kálmány mentions a few lines of it found by him in the Lowland, but he does not quote these; neither are they to be found in the Kálmány bequest.[1]

---

[1] *Kálmány Hagyaték*, II (Budapest, 1952), ed. by Gy. Ortutay. Most of the Hungarian ballad scholars talk of this reference as if it were an actual version of the ballad (cf. *Magyar Népköltési Gyüjtemény*, III, 'Kőmíves Kelemen' Notes; Gy. Ortutay, *Székely Népballadák*, Budapest, 1935, 'Kőmíves Kelemen' Notes; E. Dános, *A Magyar Népballada*, Budapest, 1938, p. 100). It is perhaps advisable to quote the words in question: 'I was able to take down fragments of some of the ballads in Kriza's collection, including a few lines of "Clement Mason" at Törökbecse. It would be interesting to discover what differences there are between this version from the Lowland and those which come from Transylvania. I tried to do some research on this subject but all my work was in vain because the School Board at Törökbecse created difficulties ... It was generally believed among the villagers that anyone found singing any sort of song would be denounced.' (Kálmány, *Szeged Népe*, Arad, 1881, II, 67.)

A Csanádi-Vargyas, *Röpülj*, no. 5 B Ortutay, *Magyar Népköltészet*, II, no. 1*a*; =Kriza, *Vadrózsák*, no. 584; =Kriza (1956), no. 3; =*MNGY*, XI, p. 422 C Csanádi-Vargyas, *Röpülj*, no. 9; =Bartók-Kodály, *SZNd*, no. 56; =Kodály-Vargyas, *MNpt*, no. 175 D *Ethnographia*, **22, 51** E Csanádi-Vargyas, *Röpülj*, no. 6; =*MNGY*, I, p. 174 F Csanádi-Vargyas, *Röpülj*, no. 8; =Bartók-Kodály, *SZNd*, no. 122; =Kodály-Vargyas, *MNpt*, no. 317 G Kerényi Gy, *Madárka*, no. 4 H *MNYr*, **15,** 287 I Csanádi-Vargyas, *Röpülj*, no. 7; =Ortutay, *Magyar Népköltészet*, II, no. 1*b*; =*Pásztortüz*, **27,** 209 J Faragó-Jagamas, *MCSNN*, no. 2 K Domokos, *Moldvai Magyarság*, no. 6; =Domokos (1931), no. 11 L *MNGY*, III, no. 40 M *Ethnographia*, **13,** 398 N *Ethnographia*, **13,** 399 O Ortutay, *Magyar Népköltészet*, II, no. 1*c*; = *Pásztortüz*, **27,** 211 P Schram, *Magyar Népballadák*, no. 2 Q *Ethnographia*, **19,** 105; =Bartók-Kodály, *SZNd*, no. 124 [with the correct tune] R Domokos, *Moldvai Magyarság*, no. 5; =Domokos (1931), no. 11 (first fragm.) S Kodály-Vargyas, *MNpt*, no. 86; =Bartók-Kodály, *SZNd*, no. 62 T Erdélyi, *Magyar Népdalok*, III, p. 151

Description of the Ballad

I. Twelve masons start building the castle of Déva.

A, B for half a bushel of silver, for half a bushel of gold; **I** for a bushel of gold, for a bushel of silver; **C** for a bushel of gold, for two bushels of silver, for three bushels of brass; **G, P** there are thirteen masons, the thirteenth is Clement Mason; **Q** the number of masons is not stated.

II. What they build up during the day collapses by nightfall, what they build up at night collapses by daybreak.

A, B at noon...by nightfall, at nightfall...by morning; **C, O, T** in the morning... by afternoon, in the afternoon...by night; **M, J** during the day...at night; **S** in the morning...by noon, at noon...by nightfall; **Q** in the morning...by noon, at noon ...by nightfall, at nightfall...by morning. **D, H, O** *My God, my God, what can it mean | That our fair castle does not want to be built? || I My God, my God, | What is happening? | My God, my God, | Have you sent this to punish us? ||* **T** ends here.

III. The masons decide to burn one of their wives and to mix her ashes with the lime in order to make the wall strong. The victim will be the first wife who arrives at their place.

E, H, L–N the victim shall be the wife who is the first to bring her husband's midday-meal. **E, I, L, P** the decision is made by Clement Mason; **C, F, G, J, N** the decision is made by the chief foreman builder (whose name is Manole in **J**); **D** is not explicit: 'My mason friends, I tell you this', but we are not told who is speaking; **S** is fragmentary, but at the end of it the mason says: 'It was I myself who decided on taking your blood.' **J, P** Master Manole and Clement Mason (respectively) have a dream, which suggests the decision. **D–F, I–Q, S** the decision is different: **E** *Let her be put between stones, let her be burnt there, | Let her be put on the top of tall castle of Déva;* **D, I, L** *Take her gently, tenderly, | Kill her gently, tenderly, | Mix her red blood with the lime; ||* **L** adds *So we can make strong | The tall castle of Déva, | With tender woman-blood; ||* **I** adds *So they will build up | The tall castle of Déva, | For a bushel of gold, | For a bushel of silver; ||* **S, Q** *Let us take her blood into the lime-bucket; ||* **F, P** *Let her be taken at once, let her blood be taken from her, | Let her tender bones be put into the stone wall, | Let her red blood be mixed with the lime; ||* **O** *To take her, to kill her, to mix her with the lime, | To* *put into the stone wall each of her tiny bones; || **K** They will cut her head off, | They will place it under the stones; || **J** Her head let them cut off, | Let them set it in the corner [of the castle]; || **M, N** This castle is not ready yet, | It calls for human life. | Let us take her, let us kill her, | Let us put her into the well. ||*

IV. Clement Mason's wife orders her coachman to prepare her coach and her horses in order to go and see her husband.

E the wife sets out on foot, carrying—according to the custom—her husband's midday-meal in a bushel-measure on her head, and her child on her arm; **K** she takes her small son with her; **D, F, I–N** the wife (**F** the foreman's wife) is prompted to go and see her husband by an ominous dream: **I** *The wife of Clement | Dreamt this dream: || There was a round little well | In her round little courtyard, || Her round little well | Was bubbling with blood, || In her round little courtyard | A brooklet of blood was running; || **F** In the middle of her courtyard | A brooklet of blood was running; || **K** In the middle of her house, | There was a well of blood; || **F, J, L–N** In the round little centre of her round little courtyard | A well of blood has sprung forth; || **N** adds And her dear husband was in mourning dress | Covered with blood from head to foot; || **L** adds Let us drive to Déva, because your Master is dead;* **D** there are two dreams: Clement Mason has a dream that his wife is approaching Déva, his wife has a dream that her husband was hit by the stone wall; **A, B** it is the coachman who has a dream, cf. **A**; **R** starts here *In front of my courtyard | There is a well of blood! | Wake up my coachman!* etc. || **O, P** are unique: **O** *Clement Mason shouted to his servant: | —My servant, my servant, my servant, I tell you this: || Do you but go home, tell your Mistress | Not to hurry at home, to be late with the midday-meal, | To be late with the midday-meal. || So the good servant set out for home. | He went through the gate, the gate closed with a bang, | The gate closed with a bang. || His Mistress ran out, asked what was the matter. | —The matter is, the matter is my fair Mistress dear, | My fair Mistress dear, || My Master sends word to you, that you should hurry to him, | Hurry out to him, hurry with the midday-meal, | Hurry with the midday-meal. || When they were half way: | —My Mistress, my Mistress!—called the servant, | Called the servant, || —My Mistress, my Mistress, I have thought a thought | —My servant, my servant, my servant, tell me your thought, | Tell me what have you thought. || —I have thought, let us turn back from here, | It will be better, it will be better for us to turn back from here, | Let us turn back from here! || **P** Mason Clement | Said to his servant: | —My servant, my dear servant, | My most truthful servant, || Go home from here, | Tell my wife | Not to come here, || Tell my wife | Not to come here, | Lest she will be beheaded. || Thereupon his servant | Set forth straightway. | —My Mistress, my Mistress, | My Master sends word to you || To come and see | The tall castle of Déva, | How they are building | The tall castle of Déva. || —How is it possible | That he has sent me this message? | But I shall not | Deny his wish. || Turn out the coach, | Place the six horses between the shafts, | I shall be ready straightway, | I am bathing my child. || My God, my God, | What can it mean, | That my clean well | Is bubbling with blood? || —It does not matter, | Hurry, hurry quickly, | Otherwise we shall be late! || —The whip belongs to you, | The six horses belong to me, | Let us go, if we can, | If God will help us. || On they go a long distance, | They have done half way. | A beautiful white pigeon | Flies towards them. || —It would be better for you, woman,[1] | If you returned,*

---

[1] 'Woman' in Hungarian = 'asszonyállat' ('woman-thing'); an archaic expression 'állat' in modern usage 'animal', but earlier it denoted simply 'thing'. Thus, e.g. 'csillag-állat'—'a star-thing', etc.

if you went home, | Do not hurry there | For your beheading. || —My servant, my servant, *It would be better if we returned, Let us not go there! || —We have done half way, We shall* *arrive there in a short time.* The dialogue between the coachman and his Mistress (cf. **A**, st. 12) appears in **B, F, G, I, P, O. C, H, Q** incident IV is missing altogether; **K** ends here.

V. Clement Mason observes that it is his wife who is the first to approach, and prays to God to prevent her coming by causing the horses to break their legs, by breaking the wheels of his coach into pieces, by sending a thunderbolt. God does not answer his prayers, and his wife arrives at Déva.

C he prays for a dark forest; **D** dark forest and rain; **H** cloud, rain; **O** rain; **R** a rain of fire, hail, storm; **E** a couple of wild beasts, a black cloud, pebbles which fall like rain; **J** wild wolf, wild bear, stone-rain; **Q** wild and windy weather, a wolf to eat up the nose of his horse. **C–E, H, J, R** God grants the mason his prayers and raises the obstructions but the wife does not turn back; **R** at first the wife orders her coachman to turn back, but then she decides again to continue the journey; **I, M, N, P** there is no prayer and there are no impediments, but when Clement Mason observes his wife's coach, he signals with his hands in order to prevent her coming; **M** nevertheless, they arrive; **J, N** the coachman understands the signals but the wife will not listen to him (**J** has the signals as well as the obstacles); **I** *Drive on my servant, | Your Master is making signs! | Perhaps he is making signs | That we should go quicker. ||* **P** *Clement Mason stood in the door, | From there he signalled that they should not come near, | But his servant did not even listen to him, | He drove there quickly. ||* **O** *My God, my God, my loving God, | Perhaps my servant has gone home with a great lie, | With a great lie! || My God, my God, give a dark shower | So that my fair love should not be able to come here, | My good wife! || When he was saying that, they arrived, | So good Clement snatched up his gun, | Shot his servant. ||* **F, G, S** Incident V is omitted.

VI. The wife greets the masons, and Clement Mason tells her her destiny. She asks for leave to say good-bye to her friends and her child.

E, G–J, L, O, S, Q nobody returns her greetings at Déva; **J** *Nobody returned her greetings | At high castle Déva. || Maybe you are in trouble? | I have been here before, || I have always greeted you, | You have always returned my greeting. ||* **E, I, O** *What can it mean? | I gave you greeting three times, | You returned me none! ||* **G, H** like **E, I, O**, but with two greetings; **Q, L** *My God, my God, what does it mean? | When I gave him greeting once, he used to return it twice, | Now I have greeted him twice, and he has given me none in return.* (**Q** the fragment is confused here, as in the previous stanza the husband did greet her); **Q, S** ends after the wife is told that she is to die; **E, G** it is not her husband but the other masons who tell her their decision; **J, M, N, P, R** the wife is not told about her destiny; **P** *She could not speak a couple of words | With her sweet one, | When the twelve masons | Seized her quickly. || Clement Mason | Said to his servant: | —My servant, my dear servant, | Go home now, || Go home now, | Go home now, | I give you your | Payment now! || —I will not go, | I will not go, | It is not Christmas yet. ||* **B** when the wife asks for leave, she addresses the masons as 'twelve murderers' and adds: *For the knell is rung three times for a dead person, | Not once will* *it ring for my hapless self.* || **C–J, L–P, R** she does not ask for leave; **C** *Good morning, good morning, Clement Mason! | —Welcome, welcome, my lady-wife! || —I have come,* [bis] *to visit you! | —You have come, you have come to be beheaded! || —I know it well, that you act in this way, | That you murder men to earn money! ||* **E** *I do not care even if it so, | If you have come so much to hate your life with me.* || **I** *Murder me, murder me | Twelve masons, | And among the twelve masons | Clement Mason. || Only give me permission, let me speak, | Speak if only three times, | For the knell is rung three times for a dead person, || —Speak, speak, speak | My dear wife, | I laid down the law, | And it has fallen upon my head! || —My golden slippers | Put upon my feet, | My silk-pile skirt | Put upon my back, || My rocking little cradle | Put in front of me, | My child | Put into it. || There will be gentle rains | Which will bath him, | There will be gentle breezes | Which will lull him to sleep. || Murder me, murder me | Twelve masons, | And among the twelve masons | Clement Mason! ||* **L** *The woman became terribly frightened, | Because she had a small child. | —Place it in front of me! | God granted her wish | God placed it in front of her. | He gave warm rain to bath it, | He gave warm breeze to lull it to sleep. ||* **F, G** *My God, my God, and my little son? | —There are rocking cradles that will lull him to sleep, | There are good women who will suckle him.* || [**F** is confused, probably with **E, K, J, R,** VI, and this stanza is told after her murder]; **H** *I do not care, I do not care, | Be my executioner, | It would not be wrong | To fasten you to a stake, | To give you nettles to eat there, | To give you water mixed with chaff to drink there, | Paint*[1] *me with my bushel measure for food on my head, | Paint me with my little son in my arms, | Paint me with my lively daughter behind me.* || **H** ends here.

VII. The masons execute their plot (cf. III) and succeed in building up the castle.

B adds *Only so could they win the rich price for it.* **G, C** they kill the wife by cutting her throat in two; **C** adds *Thereupon they were paid with a bushel of gold, | With a bushel of gold, with two bushels of silver, | With a bushel of gold, with two bushels of silver, | With three bushels of brass, with three bushels of brass.* || **L** they run her blood into the bushel measure; **P** *They took her to a hiding-place, | There they killed her straightway;* || **I** *So high they raised | The wall of the castle, | That they heard | The singing of angels.* || **I** ends here. **D, O** contrary to their original plan, the masons build her alive into the wall, like in **E, J, M, R; J** is unique, as there the husband deceives her: *Master Manole | Embraced her straightway | He sat her on his knees, | Then he took her up to the wall,*[2] *| Put her down on the wall. | —We want to make fun, | We want to wall you in;* || **E** *They took the bushel-measure with the meal from her head, | They took her little son off from her arm, | When they piled the stones up to her knees, she took it for fun, | When they piled the stones up to her girdle, she took it for just a game, | When they piled the stones up to her breast, she saw that they were in earnest.* || **D, J, M, R** she asks whether it is just for fun, or whether they are in earnest: **D** *When they built the wall up to her knees: | —My husband, my sweet husband, is it fun or true? | —It is not fun indeed, my treasure, my wife, | This is what we have decided, now it must be done. || When they built the wall up to her girdle: | —My husband, my sweet husband, is it fun or true? | —It is not fun indeed, my treasure, my wife, | This is what we have decided, now it must be done. || When they built*

---

[1] 'Paint' in Hungarian = 'Irjátok' which means both 'write' and 'paint'.

[2] In this version there are some Rumanian words in the Hungarian text, e.g. 'wall' is in Rumanian.

the wall up to her throat, | She asked her husband: ' Well, if it is not for fun, Clement Mason, | Paint¹ my name on the side of the wall, | And let my ashes fall on the black soil' | So he painted her name, to let her fame spread. // **R** she asks the question three times, when they have seized her, when they have built the wall up to her waist, and when up to her armpit; **M, J** up to her knees, up to her armpit; **R** the answer is: *Alas, we are in earnest;* **J** she addresses the question to the eleven masons, who answer: *It is true, our Mistress | It was your husband's ruling.* // **E, J, R** have a passage here analogous to that which occurs in **F, G, I, L**: **E** *Do not cry, my little son, | There are good women, they will suckle you, | There are good children, they will rock you, | The birds in the sky fly from one branch to another, | They will chirp for you, they will lull you to sleep;* // **R** *Do not be afraid, my little heart, do not be afraid | Big birds fly, they will feed you, | Warm rains will bath you, warm breezes will dry you;* // **J** *Who will bath | My child? | —There are mild rains | They will bath him.* // *—Who will dress | My child? | —There are good women, | They will dress him.* // It ends here: *Master Manole, | Master Manole, | The wall presses me, | My life is at an end.* // (The last two lines are in Rumanian.)

VIII. Here all the versions are different.

A–G are similar. Mason Clement goes home. His child asks him when its mother will return home. The mason tells him that she will be home by nightfall or by next morning. When asked again in the morning, he tells the truth to the child. **B** agrees word for word with **A** (cf. main version); the child goes to the place where his mother is immured, calls her three times, the mother replies that she cannot speak, her heart breaks, the ground splits under her, the child falls into the hollow. **C** *His daughter asked him: Father, my father, | Father, my father, where is my mother? | —She has stayed far behind, she will be back by nightfall. // Nightfall has come, yet she has not come home. // His second daughter asked him: Father, my father, | Father, my father, where is my mother? | —Your mother stands in the big stone wall, | Your mother stands in the big stone wall;* // **D** *His three-year-old son runs towards him. | —Father, my father, where is my mother? | —Do not ask it, my son, do not ask it, | She will be home by morning, | If she is not home by morning, | She will be home by noon.* // *—Morning has come, yet she has not come home! | —Do not wait, do not wait for your mother, my son, | We have put her into a stone wall, | We have mixed her with the lime. | —Well, my father, have a coffin made for me of walnut-wood, | Have me buried along my mother's side;* // **E** *Father, my father! Where is my mother? | —Do not cry, my little son, she will be back by nightfall. | He waited until nightfall, yet his mother was nowhere.* // *—Father, my father! Where is my mother? | —Do not cry, my little son, she will be home by morning. | He waited until morning, yet his mother was nowhere. Both of them died.* // **F, G** *My God, my God, where is my mother? | —Do not cry, my little son, she will be home by nightfall, | If she is not home by nightfall, she will come by morning, | If she is not home by morning, she is lost forever. | Cursed be the tall castle of Déva, | May not even the sun shine on it brightly, | I have lost my dear wife for its sake, | Now my dear son is left an orphan for its sake!* // **L** *They have built up | The tall castle of Déva, | Alas, they have built into it | The good spirit, the earthly happiness | Of Clement Mason. | He never leaves his house, | Yet he has no rest, | Even at night he is awakened | By the crying of his child.* // **M** *The husband grew desperate, | He ran up to the mountain, | He looked back from here, | He blessed her, he cried for her.* // It ends in prose: *Then they*

---

¹ See note 1, p. 25 above.

walled her up to her breast, from which a milk-brooklet sprang forth. **N** in prose: *Her dear husband did not work any more. As long as the castle held good the child suckled the mother's two breasts, because a milk-brooklet sprang forth from the wall. But now there is only a water-brooklet there.* **P** *Clement Mason | Went to the council, | He asked the council | What was their verdict on the false servant || —Have him placed between split trunks of wood | Have him burned between them, | And let his false ashes | Be blown away by the wind. || Clement Mason | Saw a dream at night | A beautiful white pigeon | Flew towards him: || —How are they, how are they, | My three beautiful children? | —They are well, they are well, | But, alas, how are you? ||—I am well, I am well | In glorious Heaven, | But my false servant | Is in eternal Hell; ||* **O** in prose: (added by another reciter) *The woman was far gone with child, and as soon as they had built her into the wall, she gave birth to her little son. For they had not killed her, but built her alive into the wall. Fortunately she could move one of her hands, and with this hand she gave suck to the child. So she fed him for seven years. During these seven years Clement Mason mourned for his wife but with the passing of the seven years he prepared for a new wedding. The woman built into the wall sensed this. She knocked apart the wall in front of her, and set out for home with her little son. When they arrived at the gate, she took off her last rags (for with the seven years her dress had mouldered away in the wall), and wrapped them around her son, who had nothing to wear. She put her wedding-ring into the mouth of the child and instructed him to go straight in to the wedding guests, to stop exactly in front of Clement Mason, to toast him, and after drinking to throw the ring with his tongue into the glass. So the child goes in. He reaches his father only with difficulty, for the wedding-guests jostle him about, but at last he comes in front of him. He toasts him, drinks, then gives him back the glass. Clement Mason,—according to the custom— drinks off the rest of the drink, something touches his lips. He looks at it. Now he sees that it is his old wedding ring. He asks the child where he got the ring. The child tells him. Clement Mason goes out. When he sees his first wife naked, he goes back into the house, takes the silk skirt, the velvet bodice, the pearls, the golden jewels off his new wife, takes them out, and puts them upon his first wife. When he leads her in through one of the doors, the new wife goes out naked with the wedding guests. Ever since they have lived always together.*

International versions

'Clement Mason' belongs to the group of ballads which tell the story of the mason's wife who was immured (or was killed and her blood was mixed with the lime) for reasons of ritual magic: in order to keep a building (castle, bridge) firm. Ballads dealing with this subject are well known in Greece, Bulgaria, Albania, Serbia, and Rumania.

Several theories have been put forward concerning the origin and spread of this ballad. The most generally held opinion is that the ballad originated in Greece, from where it spread to Bulgaria, Rumania, and to Albania, Serbia and Hungary.[1] Recently, L. Vargyas put forward a

---

[1] For the origin of the story cf. S. Solymossy, 'Kőműves Kelemenné', *Ethnographia* (1923), p. 139; also W. J. Entwistle, *European Balladry* (Oxford, 2nd ed., 1951), p. 87. For bibliographical references cf. S. Solymossy, *op. cit.*; *Magyar Népköltési Gyüjtemény* I, III, 'Kőműves Kelemen' Notes; Gy. Ortutay, *Székely Népballadák*, 'Kőműves Kelemen' Notes.

powerful argument questioning the Greek origin, and pointing out the central position of the Bulgarian ballad.[1]

The summary of a typical Greek version and of the best-known South Slavonian version will illustrate the great variety of the narratives:

In the *Greek* story ('The Bridge of Arta') 45 masons and 30 youths want to build a bridge on the river Arta. What they build up at day-time collapses by night. The master (named Manole), has a dream, in which he is told that they have to bury his wife under the foundation pier. He sends a message home, his wife arrives, wearing her jewels. Manole uses guile: he tells his wife that his ring fell down into the pier, and only the slenderest of all women can pick it up. She descends, and the masons immure her, while she is lamenting bitterly. She remembers that her sisters had died the same way.

The main variant of the *South Slavonian* type ('The Founding of Skutari of Skadar') tells a somewhat different story: Three brothers want to build the castle of Skadar by the river Bojana. For three years all their efforts are in vain, Vila the Elf destroys by morning what they have raised by evening. Finally Vila tells them to find two twins named Stojan and Stojana (N.B. 'stojiti'—'to stand'). The eldest brother, Vukasin, orders his servant to search for these twins with a chariot full of golden treasures. For three years the servant searches for them in vain. Vila gives new advice: all the three brothers are married, they should immure the wife who will be the first to bring the ration for the workers. The three brothers swear not to tell the secret to their wives. The two elder brothers break their oaths when they go home at night, only the youngest, Gojko, keeps his word. His wife is the first to arrive. Gojko sees her approach, tells her her fate. The three hundred workmen start piling the stones and beams around her. When they seize her she thinks it a jest, when they have immured her up to her girdle she smiles, when they build the stones higher she shrieks aloud in despair. Cannot they immure a slave girl instead of her? Her mother is rich, she could buy one for them. When her prayers are not heard she asks the master-builder, Rado, to leave a little window in the wall for her bosom, so that she can suckle her little son, and another window for her eyes to look at the child. When they have built the wall around her, they bring her son in his cradle there. For a long while his mother suckles him, then her voice grows faint, but for a whole year she feeds the child.

Some Bulgarian, and most of the Rumanian versions of the ballad have developed a different conclusion—there Manole falls down from the top of the castle.

---

[1] L. Vargyas, 'Kutatások a népballada középkori történetében III, Kőműves Kelemen eredete', *Néprajzi Értesítő*, **41**, 5–73 (for the same article in German cf. L. Vargyas, 'Forschungen zur Geschichte der Volksballade im Mittelalter. Die Herkunft der ungarischen Ballade von der eingemauerten Frau', *Acta Ethnographica*, 1960, **9**, 1–88) with the most complete bibliographical references. The final conclusion of Vargyas's extensive analysis of the entire ballad group, i.e. that the ballad spread from Hungary to Bulgaria, and then from Bulgaria to the other countries, rests on a comparison with certain Georgian and Mordvinian sagas, and it seems to be somewhat unjustified.

Motifs

The following motifs and incidents of 'Clement Mason' are found in the international versions:[1]

The beginning of the ballad (may be different): (a) someone employs the masons (Serbian, Bulgarian, Rumanian); (b) they agree between themselves to build some structure (Greek, Bulgarian, Serbian, Albanian); the ever-collapsing building (all versions); the suggestion of sacrificing the wife who will arrive there first with her husband's midday-meal (Serbian, Bulgarian, Rumanian); the suggestion is made (a) by common agreement between the masons (Serbian, Rumanian), (b) by the chief mason, whose wife is going to be the victim (Serbian, Bulgarian, Rumanian); the misrepeated message in our versions **O, P** occurs in a Greek version, in which the messenger is a bird;[2] the husband's prayer for miracles (Rumanian, Bulgarian); God grants the miracles (Rumanian); the mason waves to his wife (Albanian, Bulgarian); the wife arrives, greets the masons (Serbian, Albanian, Greek); the masons inform her of their decision (Serbian, Bulgarian); the incremental repetition in describing the immuring of the wife, her gradual realisation that the masons are in earnest (Serbian, Bulgarian, Rumanian, Greek); 'Who will take care of my child?—There are gentle rains', etc. (Rumanian, Bulgarian, traces in Serbian); child cries after its mother, asks its father where the mother has gone (Serbian); child goes to the place where mother was immured, speaks to the mother, the wall falls apart, the child dies there, or the mother returns home alive (Serbian); milk-brooklet from the mother's breast (Serbian, Bulgarian, Albanian); the mason's cursing the castle (Greek).

The provenance of 'Clement Mason' was the subject of much discussion during the 'Wild-Rose Trial' (cf. chapter 1). Since then, S. Solymossy has proved in his extensive analysis that the ballad did not reach Hungary via Rumania,[3] but via South Slavonia.

According to Solymossy the ballad originated in Greece, from where

---

[1] The following list indicates only the *occurrence* of the traits of 'Clement Mason' in the international versions. It should by no means create the impression that the occurrence of these traits implies a close agreement between the story as it is told in our ballad, and in the international parallels. The latter have several features which do not occur in the Hungarian ballad at all, and some of these common traits appear only at the periphery of the tradition. The great variety of the international versions may be inferred from our summary of two of these, and there are great differences between the versions within one language territory as well. The examination of these however, lies outside the field of this work.

[2] H. Lübke, *Neugriechische Volks- und Liebeslieder in deutscher Nachdichtung* (Berlin, 1895), p. 265.

[3] W. J. Entwistle also mistakenly asserts a Rumanian source of the Hungarian ballad, probably on the evidence of old (Rumanian?) sources; cf. *op. cit.* p. 277.

it spread in two directions: north-east to Bulgaria and Rumania, and north-west towards Albania and Serbia, and from Serbia to Hungary. He points out that the ring motif (i.e. the husband does not tell his wife that she is going to be immured, but says that he dropped his ring, and asks his wife to fetch it; she goes down to the foundation and they immure her) has been preserved in all versions of the north-eastern type, but it has gradually disappeared in South Slavonia, and has no traces in the Hungarian versions. Apart from the *disappearance of the ring motif*, the decisive factor which links the Hungarian ballad to the South Slavonian versions is the *active role of the child* at the end of the ballad, which motif is shared only by the Hungarian and the South Slavonian versions. The Hungarian ballad was then influenced by certain elements of the Rumanian versions: e.g. the mason's prayer for miracles, which is characteristic of the north-eastern type.

L. Vargyas, in the course of his argument pointing out the central position of the Bulgarian versions, maintains that the Bulgarian versions contain *all elements* of the Hungarian ones, and that thus there are two possibilities left: either the Hungarian ballad derives directly from the Bulgarian ballad, or the ballad reached Bulgaria from Hungary. He dismisses the South Slavonian route of 'Clement Mason' suggested by Solymossy, by stating that the *mentioning* of the child, which has been supposed to link the Hungarian ballad to the South Slavonian ones, occurs in the Bulgarian versions as well.

Certain particulars concerning the international ballad parallels in Solymossy's article certainly need revising in the light of Vargyas's comprehensive study, which takes into account several international versions recorded after Solymossy's article was published.

However, as far as the provenance of the Hungarian ballad is concerned, Vargyas cannot offer satisfactory evidence either for rejecting Solymossy's conclusions (i.e. that the ballad reached Hungary from South Slavonia and was later influenced by certain motifs of the Rumanian version) or to support his own suggestion of a direct connection between the Hungarian and Bulgarian ballads.

(1) Vargyas misrepresents Solymossy's argument when he says that it was the mentioning of the child which was supposed to link the Hungarian ballad to the South Slavonian versions. This misrepresentation of Solymossy's argument coincides with Vargyas's inaccurate statement that the Bulgarian ballad contains all elements of 'Clement Mason'. Solymossy makes it quite clear that it is the *active* role of the child at the end of the ballad (i.e. his questioning the father about the

mother's whereabouts, his visiting the castle, calling his mother, dying there, or the mother's miraculous escape due to the child in some way) which he considers to be important, and this trait does not occur in the Bulgarian version at all.

Serbian versions taken down in Dragovac, Norska, Oriov mention two children (cf. our version **C**); the elder walks in front of the wall where the mother was immured. He begs God to give his mother back. A thunderbolt falls, the walls split open (cf. our versions **A**, **B**), the mother comes out alive. This happy ending is probably a later addition, as in our version O.[1] In the versions from Komletinav and Mikanovce, the child keeps asking its father where its mother is, and wants to go and see her (cf. our versions **A–G**). In those from Banovic and Otok, the child dies in front of the mother; in the Novgorod version nobody can console the child, it keeps crying for its mother until it is taken by the father to the wall, where it dies (cf. our versions **A**, **B**, analogously **C–G**, also **L**).[2] In recently recorded versions the child keeps asking from its uncles, sisters, grandmother where its mother is; they demolish the wall, lay out the mother on the grass, the child dies.[3] In another version the child keeps asking its father where the mother is; the father curses himself for not having revealed the plan to his wife.[4]

(2) Vargyas does not deal with Solymossy's second main argument, i.e. the disappearance of the ring motif in both the South Slavonian and Hungarian ballads, although he mentions this fact when discussing the Serbian versions. This 'negative' evidence, however, cannot be neglected, since the ring motif is characteristic of *all* international versions except the Hungarian and the South Slavonian ones.

Traces of the ring motif occur in some Serbian versions, and we can follow the process of its gradual disappearance: there are only two versions in which the lost ring is used as a guile,[5] in six versions traces of the motif occur; the wife arrives, her husband starts weeping, she asks him why he is so sad, he says that his golden apple (in one version his rings and his golden apple)[6] has been immured, or lost, or dropped into the water; his wife consoles him, and it has no further relevance to the story (there is only one among these versions in which she goes

---

[1] It is interesting to observe how the familiar motifs of the South Slavonian ballads (survival under impossible circumstances, the mother who feeds her child through the wall, the milk-brooklet) are absorbed by old international folk-tale types and motifs in our version O: the recognition by ring on the wedding day (Type 506, Thompson, H 94.4; in Child, no. 17), whereupon the old bride is chosen (Type 313, Thompson, Z 211; in Child, nos. 17, 53).

[2] For all these Serbian versions, cf. M. Hrvatska, *Cuprija na Drini* (Zagrab, 1896), pp. 105–10.

[3] Cf. L. Vargyas, *op. cit.* nos. 30, Serbian versions.   [4] *Ibid.* no. 37, Serbian versions.

[5] *Ibid.* nos. 3, 19, Serbian versions.   [6] *Ibid.* no. 10, Serbian versions.

down to search for it).[1] Thus the motif has completely lost its original function (the trick) and may be interpreted as symbolic: namely, the lost or immured golden apple—his wife. In most of the versions the motif has disappeared altogether.

There is no need to introduce a direct Bulgarian-Hungarian connection in explaining the motifs of 'Clement Mason' because (1) there is no specific motif shared *only* by the Bulgarian and Hungarian ballads, whereas there are two such links between the South Slavonian and Hungarian ones; (2) apart from these two links, the South Slavonian versions can account for most of the Hungarian motifs (the two ways of beginning the ballad, the building being a castle, the ever-collapsing building, the suggestion for the necessity of human sacrifice, the nominating of the victim either by mutual agreement or by the chief mason, the victim being the wife who arrives there first with her husband's midday-meal, the arrival of the wife of the one who made the decision, her greeting the masons, her being told of the decision, the incremental repetition when immuring her, the milk brooklet from her breasts); (3) those motifs which do not occur in the South Slavonian versions (the husband's prayer for miracles, God's granting the miracles—'there are gentle rains') occur in both Rumanian and Bulgarian versions. Solymossy suggests that these motifs were borrowed from the Rumanian versions, and his suggestion is supported by the evidence of recently recorded Hungarian versions, which not only agree with the Rumanian versions in certain details not typical of the Hungarian ballad (e.g. the suggestion of human sacrifice by the mason's dream in our versions **J**, **P**) but also mix Rumanian words in the Hungarian narrative (e.g. our version **J**, in which there are two other Rumanian traits: the master's name is Manole, and he deceives his wife instead of telling her of her destiny). Neither Solymossy nor Vargyas question the Bulgarian origin of the Rumanian ballad, and it is natural that these motifs are present in the Bulgarian ballad, which lent them to the Rumanian ones. (4) From the point of view of the origins of the *Hungarian* ballad, it makes very little difference if we modify Solymossy's suggestion and shift Bulgaria to the centre of the tradition. For example: *not*

---

[1] L. Vargyas, *op. cit.* no. 16, Serbian versions.

but

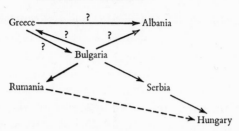

This modification explains why most (but note, not all!) motifs of 'Clement Mason' can be found in the Bulgarian ballad, without *warranting* any direct connection between the Hungarian and Bulgarian versions.

In the following we shall deal with certain motifs of 'Clement Mason' which do not figure in its international parallels. At the same time we shall point out certain devices employed in the Hungarian ballad (whether particularly Hungarian or characteristic of the entire group) which occur also in various English and Scottish ballads.[1]

I. Avarice, the additional motif which induces the masons to undertake the building of the castle in our versions **A, B, C, I** is not a frequent motif in old traditional ballads. It is probably a later modification, paralleled in many American murder-ballads in which greed for money is often an important motive.

II. Nightmare as ill omen (Thompson, D 1812.5.1) is a favourite motif of ballads (cf. Child, nos. 69, 74, 76, 88, 102, 161, 165, 178, 214, 215, 259, 262; also in Csanádi-Vargyas, nos. 82, 184, 192, 197; Gy. Ortutay, *Magyar Népköltészet*, II, no. 124/*d*; and 'The Dishonoured Maiden').

Especially sinister is dreaming of blood, as expressed in Child, no. 88:

> 'To dream o blude, mither', he said,
> 'It bodeth meikle ill'

(also Child, nos. 69, 74, 165, 259).

Premonitory dreams which *foreshow* disasters are, however, comparatively rare in English and Scottish ballads (cf. only Child, nos. 161, 262, 214 *A*). In most of the cases portentous dreams refer to events which had already taken place (cf. Child, nos. 69, 74, 88, 102, 165, 178, 214 except *A*, 215, 259), and it is some ominous sign (falling of the silver button, etc.) rather than a dream, which warns against disasters to come.

---

[1] The group of ballads to which 'Clement Mason' belongs is not represented among the Child ballads.

33

Another feature of such dreams, as treated in English and Scottish ballads, is that they very seldom concern the dreamer himself.[1] They usually signify the 'second sight' or the special awareness possessed by love, which enables the heroine (or hero) to sense when the beloved is in danger, and they often prompt her to go and search for the beloved immediately (cf. Child, nos. 74, 76, 214, 215, 216, 178). The words of Child, no. 165, come the nearest to our version **N**.

> And as shee lay in leeue London,
> And as shee lay in her bedd,
> Shee dreamed her own married lord
> Was swiminnge in blood soe red.

> Shee called up her merry men all
> Long ere itt was day,
> Saies, 'Wee must ryde to Busye Hall,
> With all speed that wee may'.

In versions **P** and **R** the sinister dream becomes reality, and occurs as an ominous sign:

> **P** My God, my God,
> What can it mean,
> That my clean well
> Is bubbling with blood?

(also in Csanádi-Vargyas, no. 192—'My watering-trough was bubbling with blood').

Here we can recognise ancient and very popular international folk-tale motifs: clean water, which becomes turbid or bloody, signifying mortal danger or death; or, the alternative of water/milk or blood springing forth (from a tree, etc.), indicating the state of the person whose safety must be watched (Thompson, E 761; Berze-Nagy, Type 303).

The same motif, but as part of the dream, occurs in version **I**, where there is a round little well bubbling with blood in the courtyard of Clement's wife, and it can probably also account for the well of blood, brooklet of blood, and the like, which figure in the dreams of the other versions.

III. False servants (stewards, 'kichie-boys', porters, nurses) appear in many English and Scottish ballads (cf. Child, nos. 61, 65, 67, 93, 97, 116, 161, 271) and are punished with death (our version **O**; also Child, no. 67), which is often carried out by burning them (Hungarian **P**;

---

[1] Only one among all the Child ballads, no. 161, falls in this latter category: 'But I have dreamed a dreary dream / Beyond the Isle of Sky; / I saw a dead man win a fight, / And I think that man was I.' There is reason to believe that these lines were written by Sir Walter Scott.

Child, nos. 93, 271). Apart from our versions **O, P**, false servants do not figure in Hungarian balladry.

IV. The motif of the pigeons warning the wife to return (**P**) may have derived from the Greek version where the message is sent home by a bird; however, as it is a well known commonplace (cf. Thompson, B 521; B 143.1; Child, no. 114, and his notes to no. 4), it may have slipped into the ballad independently. Its second appearance in the ballad (**P**), where it is the soul of the dead wife, is equally common (cf. Child, 1, pp. 180–1 nn.; Thompson, E 613).

V. 'The coach belongs to me', etc., of versions **A, B, F, G, I, P, O** is a frequent formula in Hungarian ballads, which we find in 'Kate Kádár', 'The Dishonoured Maiden', and 'Little Sophie Kálnoki' as well. Its English parallel is quoted under 'Kate Kádár', motif IV.

VI. The miraculous obstacles (**C, D, E, H, J, R**—dark forest, rain, wild beasts, rain of fire, hail, storm) placed in the wife's way are similar to the witchcraft practices related in many folk tales, in which the sorcerer or witch raises obstacles in front of the maid or youth whom he pursues (cf. Thompson, D 673). In our ballad as well as in the Rumanian versions, the miracles are produced not by witchcraft but by prayer, not by a sorcerer but by God, which is yet another example of primitive motifs appearing in Christianised form (cf. the following section on 'Christian Legendary Ballads'). The miracle in version **L** (God places the child in front of the wife) has no parallel in the international versions of the ballad.

VII. A parallel to the dramatic dialogue between wife and husband in our version **C** is to be found in Child, no. 73 B, st. 15, with the same form of repetition.

> **C** I have come, I have come to visit you.
> —You have come, You have come to be beheaded.

> Child, 73 B You're welcome here to me, Willie,
> You're welcome here to me.
> —I'm na welcome to thee, Annie,
> I'm na welcome to thee,
> For I'm come to bid ye to my wedding
> It's gey sad news to thee.

In the Hungarian ballad the incident of the wife's greeting the masons on her arrival is further elaborated. In versions **E, G, H, I, F, L, O**, none of the masons return her good wishes, being well aware of the terrible destiny lying ahead of her. In versions **Q** and **S** we have the opposite reaction: they return her greeting twice. Her surprise at the unaccustomed politeness sheds interesting light on the status of the woman and her relation with the masons. (Or does it have a ceremonial importance? She is no longer a 'lady' but a 'victim' for ritual ceremony.)

VIII. Fate, which decides to hoist with his own petard the person who commits (or is about to commit) a cruel deed, has a similar tale in Child, nos. 14, 51, 52, where the crime committed is incest.

IX. The formula:

> For the knell is rung three times for a dead person,
> Not once will it ring for my hapless self   (version **B**)

is a recurrent phrase in Hungarian ballads, which appears also in 'Balthasar Bátori'.

X. The very opposite of our version **I**, where the wife is arrayed splendidly before being murdered innocently, is given in Child, nos. 173, 194, in which the guilty woman who is to be undressed before being executed, asks for her petticoat to be left on her with which to cover her eyes.

XI. The wife's words of anxiety for her child (versions **E–G, I, J, L, R**—'who will bath the child', etc.) may be compared to that of the lady in Child, no. 76 *B*:

> O wha will shoe thy bonny feet?
> Or wha will glove thy hand?
> Or wha will lace thy middle jimp
> With a lang, lang London whang?
>
> And wha will kame thy bonny head
> With a tabean brirben kame?
> And wha will be my bairn's father
> Till love Gregory come hame?
>
> —Thy father'll shoe his bonny feet,
> Thy mither'll glove his hand,
> Thy brither will lace his middle jimp
> With a lang, lang London whang.
>
> Myself, will kame his bonny head
> With a tabean brirben kame,
> And the Lord will be thy bairn's father
> Till love Gregory come hame.

XII. The tripartite incremental repetition in immuring the wife is a device which is often used in ballads when they relate that somebody is about to die. Example: Child, no. 4 *B*:

The first step that she stepped in,
She stepped to the knee,
And sighend says this lady fair,
—This water's nae for me.

.   .   .   .

The next step that she stepped in,
She stepped to the middle,
—O-sighend says this lady fair,
—I've wat my gowden girdle!

.   .   .   .

The next step that she stepped in,
She stepped to the chin,
—O-sighend says this lady fair,
—They sud gar two loves twin!

(Cf. also Child, nos. 65 A, 68 A.)

XIII. The incremental repetition describing how Clement Mason's wife gradually realises that her fate is sealed and that it is not just a game that she is to be immured comes again from the South Slavonian variants. Here we are reminded of the antithesis which is a commonplace in English and Scottish ballads, e.g. Child, no. 173.

When she gaed up the Cannogate
She laughed loud laughters three;
But when she cam down the Cannogate
The tear blinded her ee.

(Cf. the commonplace in Child, nos. 58, 96, 99, 208, 240, 254.)

XIV. The questions of the child and the father's answers (A–G) are in the vein of those sharp questions–evasive answers which we find in so many ballads, when someone wants to conceal a crime. (Examples: Child, nos. 13, 49, 51, 68, also 4 D, 36, 173; and in the Hungarian 'The Dishonoured Maiden', 'The Maiden who was Sold', 'Merika', 'The Great Mountain Robber', 'Anna Bíró', etc.)

XV. The dead mother who speaks to her child is discussed under 'The three orphans'. In Child, no. 155 (where it is the dead son who speaks to his mother), we meet the same wording as in versions A, B.

A, B   Three times he shouted at tall castle Déva:
—Mother, sweet mother, speak but one word to me!
—I cannot speak, my son, for the stone wall presses me,
I am built in between high stones here.

Child, no. 155 C   His mither she cam to the Jew's draw-well,
And there ran thryse about:
—O sweet Sir Hew, gif ye be here,
I pray ye to me speak!

—How can I speak, how dare I speak,
How can I speak to thee
The Jew's penknife sticks in my heart,
I canna speak to thee.

A, E, G   Oh the lead is wondrous heavy, mother,
The well is wondrous deep,
The little penknife sticks in my heart,
And nae word more can I speak.

XVI. For the motif of death by sorrow, see 'The daughter of the cruel king'.

XVII. Asking for coffin made of walnut-wood (**D**) is a stock phrase in Hungarian ballads, which is repeated in 'The Maid who was Sold' and also in new-style ballads as in Csanádi-Vargyas, nos. 117, 186.

XVIII. Cursing a castle (**F, G**) is found in a Scottish fragment:

Edinburgh castle, towne and tower,
God grant thou sinke for sinne,
And that even for the black dinner
Earl Douglas got therein!   (Child, v, p. 202)

A similar expression to that in **F, G** ('May the sun not shine on it') is found in Child, no. 229 A:

And it be true that Lillie is dead,
The sun shall nae mair shine on me.

The meaning of this curse (i.e. that the castle may fall down; in Child, no. 229, that he wishes to die) is explicit in Child, no. 212:

D O landlady, landlady, what shall I do?
My life is not worth a farthing,
I paid you a guinea for my lodging last night,
But I fear I'll never see sun shining.

XIX. The moralising passage in our version **P**, where the dead wife appears before the husband in the shape of a pigeon and informs him that she is in Heaven while the false servant is in Hell, occurs in Child, nos. 72 C and 20 as well.

Child, no. 72 C   These six souls went up to heaven,
I wish sae may we a!
The mighty mayor went down to hell
For wrong justice and law.

Child, no. 20 B, G O cursed mother, heaven's high
And that's where thou will neer win nigh,
O cursed mother, hell is deep,
And there thou shall enter step by step.

E, F, C   But now we're in the heavens hie,
                   And je've the pains of hell to die!

All these are obviously later additions.

Folklore and customs

Déva, the scene of the tragedy (according to all versions except **R**) is situated in the south-east of Hungary (Hunyad county), on the left side of the river Maros. The castle in question, or its ruins, stand on the top of a mountain, which used to be the dwelling place of elves and fairies, according to local legend, and it is supposed to have been built by the Davian king, Decebalus. Its ruins have been referred to in various legal documents since the Árpád Dynasty. The first reference dates from 1269. These ruins were restored several times, and they served as state prison, royal residence, barracks for imperial garrison troops. It was auctioned in 1800, after which it became rapidly dilapidated. It took twelve years to restore it (1817-29). In 1849 it was used again by imperial garrison troops, when by chance or by treason it was wrecked by an explosion. The ruins can still be seen on the top of the mountain.

The superstitious belief on which the ballad is based has been found in many parts of the world. Where architectural techniques were still primitive, buildings, especially huge ones like castles, bridges and the like, often collapsed while being built or soon after their completion. These frequent and baffling disasters were attributed to the action of local spirits disturbed in their homes by the building operations. It was believed that there was only one way to conciliate such spirits and to gain their consent to the completion of the building: to present them with a human sacrifice.

We hear of many such ritual sacrifices in every part of the world. In some places the victims were built into the wall alive; elsewhere their blood was to be mixed with the lime.[1] This belief was well known in Scotland and England; for example, the legend of Vortigern, who could not finish the tower of Dinas Emris in Wales until the foundation stone was made wet with the blood of a child born of a mother but

---

[1] For the first alternative cf. A. Andree, 'Paralellen', *Ethnographia*, I, p. 18; Sartori, 'Über das Bauopfer', *Zeitschrift für Ethnologie* (1898); Crooke, *Popular Religion of North India*, II, p. 174; Godziher, *Orientale Baulegenden*, Globus 804, p. 64; Crawley, *The Mystic Rose*, p. 25. For the second cf. *Baring-Gould*, Strange survivals, 5; Geoffrey of Monmouth, lib. VI, cap. 17, *Ethnographia* (1911), p. 177; Gomme, Tradition and Superstition Connected with Buildings, *Antiquary*, III, p. 11; Westermarck, *Origin and Development of Moral Ideas* (1906), chap. xix, pp. 762-3.

without having a father, as related in Nennius, *Historia Britannorum*, Irish version, chap. xviii.

K. Tímár (*Ethnographia*, 1911, 177) draws attention to the fact that Robert Holkot also mentions this legend and the superstition in his *Super sapientiam Salomonis*, lectio 137 *b* (on human blood):

Sanguis autem humanus habet naturaliter ista tria scilicet quod fecundat lignum aridum, sanat corpus languidum et *causat cementum solidum*...

Tertio sanguis causat cementum solidum. Dicitur quod antiqui volentes facere aedificia perpetua, cementum cum humano sanguine commiscuerunt. Unde etiam de Vortegirno rege Britanniae in *historia Britannorum* dicitur: quod cum aedificaret turrim in monte Ererij vel monte nivis in Wallia, quidquid cementarij una die operabantur, tellus alio die absorbuit. Consulerunt ergo magistri dicto regi, quod juvenem quendam inquiri faciat qui patrem terrenum non haberet, cuius sanguine lapides et cementum aspersi praestarent solidum fundamentum. Moraliter, ante Christi passionem sic erat in mundo quod quidquid homines aedificaverunt, quantumcunque aedificarent moraliter vivendo bene, totum in morte absorbebatur a terra: quia omnes in puteum inferni descenderunt nec stare potuit aedificium meritorum: donec aspersi essent sanguine iuvenis, qui patrem non habebat in terris.[1]

The Hungarian versions of 'Clement Mason' vary as regards the way human sacrifices are used: the victim is walled up alive in **D, E, J, K, M, (O), R**; in the other versions the wife is killed and her blood is mixed with the lime (**F, I, L, P, Q, S; O**—her bones), or she is burnt and her ashes are mixed with the lime (**A–C, G, H**), according to the apparently multifarious local tradition in performing the rite.

Later this custom lost its original bloody character, but it survived as a symbol or as a superstition even during the twenties of the present century.[2] F. Deák calls attention to version **H**:

---

[1] These beliefs shed light incidentally on the hitherto unexplained motif of the *Lamkin* ballad (Child, no. 93); cf. Appendix II.

[2] It was customary for masons in Transylvania to measure the shadow of the first passer-by with a reed when they began building, and to bury this reed in the wall (cf. *Magyar Népköltési Gyüjtemény*, III, p. 443). The custom was known in Rumania as well (cf. J. K. Schuller, *Der Schattenverkaufer*, Klaster Argis, 1858). By 1882, however, the reed-measuring was dying out, as 'it happened very often that the victim, whose shadow was measured, became seriously ill, and there were even cases when he died of fear' (*Magyar Népköltési Gyüjtemény*, III, p. 443). That the measuring of a person's shadow was traditionally connected with his coming to harm is suggested by the account of a witch trial held in Debrecen in 1693, where a woman was supposed to 'measure' people, or their shadows, as preliminary to causing them harm (cf. Komáromy, *Magyarországi boszorkányperek oklevéltára*, 1910, Budapest, p. 159).

Presumably such beliefs survived in Transylvania even at the end of the nineteenth century.

An alternative to the burying of a shadow was the sacrifice of an animal in many places in Hungary. At Érendréd, when a new house was built a dog was beaten to death and placed into the wall; at Tunyog a cat or chicken was used for the same purpose; at Nagygéc a cat or chicken was thrown into the new house (*Ethnographia*, 1923, p. 106); at Nagyszalonta after having laid the foundations of a building the masons put in each of the four corners a chicken, a bottle of brandy and a few silver coins (*Ethnographia*, **38**, 260). Such symbolic objects, whose sacrifice was

Paint me with my bushel-measure
for food on my head,
Paint me with my little son on my arms,
Paint me with my lively daughter behind me.

The stanza in question refers to a custom, which was in fashion during the sixteenth and seventeenth centuries: to have a painting made of the deceased on her mourning-flag, her wooden grave-post, or on her gravestone, which immortalises her as a devoted wife and a conscientious mother.[1]

Date

Deák's reference supports the other evidence concerning the date of 'Clement Mason', which is considered one of the oldest Hungarian ballads.

The central motif of the ballad, based on the superstitious belief in the necessity of human sacrifice when a building is to be completed, harks back to very remote times. The antiquity of the story is indicated by the fact that it was well known in Greece, Bulgaria, Albania, Rumania, South Slavonia before the end of the seventeenth century.

As the Hungarian ballad has preserved the pagan rite in the same primitive and most cruel form as it is related in its international parallels, it is plausible to suggest that it should be dated, together with them, in the sixteenth-seventeenth centuries.[2]

Apart from its central idea, 'Clement Mason' has retained many international folk-tale and ballad elements (the ominous dream and

---

supposed to prevent disasters, were found recently, in 1955 at Vác during the restoration of the deaf and dumb institute (the former Episcopal palace), and in 1957 when, as a result of a fortunate coincidence, a similar object was found in the Episcopal palace of Eger.

Recent research has proved that on the north-west side of the palace of Vác there was originally a medieval dwelling house, whose remains were used when the palace was restored after the Turkish occupation, and it was in these remains that the symbolic lock of hair wedged in the wall of the entrance gate was preserved untouched. In the palace of Eger, a lock of the same kind was found folded and pressed down by a small stone. It was placed in one of the pillars 1·20–1·30 m. above the present floor, covered with about 14 cm. of plasterwork, in a hole about 10 cm. long. The location of the lock of hair would suggest that it was not immured during the construction of the building. In both Vác and Eger it seems likely that the magical effect of the lock was needed to strengthen an already existing building. (*Műemlékvédelem*, Budapest, 1958, III, p. 150.)

[1] *Magyar Nyelvőr*, **15**, 287. In France, Italy and Hungary photographs of the deceased can still be seen on gravestones.

[2] Vargyas suggests a much earlier date for the origin of the Hungarian ballad. His suggestion is based on his theory of a direct connection between the Hungarian and the Bulgarian ballad. Taking this conclusion for granted, he therefore places the transmission of the ballad in the only historical period when Hungary and Bulgaria possessed a common frontier, namely, the twelfth and thirteenth centuries.

sign, the warning of the bird, the miraculous obstacles, the false servant, the dead mother who speaks to her child, her survival under impossible circumstances, the milk brooklet, recognition by ring, old bride chosen), the presence of which would also warrant the assumption that it is of relatively early date. Several Hungarian versions have adopted folk-tale features, and the ability to do this is considered to belong only to the oldest ballads.

The fact that in some versions the hero's name is 'Clement Mason' (**A–D, I, Q**) while other versions mention him as 'mason Clement' (**E, G, H, L, P**) also indicates a late sixteenth or early seventeenth-century origin of the ballad, based on linguistic evidence: during the fifteenth and sixteenth centuries peasants and workmen had only first names. It was not until the seventeenth century that they acquired surnames as well, using at first the name of their calling for that purpose.

The lines rhymeless, with occasional suffix-rhymes, the varying number of syllables (a feature of ballads which were accompanied by recitative tunes), the repetition of half-lines, the frequent use of incremental repetition and stock phrases are also evidence for dating the ballad as suggested above.

The tune of 'Clement Mason' belongs to the oldest group of Hungarian folk-tunes.

Special Hungarian elements

W. J. Entwistle considers the Rumanian versions as the best of the international variants.[1] The Hungarian versions, I believe, are as good as the Rumanian ones. They are distinguished by the astonishing variety of the psychological motifs of a dramatic kind which they emphasise.

In versions **A** and **B**, it is the cruel superstition, Fate itself, which causes the tragedy. The masons—especially the one whose wife is going to be the victim—are as powerless to restrain it as is the wife who will not be held back by the warnings of her faithful servant. Clement, motionless, appealing in vain for a miracle, the wife galloping swiftly to face her doom, the child searching desperately for her mother—all are victims of an implacable force, breathing Death and Tragedy.

Other versions give a different picture. Now we are spectators of a more human drama. As Csanádi-Vargyas have pointed out, here it is

---

[1] W. J. Entwistle, *op. cit.* p. 309.

the mason himself who makes the decision, and it falls back on his own head (**E, I, J, L, P, S**). His wife is prompted to set out by her love and concern for her husband; and it is owing to her husband that she is to die. How does she behave at this juncture? What is the father's position like when he faces his child whom he has made an orphan? The tender grace of the wife is set against the brutality of the masons. Her dignity (**I**), her anxiety for her child (**E–G, I, J, L, R**), her horror when she gradually realizes what is going to happen to her (**D, E, J, M, R**), her resignation (**E, I**), her abuse (**C, H**), the embarrassed and evasive answers of the father when the child plagues him with questions about the mother (**A–G**), his despair which bursts out as a curse against the castle of Déva (**F, G**), or the passionless, weary answer in **C**—these multifarious, delicately shaded portrayals would make any modern author envious.

The dominant atmosphere changes too, from version to version. **I** is overshadowed by the ominous dream of the wife; **A, B** are imbued with the horror of the rite; **C** is the most lurid, the whole ballad is focused on the motif of unbridled avarice; **O, P** are interwoven with folk-tale elements; **P** concentrates on the evil intrigues of the false servant; **O** is the only ballad with a happy ending.

'Clement Mason' has contributed to the building-sacrifice set of ballads several motifs and incidents: the number of the masons (which is twelve only in the Hungarian ballad); the ominous dream and sign; the misinterpretation of the dream; the warning of the pigeon; the avarice motif; the intrigues and death of the false servant; the elaboration of the lady's arrival (her greeting the masons, their silence, etc.); and the dialogue between mother and child at the end of the ballad.

From among these special Hungarian elements, the ominous dream and its misinterpretation are the most important.

There are ballads where no notice is taken of the warnings of the one who has been made anxious by ill dreams (like our **A, B** versions), analogously in Child, nos. 216, 262, or by other ill omens (as in Child, no. 58). However, so far as my knowledge goes, there is no parallel to the genuine, highly dramatic way the dream is treated in versions **D, F, I, J–N, R**, where the heroine is given a warning by a sinister dream, but instead of understanding that it concerns herself, she presumes that it refers to her husband. This misinterpretation enhances the dramatic tension of the ballad; it is her love for her husband which makes her misunderstand the dream, and this misapprehension which springs from her love is the very cause of her death.

Thus it happens that a conventional motif (ominous dream) gains a new, *unconventional* structural-aesthetic significance in the Hungarian ballad, owing to the fact that from its two possible conventional interpretations (i.e. that it concerns the dreamer, or her beloved) the wife chooses the wrong alternative.

'THE MIRACULOUS DEAD'

'The Miraculous Dead' is a Hungarian version of 'Willie's Lyke-Wake' (Child, no. 25). It is mentioned by F. J. Child as 'Pálbeli Szép Antal'.

Version **A**

1 —I shall die indeed, mother, my mother,
For Helen Görög, for her slender waist,

2 For her slender waist, for her full lips,
For her full lips, for her rosy cheeks.

3 —Do not die, my son, do not die, Ladislav Bertelaki,
I shall have a marvellous mill made for you,

4 Its first stone will cast forth white pearls,
Its second stone will cast forth small coins.

5 Virgins, fair maids will come and see it,
Your love will come too, the fair Helen Görög.

6 —Give me leave, mother, my mother,
To go and see the marvellous mill, to go and see
the marvellous mill.

7 —Do not go, my daughter, do not go: they are casting the net,
They are casting the net, they will catch the barbel!

8 —I shall die indeed, mother, my mother,
For Helen Görög, for her slender waist,

9 For her slender waist, for her rosy cheeks,
For her rosy cheeks, for her full lips.

10 —Do not die, my son, do not die, Ladislav Bertelaki,
I shall have a marvellous tower built for you.

11 Its summit will touch the sky,
Its buttresses will reach the river Tisza.

12 Virgins, fair maids will come and see it,
Your love will come too, the fair Helen Görög.

44

13 —Give me leave, mother, my mother,
    To go and see the marvellous tower, to go and see
        the marvellous tower;

14 Its summit touches the sky,
    Its buttresses reach the river Tisza!

15 —Do not go, my daughter, do not go, fair Helen Görög,
    They are casting the net, they will catch the barbel!

16 —I shall die indeed, mother, my mother,
    For Helen Görög, for her slender waist,

17 For her slender waist, for her full lips,
    For her full lips, for her rosy cheeks.

18 —Do die, my son, do die, Ladislav Bertelaki,
    They will come here to see the marvellous dead,

19 Your love will come too, the fair Helen Görög,
    Your love will come too, the fair Helen Görög.

20 —Give me leave, mother, mother, my mother,
    To go and see the marvellous dead, to go and see
        the marvellous dead,
    Who has died for me, who has become a dead man for me!

21 —I give you no leave, my daughter, my sweet daughter,
    They are casting the net, they will catch the barbel!

22 Thereupon she slipped into her tiring chamber,
    She threw her gold-embroidered skirt[1] over her shoulder,

23 She tied her white apron before her,
    She put her red, iron studded boots on her feet.

24 —Arise, my son, arise, Ladislav Bertelaki,
    She, for whom you have died, for whom you have become
        a dead man,
    Helen Görög is coming over our land!

25 Arise, my son, arise, she, for whom you have died, for
        whom you have become a dead man,
    Is standing at your feet!

26 —I have seen corpses before, but never one like this,
    With feet ready to jump,

27 With arms ready to embrace,
    With lips ready to kiss!

    Then indeed Ladislav Bertelaki jumped up...

---

[1] 'Gold-embroidered' skirt, in Hungarian 'fontalan', probably is a corruption of 'vont arany'
which means 'gold-embroidered' and is a stock garment in Hungarian ballads. 'Fontalan' means
'not woven', so it could also mean 'a skirt that was not woven by her', i.e. it was bought.

Versions

'The Miraculous Dead' is known only in Transylvania, Moldavia, and Bukovina, where it is still sung with the greatest gusto. Nine versions and two fragments of the ballad have been recorded.

A Csanádi-Vargyas, *Röpülj*, no. 128; =Bartók-Kodály, *SZNd*, no. 97; =Kodály-Vargyas, *MNpt*, no. 334 **B** Csanádi-Vargyas, *Röpülj*, no. 127; =Bartók-Kodály, *SZNd*, no. 80; =Kodály-Vargyas, *MNpt*, no. 278 **C** Domokos, *Moldvai Magyarság*, no. 22 **D** Ortutay, *Magyar Népköltészet*, II, no. 59; =*MNGY*, III, 63 **E** Faragó-Jagamas, *MCSNN*, no. 22 **F** *MNGY*, I, no. 18 **G** *MNGY*, I, no. 19 **H** *Ethnographia*, **22**, 54 **I** Domokos, *Moldvai Magyarság*, no. 20; =Domokos (1931), no. 26 **J** Schram, *Magyar Népballadák*, no. 25 **K** *Ethnographia*, **71**, 217–19

Description of the ballad

I. Ladislav Bertelaki (**G**—Bátalaki; **H**—Bakalaki; **I**—Bogaraci; **D**—Zetelaki; **B, C, E, J**—Valentine Molnár; **K**—brave Valentine;[1] **F**—handsome Anton Pálbeli) tells his mother he is going to die for the fair Helen (**A, D, G–I**—Helen Görög;[2] **E, J**—Fair Helen; **F**—Helen Varga).

II. The mother asks him not to die, she will have a marvellous mill made for him. Its first stone will cast forth white pearls, its second stone will cast forth small change. Girls will come and see the marvellous mill, Helen will be among them.

D the third stone of the mill will cast forth swishing milk; **F** sweet kisses; **I** the mother will have 'a famous marvellous mill made'; **B** a golden mill; **E** a silver mill; **C** a brass mill; **K** the mother will have a paved-garden made, and will have flowers planted in it.

III. Helen asks her mother's permission to go and see the marvellous mill. Her mother warns her: 'They are casting the net, they will catch the barbel.'

F, H *They are casting the net, they will catch the fox;* | **I** *They are laying the snare, they will catch the fox;* || **B, C, E, K** there is no dialogue between Helen and her mother.

IV. The introductory dialogue between son and mother is repeated, and now the mother proposes to have a marvellous tower made. Its summit will touch the sky, its buttresses will reach the river Tisza. Girls will come and see the marvellous tower, Helen will be among them.

---

[1] 'Brave Valentine' in Hungarian = 'Bálint *vitéz*!' 'Vitéz' means 'soldier', 'a brave soldier', or just 'brave'.

[2] 'Görög' means Greek. As Hungarian places the surname before the Christian name, the Hungarian form of the name Görög Ilona (Ilona = Helen) means both 'Greek Helen' and 'Helen Greek'.

D the buttresses of the tower will reach the Danube instead of the Tisza; **G** 'its summit will touch the sky' only; **F** has instead of the tower a 'strong iron bridge'; **E** a golden mill; **B** a silver mill; **K** a golden mill which will grind small pearls; **C, I** there is no second marvellous building built.

V. Helen is again held back by the above-quoted warning of her mother.

G ends here; **B, C, E, K** as above III.

VI. The introductory dialogue is repeated, and now the boy is advised to feign death in order to lure Helen into his house after all.

B, C, E 'We shall have the big bell rung', i.e. to spread the news of his death; **K** the mother will have a bell made, Valentine is to have it tolled for his death.

VII. Helen, in spite of her mother's warning, dresses herself and goes to Ladislav's house.

D the mother's warning is: *They are casting the net, | They will catch the barbel, | They will take away fair Helen Görög | From her mother. || **F** Give me leave, mother, to go to the house of mourning. | —You will never come back from the house of mourning! || **D** She would not listen to her mother, | She walks into the house, | There she dresses herself | In blue silken dress, | She puts on her feet | Red, iron shod boots, | She puts on her head | A red silken scarf, | She puts her white apron | Before her; ||* **H, I** where the mother tells Helen how to dress for the occasion must have derived from this incident in versions **A, D**. **H** *Dress in black, in black silk dress; ||* **I** *Put on your skirt, | Put on your dress, | Take in your hand | Your bunch of flowers; ||* **C, E, J** add another scene here: the girl asks who has died, and gets the answer that it was her lover. **J** starts here, with the dialogue between mother and daughter; **C** *Valentine Molnár has feigned death, | The big bell has been rung. | Fair Helen runs out of the house: | —Who could have died in the village? || —Valentine Molnár has died, | Your kind, handsome lover has died! [bis] || —Mother, mother, my mother, | Give me leave to go and see the dead man, | You did not give me leave to see the marvels, | Give me leave now, to go and see the dead man. | ... || On she goes, on she goes, the fair Helen, | When she passes the gate | Her mother starts mourning for her | Her mother starts mourning for her. ||* **E, F, J** like **C**, but the mother gives Helen permission to leave. **K** there is no dialogue between Helen and her mother. *All the fair maids went to see it, | The fair maids and the fair young men, | Fair Helen was among them. ||*

VIII. Ladislav's mother tells him about Helen's movements as she approaches their house, as she walks over their land, as she stands at Ladislav's feet, and asks her son to arise in the manner of one casting a spell to arouse a dead man.

B, C she is on her way,...is at the gate,...is standing by your side; **F** she is walking in front of the gate,...is in your courtyard; is standing at your feet; **H** she is dressing herself,...she is setting off now, is on her way,...is standing at your gate,...is standing at your side; **D** is coming on the road,...has entered the house; **J** is standing at your feet; **I, K** this incident is missing; **E** 'she is coming'.

IX. Ladislav jumps up from his bier and embraces Helen. In **A–D**, **F, H, I, K** we understand the boy's movements from Helen's exclamation:

I have seen corpses before, | *But never one like this,* etc. || as quoted in the main version; **K** *Maidens, maidens, my maiden friends,* | *My friends who have grown up with me,* | *I have never seen a corpse like this,* | *Like the corpse of brave Valentine;* || **D** adds [*a corpse*] *Which is ready to wake up* | *If only I were to kiss him;* || **B** adds *Thus he jumped up and embraced her;* || **F** *He stood up gently, he embraced her gently;* || **E** ends with the mother's words: *Keep your arms ready to embrace,* | *Keep your lips ready for a kiss,* | *Keep your lips ready for a kiss,* | *Keep your feet ready to jump.* || **J** *Aye, his eyes were open,* | *Aye, his lips were smiling;* || **H** ends with Ladislav's words: *You are mine, you are mine* | *Fair Helen Görög,* | *Fair Helen Görög,* | *Rose made of pearls.* ||

Versions **C** and **I** have preserved an ending which recalls the Scandinavian:

C *Fair Helen starts mourning:* | *—I have not seen such a corpse before,* | *With feet ready to walk,* | *With eyes ready to blink,* | *With arms ready to embrace,* | *With lips ready to kiss!* || **I** *She clapped her hands,* | *She clasped her hands over her head,* | *She cried seven times more* | *Than her mother cried.* ||

International versions

F. J. Child draws attention to the fact that 'feigning dead as a means of winning a shy mistress enjoys a considerable popularity in European ballads' (Child, no. 25 nn.). He lists the Scottish, Danish, Swedish, Italian, Slovene, and Icelandic variants with which the versions of the Hungarian ballad share several motifs:[1] the hero's pining for a girl (Scottish *B, C*; Danish, Swedish, Icelandic, Italian, Slovene); his mother's questioning him about the reason for his grief (Scottish *B, C*; Danish *A–D*; Swedish); various attempts in vain to lure the girl into the hero's house (Italian, Slovene); the hero's feigning death (all versions) on his mother's advice (Scottish, Danish, Swedish, Icelandic); bells ringing for the 'dead' (Scottish, Danish *B*, Italian, Slovene); the girl's asking why the bells are ringing (Scottish, Danish, Italian); her asking for her mother's (or father's) permission to go to the house of the 'dead' (Scottish, Danish, Swedish); the parents' warnings or precautions (Scottish, Danish, Swedish); she dresses herself before setting

---

[1] Ballads similar to the Slovene versions are known in Bulgaria as well. Cf. *Deutsche Volkslieder mit ihren Melodien* (Berlin, 1957, no. 58) and L. Vargyas, ' Csudahalott', *Ethnographia*, **71**, 215–23. Vargyas calls attention to a group of French ballads similar to the Danish versions (*ibid.*): In the lover's absence the girl's parents send her to a nunnery. On his return he feigns death and eventually elopes with the girl who has stayed at his bedside to mourn over him.

off (Danish *B*, *C*); incremental repetition when describing how the girl advances towards the 'corpse' (Danish, Scottish),[1] the 'resuscitation' of the 'dead' (all versions); the girl's alarm (Scottish **A**, **B**; Danish *A*, *B*; Slovene).

Motifs

I. The Scottish and Scandinavian versions mention no tricks previous to the feigned death.

In the Italian ballad[2] the hero plants a beautiful garden, gives a ball with thirty-two musicians, builds a church; the Slovene ballad[2] has the church, and the hero has a well dug, hoping that the loved girl will go there for water.

'The Miraculous Dead' seems to preserve a more archaic form: of all the international variants, the Hungarian is the only one which brings in sorcery.

All ten versions have the marvellous mill. The original version of **B**, **E** (which have a golden and a silver mill), and **C** (which has a brass mill) probably had all the three mills, as such a triad is most common in folk tales.

Neither the marvellous mill nor the marvellous tower are Hungarian inventions (cp. Thompson, D 1263 and F 772 respectively).

The marvellous tower can be traced back as far as the Bible (the tower of Babel) and appears in several folk tales.

The best-known example of the marvellous mill is the Sampo of the *Kalevala*, which has three mills, one for flour, one for salt, one for money. F. Liebrecht (*Zur Volkskunde*, Heilbronn, 1879, p. 303, 'Eine alte Todesstrafe') mentions the Grotti-mill, which grinds gold, luck, peace and salt.

Such mills occur in the folksongs of Iceland, Sweden, Denmark,

---

[1] Danish (e.g. Grundtvig, no. 409, *E*, *F*, *I*, stanzas 9–11): 'Saa gik hun til hans Hoved / og krusede hans Haar: / 'Ret aldrig jeg dig glemmer, / hvor jeg i Verden gaar.' // Saa gik hun til hans Fødder / og bad godt for hans Sjael: / 'I Verden mens du levede / da undte jeg dig vel.' // Saa gik hun til hans Side, / klappad ham paa hviden Kind: / 'I Verden mens du levede / var du Allerkaerasten min.' Scottish *A* 'It's whan she cam to the utmost yett, / She made the silver fly roun for his sake, // It's whan she cam to the inmost yett / She made the red gold fly round for his sake, // As she walked frae the court to the parlour there / The pretty corpse syne began for to steer.' *B* 'When she came to young Willie's yate / Her seven brithers were standing thereat, // Then they did conduct her into the ha' / Among the weepers and merry mourners a'. // When she lifted the covering sae red...etc.' *C* 'When that she came to her true lover's gate / She dealt with the red gold for his sake, // And when that she came to her true lover's bower / She had not been there fore the space of half an hour, // Till that she came to her true lover's bed, / And she lifted the winding sheet to look at the dead.'

[2] Cf. Child, no. 25 nn.

Germany, Italy, Catalonia, and Greece.[1] P. P. Domokos[2] publishes a *Csángó* folksong with the same motif:

> Let your red blood and my red blood
> Run together in one stream,
> Let it drive a mill,
> And that mill should have three stones;
> Its first stone should throw white pearls,
> Its second stone should throw small change,
> Its third stone should produce love.

Marvellous mills are also familiar in folk tales: A. Waldau (*Böhmisches Märchenbuch*, Prague, 1860) has a Slovakian tale, 'The Golden Quern'. A youth, following wise advice, asks not for money but for a quern. Pure gold pours out from it. A quern of this type appears also in Arabian tales, for instance, 'The Mill that produces Gold' (G. Meyer, *Essays and Studies*, 1, p. 190). R. Köhler (*Jahrbuch für ro. and eng. Literatur*, **6,** 56) quotes a Portuguese romance: he who will bring back the husband of the Infanta will get three querns, one of them will produce all sorts of spices, another will produce cinnamon, and the third will produce delicious olives. Type 565 also has such a magic mill: it grinds an enormous amount of meal and salt when the man who stole it cannot stop it.

Although the ballad of the miraculous dead is known in Transylvania and Moldavia only, this image of the magic mill is not unknown in the Lowland. L. Kálmány in Koszorúk 1, p. 97, prints a folksong which has the motif of such a mill, but with the opposite thing to be ground:

> The windmill of Tornya is humming,
> My bright star, my sweetheart,
> The windmill of Tornya is humming,
> *Sorrow* is ground in it,
> My bright star, my sweetheart.
>
> I am going to take my sorrow there,
> My bright star, my sweetheart,
> I am going to take my sorrow there
> And will have it ground together with the other sorrows,
> My bright star, my sweetheart.

L. Vargyas has also recorded a folksong with such a mill from the Lowland (Z. Kodály, *A Magyar Népzene*, no. 34, p. 95):

---

[1] F. Liebrecht, *op. cit.*   [2] P. P. Domokos, *op. cit.* no. 29.

At the shore of the Danube there is a mill,
Sorrow is ground on it, ay,
I have my sorrow too, I shall take it there and
    have it ground, ay.

But there are, to my knowledge, no instances where such a marvellous mill is used as a decoy.[1]

II. All the Nordic versions (except Danish *B*) have the warning by the girl's mother or father against her visiting the 'dead' lover.

In Child, no. 25 *A*, the father allows his daughter to go only with her seven brothers; in *B* the father bids her to take her brother. *C* mentions her friends who were all in the bower with the girl. In the Danish *A*, *C–G* the mother (*D*, father) warns her daughter not to go, as happens also in the Swedish versions.

In the Hungarian ballad this point is much more emphasised. It is not the lovers, but the two mothers, who are the real antagonists. Their struggle for the girl has a marked similarity to struggles between sorceresses in folk tales. The boy's mother has positive magic power. She can conjure up a marvellous mill and a tower as means of temptation. The other's strength is passive. It lies in her capacity for resistance. Shrewdness and instinctive prudence are qualities cherished by every mother with a daughter. What makes them appear supernatural here is that they stand in opposition to magic; and this impression is reinforced by the rhythm and the incantatory quality of the repeated and ominous warnings which the mother gives her daughter.

Folklore and customs

'They are casting the net, they will catch the fox' could refer to the old custom of catching animals with hunting nets, but it is more likely to be merely a contamination of the expressions which occur in other versions, i.e. 'they are casting the net, they will catch the barbel' and 'they are laying the snare, they will catch the fox'.

Date

In dating 'The Miraculous Dead' we are restricted to indirect evidence when drawing our conclusions.

---

[1] L. Vargyas mentions a miraculous mill which occurs in another French ballad, 'Joli Tambour', in which a young drummer asks the King to give him his daughter, and tells the King that he has three mills: one grinds gold, the other grinds silver, the third grinds his beloved's love.

In a German ballad (recorded at Gottschee, which has a Slovene population) the mother has a white mill built, in the hope that her son's beloved will go there to have flour ground. This is, however, not a marvellous mill (Vargyas, *loc. cit.*).

4-2

Among its international variants, the earliest recorded are those Danish versions which have been found in sixteenth-century manuscripts.

As we have seen, the Hungarian ballad shares several main motifs and details with these versions, but it has also some distinctive features that do not occur in any of its international parallels.

F. J. Child, analysing the 'Willie's Lyke Wake' ballad type and comparing the Danish versions with each other, assumes that versions where elopement from a convent is involved blend two different stories, and that the convent is a later invention. Perhaps we can complete his theory of the blending of two stories, if we bear in mind the evidence of the Hungarian ballad.

Some thought should be given here to the consideration that the magic elements (i.e. the magic power of the mother and the marvellous mill) occur in *all* the Hungarian versions and that they are not accidental additions but furnish the basic construction of the ballad. Moreover, we find *no other* Hungarian ballads of wizardry, and there is no reason to suppose that an international theme would be enlarged in Hungary by the addition of motifs foreign to Hungarian balladry. Such enlargements do not occur elsewhere. There is reason therefore to suppose that the Hungarian variant has not added these motifs to the ballad, but that it has preserved them, as they were original features of the type.

If we accept that the Hungarian ballad has preserved motifs of an archetype of the ballad, it can be assumed that there was one ballad which concentrated on an elopement story (Child, no. 25; Danish C–E, G; Swedish A–C; Icelandic) and another ballad which was closely connected to another type of saga: that of the widespread folk tales of witches and fairies, who try to get hold of, or destroy, their victims by producing various alluring magic objects in front of them.

Example: AT type[1] 303, incident III, where the eldest brother goes hunting, or goes in search of another princess, or follows a fire which he sees out of the window on his wedding night (Thompson, G 241) and falls into the power of a witch who turns him into stone (Thompson, G 201, d 231); type 327, the ginger-bread house as a trap (Thompson, F 7717), lured away by birds (type 471), etc.

Our version is closely related to these folk tales, but with one difference—our heroine is not unwilling to be tempted.

This state of affairs suggests that the Nordic ballads have preserved

---

[1] 'Type' followed by a number refers to A. Aarne-Thompson's folk-tale types. A letter followed by a number refers to Stith Thompson's Motif Index.

the story which concentrated on the elopement, and some versions fused this story with another eloping ballad (i.e. that of the convent) of later origin, probably because both types had the common motif of feigning death.

The Hungarian ballad, on the other hand, has preserved the main motifs of the original elopement story as represented in the earliest Nordic ballads, and also it has preserved motifs from another archetype of the same story: the one which had magic elements and emphasised by them the events previous to the feigned death. The Italian and Slovene ballads (where the hero has a beautiful garden planted, gives a ball, has a church built, has a well dug) seem to have evolved from this second type of the ballad, and can be considered as examples of a development not uncommon in the later history of folklore, where there is a strong tendency to avoid supernatural expedients.

Although the Hungarian ballad has preserved the main motifs of the Nordic parallels as well as some details, and the magic nature of its additional motifs would suggest an earlier origin, the actual wording of the ballad does not seem to be older than the end of the seventeenth century.

Special Hungarian elements

We have already dealt with some of the specifically Hungarian features of the ballad: the introduction of magic elements into the ballad with the motifs of the marvellous mill and tower, the magic power of the boy's mother, the duel between the two mothers.

There is another point which deserves mention: the Hungarian ballad treats in a novel way the crucial part of the ballad (when Ladislav feigns death on his mother's advice).

The Hungarian versions **A**, **D**, and **H** succeed in creating a feeling of suspense not to be found in any of the international versions.

All the English, Scandinavian, Italian, and Slovenian versions leave it quite clear to the audience that the death of the hero is merely a clever device. In our **A**, **D**, and **H** versions it is not so obvious.

> **A** I am dying indeed, mother, my mother,
> For Helen Görög, for her slender waist,
> For her slender waist, for her full lips,
> For her full lips, for her rosy cheeks!
>
> —Do die, my son, do die, Ladislav Bertelaki!

The sudden contrast between her answer and her earlier prayer 'Do not die, my son, do not die, Ladislav Bertelaki' gives us the feeling of the moment when, as a result of her son's continual rumination over death, the idea of a trick comes suddenly to the mother. We are at a loss for a second, together with the son, who perhaps just like us has not caught the meaning of the words immediately. The youth's romantic desire for death and the mother's cunning device give piquancy to their dialogue. Until the very end, we are allowed only to guess at the trick, and our perplexity gives way gradually to a feeling of suspense, as we wait to see whether our conjecture will prove to be true, and whether the girl will fall into the trap.

4

CHRISTIAN
LEGENDARY BALLADS

Introduction

The Hungarian ballad tradition resembles the English and Scottish in that it makes little use of Christian themes and motifs. Among the five ballads we shall mention in this chapter, only two ('The Fair Maid Julia' and 'The Three Orphans') were recorded in several versions. The others stand solitary and fragmentary and resemble in form carols or hymns for various church festivals rather than ballads. Moreover, the stories—a virgin taken to Heaven as a bride for Jesus ('The Fair Maid Julia'), children searching for their dead mother with the help of the Virgin Mary ('The Three Orphans'), the Virgin Mary looking for shelter in which to give birth to her Son ('When the Virgin Mary was Walking'), the Virgin Mary searching for her Son who has been crucified ('The Virgin Mary set out'), Christ seeking accommodation at a rich and at a poor inn ('Good Evening, you Rich Innkeeper')—do not correspond in their detail to any conventional Christian legends. They derive their material neither from the Bible nor from the Apocrypha, and no ballads have been preserved which relate to any of the common miracle tales. The content and style of these surviving 'Christian' ballads and ballad-songs suggest that they were not written by ecclesiastics, but by lay bards who made use of legends (related in the vernacular, and circulating among the people), which have not so far been traced.

'THE FAIR MAID JULIA'

Of this group 'The Fair Maid Julia' deserves the most particular notice. It is the only 'proper' Christian legendary ballad which is represented in several versions; 'The Three Orphans', as we have said in the introduction to the Magic Ballads, stands on the borderline between magic and Christian legendary ballads. All these versions approximate in style to the proper, condensed, crystallised ballad form while the intensity of its religious emotion, its arresting simplicity and its subtle symbolism give it a claim to rank among the great ballads of the world. It is important also for reasons which have nothing to do with its aesthetic merit. The attempt to trace back its motifs will bring us face to face with that complicated process of evolution whereby the legends and symbols of pre-Christian Hungary were given Christian meanings, and then finding expression again in vernacular poetry became for a second time entangled with the popular myths surviving in curious forms from pagan times.

Version **A**

1 Once upon a time out went fair maid Julia
  To pluck cornflowers in the cornfield,
  To pluck cornflowers, to bind them into a wreath,
  To bind them into a wreath, to enjoy herself.

2 Up, up she gazed into the high heaven,
  Behold! a fine pathway came down from it,
  And on it descended a curly white lamb.
  It carried the sun and the moon between its horns,
  It carried the sparkling star on its brow,
  On its two horns were Ay! two fine gold bracelets,
  Ay! at its two sides were two fine burning candles,
  As many as its hairs, so many the stars upon it.

3 Up and speaks to her the curly white lamb:
  'Do not take fright at me, fair maid Julia,
  For now the host of virgins has fallen short by one.
  If you were to come with me, I would take you there,
  To the heavenly choir, to the holy virgins,
  So as to complete their pious host;
  I would give the key of Heaven into your hands.
  At the first cockcrow I would come and see you,
  At the second cockcrow I would propose to you,
  At the third cockcrow I would take you away.'

4 Fair maid Julia turns to her mother,
  And up and speaks to her: 'Mother, my mother,
  I did but go out to pluck cornflowers,
  To pluck cornflowers, to bind them into a wreath,
  To bind them into a wreath, to enjoy myself.
  Up, up I gazed into the high heaven,
  Behold! a fine pathway came down from it,
  And on it descended a curly white lamb.
  It carried the sun and the moon between its horns,
  It carried the sparkling star on its brow,
  On its two horns were Ay! two fine gold bracelets,
  Ay! at its two sides were two fine burning candles,
  As many as its hairs, so many the stars upon it.

Up and speaks to me the curly white lamb:
"Do not take a fright at me fair maid Julia,
For now the host of virgins has fallen short by one."
If I were to go with it, I would be taken there
To the heavenly choir, to the holy virgins,
So as to complete their pious host.
It will give the key of Heaven into my hands,
At the first cockcrow they will come and see me,
At the second cockcrow they will propose to me,
At the third cockcrow they will take me away.
Lament for me mother, lament. Let me hear while I still live,
Let me hear while I still live, how you will lament when I am dead.'

5 'My daughter, my daughter, in my flower garden,
You the wee honeycomb of my first bee-swarm,
You the yellow wax of this wee honeycomb,
The earth-spreading smoke of this yellow wax,
The earth-spreading smoke, its heaven-breaking flame!

6 The heavenly bell, untolled it tolled,
The heavenly gate, unopened it opened,
Alas! my daughter, she was led in there!'

Versions

This ballad has survived in ten versions, all of which come to us from Transylvania or Moldavia.

A Csanádi-Vargyas, *Röpülj*, no. 17; =Kriza, *Vadrózsák*, no. 270; =Kriza (1956), no. 4; =*MNGY*, XI, no. 175; =Ortutay, *Magyar Népköltészet*, II, no. 22 a[1] B Csanádi-Vargyas, *Röpülj*, no. 18; =Domokos, *Moldvai Magyarság*, no. 11; =Domokos (1931), p. 226 C Ortutay, *Magyar Népköltészet*, II, no. 22 b; =Kriza, *Vadrózsák*, no. 318; =Kriza (1956), no. 5; =*MNGY*, XI, p. 214 D Csanádi-Vargyas, *Röpülj*, p. 446; =*Ethnographia*, 70, 23 E Csanádi-Vargyas, *Röpülj*, p. 448 F Faragó-Jagamas, *MCSNN*, no. 4 G *Néprajzi Közlemények* (Budapest, 1958), III, 1–2, no. 9 (pp. 61–2) H *ibid.* no. 10 I *MNYr*, 7, 143 J *MNYr*, 16, 48 K *Ethnographia*, 70, 24, no. 9 L *ibid.*, no. 10. (All versions may be found together in *Ethnographia*, 70, 14–27.)

Description of the ballad

I. The fair maid Julia (**B, D, F–H, K** fair Helen Márton; **E** fair maid Martha woman; **I, J** fair maid Susannah; **L** virgin martyr woman) goes out to the field to pick flowers for a wreath; (**E**—she goes to the rose-vineyard (?) to pick roses; **B–D, F–H, K, L** she sits under an apple

---

[1] A. B. Vikár, *Magyar Népköltés Remekei*, II (Budapest, 1906), p. 7, published a text which is obviously a retouched version of **A**. He does not give any references, and elsewhere in the same anthology he mixes arbitrarily several versions of certain ballads. S. Solymossy, *Magyarság Néprajza*, III (Budapest, 1941), pp. 97–8, uses Vikár's unreliable version in describing 'The Fair Maid Julia' while incorrectly giving the reference to our version **A**.

tree; **I, J** she walks out to the rose-meadow, lies down under the roses, tousles her golden hair, washes her rosy cheek).

II. She looks at the sky. A path comes down from Heaven (**C**—the two sides of the path are pure silver, its middle pure gold). Along the path a curly white lamb[1] descends towards her. It carries the sun and the moon between its horns. It has a bright star on its forehead. On its two horns are two fair golden bracelets. On its two sides are two burning candles. It has as many stars on it as it has hairs.

B on its right side are eighty mass candles, on its head is beautiful sunlight; **C** (which ends here) and **G** on each hair is a star; **D** on its forehead is a beautiful bright star, on its right side is beautiful bright sunlight, on its left side is beautiful bright moonlight, on its head are eighty mass candles; **H** on its right side, it carries the light of the blessed sun, on its left side the light of the blessed moon, on its hairs the tiny stars, on its forehead eighty mass candles; **K** it has the light of the blessed sun on its left side, the light of the blessed moon on its right side, between its two horns sixty mass candles; **L** similar to **K**, but sixty mass candles on its hairs, and the heavenly bell between its horns; **E** (very corrupt), **F, I, J** mention only the curly lamb without further details.

III. The lamb tells the maiden not to be frightened. She is needed to join the heavenly choir, in which one is missing from the legion of virgins. The lamb would give the key of Heaven into her hands; at the first cockcrow it would come to see her, at the second cockcrow it would propose to her, at the third cockcrow it would take her away.

B, D, G, H the lamb says God has sent him, because there is one fair virgin short; **E** he asks her to complete the number of the ninety-nine virgins; **F** a lamb is missing from the legion of virgins; **F, I, J** the girl asks the lamb to wait while she bids farewell to her parents; **I**—to her girl and boy friends; **J**—and to her betrothed; **I, J** the lamb says: 'I am not a phantom. I am a messenger from Heaven. The Lord Jesus Christ sent me as the legion of virgins is one short'; **K, L** incident III is missing.

IV. Julia turns to her mother (having presumably returned home in the meantime) and repeats sections I–III (transposed into the first person) to her. The repetition is preserved only in version **A**.

E she goes home and loosens her golden hair; **H** she turns away and weeps and her mother asks why she is weeping; **F, H** she thanks her mother for the care she has received: *May God repay you | My mother dear, | That for nine months, | You carried me in your womb, | That after nine months | You gave me birth, | That you kept awake | By the rocking cradle.* (**F** ends here) || **H** adds: *Because I have to go to Heaven, | To the kingdom of Heaven, to the legion of fair virgins.* || **A, E** the maid asks her mother to lament for her.

V. The mother then laments.

A cf. full translation of **A**, sts. 5–6; **E** like **A**, st. 5, but adds: *Indeed, at the first cockcrow*

---

[1] The Hungarian 'bárány' means lamb. For its horns, cf. pp. 70–72.

it was proposed to her, | *At the second cockcrow she was promised away,* | *At the third cockcrow she passed away from this world.* | *The heavenly gates, unopened they opened,* | *The key of Heaven was given into her hands,* | *'Take care of this, fair maid Martha woman.'* | *'It is enough, mother, my dear mother,* | *Now I have heard how you will lament when I am dead.'* || In **B, D, G–L** the concluding passage is of a descriptive nature instead of being part of a lament as in **A, E.** Instead of IV **B** has: *My God, my God, my beloved God,* | *I have not heard such a thing before,* | *That heavenly bells should toll themselves,* | *That heavenly tables should set themselves,* | *That heavenly glasses should fill themselves;* || **D** *The heavenly gates, unopened they open,* | *The heavenly bells, untolled they toll,* | *On twelve altars are twelve priests,* | *The greatest of them is Jesus Christ.* || **G** *The wreath of virgins alighted on her head.* || **H** *The heavenly gates, unopened they opened,* | *The heavenly bells, untolled they tolled,* | *The heavenly glasses became full, unfilled.* || **I** has: *At the second cockcrow, they went out to see her,* | *At the third cockcrow they proposed to her,* | *At the fourth cockcrow, they proposed to her,* | *At the fifth cockcrow, they took her away.* || *The heavenly gate, unopened it opened,* | *The heavenly bell, untolled it tolled,* | *The key of Heaven is put into her hands:* | *'Take care of this, fair maid Susannah,* | *Take care of this, forever, Amen.'* || **J** like **I**, but: *At the first cockcrow, they went out to see her,* | *At the second cockcrow, they came to her,* | *At the third cockcrow, they proposed to her,* | *At the fourth cockcrow, she was promised away,* | *At the fifth cockcrow she was taken away, etc.* || **K** *Let the candles of Heaven flare up, unlit,* | *Let the heavenly bells toll, untolled,* | *Let the heavenly gate open, unopened.* || **L** like **K**, but without the heavenly gates.

International versions

Ballads and legends with a theme similar to 'The Fair Maid Julia' were recorded in German, Dutch, Swedish, and Danish language territories. R. Gragger was the first to supply references in this direction.[1] His bibliographical references were completed by Gy. Ortutay,[2] E. Dános,[3] and P. P. Domokos.[4]

I. *Danish versions.* (Danish: S. Grundtvig, *Danmarks Gamle Folke-viser,* Kopenhague, 1856, no. 104 [*A, B, C*].)

God sends an angel from Heaven to the earth to fetch a virgin for him. A virgin goes into a rose garden, she is picking flowers and she wishes that she could meet the Master. (*C*) A bird appears on a tree in her garden, and sings beautifully (of Jesus and of God). It has to wait for three days before the maid notices it. She loves the song, and wants to have the bird. She would put it into a golden chest, on a golden bar. She opens first three, then five, windows, but the bird would not be lured inside. Finally she goes out to entice it. The bird greets her sweetly and informs her that by the next day she will be in Heaven.

[1] R. Gragger, *Ungarische Balladen* (Berlin, 1926), pp. 11, 180.
[2] Gy. Ortutay, *Székely Népballadák* (Budapest, 1935), 'Júlia szép leány', notes.
[3] E. Dános, *Magyar Népballada* (Budapest, 1939), p. 136.
[4] P. P. Domokos, 'Júlia szép leány', *Ethnographia*, **70**, 1–3, pp. 13–75.

'Then I shall see my Saviour.' The virgin is healthy when she goes out, but she is ill when she returns home. She asks her sister to prepare her bed, her mother to stand by her, her brother to fetch a priest for her, and her father to be near her. They should not grieve for her for they will meet in Heaven. Between four and five o'clock she gives up her soul, between eight and nine o'clock she dies. The Virgin Mary dresses the corpse. Angels take her soul to Heaven.

In the Swedish versions (E. G. Geijer and A. A. Afzelius, *Svenska Folkvisor*, Stockholm, 1880, I, no. 56, 2 versions, and II, pp. 249–51) a bird sings beautifully of Jesus Christ. A maid listens to it, and the bird informs her that in the same year she will die. (In some versions she protests.) Her heart aches, she goes home, and asks her mother to prepare her bed. The mother tells her not to talk like that, she is to be a queen. She says it is better to be Christ's bride, asks her father to fetch a priest, her brother to make her bier, her sister to arrange her hair. The maid dies, angels escort her coffin, singing.

II. *Regina-songs*. (For representative texts cf. Erk-Böhme, *Deutscher Liederhort*, Leipzig, 1894, nos. 2123, 2124, 2125.)[1]

Known mostly in Switzerland and Germany. Regina goes into her enclosed garden. She is picking flowers (occasionally making a wreath) when suddenly she notices a youth next to her. 'How did you come in?—she questions him—all the gates are locked, and the walls are high.' 'I am Jesus for whom there are no high walls or locked gates.' Regina wants to follow him and they write a letter to her parents informing them that she is in Heaven.

III a. *The Sultan's Daughter*. Known in German and Swedish language territory. (For representative texts cf. Erk-Böhme, *Deutscher Liederhort*, Leipzig, 1894, nos. 2127, 2128.)[2]

The Sultan's daughter goes into her garden. She admires the flowers and wonders who has created them. If she could see him only once she would leave her father's kingdom for him. At midnight Jesus appears to her. He betrothes the maid with a ring. She questions him about his name, and about his father and mother. He reveals that he is Jesus, and describes his father as the creator of everything and his mother as a pure virgin. She wants to follow him. 'You must be pure.' He takes her to the gates of Heaven, which he enters. The maid waits for her betrothed. She has forgotten his name, but describes him. The gatesman recognises Jesus from the description, and admits her into Heaven.

---

[1] For further bibliographical references, cf. P. P. Domokos, *op. cit.*
[2] *Ibid.*

Jesus comes to welcome her, and leads her into his kingdom through a golden gate.

III *b*. Two versions belong here (Erk-Böhme, *Deutscher Liederhort*, Leipzig, 1894, nos. 2121, 2122) which contain elements of both II and III and which were apparently influenced by prose legends current in the fifteenth century.[1]

The daughter of a pagan king goes into her garden. She admires the flowers and wants to serve their creator who must be even mightier than her father. A beautiful youth appears suddenly in spite of the locked gates. The dialogue of the Regina-songs follows. She wants to accompany him. This is possible if she leaves her worldly wealth behind. Jesus takes her to a monastery gate. She knocks and asks for her bridegroom; the nuns inform her that no man could have entered their nunnery. She describes him as Jesus, and is admitted into the house of the nuns where she serves God for the rest of her life.

IV. *The Captain's Daughter*. (For representative text cf. Arnim-Brentano, *Des Knaben Wunderhorn*, Berlin, 1873, pp. 99–103.)[2]

The daughter of the captain of Grossvarden chooses Christ as her bridegroom. Her parents arrange a marriage for her in spite of her protests. She goes into her garden, calls Jesus. Jesus, a beautiful youth, appears. He gives her a ring, she gives him a rose. Jesus invites her to see his garden. When she returns, it turns out that she has been away for a hundred and twenty years although she has not aged at all. No one knows her in the town any more. She goes to the church, starts to grow old rapidly, and dies.[3]

---

[1] These prose legends constitute group IV in P. P. Domokos's article. Their story goes as follows: The daughter of a pagan king goes into her garden. She admires the flowers and wants to serve the God that created them. She becomes engaged, but before her wedding she asks her bridegroom's permission to go into her garden to pray to the God of flowers. A beautiful youth appears to her, declares himself to be the angel of God. She asks the angel's advice how she should serve God. She should remain pure and must not get married, the angel replies. Then he takes the maid to a church (or nunnery) in a Christian country, and places her in front of an altar. The nuns (or guardian of the church and his companions) believe her to be the Virgin Mary and sing 'Salve Regina' to her. Later they find a letter in her hand which describes her story. The bishop christens her, and the maid serves God as a nun till the end of her life.

[2] For further bibliographical references, cf. P. P. Domokos, *op. cit.*

[3] The story was known in Hungary early in the sixteenth century. It appears in the Érdy codex of 1527. In this 'Exemplum Mirabile' a noble knight goes to a church to pray before his wedding. On his way back he meets a fine old man who is riding a white mule. He invites him to his wedding. The old man tells the night that he is God's messenger, and has come to take part in the feast. He stays with the knight for three days during which neither he nor his mule eat or drink. Then he is ready to leave. The knight escorts him to the path where they met and weeps in his sorrow. The visitor from Heaven invites him to return the visit: in three days' time he will find the mule at the same place and it will take him to the old man. The knight goes home, does not eat or drink, is not interested in his young wife. In three days' time he goes to the appointed

Motifs

Csanádi-Vargyas (*Röpülj*, p. 44) remark that the only feature common to the whole collection is that a girl is taken up to Heaven as a bride of Christ. But if we analyse the motifs of the ballad we shall discover a number of other more particular connections.

All versions, Hungarian and otherwise, introduce the heroine among flowers. In the Hungarian ballad, as in Danish *C*, and Regina-type she is picking flowers (making a wreath); in 'The Sultan's Daughter' she is admiring them and wonders who has created them. In 'The Captain's Daughter' she goes into her garden to call for Jesus.

The sudden, unexpected appearance of Jesus or of the heavenly messenger also occurs among flowers or in a garden in the Hungarian, Danish, and Swedish versions in the Regina-songs and in 'The Captain's Daughter'.

According to Domokos it is the Regina-type that stands closest to the Hungarian ballad in its present form. In his comparison of motifs he illustrates the similarity in the following:

Julia	Regina	Common motifs
1. Julia	1. Regina	1. a pure virgin
2. in a cornfield	2. in a closed rose garden	2. among flowers
3. is making a wreath	3. is picking flowers	3. is picking flowers, making a wreath
4. she looks up	4. she looks around	4. she looks around
5. observes a shining white lamb	5. observes a youth clad in white with golden hair	5. observes a heavenly messenger
6. they talk to each other, the lamb invites Julia to Heaven	6. they talk to each other, Regina is ready to follow Jesus	6. they talk to each other

place and the mule takes him to the land of eternal life. A description of Heaven follows: beautiful trees, flowers, fruit, birds singing. He meets the old man and various knights, all beautiful and glittering, each wearing a royal crown. His family in the meanwhile searches for him in vain. They give away their wealth and transform their castle into a monastery where they live till their death. After what has seemed to him a three-hour visit the knight asks leave to go back to his family and to his guests. The mule takes him back. Instead of his friends and family he finds the monastery there. It turns out that he has been away for three hundred years. They arrange a feast for him, but when he tastes food he grows old rapidly and dies.

L. Katona ('Az Érdy codex egy fejezetéről', *Akadémiai Értesítő* (1909)) has established the fact that the author of the 'Exemplum Mirabile' took his material from the thirteenth-century 'Visionslegende', which has been preserved in many versions in Latin from Germany and Italy, and which appears to have been well known between the thirteenth and fifteenth centuries.

| 7. the lamb takes the maid to Heaven in a miraculous fashion | 7. Jesus takes Regina to Heaven in a mira- culous fashion | 7. the messenger takes the maid to Heaven in a miraculous fashion |
| | | 8. the maid has arrived at the place for which she was longing |

In this summary, however, certain elements of the Hungarian ballad are completely ignored (e.g. the proposal, her return home, her death, the mother's lament) while others are overemphasised (e.g. (4) in both the Hungarian and Regina-songs this is a secondary motif which is not mentioned at all in most of the versions; (7) neither the Julia nor the Regina-type describe the actual journey to Heaven;[1] and (8) is implicit only in the Regina-songs).

The Scandinavian (group I) ballad also introduces the heroine among flowers. In addition to this it offers some further interesting points of similarity with the Hungarian ballad which do not occur in the other international versions:

1. In Danish *A, C*, God sends down one of his angels to the earth to fetch a virgin to Heaven:

> Vor Herre han sidder i Himmerig:
> han talede til Engelen saa trøstelig.
> 'Og du skal ned til Jorderig
> og hente den Jomfru hid til mig.'

(*The Lord sat in Heaven, and | spoke to his angel kindly: | You shall go to the earth and | bring up a virgin to me.*)

This parallels the lamb's statement in our **B, D, G, H**, that God (**I, J** that Jesus) had ordered its mission.

2. The girl's destination is revealed by a magic animal, though in the Scandinavian it is not a lamb but a bird which sings beautiful songs about Jesus and God.[2]

3. The girl returns home and tells her family that she is going to die as she does in our **A, E, F, H, I, J**.

4. The virgin's journey to Heaven is felt to be an earthly death only in the Scandinavian and in the Hungarian ballad.

5. Danish *B* ends with a passage that is the only counterpart in the international versions to the mother's lament.

---

[1] In the two versions which I described under III*b*, Jesus takes the maid to the nunnery over fields, but this trait is not typical of the Regina-songs.

[2] The maiden's rather irrelevant attempt to entice the bird in the Danish ballad has no counter- part in the Hungarian ballad. This passage, however, as Grundtvig has pointed out (*op. cit.* no. 68), comes from another Danish ballad in which it has its structural point.

Ja, hun havde Haar, som spinden af Guld:
de Øjne de vare saa frydefuld.
Ja, hun havde Haender og Fødder saa smaa:
of liflig var Talen at høre oppaa.
Ja, jeg haver vaeret i fremmede Land:
ja, udi syv Kongeriger forsand,
Men aldrig fandt jeg saa vaen en Maar:
nu hviler skjøn Jomfru i sorten Jord.

(*Her hair was golden, her eyes were full of joy, her hands and feet were so small; her voice was delightful to hear; I have been in many foreign lands, have seen many princesses, but never have I seen such a fair maid, or such a lovely virgin in the world.*)

It follows then from (4) and (5) that there is a structural similarity in the last part between the Hungarian and the Scandinavian ballads which is not to be found elsewhere in the international versions:

> virgin hears the message
> goes home
> says goodbye to her family
> the lament (Danish)
> she arrives in *Heaven after* her death.

Elizabeth Dános (*Magyar Népballada*, p. 136) puts forward the theory that the Hungarian ballad derives from 'The Captain's Daughter' type. She conjectures that the Hungarian ballad might once have had the same ending as the former, and that the girl might have escaped to the field in her despair at a forced marriage. But she offers no supporting evidence for these conjectures and finds no other points of similarity.

P. P. Domokos agrees with Dános, and suggests that the ultimate source of the *entire* group (including 'The Fair Maid Julia', the Danish and Swedish versions as well as the Regina-songs and groups III and IV) is to be sought in the 'Visionslegende', i.e. in a body of legends which were to illustrate the words of the Psalm: 'For a thousand years in thy sight are but as yesterday when it is past, and as a watch in the night' (Ps. 90: 4).

According to his theory in these works (i.e. legends, etc.) the youth should be taken as a symbol of the young heathen people unaware of the teachings of Christianity, for whom Christ, who was crucified for humanity (or a heavenly messenger, a mule, a bird, or a white lamb) opens the gates of Heaven. Accordingly, the youth's journey (over hills and dales, without touching bridges, etc.) symbolises the spreading of Christian doctrines. These parables were the source of legends, ballads and songs, which were modified during the process of oral transmission. Thus, in Domokos's opinion, the duke or graf in the 'Visionslegende', the noble knight in the 'Exemplum Mirabile' (i.e. the bridegroom) becomes a bride in 'The Captain's Daughter'. Both bridegroom and bride reach Heaven in a miraculous way, and they die on their return. In the prose legends the bride-princesses also reach Heaven, but they do not return from there. The same happens to the Sultan's daughter, to the Reginas, and to the heroines of the Hungarian ballad, but in the latter forms the maids are not brides yet. In the case of 'The Captain's Daughter' roles are exchanged (bridegroom becomes bride), in the latter cases the change is due to structural decomposition—both well known processes in folklore.

This theory is most convincing as far as the interpretations of the 'Visionslegende'-'Exemplum Mirabile' type legends are concerned. Considering, however, the development of the international ballad versions Domokos has not, in my view, succeeded in establishing sufficiently that the idea represented in the Visionslegende-type can alone account for 'The Captain's Daughter'-'Sultan's Daughter'-Regina-Danish-Hungarian type ballad tradition. The fact that the central figure is a 'bride' in 'The Captain's Daughter' and not a 'bridegroom' (as in the Visionslegende and Exemplum Mirabile) is not due to arbitrary role exchanges (which are common indeed in oral tradition) becomes apparent if we compare this ballad with the rest of the group. Throughout his analysis Domokos ignores completely the motif which is prominent in most of the international versions, namely, that a maid is taken into Heaven *as a bride of Christ*. This is greatly emphasised in the Hungarian ballad (the proposal) as well as in the 'Sultan's Daughter':

> Schöne Magd, ich hab euch lang geliebt,
> Um euch bin ich gekommen
> ...Mein Garten liegt in Ewigkeit
> Von hier viel tausend Meilen,
> Da möcht ich dir zum Brautgeschmeid
> Ein Kränzlein roth ertheilen!
> Da nahm er von dem Finger sein
> Einen Ring von Sonnengolde
> Und fragt, ob Sultans Töchterlein
> Sein Bräutlein werden wollte.

(K. Simrock, *Die Deutschen Volksbücher*, VIII [Basel], no. 78, p. 155.)

In the Danish ballad:

> Hun havde trolovet den Herre Christ:
> nu lever hun udi Himmerig vist   (version *A*)

(*She has betrothed Jesus Christ, and now she certainly lives in Heaven.*)

In 'The Captain's Daughter':

> Der Jüngling an zu reden fing
> Verehrt ihr einen goldnen Ring:
> 'Schau da, mein Braut, zum Liebespfand
> Tragt diesen Ring an eurer Hand.'
> Die Jungfrau da schön Rosen brach,
> 'Mein Bräutigam', zu Jesu sprach,
> 'Hiermit seh du von mir beehrt,
> Ewig mein Herz sonst keinen begehrt'.
> Da gingen die verliebte Zwei,
> Brachen der Blumen mancherlei, etc.

(Arnim-Brentano, *Des Knaben Wunderhorn* [Berlin], pp. 99–103.)

Compared with the significance of this idea in the ballad versions, the circumstance that in 'The Captain's Daughter' the heroine is 'a bride', i.e. engaged for an earthly wedding, is a matter of secondary importance. The latter motif is characteristic of the prose legends and among the ballads it was introduced into 'The Captain's Daughter' only, apparently taken from the Visionslegende-type Exemplum Mirabile.

The evidence of the comparison of the various versions with each other would indicate that rather than having to deal with the Visionslegende-type as ultimate source of the entire ballad group and a 'structural decomposition' in the rest of the ballad types (as Domokos would have us), we have to recognise the confluence of two different traditions: (1) a maid is taken up to Heaven as a bride of Christ; (2) the Visionslegende-Exemplum Mirabile type of legends. The latter influenced group (1), owing probably to the common motif of a journey to Heaven. As a result we have 'The Captain's Daughter' which has the main elements of tradition (1) in its first part, but the ending of (2), and the virgin heroine of tradition (1) becomes engaged for an earthly wedding, as the hero in (2).

'The Fair Maid Julia' obviously belongs to tradition (1)[1] and, as I

---

[1] Domokos attempts to link it with tradition (2) by three common features: (a) the apparition of the lamb as compared with the words of the Visionslegende (the heavenly visitor, riding his white mule, descends on a mountain path, enveloped in full splendour) 'semita illic angusta ducit in montana, qua virum veneranda canicie venientem vidit sedentem mulo, indutum albis ex toto splendidum id quoque sedit animal candidum'; (b) in 'The Captain's Daughter' the identity of the maid has to be established by opening old documents on her return from Heaven, and this would parallel the repetition element in 'Fair Maid Julia' (also the letters in the Regina-songs, the description of Jesus to the gatesman in 'The Sultan's Daughter', and the letters of the prose legends described in our note, p. 61, above; and (c) finally, Domokos derives the three cockcrows in 'Fair Maid Julia' from certain passages of the 'Exemplum Mirabile'. 'The heavenly messengers who appear surrounded by dazzling splendour look up, choose, estimate the pure youth who is ready to listen, understand and follow their teaching. They give the key of Heaven into his hands: i.e. teach him the Christian doctrines by words and by their personal example. During the first

have tried to show, within this tradition it seems to be most closely related to the Scandinavian, and especially to the Danish versions.

Folklore and custom

Before examining the wider affiliations of this ballad in European religion and mythology, we shall do well to consider certain of its details which seem to refer to traditional peasant customs. The maiden becomes the bride of Jesus; but when he comes to describe this mystical union, the singer of the Hungarian ballad has an earthly wedding in mind. Just because he is deeply moved by his theme, he has recourse to associations which have a real and deep meaning for him and for his audience. He evokes the familiar details of a village wooing, the circumstances of a village marriage feast; and his ballad gains in vividness even for us and must have gained much more for its original hearers.

'At the first cockrow, I will come and *see* you' refers to the suitor's traditional reconnoitring visit to the girl's home prior to a marriage proposal. This was the 'háztűznéző', or 'inspection of the hearth'. The suitor arrived alone or accompanied by an older female relative to make himself familiar with the household. Another name given to this type of visit was the 'leánynéző', or 'inspection of the girl'. Where a marriage had been arranged by the parents, as happened often enough, this was perhaps a couple's first opportunity to meet. No mention was made of marriage, and we hear of various tricks which were employed to lure the shy maiden near enough for her face to be seen.

The formal proposal (**A, E, I, J**) and the 'promise away' (**E, J**) could be made only when the suitor and his prospective parents-in-law had arrived at a financial agreement. The proposal was framed in allegorical terms and had to be repeated two or three times to obtain a favourable answer. When that answer had been given, the dates of the betrothal and wedding could be decided.

---

three days spent in this world they accomplish the teaching. Thus the meaning of the words: "I would give the key of Heaven into your hands, at the first cockcrow I would come to see you" becomes apparent (First triduum), the guest asks the youth to meet his mule in three days' time. That is to say, the heavenly messenger leaves the youth to himself to see whether he follows the heavenly teachings and remains pure even after the wedding. If he remains pure he will be able to go to heaven. "At the second cockcrow I would propose to you" (Second triduum). At the end of his "three hour stay" in Heaven the youth goes home. He has to die after having tasted the earthly food, but he is not afraid of death, i.e. to go back to the land of eternity. "At the third cockcrow I would take you away" (Third triduum).'

The resemblance offered by the first two of these parallels is just acceptable though rather vague; the third point, however, is too tenuous to be convincing. We shall deal with the particular symbols of the lamb and with the significance of the cockcrows at a later stage of our study.

Bearing in mind the text of **A, E, I, J**, it seems reasonable to interpret the last lines of the **B, H** versions as an allusion to a heavenly wedding feast (That heavenly tables should set themselves/That heavenly glasses should fill themselves). The bride's leave-taking occurred at the end of the wedding feast which usually followed four or five weeks after the proposal and lasted several days. Therefore the mention of the three cockcrows which locates the whole sequence of the preliminary visit, the proposal and the wedding within at most the compass of a single morning was admirably calculated to convey to a contemporary audience the suddenness of the girl's taking-away, and heightened the tragedy in so far as the mystical marriage was felt to be an earthly death.[1] The sense of untimely or tragic speed was emphasised by the stylistic device of the incremental repetition of the three (**I, J**—five) cockcrows. This significance of the cockcrows (contrary to Domokos's interpretation) is borne out by the fact that a similar repetition for a similar purpose is found in the Danish version:

> Danish, *B* Imellem Klokken var fire og fem,
>   da fulgte de den Jomfru til saeng.
>   Imellem Klokken var fem og sex,
>   da blegned Kinden, gik Maelet vaek.
>   Imellem Klokken var ni og ti,
>   kom Engelen, tog Sjaelen til Himmerig.

(*Between four and five o'clock the virgin was put into bed, between five and six o'clock her cheeks grew pale and voice grew faint, between nine and ten o'clock the angel came to take the soul to Heaven.*)

The final section of the ballad, the 'lament' (or, according to the Scottish expression, 'keening') appears at first sight to refer to the funeral custom, common in Hungary as elsewhere, which obliged the nearest female relative of the deceased to lament over her in an improvised recitative, and so would seem to fit in only with the tragic aspect of the ballad, emphasising not her heavenly marriage but her death here and now. This first impression is not, however, wholly correct. The 'keening' had its place also in the traditional wedding ceremony. Version **F** has none of the references we have been discussing, but it has a final section agreeing with version **H** which closely resembles the song traditionally sung at a point in the wedding ceremony which we

---

[1] The tradition works the other way as well: the earthly death is considered to be a mythical marriage. We read in *Monumenta Hungariae Historica Scriptores*, xi, 480, that in the sixteenth century when a young maid died in Hungary she was buried in white, as a bride of Christ, and a wedding dance was performed at her funeral.

have not yet had occasion to discuss—namely, the bride's leave-taking.
Z. Kodály, *Magyar Népzene Tára*, III/A (Lakodalom), describes this as
'the most moving, the most dramatic, almost the climactic scene of the
wedding'. The best man led the bride to her parents' table. Here she
rested her head first on her father's, then on her mother's lap and said
good-bye to them weeping bitterly. Versions **F** and **H** agree almost
word for word with the text given by Kodály (cf. *ibid*. nos. 242–4) for
the girl's lament:

> Mother, dear mother,
> my nurse
> who for nine months
> carried me in her womb,
> who after nine months
> gave birth to me,
> who gave birth to me,
> who suckled me, etc.

Moreover, in some parts of Hungary (South Danubia and Moldavia)
songs of this type were described as 'keening' and, according to
Kodály, their tunes recall those of mourning-songs. Sometimes too the
mother joined in the lament and bewailed the loss of her daughter:

> My dear sweet daughter, my dear single flower, you my carnation, the tulip that has
> blossomed in my little garden. You the glory of my courtyard, the ornament of my
> household, my tender rosemary, my dear little bird... (*ibid*. no. 294).

The resemblance of this passage to the corresponding portions of **A** and
E is evident. They make use of the same allegorical style and the same
rhythmic patterns. Other examples of this type of lament, which we
find in Domokos-Rajeczky, *Moldvai Magyar Népdalok és Balladák*
(Budapest, 1956, pp. 166–7), provide similar parallels. We can establish
beyond any doubt that the 'keening' in 'The Fair Maid Julia' fits in
not only with the tragic interpretation, but also simultaneously with
the more hopeful picture of a heavenly wedding, as do so many of the
other realistic elements in the ballad.

Date

That these references to traditional customs made the ballad more real
and immediate is borne out by what we know about its date. The
international ballad variants are generally regarded as belonging to the
sixteenth century and the same is probably true of the Hungarian versions. They are all isometric, written in twelve syllable lines with halving
cesura. This metre, together with the octosyllabic line divided by the
same halving cesura, is known as Hungary's national verse form, and

it became fashionable at the beginning of the sixteenth century (J. Horváth, *Vitás Verstani Kérdések*, Budapest, 1955, pp. 51–4). For the tune of the ballad, cf. P. P. Domokos, 'Egy ballada dallama', *Ethnographia* (1952), pp. 150–60.

The oldest of the versions is probably **A**, with its frequent use of alliteration (*koszorúba kötni, magát ott mulatni . . . hadd halljsm éltembe hogy siratsz holtomba . . . földön futó füstje*), its intertwining repetition of half lines and its full description of the lamb. This version, as B. Vikár pointed out (*Ethnographia*, 1938–9, p. 315), is similar in its structure to certain Estonian folksongs which also consist of three parts. In these folksongs we find:

(*a*) The Narrative (a child loses some animal while being away from home.

(*b*) Its Repetition (the child repeats the story verbatim to its parents as a complaint).

(*c*) The Parents' Consolation. (This is replaced in the Hungarian ballad by the mother's 'keening'.)

The parallel suggests a remote and traditional origin for the ballad.

The ballad's affiliations

Bearing these facts in mind, we can now turn to the connections which appear to exist between our ballad and myths found elsewhere in the European tradition, both pagan and Christian. It will be convenient to begin by considering the magic lamb, for this has—as suggested first by Sebestyén, see below—much in common with a well-known motif in Hungarian folklore: the magic stag of the *regös* lays.

These lays were a survival from the celebration of the pre-Christian feast of the winter solstice. Sung by the *regös* or bards, their purpose was to draw together couples in marriage through the repetition of verbal charms and also to bring prosperity during the coming year. There is some evidence (Gy. Sebestyén, *Regösénekek, Regösök*, Budapest, 1902) that they were originally performed by shamans wearing the mask of the Sun-Stag, a figure of primitive mythology. As a result of ecclesiastical persecution and the coincidence of dates, made more influential by the uncertainties of the medieval calendar,[1] this custom became incorporated into the celebration of Christmas. In some villages even today remnants of these lays are still sung by village lads between Christmas and the New Year outside houses where there are marriage-

---

[1] Until the Gregorian calendar was introduced in 1583, Christmas and the New Year were celebrated simultaneously.

able daughters or newly wed couples; and some of these lads still wear the stag disguise.

The *regös* lays—or such of them as are not mere fragments—consist of three parts:

(*a*) The Inaugural Address. This has in most cases preserved the line: 'we are not devils, but the servants of St Stephen.' St Stephen I, it will be remembered, was the king (1000–38) who Christianised Hungary. The *regös* while clinging to their old practices were presumably anxious to avoid persecution by declaring their loyalty to the new religion.

(*b*) The Song about the Magic Stag which concludes with the charms mentioned above.

(*c*) The Farewell in which the *regös* asks for a present.[1]

In the second part of these lays we often have the magic stag addressing St Stephen and claiming that it is the messenger of God, as was the magic stag that appeared to St Hubert or St Eustace. The legends of these saints had apparently inspired a Hungarian story about the miraculous conversion of the first Christian king of Hungary.[2]

The stag in the *regös* lays still carries the sun, the moon and the stars as did the Sun-Stag of the earliest Magyar legends but it also carries candles for the mass as does the lamb in our versions **B, D, H, K, L,** and as does the stag in the St Eustace (St Stephen?) legend.[3]

---

[1] For texts see Z. Kodály, *Magyar Népzene Tára*, II Jeles Napole (1953), the chapter 'Regölés'.

[2] In connection with the concept of angels appearing in the shape of animals, which seems to be related to the witchcraft tradition, it may be of some interest to quote Gerald of Wales, who wrote in his *Topographia* (quoted by R. M. T. Hill, 'Some beasts from the medieval chronicles of the British Isles', *Folk-lore*, 1954–5, pp. 213–14): 'We agree with Augustine, that neither demons nor wicked men can really change their natures, but that those whom God has created can, by his permission, become transformed, so that they appear to be what they are not. It is believed as undoubted truth that the Creator can when he pleases change one thing into another, as in the case of Lot's wife, who looking back contrary to her Lord's command, was turned into a pillar of salt.'

[3] This stag appears in a different legend in a fourteenth-century Hungarian chronicle that drew its material from a lost eleventh–twelfth-century Gesta Ungarorum. 'Post coronationem autem veniens in locum ubi facta visio fuerat, et ceperunt cum fratre suo Ladizlao proponere de loco fundamenti ecclesie ad honorem Virginis matris fabricande. Et dum ibi starent iuxta Vaciam, ubi nunc est ecclesia Beati Petri apostoli apparuit eis cervus habens cornui plena ardentibus candelis cepitque fugere coram eis versus silvam et in loco, ubi nunc est monasterium, fixit pedes suos. Quem cum milites sagittarent, proiecit se in Danubium, et eum ultra non viderunt. Quo viso Beatus Ladizlaus ait: "Vere non cervus, sed angelus Dei erat." Et dixit Geysa rex: "Dic mihi dilecte frater, quid fieri volunt omnes candele ardentes vise in cornibus cervi?" Respondit Beatus Ladizlaus: "Non sunt cornua, sed ale, non sunt candele ardentes, sed penne fulgentes, pedes vero fixit, quia ibi locum demonstravit, ut ecclesiam Beate Virgini non alias, nisi hic edificari faceremus"' (*Chronici Hungarici compositio saeculi XIV*. Praefatus est, textum recensuit, annotationibus instruxit A. Domanovszky. Scriptores Rerum Hungaricarum (Budapest, 1937), pp. 394–5). For further connections between Christian and pre-Christian aspects of the stag see an excellent article by T. Dömötör, 'Les variantes hongroises des légendes médievales du cerf', *Littérature hongroise—littérature Européenne*, ed. I. Sőtér (Budapest, 1964), pp. 51–68.

Here is its description in one of the oldest of such lays:

> Do not hurry, do not hurry my death,
> Your Majesty, my king St Stephen,
> For I am not the wild beast for you to shoot at,
> But I am, indeed, a messenger sent to you by God the Father.
> On my brow I have the bright rising sun,
> On my side I have the...[1] fair moon,
> On my right kidney I have the stars of the sky.
> I have antlers, antlers a thousand,
> On the tips of my antlers there are a hundred thousand torches,
> Unlit, they flare up, unextinguished they go out.

In this lay the stag, like the lamb of the ballad, appears on a beautiful broad road. In most of the other lays the stag appears from a black cloud, i.e. from the sky.

The process of Christianisation had only one step further to go before this stag became entwined with the image of the Lamb of God. As a result of this union a heavenly lamb messenger appears in the ballad, curiously enough in the full splendour of the Sun-Stag.[2]

At the same time other, not specifically Hungarian, connections also suggest themselves. Strip the ballad of all its Christian attire and we recognise underneath it a much older theme: the girl ravished by the god, who, as in the Greek myths (e.g. Leda and the Swan; Europa and the Bull) often assumes an animal form. The same myth is to be found in the totemistic legend of the first Hungarian dynasty as related in the *Gesta Hungarorum* of Anonymous, written about 1200.[3]

This myth had found its way into the medieval Christian poetry.

In some French and German poems not only has the Virgin Mary

---

[1] 'ardeli' is an unexplained word.

[2] In some cases the heavenly lamb messenger of the ballad even introduces itself with words echoing the *regös* lays: 'We are not devils but the servants of St Stephen' (or 'the messengers of God') of the *regös* lays echoes **I, J**: 'I am not a phantom, I am a messenger from Heaven.' In the *regös* lays the number of candles are 1000, 100, 3, 9. The 80 candles in our **B, D, H** is certainly a curious number; 81 would be logical as 9 × 9. It is perhaps due to the one virgin who is wanted in Heaven that instead of 81 the lamb has only 80 candles on him.

[3] Emese the ancestress dreams that the mythical eagle (the genus-symbol of the dynasty) descends upon her and foretells her the birth of her son Álmos, who will be the ancestor of the first Hungarian dynasty, the Árpád-s: 'Anno dominice incarnationis DCCC-o XVIIII-o Ugek, sicut supra diximus, longo post tempore de genere, Magog regis erat quidam nobilissimus dux Scithie, qui duxit sibi uxorem in Dentumoger filiam Eunedubeliani ducis nomine Emesu, de qua genuit filium, qui agnominatus est Almus. Sed ab eventu devino nominatus est Almus, quia matri eius pregnanti per sompnium apparuit divina visio in forma asturis, que quasi veniens eam gravidavit et innotuit ei, quod de utero eius egrederetur torrens et de lumbris eius reges gloriosi propagarentur, sed non in sua multiplicarentur terra. Quia ergo sompnium in lingua Hungarica dicitur almu et illius ortus per sompnium fuit pronascitatus, ideo ipse vocatus est Almus.' P. Magister, Quondam bele regis hungarie notarius, *Gesta Hungarorum*, ed. by L. Juhász. Bibliotheca scriptorum medii recentisque aevorum (Budapest, 1932), p. 4, 'De Almo primo duce'.

been described as a bride but, 'quite without reserve', God himself has been made into a lover.

Even in so ecclesiastical a work as Bonaventura's (?) Psalter, it is expressly said that it was Mary's beauty which drew God down from Heaven: 'Speciem tuam et decorem tuum / Altissimi filius concupiscit' (Bonaventura, *Psautier*, p. 105, Psaume xlix; quoted by Y. Hirn, *The Sacred Shrine*, London, 1912, p. 522). E. Male refers to a similar passage in 'De Laudibus beatae Mariae': 'Mais bien souvant le grave docteur s'émeut: il s'attendrit sur l'humilité de Marie. C'est cette humilité, dit-il, qui fit violence a Dieu, qui attira le Seigneur du ciel sur la terre (lib. i. cap. v (E. Male, *L'art religieux de XIIIe siècle en France*, Paris, 1910, p. 277)). Paul Küchenthal (*Die Mutter Gottes*, Braunschweig, 1898) gives ample references to this concept as it is represented in the poems of German minnesingers before the end of the thirteenth century.

Examples:

Das heilige, edle Minneverhältnis empfängt die Einwirkung französischer Galanterie und wird schliesslich ganz sinnlich, ja frivol...Maria ist jetzt 'gotis gemahele' ...Ihre wunderbare Schönheit, die alle Weiber überstrahlt, und ihre Keuschheit und Reinheit haben Gott mit heisser Minne erfüllt. Er ist aber auch der schönste und stärkste aller Männer, und so ganz dafür bestimmt der Gatte der holden Schönen zu werden. Und der Verfasser schildert die 'brutlouft' des edlen Paares und singt ihm den 'brutgesang' (p. 41).

Der schönste Freier, der Herr des Himmels, hat an dem reinen, lieblichen Leibe der Jungfrau Gefallen gefunden und sie, die schönste aller Frauen, zu seiner Braut erwählt. Unter dem Einfluss der französischen Minnepoesie wird sie zu seiner 'amie', während Gott die Rolle des 'amis curteis'. In rechtmässiger Weise verbindet sich der Herrscher seiner Braut durch den Mahelschatz...Wie der Ritter der Minnezeit heimlich zu seiner geliebten 'frouwe' schleicht, um der Minne Lohn zu empfangen, so kommt Gott, durch die strahlende Schönheit der Maria verlockt, der 'götlich minnendiep', zur Jungfrau durch die Pforte, um der 'tougenlichen minne' zu pflegen (p. 42).

More startling is Meister Friedrich von Sunnenburg's address to the Virgin.

He wants to extract favours for himself by threatening the Virgin to ruin her reputation: he will make it public that she had a love affair with a 'high Lord' who had courted her, used Gabriel as his love messenger, and to whose wooing she had given way not only once.

> Sich, Gotes tohter, wiltu mich
> niht mieten, küniginne,
> so sage ich, was ein hoher man
> mit dir begungen hat:
> Er nam sich dir ze dienen an
> in minneklicher minne,

er warb ez tougen wider dich;
do taet' du, swes er hat.
Dir gienk sin bet unt sinin wort
durch oren unt durch ougen;
al dar kam siner Bröuden hort
ze dir geslichen tougen,
er was dir minneklichen bi
mit warheit, sunder spot;
doch weiss ich diner hulde dri,
der du verholne pflaege, unt was des Gabriel din bot.

(*Minnesinger, deutsche Liederdichter des XII.–XIII.–XIV. Jahrh.*,
ed. F. H. von der Hagen [Leipzig], 1838, p. 353.)

The eleventh-century 'Quis est hic qui pulsat ad ostium' brings us closer to our entire ballad group. The theme: Christ visiting his beloved at night, his disappearance, her grief and search for him, followed by her entry to heaven as Christ's bride is closely related to 'The Sultan's Daughter'. The revelation that the 'beloved' of this famous poem is the Virgin Mary herself we owe to E. P. M. Dronke, who was the first to point out that the title of the original MSS is 'Rhytmus de b/eata/ Maria virg/ine/'.[1]

The further development of the assimilation of pre-Christian myths into eleventh-century Christian hymnology can be seen in 'Virginis castae, virginis summae'. Here we are allowed, as it were, to get an insight into the blessed state of happiness that will be the share of all our Sultan's daughters, Reginas and Julias. In this curious piece, where mystic vision is set aglow by sensuous passion, the concept of Christ the Lover is entwined with his image as the Lamb of God. In the mystic union envisaged by the poet the brides are now chaste virgins carrying roses and lilies, now flowers themselves; Christ is now the Heavenly Bridegroom, now the frisky lamb, and sts. 17 and 20 leave us in no doubt that we are to take the Lamb-image quite literally:

11. It is a Holocaust they offer again to the Lord: Virgins, pure in body, whose hearts chose an immortal bridegroom, Christ Himself.

12. Happy their nuptials which know no stain, nor the grievous pains of childbirth, the fear of rival mistress or vexatious nurse!

13. Their couches which await the Lord are walled by angels who guard them against pollution. With drawn swords these ward off the unchaste.

Here Christ sleeps with them. Happy that sleep! Sweet the repose when the faithful virgin is cherished in the arms of her Heavenly Spouse!

---

[1] P. Dronke, *Medieval Latin and the Rise of European Love Lyric*, I (Oxford, 1965), pp. 269–70, with English translation. For the Latin text see *The Oxford Book of Medieval Latin Verse*, ed. F. J. E. Raby (Oxford, 1959), p. 158, no. 115.

14. The Bridegroom's right arm encircles the bride and on his left she rests her sleeping head. With wakeful heart, though her body is at rest, she reclines on her dear Bridegroom's bosom.
Her Holy Spouse blesses her sleep and bids the happy bride be not disturbed. He says: 'Waken not my beloved, let her rest to her heart's content.'

15. Here does the growth of Holy Church come to full flower, rich in roses and lilies without number, whose fragrance exalts the Bridegroom's domain delectable alike in its scenes and its odours.

16. Splendid in delicate, shining apparel, they hold lilies in their left hands, roses in their right, and crowned with jewelled diadems, they walk in the Lamb's immaculate ways.

17. And with these flowers, which never wither, are woven garlands for the saintly heads.
On these the Lamb feeds and is refreshed, these flowers are his chosen food.

18. Ringed by these dancing bands, he runs hither and thither through the garden's delights. Now they hold him. Now he has slipped away and gambols wantonly in pretended flight.

19. Here the Lamb gives many a bound as he prances among the maidens, and then he rests with them in the noon-day heat. It is on their bosom that he sleeps at mid-day, making his bedchamber between their virgin breasts.

20. For a Virgin Himself, born of a Virgin Mother, he loves above all and seeks the retreats which Virgins offer. Peaceful his slumber in their chaste embrace; only let no spot soil by chance his fleece.[1]

At this point we have to return to 'The Fair Maid Julia', taking up the thread of the Virgin Mary cult in connection with our ballad.

---

[1] The original text of the quoted passages runs as follows: '...11. Holocaustum Domino / offerunt ex integro / virgines carne / integrae mente / immortalem sponsum / eligentes Christum. // 12. O felices nuptiae, / quibus nullae maculae, / nulli dolores / partus sunt graves, / nec pelex timenda / nec nutrix molesta! // 13. Lectulos harum / Christo vacantes / angeli vallant / custodientes; / ne quis incestus / temeret illos, / ensibus strictis / arcent immundos. / Dormit in istis / Christus cum illis; / felix hic somnus, / requies dulcis, / quo confovetur / virgo fidelis / inter amplexus / sponsi caelestis. // 14. Dextera sponsi / sponsus complexa / capiti laeva / dormit submissa; / pervigil corde / corpore dormit / et sponsi grato / sinu quiescit. / Approbans somnum / sponsus beatam / inquietari / prohibit illam; / "ne suscitetis," / inquit, "dilectam, / dum ipsa volet, / ita quietam". // 15. Hic ecclesiastici / flos est ille germinis, / tam rosis quam liliis / multiplex innumeris, / quorum est fragrantiis / ager sponsi nobilis, / naribus et oculis / aeque delectabilis. // 16. Ornatae tam byssina / quam veste purpurea / laeva tenent lilia, / rosas habent dextera,/ et corona gemmea / redimitae capita / agni sine macula / percurrunt itinera. / 17. His quoque floribus / semper recentibus / sanctorum intexta / capitum sunt serta; / His agnus pascitur / atque reficitur, / hi flores electa / sunt illius esca; // 18. Hinc choro talium / vallatus agminum / hortorum amoena / discurrit hac illac, / Qui nunc comprehensus / ab his, nunc elapsus / quasi quadam fuga / petulans exsultat. // 19. Crebros saltus / dat hic agnus / inter illas discurrendo / et cum ipsis / requiescit / fervore meridiano; / In earum pectore / cubat in meridie, / Inter mammas virginum / collocat cubiculum. // 20. Virgo quippe / cum sit ipse / virgineque matre natus, / Virginales / super omnes / amat et quaerit recessus; / Somnus illi placidus / in castis est sinibus, / Ne qua forte macula / sua foedet vellera.' // (*Analecta Hymnica Medii Aevi*, ed. C. Blume, vol. 54 [Leipzig, 1915], pp. 133–4. I am indebted to P. Dronke for drawing my attention to this interesting piece.)

First of all we have to deal with the hitherto unexplained apple-tree motif at the beginning of our versions **B, C, D, F, G, H, K, L**.

I. *Over there is a round little hill,* | *A sweet apple-tree grows on it.* || II. *Its apple is sweet, its flower is full blooming* | *And yellow edelweiss grows under it.* || (**F**—its owner is gentle) III. *And a fair maiden sits under it.* | *She binds red and white flowers,* | *And those which she presses against her breast* | *become silver.* (**C**) || (**F, G, H, K, L** she binds her wreath; **G** with white narcissus, roses and lilies; **K** with roses and lilies; **F** with white lilies; **H** with branches, seedlings, lilies and roses; **L** with branches, thistles, white seedlings and lilies.)

In comparison with this beginning, an interesting Hungarian fragment might be quoted:

> Outside St John [village], there is a round little hill,
> A sweet apple-tree grows on it,
> Its apple is sweet, its rose is full blooming,
> *The Virgin Mary* sits under it.
> So she binds, so she binds her adorned wreath
> With white and red (flowers), where it is not enough,
> She finishes it with golden ones.

(P. P. Domokos, *Moldvai Magyarság*, II, 258.)

This fragmentary song is performed on St John's and St Stephen's day when the children go from house to house to greet the Johns and Stephens of the villages.[1] This custom is called 'Jánosolás' ('János' is 'John' in Hungarian).

The songs on this occasion invariably mention the apple-tree symbol of the Virgin Mary.[2]

---

[1] P. P. Domokos (*Ethnographia*, **70**, 21) draws attention to the customary wreath of corn-flowers worn by the participants. In connection with the 'Susannah' in our **I, J**, he also points out that the children are organised in three rows for the greeting, and the ones in the middle row are called 'Susannahs'.

[2] The apple tree was linked in the Bible to Eve. She in turn was a figure of the Virgin. There-fore, the apple tree became one of the Virgin's symbols, but this time without the association of sin. Cf. the hymn 'Ave Maris Stella': 'mutans nomen Evae' where we are reminded that Ave is the palindrome of Eva. For representation in art of 'Mary as Antithesis of Eve' cf. M. L. D'Ancona, *The Iconography of the Immaculate Conception in the Middle Ages and Early Renaissance* (1957), fig. 15; Burgundian, 1477, MS in Jena Library; also Fra Angelico's 'La chute et la répara-tion' (Musée du Prado, Madrid), reproduced by M. Vloberg, *La vie de Marie* (Paris, 1949), p. 108; for representations of the Virgin with the apples cf. Crivelli's *Virgin and Child* (Breve Gallery, Milan), Titian's *Annunciation*, etc. The same idea is expressed by Guillaume de Deguilleville in the fourteenth century, *Pèlerinage de l'âme de Guillaume de Deguilleville* (J. J. Stürzinger, London, 1895), pp. 188–94. For illustrations and commentary cf. D'Ancona, *op. cit.* pp. 49–50. For a striking parallel to both our ballad and the 'Jánosolás' songs cf. the Song of Songs, the descriptions of which are so frequently adapted when praising the Virgin Mary: viii. 5—'Who is this that cometh up from the wilderness, | Leaning upon her beloved? | Under the apple tree I awakened thee.' Cf. also the Virgin awakened by her heavenly bridegroom in *Minnesinger*, 2. 342: 'suoze im troume | nam er min goume, | under einem apfelboume | wart erwekket ich so suezlich: | seht, daz tet der jungelink.'

In the garden of Paradise
There is a fair apple-tree,
Flower of the apple-tree,
Apple of its flower:
Apple-begetting Holy Mother.

(Z. Kodály, *op. cit.* ch. 'Jánosolás', no. 907.)

On the market of heaven
They pick violets,
They make a bunch of them
A crown for St Stephen.
In the courtyard of St Stephen
There is a beautiful apple-tree,
Earth gives its roots,
Its roots give its tree,
Its tree gives its blossom,
Its blossom gives its apple,
Let us praise its apple:
Happy Virgin Mary.

(*Ibid.* nos. 906, 908, 909, 911, 924.)[1]

In the little garden of Paradise
There is a red apple
The angels pick it up
And place it in the bosom of Mary.   (*Ibid.* no. 905.)

This last example of 'Jánosolás'-songs becomes easier to interpret if we bear in mind that the apple symbol has another significance in Hungarian folk poetry: it is the symbol of love.

Examples:

High trees have tasty apples
But their branches are very high up,
My sweetheart is of slender shape,
But it is forbidden to embrace her.

*

Apple grows on the hemp,
Two or three apples on each of them,
I have sweethearts thirteen.

*

How high is the spire of the church of Szeged,
An apple is on the top of it, how red it is,
It is easy to cut that apple in two,
If you do not love me, you need not visit me.

---

[1] This song can be compared to another Latin verse, connected with the Virgin Mary's symbol as the Rod of Jesse. 'Virga Jesse floruit, / radix virgam, virga florem, / virgo profert salvatorem / sicut lex praecinuit / radix David typum gessit / virga matris quae processit / ex regali semine; / flos est nobis puer natus, / iure flori comparatus / prae mira dulcedine.' // (F. J. E. Raby, *A History of Christian Latin Poetry from the Beginning to the Middle Ages*, 2nd ed., Oxford, 1953, p. 372.)

A red apple rolled out into the mud,
He, who picks it up will not do so in vain,
I pick it up and wash the apple,
I embrace and kiss my sweetheart.[1]

The apple was well suited therefore to figure at the beginning of a poem like 'The Fair Maid Julia'. As a love-symbol it served to fore-shadow the heavenly proposal; as the symbol of the Virgin Mary it was peculiarly appropriate in a story which dealt with a virgin's mystic betrothal to Jesus, since in the Middle Ages Mary was, as we have seen, the archetype of the maidens who gave themselves to God.

The relation of 'The Fair Maid Julia' to the myths 'The Girl Ravished by God who assumed an Animal Form' and 'Christ coming to the Virgin Mary as a Lover' suggest indeed a new possible interpretation of the ballad. The heavenly gates opening without anybody opening them (**A, D, E, H–K**); the heavenly glasses being filled without any-body filling them (**B, H**); and the heavenly tables being laid without anybody laying them (**B**) could be taken as indirect references to the Virgin conceiving.

Examples:

The *closed door of Ezekiel*. Ezekiel beheld a door always shut, through which the King of King's alone passed and left it shut. The Blessed Virgin Mary is the gate of Heaven for, before the birth and during the birth, she was a virgin, and remained a virgin after the birth.

Daniel's mountain. The stone which was cut out of the mountain without the hands of any one breaking it off is Christ, born of a Virgin without the hand of anyone embracing her.

(For these and for symbols of the same idea, cf. F. J. E. Raby, *op. cit.* pp. 373–4.)

She was *The fleece of Gideon*, for just as the fleece, i.e. Mary, absorbed the moisture of the air while the surrounding earth was dry, so she alone remained untouched while all the ground was drenched in dew' (Y. Hirn, *op. cit.* p. 309).

The Virgin was the *unploughed field* which gives seed without having been cultivated (*ibid.* p. 469).

She was also the *hortus conclusus*, 'the spotless, enclosed garden, full of flowers', because her womb remained closed before, during and after the miraculous birth (*ibid.* p. 446).

In art the representation of the Virgin's Immaculate Conception was often depicted in a garden or in a field. This 'idyllic and colourful *garden-type*' representation of the Virgin became especially popular in the early fifteenth century (cf. references and quotations, M. Meiss, article in *Art Bulletin*, XVII, 1936, 448–50). 'It was developed chiefly in

---

[1] Gy. Ortutay, *Magyar Népköltészet* (Budapest, 1955), I, 'Dalok, Szerelmes Dalok', nos. 226, 74, 49, 48.

78

Northern Italy [exx.: Stefano, Pisanello, etc., *ibid.*] but spread rapidly to France.' 'C'est à la fin du moyen age qu'on vit apparaître sur les vitraux, les tapisseries, ou dans les livres d'Heures, la jeune fille aux long cheveux qu'entourent la rose, l'étoile, le miroir, la fontaine, le jardin fermé' (E. Male, *op. cit.* p. 280).

An interesting example of this type is reproduced in D'Ancona (*op. cit.* fig. 51) and in another painting, reproduced in the catalogue of *The Worcester-Philadelphia Exhibition of Flemish Painting*, 1939 (pl. 5, described by D'Ancona, p. 26): 'The Virgin sits in an enclosed meadow (the enclosed garden) and holds the Child. A scythe-like crescent is shown at her feet, and the lily, symbol of her purity, is placed on the low wall which encloses the meadow. A rose-hedge, another attribute of Mary Immaculate, grows on top of the low wall. The Child holds an apple, a reminder of the fatal apple which caused the Fall of Man.' In accordance with the gradual humanisation of the Divinity, which reached its peak during the Renaissance, artists of the latter period no longer represent Mary carrying the Christ Child. They represent Mary as a maiden, and 'emphasise her purity, no longer her motherhood' (D'Ancona, p. 52).

This young maid with the long hair (cp. our **E, I, J**), surrounded by roses and lilies (Hungarian, Danish, Regina, Sultan's daughter) with the apple (Hungarian), in a garden (Regina, Sultan's daughter, Captain's daughter) or in an open field (Hungarian, Danish) represented so frequently in Renaissance paintings, recalls the opening scene of our entire ballad group. The associations with the enclosed garden and the shut gate through which only the King can pass, echo the Regina-songs:

'Wo bist du ine kume?	Kei Schloss ist mir zu stark:
ist Alles wohl vermacht.'	Ich bin der Herr Jesus selber
'Kei Mur ist mir zu hoche,	Der alles erschaffe hat.'

(Erk-Böhme, *op. cit.* no. 2123.)

or   'Wer hat dich eingelasse wohl in den Garten mein?
Ist er doch wohl beschlossen, du must behende sein.'
'Ist dein Garten wohl beschlossen, das acht ich schlecht und kein,
All Ding die seind mir offen, auch gar die harten Stein!
Kein Schloss kann mich ve schliesen, kein Stein ist mir zu hart,
Mit meinen freien Künsten bin ich in Allem stark.'   (*Ibid.* no. 2122.)

The stag of the *regös* lays had candles, which 'Unlit, they flare up, unextinguished, they go out'. This construction (repeated in our versions **K, L**) might have recalled the popular motif of 'heavenly bells tolling untolled' (**A**, **B**, **D**, **E**, **H–L**) that occurs in folk literature when an innocent human being dies usually an unnatural death.[1]

The construction was then developed further according to the pattern of the incremental repetition, following the heroine's ascent into heaven (heavenly gates), and her presence at a mystic wedding feast (there: tables, glasses).

But since there were these parallels between our ballad and the story of Christ coming to the Virgin, it is possible that they influenced the poet and decided him to use the symbols suggested by the repetition, which happened to fit in really with the idea of a divine conception.

This conjecture can perhaps account for the otherwise inexplicable name of the heroine in our version **E**, where she is called 'Fair maid Martha *woman*'. 'Asszony', which I translated 'woman' expresses also in Hungarian the loss of her virginity.[2] In earlier Hungarian texts, on the other hand, it meant 'queen, noble woman' and it was often used in connection with the Virgin Mary.

Whatever the explanation of this correspondence may be, here we have a case similar to that which M. J. C. Hodgart describes in a different context:

The fragments work imaginatively on us as symbols, though how they do it is by no means clear. Sometimes we can see at last part of the image and then our response to what the symbol refers to is part of our total response to the poem: the pleasure of recognition is added to our enjoyment.[2]

---

[1] Cf. 'Sir Hugh, or the Jew's Daughter' (F. Child, no. 155 *A*, references given p. 335). However, considering the line in version **A** which precedes the bell motif (where the heroine is described as one whose smoke spreads on earth and whose flames reach heaven, also in **E**; cp. Cornelius a Lapide's description of the Annunciation: 'The heaven sinks down and the earth rises', quoted by Y. Hirn, *op. cit.* p. 302) recalls another 'purely religious meaning the message of evening bells acquired' (Y. Hirn, *op. cit.* p. 278): 'There was a natural symbolism in the idea that God joined himself to man [referring to Gabriel's Annunciation] just at the moment, when the sun sinks to the earth. This thought was impressed on the minds of the faithful when the Church during the 14th century began to ordain the saying of an *Ave Maria* during the moments, when the bells rang in the evening rest.'

[2] It may also be that the 'key of heaven' that is put into Julia's hand (**A, I, J**) was suggested by the various connections of the ballad with the Virgin Mary. The latter is often represented in art as the 'Virgo Clavigera' with the keys of heaven in her hand (cf. 'La Vierge à la clef', Tableau offert on Puy d'Amiens en 1513; as well as the works of C. Crivelli, Jean de Sachy, Nicolas Blasset, Wolfgang de Chemnitz, Dürer, etc.). For references and reproductions cf. M. Vloberg, *La Vierge, notre médiatrice* (Grenoble, 1936), pp. 182–8.

The idea is suggested by the Virgin's symbol, as 'porta coeli', 'gate of heaven'. 'A la porte va la clef: le symbole de l'une devait suggérer celui de l'autre. Parfois la Vierge est comparée à la clé elle-meme, comme en ce salut d'un trouvère: "Dame, vos estes la clef d'aler en paradis/Dont Evain et Adam nos geterent jadis..." Plus souvent on donne à la Vierge le titre de "Clavigère" ou Porteclés, ainsi dans l'Oratio devota attribué à saint Bernard: "Summa summi tu Mater Filii./Clavem nostri tenens auxilii."' (*Ibid.* p. 184.)

[2] M. J. C. Hodgart, *The Ballad* (London, 1950), p. 36.

We may summarise diagrammatically the lines of development of the intertwining of pagan and Christian elements in connection with our ballad:

I. The Lamb

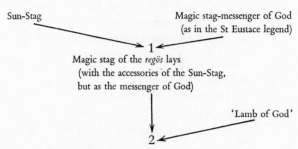

II. The Theme

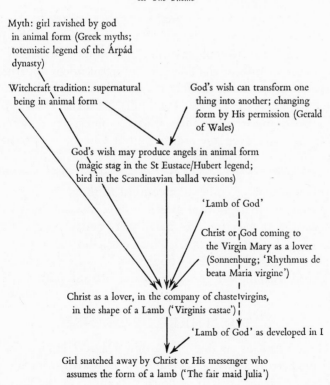

The hints which remind us of these ancient beliefs increase the field of association opened up by the ballad, and so increase its emotional impact. Keeping the beliefs in mind we have come to see more clearly why certain motifs are introduced and how they fit in with the rest.

Special Hungarian elements

The originality of the Hungarian ballad lies in its being exclusively interested in the miraculous vision and in its emotional impact. The particular images employed for the representation of this vision: the lamb adorned by the symbols of the Sun-Stag of the *regös* lays, and another, the miraculous gate that swings open unopened, the glasses that wax full unfilled, and the tables that set themselves are also unparalleled in the international versions and lend, in their context, a transcendental air to the very earthy folk-tale motif of the peasants' treasured magic table.[1]

The simplicity of style in the first narrative part, the long lines that run with almost liturgical dignity, the interweaving of the notably Hungarian wedding customs leave an impression of 'actuality' in spite of the illusory nature of the content: the resplendent apparition and the heavenly proposal. In the international versions the heroines have some initiative role. In 'The Fair Maid Julia' we are allowed to perceive the maiden's amazement only through interspersed ejaculations (Behold! Ay) and even these are expressed in an impersonal way. Throughout the ballad she remains passive, like Michelangelo's 'Leda', accepting her fate with an air of dazzled resignation. The poignant keening of the mother comes as a contrast to the preceding part. Her agony bursts into metaphorical speech at the climax of the ballad, later to give way to quieter tones of naïve piety and wonder. Her subtle allusions of the heavenly betrothal, which recall the Virgin's conception, are as if set against the maiden's tragic death, and conclude the ballad with a chord recalling the grandeur of sacrifice and purity.

'THE THREE ORPHANS'

'The Three Orphans' is one of the few classical Hungarian ballads which have been recorded in several versions drawn from all over the Hungarian language area. It is equally popular in the Lowland in

---

[1] Thompson, D1472.1.7.

Transylvania and in Moldavia, and in some places it is even sung and danced by children.[1]

Version A

1 Three orphans have set out
For a long journey, to wander away.
The fair Virgin Mary asks them:
—Where are you going, you three orphans?

2 —We are going to wander away
From one door to another.
—Do not go away, come back,
I give you three wands,
I give you three wands,
Strike the cemetery.

3 —Arise, arise, our mother,
For our mourning dress has become ragged,
For our mourning dress has become ragged,
There is nobody to put fresh linen on us!

4 —I cannot rise, three orphans,
I am locked up in a coffin.
You have a stepmother,
Who takes care of you.

5 —When she combs our hair,
Our red blood streams on our heels,
When she puts bread into our hands
The tears flow on to our breasts!

6 My God, look
At last at the orphan,
That she may not have to wander
From one door to another!

Versions

Twenty-six versions and some twenty fragments of the ballad have been recorded.

A Kodály-Vargyas, *MNpt*, no. 90   B Csanádi-Vargyas, *Röpülj*, no. 100; =Kodály-Vargyas, *MNpt*, no. 137   C Faragó-Jagamas, *MCSNN*, no. 11/d   D Faragó-Jagamas, *MCSNN*, no. 11/e   E Bartók-Kodály, *SZNd*, no. 68; =Kodály-Vargyas, *MNpt*, no. 321   F Bartók-Kodály, *SZNd*, no. 105   G Csanádi-Vargyas, *Röpülj*, no. 101; =*MNGY*, xiv, p. 21   H Ortutay, Gy., *Magyar Népköltészet*, ii, no. 24/a; =*MNGY*, i, p. 185   I Kálmány, *Hagyaték*, ii, no. 5/a   J Domokos, *Moldvai Magyarság*, no. 29   K Domokos-Rajeczky, *Csángó Népzene*, ii, no. 50   L Faragó-Jagamas, *MCSNN*, no. 11/b   M Schram, *Magyar Népballadák*, no. 16   N *MNYr*, 1875: 432   O *Ethnographia*, 19, 108, v. B   P Domokos-Rajeczky, *Csángó Népzene*, i, p. 153

[1] Cf. Kodály, *Magyar Népzene Tára*, i (Gyermekjátékok), nos. 1001–2.

Q Bartók-Kodály, *SZNd*, no. 69   R Csanádi-Vargyas, *Röpülj*, no. 102; =*MNGY*, III, p. 78
S Ortutay, Gy., *Magyar Népköltészet*, II, no. 24/*c*; =Domokos, *MM*, no. 27; =Domokos, *MM* (1931), no. 21   T Domokos, *Moldvai Magyarság*, no. 28; =Domokos, *MM* (1931), no. 22
U Kálmány, *Hagyaték*, II, no. 5/*b*   V Kálmány, *Hagyaték*, II, no. 5/*c*   W Kálmány, *Hagyaték*, II, no. 5/*d*   X Kálmány, *Szeged Népe*, II, no. 9   Y Kálmány, *Koszorúk*, I, no. 3   Z Kriza, *Vadrózsák*, I, no. 347; =Kriza (1956), no. 32   AA Faragó-Jagamas, *MCSNN*, no. 11/*f*   BB Kálmány, *Koszorúk*, I, no. 4   CC *MNGY*, III, no. 43   DD Bartók-Kodály, *SZNd*, no. 26; =Kodály-Vargyas, *MNpt*, no. 324   EE Faragó-Jagamas, *MCSNN*, no. 11/*c*   FF Ortutay, Gy., *Magyar Népköltészet*, II, no. 24/*b*, =Kálmány, *Hagyaték*, II, no. 5/*e*   GG Berze Nagy, *Baranyai Néphagyományok*, I, p. 142   HH Kálmány, *Szeged Népe*, I, no. 1   II Kálmány, *Hagyaték*, II, no. 5/*f*   JJ *MNGY*, VIII, no. 19   KK *MNGY*, VI, no. 2   LL *MNGY*, VI, no. 2/*b*   MM Kodály, *MNT*, I, no. 1002   NN Kodály, *MNT*, I, no. 1001   OO Faragó-Jagamas, *MCSNN*, no. 11/*a*
PP Bartók-Kodály, *SZNd*, no. 31; =Kodály-Vargyas, *MNpt*, no. 366   QQ *Ethnographia*, 19, 108 v. A   RR *MNGY*, VII, no. 3/*a*   SS Domokos, *Moldvai Magyarság*, no. 81; =Domokos, *MM* (1931), no. 12   TT Bartók-Kodály, *SZNd*, no. 95; =Kodály-Vargyas, *MNpt*, no. 136

Description of the ballad

I. Three orphans have set out to wander away.

N, O, AA, BB to the cemetery; G–L, P, Y, Z, DD to take service with somebody; E, U–X, FF, II they are in the gate of the cemetery; GG (which has two orphans only); HH, JJ, LL, MM, NN they are walking in the cemetery; C–F, J, K, S, DD, EE, KK, PP, SS they sit together under a tree crying; QQ they are lying in a little bed under the tree; K, T, Y, BB have an introductory stanza. T *Beyond the water, in Slovakia, / Plums grow on beautiful green branches, / I picked some of them, but I have not eaten them, / Because I have been made for sorrow, / My mother bore me for misery, / And for this sad world. // K A poplar tree has grown in Barasso, / It has thirty branches, / Three orphans are sitting under them. // Y Long roads have much dust; my heart has great sorrow. //* BB (Like the first part of Y.) As for the beginning of S, PP–RR, cf. incident VII.

II. The three orphans meet the Virgin Mary.

N, S they meet a man; G–L, O–R, T, W, Y, BB, DD, EE, OO, TT they meet somebody (who may be the Virgin Mary or somebody else), the presence of whom is indicated indirectly, by his or her asking the orphans where they are going.

III. The person the orphans meet gives them three wands.

B, J, W a golden wand; K three golden wands; PP has the golden wand, but one of the orphans seems to have it: *I wish my brother would give me a golden wand.* G a birch wand; Z the children carry in their hands three wands. They are told to strike the cemetery with the wands. K, N, P, S–U, W, Y, AA to strike the mother's grave; K (corrupt) the father's grave as well; C to strike it from three different directions; AA *we are going to strike the cemetery;* L, S add *So that your mother should rise from her grave;* X, CC, FF–NN, QQ–SS do not have incidents II–III; BB, OO, TT do not have incident III; DD ends here.

IV. The children entreat their mother to return from her grave, because their clothes have become ragged.

X adds *to wash our clothes, to dry our hair, for we have no mother who would sew for us;* U, V to comb our hair, to sew our dresses; TT ends here.

V. The mother answers that she cannot return, because she is locked up in the coffin.

FF–HH, KK because her bed is too deep; **Q** because she is in the stomach of the earth; **C, J, L, O, Q, R, AA, EE, PP** because she is covered with the moss of the earth; **B, E, M, S, U, X** because her tendons have been torn; **E, F, U, X** because her bones have fallen away; **W** because the yellow earth is sucking her feet; **Y** because earth has sucked her flesh; **S** because her body has decayed; **D, G, K, M, P, T** because her feet, **B, D, K, M, P, T, V** her arms, **S** her right arm—have rotted away; **G, U** because she is hollow-eyed; **G** because her tears keep on falling on her cheek; **T, Z** because her rosy cheeks have withered; **B** her blood has flowed away, and her soul has left her; **N** has only *I cannot rise, my children;* **BB** God has not allowed her to rise; **B, J, K, O, T, PP** add here—the orphans ask for the key of their mother's coffin in order to kiss her; **F, Y** end here. **Y** adds an additional lyrical stanza: *Fly, fly, little bird to the gate of the cemetery, to our mother's grave.* | *Who will mourn for me if I happen to die?* | *Mourn for me mother, while I am still here,* | *For I am going to leave for a long journey.* ||

VI. At this point the versions are slightly different. Either (1) the mother refers to the orphans' stepmother, who is supposed to take care of them, and this is followed by the lyrical complaint of the orphans (**A, G–I, R, U–W, G, II**), or (2) it is the mother who describes the orphans' sufferings caused by the cruel stepmother (**B–F, K, L, N, O–Q, S, T, Z, AA, BB, FF, KK–MM, OO, PP**). **J** is a compromise between (1) and (2), partly the mother, partly the orphans describe the stepmother's cruelty.

(1) Examples:

G *We have a stepmother,* | *But she does not take care of us,* | *When we ask her for some bread,* | *She puts stone in our hands,* | *When she puts fresh linen on us* | *She lets it down on us with blood,* | *When she combs our hair* | *Our blood streams on our heels,* | *She tortures us always,* | *Please, return, mother!* || **R** *When she puts fresh linen on our back,* | *Its bottom blooms with blood.* || **U, V** *A stepmother is only a stepmother,* | *She is not like a mother:* | *Her comb is iron, her stitch is iron,* | *Her towel is iron.* || **J** *We have a father, but he is dull-witted,* | *We have a mother, but she is a stepmother.* ||

(2) Examples:

OO *When she washes your dress* | *Your back lathers with blood.* || **L** *When she combs your hair,* | *Your eyes lather with tears.* || **T** *Your faces bloom with tears.* || **H** *When she puts bread in our hands* | *Seven devils are in her eyes.* || **FF** *She combs your hair,* | *Blood beats your heels,* | *She puts fresh linen on you,* | *It blooms with blue on your back.* | *She takes in the empty dish:* | *—Swallow, orphan, the saliva of hunger!* | *She takes in the empty jug:* | *—Swallow, orphan, your last gulp!* || **KK** *When she makes your little beds,* | *She beats them with the wild rose.* || **P** somewhat meaninglessly adds, that the stepmother combs the orphans' hair only at Saturday midnight. In **HH** and **JJ** the suffering of the orphans is told in third person. **JJ** adds a new description: *She prepares the midday* meal, | *The three orphans look at her crying.* | *She pushes out the three orphans* | *She invites her own daughter in.* || **HH** has interwoven one of the stock phrases found in curses: *When the three orphans wash themselves,* | '*The water turns into blood*', | *When the three orphans are combed,* | *They are hit in the face from three directions.* || In **B, L**, curiously enough, the mother tells the children in advance who their stepmother will be: **B** *There is a young woman yonder walking along,* | *There is paint on both of her cheeks,* | *She will be your stepmother,* | *Who puts fresh linen on you.* | *When she puts fresh linen on you!* etc. || **C–L, N, O–Q, S, Z, AA, BB, FF, GG–II, OO, PP** end here. The rest of the versions have various endings.

VII.

B ends like **A**. **JJ–NN** *Come, let us go to the barn,* | *Let us embrace each other,* | *Let us mourn for our good mother,* | *For our good nourice, who has born us.* || **W** ends with the mother's curse: *Cursed be your stepmother,* | *May thousand curses take an effect on her,* | *May her child die in her womb* | *Because she has not loved mine!* || **EE** has no stepmother, it ends with a lyrical complaint: *I have been an orphan without my father,* | *But even more an orphan without my mother.* | *I have been an orphan and I remain one,* | *As long as I am in the world.* || *The sunbeam has begun to shine* | *On everybody's window,* | *Oh, my God, why is it* | *That it never shines on mine?* || **R, T** end with a complaint, which is stereotype in Hungarian ballads (cf. 'Anna Betlen' and 'The Great Mountain Robber'). **R** *The three orphans have set out again* | *For a long journey, to wander away.* | *The eldest orphan said:* | *—Let us go, let us go to wander away,* | *For a long journey, to Moldavia!* | *The youngest orphan said:* | *—Let us not go to Moldavia,* | *For a long journey, to wander away,* | *You should rather kill me,* | *Take out my heart and my liver,* | *Cover them with tender crimson,* | *Put them into a green chest,* | *Take it to Barasso,* | *Place it on the iron gate,* | *So, that it may be an example for every orphan* | *Who does not have a mother!* || (**T** ends the same way, but instead of the green chest it has paper, instead of the gate of Barasso it has a stone castle, and it adds *Wash me in sweet wine;* **S**,[1] **PP** have the complaint at the beginning of the ballad. **S** has: *Wrap them in paper,* | *From the paper in a lovely cloth.* Here these versions get confused with the complaint of 'The Great Mountain Robber', where it is not an orphan who complains: *Send it to Moldavia,* | *To my mother's and father's courtyard,* | *Place it on their window,* | *From their window on their table,* | *So, that it may be an example for the whole world,* | *Of what orphans' lives are like.* || **PP** is very much corrupted: *Yonder there is a walnut tree,* | *It has three branches* | *Three orphans sit under it* | *Three murderers go there.* | *The eldest brother says only this:* | *—Kill the youngest of us.* | *—I do not mind it, my dear brother,* | *Take out my heart...* || It has the sweet wine, the tender crimson, the green chest and *Take it to Barasso, place it at the market;* **QQ–SS** are fragmentary, and have preserved only this complaint from the whole ballad. **QQ, RR** it is the eldest brother who suggests killing the youngest, without giving any reasons for it. **QQ** *Take me to the waterside,* | *Take out my heart,* etc., sweet wine, fine crimson, but *Nail it on to the door-post;* **RR** like **QQ**, except the waterside; **SS** *There are three green trees in a small garden,* | *Three orphans cry under them.* | *The eldest one keeps on crying,* | *That there is no one to teach him,* | *The middle one keeps on crying,* | *That for full nine years* | *He has been an orphan,* | *The youngest one keeps on saying:* | *—Take out my heart,* | *Cut it into five or six pieces,* || etc., like version **R**.

---

[1] Gy. Ortutay does not quote the two introductory lines to version **S**, 'I crossed the cemetery, | I remembered my sweetheart.'

U–X the mother not only answers her children, but she rises from her grave in order to sew their dresses, to comb their hair. **X** *Their mother rose, | She washed their hair, | Not in water, but in her tears, | She combed their hair, | Not with a comb, but with her ten finger-nails. || * **V** *She washed their dresses, | Not in water, but in her tears, | She sewed their dresses, | Not with threads, but with her hair. || * **U, V** the mother advises the children to tell the stepmother that it was the neighbour who has tidied them; **S, T, V** the children say so; **V** the mother arises three times successively. On the second occasion the orphans tell the stepmother that it was their godmother who helped them. The stepmother abuses first the neighbour, then the godmother.[1] **U** has a curious ending in prose: *The third time, when the orphans went out [to the cemetery], their mother said to them: 'Go home now, my children, and do not come here any more, because the Blessed Virgin Mary has allowed me to rise three times, but no more! You can tell your stepmother now, that it was your mother who has combed your hair, who has sewn your dresses. The stepmother went to the cemetery, scolded the dead woman, asking why she had combed the children. But she disappeared straightaway. There was one good stepmother, even she was carried away by the Devil.* (The stepmother who quarrels with the dead mother at her grave is an obvious vulgarisation. It is a most unnatural reaction, as in folk tradition even the most depraved people respect the dead and are afraid of their ghosts [cf. e.g. the Danish versions].) **CC** has instead of V–VI–VII: *Go to the house of your step-mother, three orphans, | Tell her it is my message | That I will not forget her meanness. | If I learn that you are unwell, | I shall turn in my grave, | I will come home, I will suckle you, | I will visit you even at night-time.*

International variants

Ballads with a theme similar to 'The Three Orphans' are well known throughout Europe. In the Scandinavian and French ballads the dead mother is given permission to rise from her grave by God, by Christ, or by a Saint. In other European ballads the mother does not rise, but is awakened to be told of the sufferings of her children.

(The Scandinavian variants are given by S. Grundtvig, *DGF*, no. 89; other variants are listed by W. J. Entwistle, *European Balladry*, pp. 84, 222, etc.; the French versions (as well as some Flemish and German versions recorded in French regions) are given by L. Vargyas, *Ethnographia*, **71**, 174. The German version (Erk-Böhme, 190) is a variant of 'Lord Randal' (Child, no. 12).)

The Slovakian, Latvian, Lithuanian and Estonian variants consist

---

[1] The Ortutay edition of the *Kálmány* bequest joins another two stanzas to version **V**. *Three orphans set out together, | To the gate of the cemetery. | —Wait, wait, three orphans, | I give a wand in your hand, | Beat your mother's grave with it! | —Arise, arise, our dear mother, | For our dresses have worn away! | —I cannot arise, my three orphans, | For my two arms have fallen away! | For my ashes have become dust. | I shall rise only to render account | At the harsh sound of the trumpet. || * Though the final two lines would make an attractive ending of the ballad, the first stanza, which is inseparable from the second, has no meaning in such a position. I consider these stanzas to be more probably the fragmentary beginning of a different version.

entirely of the orphans' complaints and in these cases the ballad is purely lyrical. These variants are connected with 'The Three Orphans' only through their central idea: that orphans tell their dead mother about their suffering.

The Danish, Dutch, French, and Lusatian variants offer more similarity with the Hungarian ballad.

In the *Danish* ballad a man sets out to marry a young girl who dies later, leaving seven (three, five, nine) children after her. The father marries again, gives his second wife red gold and blue bolsters to induce her to like his children, but she lets them starve for bread, and 'straw for their bed is all their due'. In some of the versions (Danish *C–F*, *M*, *N*) the children go to their mother's grave and cry there. The children's tears wake their mother, who asks Jesus Christ (God) for leave to go and see the orphans. She is given leave, on condition that she will not stay too long. She rises from her grave, carries her coffin on her back and goes home. Her eldest child does not recognise her: 'How could you be our mother, when your face is so pale?' '—How could I be fair and good looking, when I have been dead and that makes the cheeks turn pale.' She combs her children's hair, she washes them, lifts one to her lap, suckles the youngest, dresses them in blue silk, and lights candles for them in the dark room, where they are compelled to sleep; then she wakens their father and stepmother, reproaches them for treating the children so heartlessly, threatens them with death and Hell, unless they will treat her children better. Ever since then, the stepmother is kind to the orphans.

The *Dutch* version has three orphans who have a cruel stepmother, who beats them, and gives them only bread to eat. The orphans go to their mother's grave, they pray and sing and kneel at the grave until the three stones of the grave open and the mother arises. She puts the elder son on her lap, the younger she lifts to her breast and suckles him. The version is somewhat corrupted, as when the orphans ask their mother to go home with them because they are hungry, the mother answers: 'I cannot go home with you, because my body is under the earth.'

In the *French* ballads there are three children whose mother died. The father marries again, the stepmother beats the children. The smallest one asks for bread, she kicks him so that he collapses. The eldest brother tells the others to come to the cemetery. On their way they meet Jesus Christ (St Nicholas, St Peter, St John). He asks them where they are going, gives the mother permission to rise from her grave, and allows her fifteen years (a week) to live. At the end of this period the mother starts crying that she has to return to her grave. Her children say: 'Do not cry, we shall come with you.'

In the *Flemish* and *German* versions recorded in Flanders, Lotharingia, and Mosel (i.e. in French regions), the mother's return from her grave gradually disappears; in the Flemish ballad she rises, suckles her smallest child but says that she cannot go with her children; in the German versions the three orphans go to the cemetery and ask their mother to rise. She tells them that this is impossible: her bones are pressed with heavy earth. An angel appears from Heaven, brings a chair to the mother to sit on it and to teach her children to take their hats off. They are to tell those who question them that they were taught this by their dead mother.

The two *Lusatian* versions seem to be the closest to the Hungarian ballad. In *A* (Haupt-Schmaler, I, no. 132) the child sets out to find her mother, who has not come home from the church. She meets a man, who asks her why she is crying and advises her to go to the cemetery, to kneel down at the first green grave, to repeat the Lord's Prayer and then to shout three times 'Mother, come home again!' The mother tells her child to go home, where it has its father and its stepmother. 'She beats me and abuses me: I would prefer you to be dead.' The mother answers: 'Go home, my child, there is earth on my eyes, there is a heavy stone on my heart, and grass grows on my legs.' Two angels take the child to Heaven.

In *B* the orphan bows three times in the cemetery, and finds her mother's grave. 'Come home, my mother, and cut a slice of bread for me!' '—You have a stepmother, she will cut it for you.' '—She has her own child to whom she gives bread, but she does not give me even the bread-crust! Come home, mother, and wash my little shirt!' '—You have a stepmother, she will wash it for you.' '—When she washes it, she tears it to pieces! Come home mother, and comb my hair!' '—You have a stepmother, she will comb it for you!' '—When she combs my hair, she beats me at the same time!' The mother answers, 'I cannot go home, my child. There is a heavy stone on my breast, there is white sand on my eyes, and green grass grows on my legs.' As in version *A*, two angels take the orphan to Heaven.

Motifs

Collating 'The Three Orphans' with these variants we find several motifs which the Hungarian ballad shares with the Dutch, Lusatian, French, and with some of the Danish versions. Thus:

1. The *three* orphans (Hungarian, Dutch, French, Danish D–F).
2. The children's walk to their mother's grave (Hungarian, Lusatian, French, Dutch, Danish C–F, M, N).
3. Introducing Christian elements (Hungarian **A–F, M, U, T, V**, the Virgin Mary; Danish, God or Jesus Christ; Dutch and Lusatian A, prayer; Lusatian, angels; French, Jesus Christ or Saints).
4. Description of the stepmother's cruelty (Hungarian, Lusatian, French, Dutch, analogously Danish).
5. Reference to the state of the dead (Hungarian, Lusatian, Dutch, German from the French regions and vaguely Danish A, B, O, in the mother's answer when her eldest child does not recognise her).

Some other motifs of the international variants correspond only with certain versions of the Hungarian ballad. Thus:

6. The resuscitation of the mother, who washes and combs her orphans (cp. Danish and Dutch), occurs only in our **U, V, X**.
7. The mother's threats against the stepmother (cp. Danish ballads) occur in Hungarian **CC** only.
8. The reference to the stepmother's own child, whom she treats better than the orphans (cp. Lusatian B) occurs in Hungarian **JJ** only.

The Lusatian versions share several motifs with the Hungarian ballad, which do not occur elsewhere:

the man, who meets the orphan and advises it to go to the cemetery (Lusatian A);
reference to some ritual at the mother's grave (Lusatian A: kneel down, pray, shout out loudly three times; B: bow three times);
the mother's reference to the stepmother who is supposed to take care of the orphans;
verbal agreement when describing the state of the dead and motif 8 above.

There is one trait, however, in which the Hungarian ballad differs significantly from *all* the international versions: none of the latter mention the three wands which the orphans receive in twenty-nine Hungarian versions, together with the instruction to strike their mother's grave with them.

Folklore and custom

There are certain features about these wands in the Hungarian ballad which remain obscure.

What was the use of these wands? After the orphans have received them, *none* of the versions refer to these wands again. Except for three versions the only miraculous thing that happens is that the dead mother talks to her children. But dead people who talk are treated in a most matter-of-fact way in ballads, and it is not usually felt to be necessary to explain their appearance by the introduction of special magic instruments. Examples of dialogues between the dead and the living are to be found in many Hungarian ballads ('Mason Clement', 'Kate Kádár', 'The Boy who was Murdered', 'The Maiden who was Sold').

The fact that the magic wands appear in most of the Hungarian versions and in the Moldavian versions as well suggests that the motif was present before the *Csángós* took the ballad out with them to Moldavia, and suggests too that the motif had a perfectly well understood justification at that time, otherwise it would have been forgotten or displaced as meaningless.

Its justification in the ballad can be explained in only one way: that the wands were magic wands to resuscitate the dead.

Such wands are familiar in tales listed in Stith Thompson's Motif Index (D 1663.1). The resuscitation of the dead is a more serious matter in ballads than a dead person talking, and it usually requires a good reason to explain it. In fact, two Hungarian versions (**L, S**) are explicit about this, and the wands are given to the orphans by the Virgin Mary together with the instruction: 'Strike your mother's grave with them, so that she may rise' (cf. incident III).

But, if the mother's rising from her grave was part of the original Hungarian telling, why has it disappeared from most versions? This question raises another problem concerning these wands.

Who gave the orphans these magic wands in the first place? It is certainly strange to find these pagan magic instruments in the Virgin Mary's hands. Her appearance must be a (later) adaptation, made probably under the influence of religious songs and legends, where the Virgin Mary appears as the protectress of the poor orphans and the deserted.

There is a charming traditional song of the type from which the borrowing might have been made.

> The little girl is crying in the cemetery,
> She cries wailing in her sorrow.
> Her mother has died.
> Now she has not got anybody to comfort her.
> She is just praying about midnight,
> When the fair Virgin Mary descends to her.
> She has brought her flowers from Heaven,
> She speaks to her: —Do not mourn for your mother,

—Virgin Mary, but I do not have a mother
Who would take care of me in this world;
And Oh, but how hostile is the world,
One spits on me, another hits me on the face!
—Do not cry my child, I will be your mother,
Who will take care of you always.
I will open the gate of Heaven
You will find your mother there![1]

The adaptation seems to have worked in two ways. It influenced our original ballad by bringing the Virgin Mary into it, and our ballad, on the other hand, lent some of its motifs to the Christian legend. We can follow the process of borrowing from another version of the legendary song. There the orphan tries to arouse her mother after the first four lines of the above quoted version:

Arise, arise, my dear mother,
For my dress has worn away.

The Virgin Mary answers:

My child, do not mourn for your mother,
You have a mother in Heaven,
The Virgin Mary, who takes care of you.

Whereupon the orphan says:

I know you will be my mother in Heaven,
The Virgin Mary, who takes care of me,
But in this world there is nobody who takes care of me,
Who will sew my ragged dress.[2]

Mixing magic elements with Christian tradition is a very common feature in Hungarian folk poetry (cf. especially 'Fair Maid Julia').

But who was the donor then of the magic wands in the original versions if it was not the Virgin Mary?

Most of the Hungarian versions leave this point obscure, giving only the dialogue between the orphans and an unknown person without any further details.

The foreign parallels are of no help here, since they do not mention the wands. Laime, the goddess of luck, is known to have been regarded as especially kind to orphans in the Latvian tradition (cf. Entwistle, *op. cit.* pp. 84, 291), but there is no trace of her in the Hungarian tradition.

---

[1] Gy. Ortutay, *Magyar Népköltészet*, II, no. 23.
[2] Kálmány, *Hagyaték*, II, 59.

There is no hope of identifying the original donor. She could have been the mysterious old woman (or, if 'he', the old man, as in our **N, S**; also in Lusatian *A*), who often presents magic instruments to folk-tale heroes and heroines, or it could have been some other figure of pagan tradition whose name was not to be mentioned in the new Christian state, and so it was omitted from the ballad and later replaced by the Virgin Mary. (Such omissions of pagan gods and heroes, and their replacement by God, Christ or the Virgin are especially prominent in Anglo-Saxon charms—cf. A. von Gennep, *The Rites of Passage*, Chicago: Phoenix Books, 1962, p. 64.)

But in the changed cultural surroundings the resuscitation itself, which embodied a primitive belief according to which magic wands and the ritual of striking the grave of the dead with them was thought necessary to rouse the dead, had also to be omitted from the ballad. Thus the presence of the magic wands and their donor lost its significance and became a meaningless episode, and the resuscitation was replaced by the orphans' stereotype lyrical complaint (cp. VII, versions **R–T, PP** and **QQ–SS**. See the discussion of this motif under 'Date').

In some versions, however, the Virgin Mary replaced the anonymous donor at a time when the resuscitation motif was still alive in the ballad. In these versions the resuscitation appeared now, with her approval as her gift. The emphasis shifted back again to this incident, and the magic wands became connected with the Virgin Mary, though by weak and uncertain links.

Thus in version **V** the Virgin Mary says:

> Have these three wands,
> Beat the cemetery with them,
> Then your mother will arise.

In version **U** the connection is more ambiguous. Here the mother says (N.B., not in the ballad itself, but in a prose supplement) that the Virgin Mary allowed her to rise from her grave three times only. This could be a reference to the three wands, but can just as well be independent of them, the symbolical number three being so often used in folk tradition that it does not need any further explanation.

The fact that out of the twenty-nine Hungarian versions which introduce the magic wands, only nine bring the Virgin Mary into the story, and in the other twenty cases the wands are present as a meaningless survival, will illustrate this point.

Date

Bearing these possibilities in mind, we can now turn to the problem of dating 'The Three Orphans', and here we must pay special attention to the versions **U** and **V** which have preserved *both* the wands *and* the resuscitation.[1]

These versions have their closest parallels in the Danish variants. They share the central motif of the Danish ballad (the resuscitation) and have also certain other details in common with it (the mother washes and combs her children).

We are faced therefore with two possibilities. Either the Hungarian versions are derived from the Danish, or the Hungarian and Danish versions are both related to some common archetype. But the first of these possibilities can, I think, be disregarded, since the Hungarian versions contain a great many details bearing on the actual mode of the resuscitation, which could not have come from a Danish source. It seems likely therefore that the links between the Hungarian and Danish traditions belong to a period before 1689, the date of the earliest re- corded Danish version (Grundtvig, no. 89 *B*; it appeared in P. Syv's collection, 1689).

This hypothesis that the two traditions were linked at some time previous to the seventeenth century seems to find support when we consider the history of the ballad.

Our examination of the Hungarian material led us to conclude that probably:

(*a*) The wands in the Hungarian ballad were magic instruments designed to resusci- tate the dead;

(*b*) the striking of the grave referred to the rite required to make these instruments effective;

(*c*) a resuscitation did occur in the original Hungarian telling;

(*d*) its disappearance from the ballad was due to a process of christianisation;

(*e*) the resuscitation motif survived however in some versions in spite of christian- isation, because the Virgin Mary was introduced as the donor of the wands;

(*f*) the Virgin's presence in the ballad was therefore the product of an adaptation of the original ballad.

This final hypothesis receives further support from the facts that:

(i) The Virgin is mentioned in only nine Hungarian versions as against twenty which leave the identity of the donor undefined;

---

[1] When using the term 'resuscitation' I have always meant that the mother actually rises from her grave. It is not intended to cover the instances where she merely talks to her children.

(ii) songs which have Christian legends for their theme of a type that might have served as models for the adaptation have been actually found in Hungary.

But when we turn to the Danish material, we find there too, in some of the variants, an indication that the ballad might have existed in an earlier non-Christian form. In versions **D–F** and **N** the granting of God's permission for the mother's rising is preceded by the following lines:

> The first orphan cried tears,
> The second orphan cried blood,
> The third orphan roused the mother from the
> grave with her weeping.

This would seem to be a survival from a more primitive form of the ballad in which the orphans' tears had in themselves been sufficient to effect the resuscitation.[1] Such a version in which the orphans' tears have a magic power would not be so far removed from the original Hungarian version where the children actually perform magical rites; and the existence of a link between the two is not out of the question. But if we accept this hypothesis then the original Hungarian ballad must be placed in a period some time before the first recording of the Danish ballad, that is, in the sixteenth century if not earlier. The fact that the resuscitation motif has been preserved in only a few of the Hungarian versions while it is present in all the Danish versions can be explained by the following hypothesis.

It is possible that in Hungary the resuscitation motif was omitted for religious reasons from a great many variants before the story of the ballad was given a Christian form, while in Denmark the Christian element was introduced at a time when the resuscitation was still a central part of the story. This explanation is confirmed by the evidence that the resuscitation is justified in Christian terms in all the recorded Danish versions, while out of the twenty-nine Hungarian versions which mention the wands, only nine introduce the Virgin Mary into the story. Moreover, out of the nine which preserve both the wands and the intervention of the Virgin, two only have preserved also the incident of the resuscitation.

L. Vargyas (*op. cit.*) derives both the Danish and the Hungarian ballads from the French. His derivation is based on his assumption that in the original form of the ballad Jesus Christ, the Virgin Mary, etc., give permission to the mother to rise from her grave. Vargyas, how-

---

[1] In other Danish ballads the belief in the magic power of tears that can rouse the dead is openly manifested. Cf. Grundtvig, *DGF*, II, 495, also Entwistle, *op. cit.* p. 221.

ever, does not take into account the old pre-Christian traits in both the Danish and the Hungarian ballad: the orphans' tears which originally wake the mother in the Danish ballad, and the similar significance of the magic wands in the Hungarian versions.

Other less important indications also support a sixteenth-century date. The cult of the Virgin Mary, as the protectress of orphans and the deserted, was at its height in Hungary during the early part of the seventeenth century. A date for the original ballad, which would allow its christianisation to occur during the first half of the seventeenth century, would therefore fit in very conveniently with the dominance of this cult.

Similar corroboration can be drawn from the presence of the 'heart' motif in the orphans' complaint. The gift of a heart (usually the lover's heart offered to the beloved) was a popular motif in the courtly romances and paintings of the fifteenth and sixteenth centuries (cf. the ballad 'The Daughter of the Cruel King'). Moreover in our ballad here the motif is combined with the wish that the heart might be placed on Barasso's iron gate or on the wall of a stone castle. This seems to be a reference to the custom of exposing the body of a criminal in some prominent place which was still common in the sixteenth century.[1] The phrase 'cut my heart into five or six pieces' evokes the particular form of the custom by which the criminal's body was quartered, and the quarters hung on the four corner towers of the town wall, so that they might be visible from all points of the compass and serve as an example to the whole world. The implication behind the phrase appears to be that as the body of a criminal evokes horror and hatred so the heart of an innocent orphan would evoke a universal pity, and the reference suggests a fairly early date.

Finally, the tune of 'The Three Orphans' is one of the oldest pentatonic tunes known for Hungarian folksongs; and the rhymeless octosyllabic lines are of a type that was popular in the sixteenth century. Such rhymes as do occur irregularly are produced by employing the same suffix at the end of successive lines.

In this discussion on the date of the Hungarian ballad, I have not drawn any conclusions from the evidence offered by the Lusatian and Dutch versions. The Lusatian versions show some verbal agreement with the Hungarian particularly in the passages describing the condition

---

[1] Apparently not only criminals but all objects of interest were placed on the castle wall. The Wenzel Codex (1588), p. 334, records that a gander with two heads and four wings and legs was nailed to the gate of the upper castle at Fehérvár.

of the dead woman and her dialogue with the orphans. But while the Lusatian version **A** has the anonymous donor, it has not the wands; and instead of beating the cemetery, the orphans offer up a prayer. So it seems likely that these versions were derived from the Hungarian ballad at a time when the wands had already lost their significance, but the Virgin Mary had not yet been introduced into the story. The somewhat corrupt Dutch version also seems to have been derived from the Hungarian tradition.

Special Hungarian characteristics

The inclusion of the magic wands and the striking of the grave are, as we have seen, genuine Hungarian contributions to the orphan-ballad, and so is the inclusion of the complaint of the orphans with the heart-motif. (The wish to have one's heart [body, head] washed in sweet wine, covered with cambric and placed on the gate of a town or the wall of a castle is a stereotyped form of complaint, which appears in many Hungarian ballads, for example, 'The Great Mountain Robber' and 'Anna Betlen'. Covering a corpse with white cambric was a common Hungarian custom, while washing the corpse in wine would seem to refer to a practical method of attempting to preserve it.) The folktale-like conclusion of **U**, **V**, **X** in which the orphans tell their stepmother that it was a neighbour who combed their hair and sewed their dresses, is another motif not found elsewhere.

There are also some fine poetical devices which belong only to the Hungarian variant, such as the expressions which describe the stepmother's cruelty (the orphans' backs 'bloom with blood', or 'bloom with blue', their faces 'lather with tears', etc.), and those which describe the self-sacrificing love of the dead mother, who 'washes the orphans not in water but in her tears', combs their hair 'not with a comb, but with her ten finger-nails', sews their dresses 'not with threads but with her hair'.

These poetical details together with the inclusion of old Hungarian folk-beliefs make 'The Three Orphans' an important piece in the European ballad-tree.

5

BALLADS OF LOVE AND
INTRIGUE

Introduction

Of all the themes, that of love and intrigue is the most popular in Hungarian ballads. Not only do we find that more than half of the old-style ballads belong to this group, but also that they are recorded in more versions and variants than any other group of ballads we have to discuss.

Out of the eighteen ballads in this group, fourteen relate events of a tragic nature. Love itself is seldom allowed to remain a private affair between the two lovers concerned, though it proves to be the strongest of all emotions, as in 'The Asp' (the Hungarian representative of 'The Maid Freed from the Gallows'). Lovers are devoted and faithful unto death. In no instance do they forsake each other for the prospect of a more advantageous match. It is remarkable that there is only one ballad that recounts conflict between lovers ('The Maid who was Danced to Death'). The reason for the tragedy usually lies outside the lovers' personal relationships: most often it is the opposition of their families to their love, due to differences in social position ('Kate Kádár', 'Anna Betlen', 'The Daughter of the Cruel King', 'The Dishonoured Maiden'). Married life is full of cruelty, unhappiness and hatred. Maidens are sold in marriage or hurled into it by parental will. Adulteresses and innocent wives are treated with the same unbridled brutality by their husbands. Elopement, ravishment and seduction through treachery also lead to disaster, though these themes occur in three ballads only.

Twelve ballads derive their material from the international stock of ballads and romantic tales, the rest of them appear to be indigenous to Hungary; their stories are based on local legends about passion and violence.

'THE TWO ROYAL CHILDREN'

This ballad drew its material from the international stock of tales and romances. It is the Hungarian representative of the group of ballads that may be traced back to the Hero and Leander tale, and even earlier.

Version **A**

1 —Harken to me, Prince,
  Come to me in the spinning-room!
  —I will not come, for it is dark,
  It is very dark, very dark indeed,

2 And I shall fall in the sea,
  Into the midst of the sea,
  I shall fall in the sea,
  Yes, into its deepest part.

3 —I will light my golden candle,
  You can come by its light,
  I will light my golden candle,
  You can come by its light.

4 The Prince sets out,
  To the spinning-room, late in the evening,
  He has fallen into the sea,
  Into the midst of the sea,

5 The Princess weeps so sore, she weeps so sore
  As if she would weep herself dry.
  The Princess weeps so sore, she weeps so sore,
  As if she would weep herself dry.

6 Up and asks her mother dear:
  —Why are you weeping, why are you weeping,
      my dear daughter?
  —How should I not weep my dear mother;
  I have lost my pearly headdress,

7 It has fallen into the sea,
  Into the midst of the sea,
  It has fallen into the sea,
  Yes, into its deepest part.

8 —Do not weep, do not weep, my dear daughter,
  I will give you mine!
  —I do not want yours,
  I want only mine!

9 They have hired a diver,
  They have set out to seek,
  And they do not find the pearly headdress,
  But they find the Prince.

10 The Queen herself says:
  —Pull him out to the shore,
  Take him to the Palace,
  And place him on the bed that is made ready.

99

11 Let us have a stone coffin made for him,
Let us have the bells tolled,
Follow him out to the crypt,
Shed three tears upon him...

Versions

'The Two Royal Children' has been recorded only in Transylvania. There are only two versions which seem to be authentic:

A Csanádi-Vargyas, *Röpülj*, no. 47; =Bartalus, *Magyar Népdalok*, II, no. 5 **B** Ortutay, Gy., *Magyar Népköltészet*, II, no. 6; =*MNGY*, I, p. 183; =Kriza (1956), I, no. 9

Description of the ballad

I. A Princess invites a Prince to come and see her in her spinning-room. He is reluctant to go: it will be late in the evening, he may fall into the sea.

B instead of sea, Danube; the Princess is called little Julia.

II. The Princess reassures him: she will light a golden candle, the Prince will be able to find his way by its light.

B she will light a taper, and put it on her balcony.

III. The Prince sets off, late in the evening, but he drowns in the sea.

IV. The Princess is weeping sorely, her mother questions her as to the reason for her tears. She gives evasive answers: her pearly head-dress has fallen into the sea (**B** Danube). The mother offers her her own headdress. She is not consoled: she wants only hers.

V. They hire a diver to search for the headdress. Naturally, he cannot find it, but he finds the Prince.

B this part is narrated in dialogue. Julia asks John Biró the diver to find her pearly headdress. He informs her that all he has found is the Prince's body.

VI. The two versions are different as far as this incident is concerned.

A the Queen bids the diver to take the Prince to her palace, to place him on the bed that is made ready, they will have a stone coffin made for him, they will have the bells tolled, follow him to the crypt; and it is the Queen who says (presumably addressing her daughter), 'Shed three tears upon him'. **B** it is the Princess, little Julia, who gives orders to the diver: the Prince is to be taken to her palace, placed on her bed. The Princess weeps so sorely that her heart breaks, and she dies. One of them was placed in a white marble coffin, the other was placed in a red marble coffin. They were buried next to each other in the flower garden. A tulip with white stripes was planted on one grave, a tulip of pure scarlet on the other one. 'The souls of the lovers become living tulips', and they intertwined.

International versions

Ballads and tales relating the tragic story of two lovers who are separated by deep water in which the knight is drowned when swimming to his lady have a world-wide circulation. The story has found its way into literature: Ovid, Musaeus, Marlowe, Schiller, Byron are only the greatest names among those who elaborated this subject in their works.

Ballads with the same theme are found in Scandinavia, Germany, France and Italy, and several ballad scholars have written about the origin and spread of the story.

Rosenmüller[1] describes the motifs which all of these ballads share in the following order:

1. Two lovers are separated by deep water.
2. The lady shows the way to her lover by a light signal.
3. The light gets extinguished for some reason.
4. The lover is drowned in the water.
5. The lady, in her despair, throws herself into the water and dies.

Most probably the Hungarian ballad drew its material from the High German versions, as Katalin Benkő points out in her dissertation, 'A Hero és Leander Monda' (Marosvásárhely, 1933), which gives an extensive analysis of the entire ballad group.

In the *High German*[2] ballad we have an expository stanza: there were two royal children, they loved each other dearly, but they were separated by water (*Das Wasser war viel zu tief*). The Princess advises the Prince to swim, she will light three candles to direct him (*Lieb Herze, kannst du nicht schwimmen? | Lieb Herze, so schwimme zur mir: | Drei Kerzen will ich aufstecken, | Und die sollen leuchten dir*). A false nun puts the lights out, and the Prince is drowned. On Sunday morning everyone is joyful, only the Princess is sad. She asks her mother to give her leave to walk to the seashore, for her head is aching. The mother does not want to let her go alone, she should take her young sister to accompany her. This she would not do, her sister is too young, she will pluck all the flowers. The mother then tells her to take her young brother along. Again she refuses the advice: he is too young, he will chase all the birds away. Finally she leaves home alone, and walks till she finds a fisherman. She asks him whether he would like to earn some money, if so he must pull the Prince out of the water. (*Ach Fischer, guter Fischer, | Willst du verdienen Lohn? | So greif mir aus den Wellen,*

---

[1] E. Rosenmüller, *Das Volkslied; Es waren zwei Königskinder* (Dresden, 1917).
[2] L. Arnim and C. Brentano, *Des Knaben Wunderhorn* (Berlin, n.d.), pp. 114–16.

Einen reichen Königssohn). The fisherman casts his net into the waves, and pulls out the Prince. (*Sieh da, du liebe Jungfer, Hast einen Königssohn.*) She takes him in her arms, kisses him, and talks to him, then she gives the fisherman her crown and her gold ring. She takes off her gown, and throws herself into the sea with the words 'My father and my mother will not see me again!' The ending of the ballad tells that one can hear the bells tolling, one can hear lament in distress, two royal children lie next to each other, both of them dead (*Da hört man Glocken läuten, | Da hört man Jammer und Not, | Da liegen zwei Königskinder, | Die sind alle beide tot*).

Motifs

The Hungarian ballad agrees with the German in the following details:

1. The lovers are both 'royal children';
2. the Princess tells the Prince to come to her;
3. she will light candles to direct him;
4. the Prince gets drowned in the water;
5. there is a dialogue between the Princess and her mother;
6. neither the Hungarian nor the German Princess tells her mother the real cause of her grief;
7. she hires a man to pull her beloved out of the water;
8. the man tells her that he has found the Prince, and pulls him out of the water;
9. the Princess dies (our version **B**);
10. reference to the bells tolling.

There are, however, considerable differences between the German and the Hungarian ballads:

1. There is no exposition in the Hungarian ballad. It starts with a dialogue between Prince and Princess.
2. In the Hungarian ballad we are not told that the light is extinguished.
3. The passage in which the joyful Sunday crowd is contrasted with the sadness of the Princess is omitted in the Hungarian ballad.
4. The incident which relates that the Princess asks her mother's permission to go to the seashore, and the mother's objections to her going alone (a passage prominent in the Scandinavian and other international versions as well) is missing. In its place we have the dialogue of the mother's questioning her daughter as to the cause of her tears, and her reply about her headdress which has fallen into the sea.
5. In the Hungarian ballad the mother is sympathetic to her daughter, and is most co-operative, while in the international ballads she raises objections to her leaving the palace.
6. Instead of the fisherman we have a diver in the Hungarian ballad.
7. In the German ballad the Prince is not taken to the Princess' palace.

8. Although the Princess dies in our version **B**, she does not throw herself into the water, but dies from sorrow.

9. The sympathetic plants which intertwine do not appear in the German ballad.

These divergencies are due to several reasons: certain details sunk into oblivion during the course of oral transmission; certain changes are made in the narrative according to the true ballad tradition; and finally, there is contamination with other ballads and ballad-motifs.

1. The omission of the expository stanza of the German ballad does not affect the narrative seriously. Its content (the information about the water which separates the lovers) is sufficiently given in the initial dialogue of our ballad. It is a characteristic feature of Hungarian ballads to open with a dialogue, and to carry the narrative forward by dialogue rather than by description. (Cp. 'Clement Mason', 'The Dishonoured Maiden', 'The Maid who was Sold', 'Barcsai', etc.)

2. The extinguishing of the light must have dropped out of the ballad merely with the passage of time. Here we must draw attention to the fact that since the time of the first recording of this ballad at the end of the nineteenth century, it has been altogether forgotten. Recent ballad collectors could not find anyone who knew, or who remembered this story, in Transylvania or elsewhere. This omission of the lights renders the ballad fragmentary. The fact that in the previous passage we were told that the Princess would light a candle indicates that originally the second part of this motif (i.e. the extinguishing of the light) must also have been present in the Hungarian telling.

3. The reference to the joyful Sunday crowd in the German ballad seems to be a later insertion, and it is not surprising that it does not occur in our ballad.

4. The mother's questioning her daughter as to the reason for her tears, the Princess' evasions: her pearly headdress has fallen into the sea, are motifs entirely peculiar to the Hungarian ballad. Up to this point, as we have seen, the Hungarian ballad follows more or less closely the German and international versions, although with certain omissions. The differences between the German and Hungarian ballads in the previous parts are either insignificant or negative (omissions). Here, however, we have a 'positive' difference, an entirely new motif is introduced into the narrative.

The symbolic, riddling quality of the girl's answer brings to one's mind the similar passage in the Scottish 'Leesome Brand':

Child, no. 16 *A*:

> O Willie, O Willie, what makes thee in pain?
> —I have lost a sheath and knife that I'll never see again.
> —There is ships o' your father's sailing on the sea,
> That will bring as good a sheath and a knife unto thee.
> —There is ships o' my father's sailing on the sea,
> But sic a sheath and a knife they can never bring to me.

Child, no. 15 *B*:

> 'Oh' said his father, 'son, but thou'rt sad
> At our braw meeting you micht be glad!'
> 'Oh', said he, 'Father, I've lost my knife
> I loved as dear almost as my life.

But I have lost a far better thing,
I lost the sheath that the knife was in'
'Hold thy tongue, and mak nae din,
I'll buy thee a sheath and a knife therein.'
'A' the ships eer sailed the sea
Neer'll bring such a sheath and a knife to me.
A' the smithes that lives on land
Will neer bring such a sheath and knife to my hand.'

In the oldest Scottish version published by H. M. Shire (*Poems from Panmure House*, Cambridge, 1960), this passage is told in a similar fashion:

'Mother' quoth he 'can so mak my bed
can se mak it long and nothing bread.
mother alas I tint my knife
I lovid better then my lyffe.
mothir I have als tint my shead
I lovid better then them bead.
ther is no cutlar in this land
can mak a kniffe so at my command.'

The Scottish ballad is a story of incest and flight, the knight loses his beloved and his young son: the lady dies in childbirth. The sheath is his beloved, and the knife is his young son. In both the Scottish and the Hungarian passages a parent questions a child about the child's grief. In both symbolic answers are given. In both the questioner fails to understand the meaning of the riddling answer and offers new objects instead of the lost ones. In both this is refused by the one who is grieving for the dead beloved. The pearly headdress is a special Hungarian symbol here; it is usually worn by brides at their wedding.

5. This parallel would seem to provide a background to the mother's sympathy in our ballad since the symbolic answers are given in both ballads to the mother/ father who wants to know the reason of the sadness of her/his child.

One wonders how this passage got included in the Hungarian ballad. A direct Scottish-Hungarian connection is surely out of the question, and we do not find the motif in German or indeed in any other ballads, whether in our group or elsewhere. All I can make is a conjecture, which cannot be established. We have seen that the Hungarian versions of 'Es waren zwei Königskinder' have lost several motifs of the original story. This is obvious from the missing motif of the extinguished lights, and from the different ending of the Hungarian ballad. According to K. Benkő, the sympathetic plants were borrowed into our ballad from 'Kate Kádár', which also lent the diver-motif to our ballad, instead of the original fisherman. Without questioning this borrowing from 'Kate Kádár', we may point out that death from sorrow, or suicide, and the sympathetic plants occur also in 'The Sheath and Knife, or Leesome Brand'. Is it not possible that the sequence of motifs: the grief of someone who has lost her/his beloved, the mother's questions; her/his symbolic answers; the literal interpretation of this answer on the part of the questioner, her/his offering new objects to replace the lost ones; the refusing answer of the one who grieves; her/his death from sorrow/suicide; the sympathetic plants; were commonplace at the time of the currency of our ballad, and thus got included in our present story when the original ending was forgotten? Or is it possible that once upon a time the story which related the tragedy of the two lovers who were separated by a deep water became connected with the incest story of Leesome Brand? This would be a very far-fetched suggestion, were it not for the Wendish versions of our group. 'Der ertrunkene Geliebte'—A man approaches his beloved by boat, with eighteen musicians, but the boat sinks into the sea. The maid observes the tragedy from her tower, goes to her mother, and asks her to give her leave to go to the meadow. The mother asks her to take her younger sister along. She goes to the seashore, and meets two fishermen. She asks them to catch a gold fish for her. First they catch a gold fish, then they catch her beloved, finally they catch *two knives*. One knife the maid throws back into the water, with the other she stabs herself to death with the words: 'He has died for me, I will die for him.' She asks the fishermen to bury them in the same grave. Rosen-müller remarks that the Wendish tunes of this story are akin to the German ones.

One cannot, of course, arrive at any conclusions with certainty, since the Wendish and the Hungarian ballads are both incomplete representatives of the group we are dealing with. There is, of course, always a third (and safest) possibility that the re-semblance between the passage of 'Leesome Brand' and our ballad is merely accidental.

Whichever was the case, the occurrence of this trait in quite separate ballads bears witness to a shared climate of beliefs and attitudes. The riddling answer: the ritual avoidance of naming the dreadful fact.

6, 9. The diver in our ballad instead of the German fisherman derives, according to Benkő, from the influence of another Hungarian ballad, 'Kate Kádár', which also lent the sympathetic plants to the Hungarian 'The Two Royal Children'.

7, 8. The death from sorrow, the Prince being taken to the palace, are motifs which the Hungarian ballad adopted in order to conclude the story, the original ending (she throws herself in the sea) being forgotten. Death from sorrow is a very general trait (cf. 'The Daughter of the Cruel King'), the order to take the Prince to the palace and the Queen's words addressed to her daughter in version **A** come probably from a version of 'The Maid who was Sold'. There the dead person is the bride, and the mother orders her son to take her to the palace, place her in the dining room: 'When-ever you will turn you will kiss her, whenever you will turn back you will lament/ weep over her' (cf. Appendix I, 'Gabriel and Clara Bátori').

Folklore and custom

We have already remarked that the 'pearly headdress' referred to in the girl's answer has a special function in the life of Hungarian girls; it is their headgear at the wedding. We find it in several other Hungarian ballads: reference is made to it in 'The Fair Maid Julia', in 'The Maid who was Sold', and in 'The Dishonoured Maiden'. The 'loss of a pearly headdress' has implications similar to the 'loss of a wreath', it suggests the loss of maidenhood. (Cf. 'Bagolyasszonyka', Csanádi-Vargyas, no. 109.) Such an implication is appropriate to our ballad and it would add another puzzling link to its elusive resemblance to 'Leesome Brand'.

Date

In dating the ballad we have to rely on the circumstantial evidence of the international parallels, and the style and tune of the Hungarian ballad.

The oldest recording of the German ballad dates from the sixteenth century, but most probably it had a wide circulation before this time. This is, however, of little use to our problem, since the Hungarian-German connections were extremely close even at the time when the first Hungarian ballad collections were made, and it could have reached Hungary any time before this.

The stylistic evidence, the frequent repetition of half lines, and half stanzas, the rhymeless octosyllables suggest an early origin of the ballad, that is, 'early' by Hungarian ballad standards: late sixteenth or early seventeenth century. The frequent alliterations are a feature characteristic of the oldest Hungarian ballads (cp. 'Clement Mason', 'The Maid who was Sold', 'Anna Molnár', 'The Fair Maid Julia').

Examples: 'király-leány kis Júlia'; 'nem kell nekem senki másé'; 'csak kapok én király fiát'; 'Mindjárt szörnyű halált hala'; 'tiszta vörös tulipántot'; 'nem megyek mer setét vagyon'; 'az királné maga mondja'; 'kísérd ki őt a kriptába'; 'három könnyet hullass rája'. The fact that the ballad has altogether sunk into oblivion since its recording in the late nineteenth century, and the incomplete narration of the recorded versions are also suggestive of the age of the ballad. The evidence of the tune also corroborates an early date of the ballad: as B. Fabó points out, it derives from the tune of the St Bernard Hymn which was probably composed in the twelfth century (Fabó, *A Magyar Népdal Zenei Fejlődése*, Budapest, 1908, p. 210).

Special Hungarian elements

The most important feature of the Hungarian ballad is the dialogue about the lost pearly headdress of the Princess, on which we have already commented. The ending of the ballad is also different from the international versions. This, however, must be due to the minstrel's attempt to complete the story the original ending of which he had forgotten.

The Hungarian ballad has preserved the original princely setting of the ballad, but the invitation to the spinning-room sounds somewhat strange, coming from the mouth of a Princess. This invitation would suggest that the ballad was sung in the spinning-room, and the fact that this trait is present in both versions indicates its popularity at the time on such occasions. Another localisation of the story is the substitution of the Danube for the original sea in which the Prince was drowned.

'ANNA MOLNÁR'

This ballad is the Hungarian representative of 'Heer Halewijn' known throughout Europe. It is included among the few Hungarian ballads which were known to F. J. Child. He describes five of its versions in his notes to 'Lady Isabel and the Elf-Knight' (no. 4).[1]

Version **A**

1 —Come, let us go away, Anna Molnár,
  On a long journey, into the vast forest
  To a land of milk and honey!
  —I will not go Martin Sajgó,
  I have a gentle husband,
  A gentle husband, a little son.

2 Anna Molnár could not resist.
  She set out on a long journey,
  To the land of milk and honey.
  They find a citrus-tree
  They sit down in its shadow.
  —Listen, my sweet treasure,[2]
  Search a little among my hair[3]
  My sweet treasure, Anna Molnár,
  Do not look up at the citrus-tree!
  Anna Molnár could not resist,
  She looked up at the citrus-tree:
  Behold, there are six fair maids there,
  Hanged one next to the other.
  Anna Molnár began to weep:
  She will be the seventh today!
  One drop of her tears fell
  On the face of Martin Sajgó.
  Martin Sajgó awakened:
  —Why are you weeping, why are you
      weeping, Anna Molnár?

---

[1] Child refers to these five versions under the letters **A–E**. Child, Hungarian **A** = our **G**; **B** = our **C**; **C** = our **I**; **D** = our **A**; **E** = our **H**.
[2] 'My sweet treasure' in Hungarian *édes kincsem*, a common term of endearment.
[3] 'Search a little among my hair' translates literally 'look into my head for a little while'.

—I am not weeping, Martin Sajgó,
But the tree is shedding its dew.
—The tree is not shedding its dew,
For it is sharp on midday now;
Listen, Anna Molnár,
Go up into the citrus-tree,
Up, into the branches of the citrus-tree!
Up Anna Molnár replies:
—I am not used to climbing trees,
Let Martin Sajgó lead the way,
And I will go after him.
Martin Sajgó leant his shining sword against
    the tree,
And he set off.
She just snatched up his sword,
And hewed his head off with one stroke.
She put on his clothes,
She mounted on his horse,
So she set out for home
For her gentle husband's courtyard.

3 —Good day to you, gentle master!
  —Welcome to you, (my) gallant soldier,
  —Listen, gentle master,
Will you take me in for the night?
  —I cannot take you in, my gallant soldier,
My wedded wife has deserted me,
My little son is crying all the time,
And your gallant lordship will not be able to sleep.
  —Never mind, never mind, good master,
Take me in for the night!
So he did, the gentle master,
And she sent him for wine to the village.
She picked up her son,
She suckled her crying son.
The gentle master came home.
And he asks her: —My gallant soldier,
What can be the reason
That my little son is not crying now?
Perhaps he knows, my gallant soldier,
That there is a stranger in the house.
  —Listen, gentle master,
I ask you one question, answer it:
If your wife were still alive,
If she were to come home suddenly,
Would you scold her, would you beat her,
Would you ever in her life reproach her?

—I would neither scold her, nor would I beat her,
Nor would I ever in her life reproach her.

4 She sat down on the couch,
She picked up her little son,
She unbuttoned her dolman,[1]
She revealed herself.

Versions

'Anna Molnár' has been recorded in numerous versions and fragments from all parts of Hungary. There are several versions which have hitherto remained unpublished.

A Csanádi-Vargyas, *Röpülj*, no. 11; =*MNGY*, I, p. 146 =Kriza (1956), no. 7 **B** Csanádi-Vargyas, *Röpülj*, no. 12; =Bartók-Kodály, *SZNd*, no. 93; =Kodály-Vargyas, *MNpt*, no. 341 **C** Ortutay, Gy., *Magyar Népköltészet*, II, no. 3 a; = *MNGY*, I, p. 138 = Kriza (1956), no. 8 **D** *Ethnographia*, **24**, 38 **E** *Ethnographia*, **21**, 131, no. 2 **F** *Ethnographia*, **21**, 131, no. 1 **G** *MNGY*, I, p. 141 **H** *MNGY*, I, p. 137 **I** *MNGY*, I, p. 144 **J** *MNYr*, **3**, 334 **K** *Ethnographia*, **16**, 222 **L** Faragó-Jagamas, *MCSNN*, no. 3 a **M** Faragó-Jagamas, *MCSNN*, no. 3 b **N** Faragó-Jagamas, *MCSNN*, no. 3 d **O** *MNYr*, **21**, 47 **P** Csanádi-Vargyas, *Röpülj*, no. 13; =*Ethnographia* (1908), 109; =Bartók-Kodály, *SZNd*, no. 10; =Kodály-Vargyas, *MNpt*, no. 79 **Q** *Ethnographia*, **19**, 110 **R** Domokos, *Moldvai Magyarság*, no. 2; =Domokos, *MM* (1931), no. 48 **S** Domokos, *Moldvai Magyarság*, no. 3; =Domokos, *MM* (1931), no. 48, part 2 **T** Bartók, *A Magyar Népdal*, no. 307 **U** *MNGY*, VIII, p. 186 **V** *MNGY*, VIII, p. 188 **W** Csanádi-Vargyas, *Röpülj*, no. 10; =Ortutay, *Magyar Népköltészet*, II, no. 3 b; =Bartók, *A Magyar Népdal*, no. 315; =Kodály-Vargyas, *MNpt*, no. 216 **X** *Ethnographia*, **2**, 79 **Y** *Ethnographia*, **39**, 108 **Z** Faragó-Jagamas, *MCSNN*, no. 3 c **AA** Domokos-Rajeczky, *Csángó Népzene*, II, no. 40, version I, p. 209 **BB** Domokos-Rajeczky, *Csángó Népzene*, II, no. 40, version 2, p. 210 **CC** Domokos-Rajeczky, *Csángó Népzene*, II, no. 40, version 3, pp. 211–12 **DD** Domokos-Rajeczky, *Csángó Népzene*, II, no. 40, version 4, p. 212 **EE** Domokos-Rajeczky, *Csángó Népzene*, II, no. 40, version 5, pp. 212–13 **FF** Domokos, *Moldvai Magyarság*, no. 4

International parallels

The international parallels are too well known to need description, and the history and the spread of the ballad have a bulky literature. For these reasons, instead of my usual way of presenting the ballad, I shall follow the descriptive part of a recent general study of the entire ballad-group: that of H. O. Nygard ('The Ballad of "Heer Halewijn"', *FF. Communications*, no. 169, Helsinki, 1958), pointing out how the Hungarian ballad fits in with his list of incidents ('stages', as he calls them) and making certain observations which may be of general interest. (Nygard unfortunately does not deal with the Hungarian ballad in detail for the reason that in his opinion it has come from the

---

[1] 'Dolman' in Hungarian *dolmány*, a short jacket used for riding by the barons and soldiers, especially during the reign of King Matthias (1458–90).

German tradition, and therefore in so far as the origin of the ballad is concerned it need not be discussed.) The collation of the Hungarian versions with the forms and variations of the ballad in Western Europe may prove particularly useful, since the main body of the Hungarian material has remained inaccessible to the Western scholars. I shall make a special distinction between those traits of 'Anna Molnár' which appear to be genuine Hungarian additions to the international story and those which are included in the various national narratives of this group. It will also be necessary to make a further distinction between traits in the latter group, and decide (1) to what extent the Hungarian ballad has retained traits of the oldest traditional narrative of this group, and (2) which are the motifs it has taken from secondary forms of the ballad, and (3) to what degree it has altered both (1) and (2).

I. *The solicitation*

(a) *come, let us go*... (or *come with me*...) **A–R, T, Y, Z, AA–FF**
(b) for a long journey **A, C–E, H, T, FF**
(c) to the forest (greenwood) **A, C, D, H, J, O, W–Y, EE**
(d) to wander away **G, P**
(e) in the shadow of a branchy tree **I, P**
(f) for a visit **F**
(g) for a walk **K, FF**
(h) to a foreign land **U**

Promises

(i) to a land which flows with milk and honey **A**
(j) *I have six palaces I will put you in the seventh* **G**; *I have six stone castles* **I, R, AA**; *I will give you the seventh* **I, AA**; *I am having a seventh made now* **R**; *I have seven stone castles I will give you the seventh* **K, Q**
(k) *I will buy you dresses and boots for Sunday* **B**

Almost all readings have their international parallels:

(a) is the most frequent. It appears mostly in the French ballad 'Allons-y, donc nous promener'. But, while 'promener' means not a long journey in these (later) French versions, in the Hungarian it is usually made clear that they will have to go for 'a long journey'. Exceptions to this are only **K, F** (readings (f), (g)). This opening, 'let us go for a walk', is characteristic of the German Ulrich versions as well: 'Schön Ulrich wollt spazieren gehn, Traut Ann wollte mit ihm gehn.'

(c) occurs in Danish *K, L*. Its frequent occurrence in the Hungarian ballad would point to the fact that it was included in the original Hungarian telling.

(*h*) is most common in the British and Scandinavian versions, in which the villain is often 'an Outlandish Knight' (cp. our **F**, in which he is made a Turkish outlaw).

The villain's promises are also paralleled in the international versions:

(*j*) occurs in the Halewijn form: her dwelling will be a prince's castle; in the Danish versions there are eight golden castles promised to her (Nygard seems to be mistaken in saying that it must be a corruption of the eight ladies, for it is repeated not only in the Danish and Hungarian versions but also in other national forms: e.g. nine golden castles in the Norwegian versions), and the promise is repeated at a later stage also: when the villain is pleading for his life he offers her fifteen gold castles. At this later stage it occurs in the French ballad as well: the villain offers her the keys of his castles.

(*i*) is more significant, for here the promise of the wonderland occurs, similarly to the Danish, Swedish, and Norwegian versions. We shall refer to this motif later.

(*k*) is a more plebeian reading; a similar process of changing from the miraculous to the theme of everyday comfort is to be observed in the British and Norwegian versions.

II. *The lady's reply to the solicitation*

(*a*) *I will not go* **A–R, T, Z, AA–FF**

(*b*) *I have a gentle husband | Who is in the forest* **A–R, T, Z, AA–DD, FF**

(*c*) and *I have a small son* (in the field—**EE**) **A–R, T, Z, AA–CC, EE**; a babe in the cradle **B, F, K–M, O, Q, R, AA–FF**; who is crying in the cradle **I, N, T, Z**

(*d*) *a quiet house* **H, J, P, T**

At this stage it is revealed that Anna Molnár is a married woman, a trait entirely peculiar to the Hungarian ballad. The reply to the solicitation, namely, some reluctance on her part to listen to the villain's entreaties, occurs in all international versions except in the French and Norwegian.

III. *The departure for the journey*

This stage is very much curtailed in the Hungarian ballad. There appear to be two groups:

(*a*) usually he woos her till she cannot resist him any more and goes away with him: **A, B, E, G, I–W** (twenty-one versions altogether), **AA, BB**.

(*b*) she resists, the villain seizes her, lifts her on his horse's back, and carries her away by force: **C, D, H, Z**.

The first reading is the more general in the international versions; (*b*) is found only in the Scottish *C*, *D*, in which she is forcibly abducted ('as nowhere else in the tradition of the song', Nygard mistakenly comments).

IV. *The journey*

(*a*) they go along a big road **B, H**
(*b*) they pass through a vast forest or a greenwood **C–E, G, H, J, O, Q, U–Y, CC**
(*c*) the banks of the Danube **L**
(*d*) a field **U, V**
(*e*) in the forest she wants to rest **J, BB, DD**; *Let us sit down in the forest, | I have grown very tired | I am feeling faint* **J**; *Sit down, sit down, good soldier, | My weak legs have grown tired* **O**; *Let us rest here* **Q**

His reply

Let us go further in the greenwood **J**; *When we shall arrive at the branchy tree* **J, O, Q, BB**; *At the very tall tree* **J**; *The branchy tree has six branches | We shall rest in its shadow* **O**

The principal scene of the action is a greenwood in the Halewijn group, Ulinger and other German groups, in the Scandinavian ballad and in English *A*.

Readings (*e*) occur only in five versions, all recorded in Moldavia. They correspond with the German, Dutch and French forms in which the lady is thirsty, hungry, and wants to be reassured of shelter for the night.

(*f*) the villain's reply is found in the German and French ballads. The Hungarian versions resemble the German rather than the French reply, they lack the brutality of the villain's reply in the French. Especially close to the Hungarian reply is the German *H* (belongs to the Halewijn group) and the Ulinger versions (only the Swiss versions have this trait), in which the villain answers that they would rest under the linden—'a reply ominous enough in itself, but not as revealing as to the villain's intentions as the brutal remarks the French Renaud makes' (Nygard, *op. cit.*).

V. *The wish to rest, the delousing-scene*

(*a*) they arrive at a tree **E, T, V**; a branchy tree **C, D, F, G–J, M–R, AA–EE**; citrus-tree **A, L**; tall/big tree **B**; beautiful tree **U**; tree of murders **K**
(*b*) the villain asks Anna to *search among his hair*, i.e. to delouse him **A–Y, AA–EE**
(*c*) he forbids Anna to look up at the tree **A, B, E, G, J, K, S, BB, DD**
(*d*) he falls asleep **A, C, D, F, J, L, R, X, Y, BB**

Reading (*a*) is found in the Ulinger and Halewijn versions (cp. previous stage—reference to the linden); (*b*) occurs in the Ulinger versions and in the Western Nicolai form; traces of this motif are found in the

Dutch Halewijn form as well; (*d*) occurs in nine versions. This is a prominent motif in the Danish ballad, in which the delousing-motif is identical with the lady's ruse: it is she who makes the suggestion to delouse the villain, she charms him to sleep, binds him, then she wakes him, and eventually kills him.

VI. *The murderer's tree*

(*a*) she looks up into the tree and sees the previous victims hanging there **A–G, I–N, P–S, BB**

(*a₁*) six fair maids hanging there **A, C–G, J, K, Q, BB, DD**; six women **R, S**; seven women **P**

(*a₂*) six maids decapitated **I**; seven maids decapitated **L**; she sees *many fair heads* **B**

(*a₃*) sees her sibling hanging there **M**

(*a₄*) nine persons hanging there, the tenth is her brother **N**

(*b*) six birds appear above her head, they weep and they twitter, then she looks up into the tree **R, AA, CC**

Reading (*a*), namely, that the lady *actually sees* the previous victims, occurs in the Ulinger and Halewijn groups only, but only in the Ulinger versions and in the Hungarian ballad is the lady not made aware of the murderer's tree on which hang the previous victims until the two have sat down and the lady has deloused the villain as requested.

The number of the previous victims is mostly six in the British versions, seven in the Halewijn versions (in three versions); eight or nine (seldom fifteen or eighteen) in the Norwegian ballad, eight in Denmark, and three in the French ballad.

(*a₃*) and (*a₄*) appear to be corruptions, probably due to the influence of the Ulinger form, in which the lady's brother appears.

Reading (*b*), the warning of the birds which are in fact the souls of the previous victims, is found only in the Ulinger version.

VII. *The lady's tears*

(*a*) she starts weeping at the sight of the previous victims **A, C–J, L–P, R–T, AA, CC, DD**

(*b*) he will make me the seventh/eighth **A, C, D, G, J, L, P, S, BB–DD**; *if I were not clever he would have made me the seventh* **K, Q**

(*c*) a drop of her tears falls on the villain's face **A, C–F, J, L–O, R–T, AA, CC**

(*d*) it awakens him **A, C, D, F, H, J, L, R, BB, CC**

The villain's questions

(*e*) why are you weeping? **A, C–I, L–P, T, AA, CC–EE**

(*f*) have you looked up at the tree? **G, J, S, BB**

Her reply

(*g*) I am not weeping **A, C–E, H, I, K, L, O, P, T**; the tree is shedding its dew **A, C–E, H, I, K, L, O, P, T, AA**

(*h*) a few drops of rain fell from a cloud **F, M, N, EE**

(*i*) three orphans passed this way, and I remembered my young son and my husband **G, J, S, DD**; remembered home **BB, CC**

His retort

(*j*) how could the tree shed its dew when it is sharp noon **A, C, D, H, K,**[1] **L, O**

Readings (*a*) and (*e*) are paralleled only in the Ulinger versions; there, however, she gives a direct answer to the villain's question, while in the Hungarian ballad the lady evades the answer.

(*b*) is a most common feature in this ballad tradition; it occurs in all groups, but only in one version of the Dutch Halewijn form. In the Hungarian ballad this passage is shifted from the villain's speech to the lady's thought, according to the conception that she comes to her own conclusions as to the villain's intentions.

(*d*) the villain is awakened in the Danish ballad, but not by the maid's tears: she wakes him, after having safely bound him.

VIII. *The villain's order to climb into the tree—the lady's ruse*

(*a*) the villain bids Anna to climb into the tree **A–G, I, J–L, N, O, R, S, AA, BB, DD**

(*b*) the ruse: she asks the villain to climb first, for she does not know how to climb **A–G, I–L, N, O, R, S, AA, BB, DD**

Neither the villain's order, nor Anna's particular ruse have exact counterparts in the international forms of the ballad.[2] Traits of these, however, can be detected in Halewijn (German versions *E–J*) in which a similar passage occurs included in the passage of the choice of deaths available for the heroine:

> Und willst du klimmen den Lindenbaum?
> Or willst du schwimmen den Wasserstrom?
> Or willst du sterben des blanken Schwerdts?

The ruse of the Hungarian lady is also suggested:

> Ich will nicht klimmen den Lindenbaum...

and especially in version *J*:

> Ich *kann nicht* klimmen den Lindenbaum

---

[1] **K** is corrupted, it is the villain who tells Anna not to look into the tree for it is shedding its dew, and the retort is given by Anna.

[2] Cp., however, similar ruse in Berze Nagy, Type 327 A, nos. 3, 7, 12, 14, incident C.

IX. *The decapitation*

(*a*) the villain leads the way up into the tree **A–O, R, S, AA, BB, DD**

(*b*) he takes his clothes off **E, K, O, Z, AA, DD**

(*c*) he leans his sword against the tree **A, K, O, DD**; sticks it in the ground **AA**

(*d*) she snatches up his sword **A, B, E–G, I–K, O, R, S, AA, BB, DD**

(*e*) and hews his head off **A, B, E–G, I, J, R, S, AA, BB**

(*f*) he drops his sword from the tree accidentally **C, D, H, L, M, N**

(*g*) asks her to hand it up to him **C, D, L, M, N**

(*h*) she promises to do so **C, D**

(*i*) she throws the sword up in such a way that it cuts his head off at once (**H** his waist) **C, D, H, M, N**

(*j*) she cuts him into pieces **K, L, O**

(*k*) seven versions (**P, Q, U, V–Y**) move directly from the delousing scene to the decapitation: as soon as the villain falls asleep the lady snatches up his sword and hews his head off. This is done without any apparent reason in **U–Y**, in which the multiple murder motif has not been preserved. Among these versions **Q** is the most logical: as soon as the lady looks up into the tree and sees the previous victims she snatches his sword and decapitates him; in **P** the order of the stages is changed: the delousing scene follows the discovery of the victims and her tears. The peculiar reading of version **O** has probably come from one of these truncated versions: since the lady has no apparent reason to kill the villain with whom she has eloped, a confused and unintelligible story is made up to fill in the gap: it is she who has killed six knights previously, and now the seventh.

X. *The villain's pleas and her retorts*

This part of the story is almost altogether missing in the Hungarian ballad.

(*a*) *Spare my life, I will give you the money I possess* version **O**. Retort: *I do not need your money, but I need your red blood. | I will take your life and your money as well.*

(*b*) *Spare my arms so that I can put away my...* version **K**. Retort: *I will not spare your arms, for if I did you would cut my neck.*

(*c*) There is only one version in which the villain pleads after decapitation: version **E** *His head spoke: | —Pick me up, Anna Molnár, | Cover me with your handkerchief, | Take me to my father's table. | Anna Molnár did not answer. ||*

(*d*) her taunt: *Rightly served, Martin Ajgó, | Why did you lure me away from my home?* versions **C, D**

Reading (*a*) may be compared to the Danish and Swedish versions in which the villain asks the maid to release his arms, and in which the maid cuts his head and his arms off; however, the crudeness of this passage in our version **O** leaves it without doubt that it is a later fabrication.

(*b*) has its parallels in Norwegian, French, in which the villain offers gold, or his castles, etc., to the maid if she spares his life.

We shall refer to reading (*c*) later.

XI. *The departure for home*

(*a*) the lady puts on the villain's clothes **A–Q, S, U–Z, AA–CC**
(*b*) she mounts on his horse **A, C, G, J, L, V, W, Y, BB**
(*c*) she sets off for home **A–H, J–Q, S, U–Z, AA–DD**

Reading (*a*) is singular to the Hungarian versions, but (*b*) and (*c*) are repeated commonly in the international versions.

XII. *The lady and her husband, the reconciliation*

With stage XII we enter upon narrative substance that has no parallel elsewhere in the tradition of the ballad.

(*a*) the lady, disguised in the villain's clothes, asks accommodation from her husband (for the night) **A–Q, S, U–Z, AA–DD**
(*b*) he cannot take her in **A–L, N–Q, S, U–Z, AA, BB, DD**; for his wife has left home **A–C, E, F, N, P**; his small son is crying all the time **A–L, N–Q, S**; the child has been crying for three days **M, Z**; for four days **P**; for three weeks and three days **G**; for a year **K, O**; and three days **O**; and six months **K**; and *he* will not be able to sleep **A**; there is nobody to cook dinner for *him* **U–Y**
(*c*) she persuades him, and sends him for wine **A–Q, Y, Z, AA–DD**; for water **DD**; sends the servant to fetch some logs **G, I, J**
(*d*) while the husband is away she suckles the child **A–Q, U, W–Z, AA–DD**; and lulls him to sleep **C, D, J, L–N**; and washes the child in her tears **J**
(*e*) on his return the husband is amazed that the child has stopped crying **A, C, F, G, J, K, L, N–Q**; *perhaps he knows that there is a stranger in the house* **A, C, F, J, L, BB**
(*f*) she asks him whether he would reproach/beat his wife if she returned **A–G, I–Q, AA**
(*g*) he would never do that **A–G, I–P**; *have you seen Anna Molnár?* **N**

Anna reveals herself

(*h*) 'She opens her *dolman*' **A, E–I, M, N, O, U, W, Z, AA, CC, DD**; she reveals herself **A, E–I, K, M–O, U, W, Z**; *She let down her fair hair | —I am Anna Molnár | —You are not Anna Molnár. | She went to her chamber, | Put on her own dress: | —Am I Anna Molnár?* | —*Yes, yes, you are Anna Molnár* **K** || *Even if you reproach me, | even if you beat me | I am your wife* **B, L, P** || *I am your wife, | With whom you pledged. | He recognized her, | They embraced each other, | They had a gay dinner, | They stayed together till | They died* **C, D** || *I am the mother of this child | Who was lured away by a stranger. | Go into your stable, | There is a saddled horse there. | He came back, embraced her, | He recognized his dear wife. | He almost died with joy, | He thanked God for this* **J** ||

Mother-child

(*i*) she asks her husband to take her boots off, to dry her foot-cloth **U, V**; she asks her son... **W**
(*i₁*) the husband tells his son to help the stranger **V**; daughter... **U**
(*i₂*) *Father, father, | This is my mother* **U–Y**; *I know her by her foot* **U–W**; *I know her*

by her black hair **V, W**; *I know her by her slender waist* **V**; *I know her by her way of walking, and by her apron* **X**

(*i₃*) *You have no mother,* | *For the soldiers have lured her away* **V, W**; *For she has left her home,* | *She did not pity her brown-haired son* **V**; *What has got into your mind?* | *Your mother is not a soldier,* | *She has become a wanderer* **Y**

Names

The villain's name:

Martin Sajgó **A, F, I, R, T, AA–DD** (In version **F** Martin Sajgó is made a 'Turkish outlaw' by an introductory stanza: *A Turkish outlaw set off* | *From one country to another,* | *To behead seven fair maids,* | *To take them to Turkey.* | *But God did not allow him this:* | *The seventh maid beheaded him.*) Martin Ajgó **C, H**; Martin Jajgó **D**; Martin Zajgó **P**; *a soldier* (**A**), **B, E, G, K–O,** (**P**), **Q, S, U–Z**; *a stranger* **J**; *a Turkish outlaw* (**F**)

The heroine's name:

Anna Molnár **A–I, K–T, Z, AA, BB**; *a young wife* **J, U, W, X, Y**; *the sheriff's wife* (**U**), **V,** (**W**), (**X**), (**Y**)

The husband:

a miller, a sheriff **E, K, O, V–Y**

Comparing now the Hungarian ballad with the various groups of the international versions we find, first of all, that with certain modifications all the complete versions of 'Anna Molnár' have retained what Nygard considers to be 'the narrative core' of the ballad: 'a villain entices a girl (in the Hungarian ballad, a married woman) from her home to kill her as he has killed others; she through bravery and presence of mind defeats his designs by a ruse, and he (pleading for his life) is destroyed by her.'

Beyond this 'narrative core' of the ballad, a considerable diversity has developed in the narrative of the national versions. In order to trace the origin of the Hungarian ballad, we have to examine its central body (i.e. stages V–IX) and compare it with the international parallels. These stages are present in all Hungarian versions which tell a complete story.

	Hungarian	Ulinger	German E–J (Halewijn group)	Danish (Scandinavian)
1.	principal scene of the action: greenwood	yes	yes	yes
2.	delousing scene	yes	(traces)	(yes, but in the maid's ruse)
3.	the lady notices the previous victims	yes	yes	—
4.	tears	yes	(traces)	—

Hungarian	Ulinger	German E-J (Halewijn group)	Danish (Scandinavian)
5. *he will make me the* [nth] *victim*	(*you* will be, etc.)	(yes)	(yes)
6. villain's questions: *why are you weeping?*	yes	—	—
7. lady's evasive answers	(she tells the truth)	—	—
8. villain's order: climb into the tree	—	(included in the choice of death: the first)	—
9. her ruse:	—	yes	yes
I cannot climb	—	(included in the lady's answer to the villain in *J*)	—
You lead the way	—	—	—

Placing these motifs and incidents side by side, it is unquestionable that the Hungarian ballad is linked to the Ulinger version and to the German E-J of the Halewijn group, and more distantly to the Danish ballad.

Traits which are shared by the Hungarian and the Ulinger ballads include:

> the ominous reference to the tree under which they will rest
> the delousing—it is the villain's wish
> the lady's actually seeing the previous victims
> her weeping
> the villain's questions as to why she is weeping

Only in the Ulinger and in the Hungarian ballad is the lady not made aware of the murderer's tree on which hang the previous victims until the two have sat down and the lady has deloused the villain as requested.

From point 7 onwards there is a considerable difference between the Ulinger group and the Hungarian versions: (1) in the Ulinger version the lady tells the villain the true cause of her tears, in the Hungarian ballad she evades the answer; (2) in the Ulinger ballad the lady's ruse is replaced by her three cries for help, she is incapable of saving herself by her own wits; it is her brother who hears her cries for help and comes to her rescue.

In order to find further agreements with the Hungarian ballad, we have to turn to the source of the Ulinger ballad, namely, the German forms E-J of the Halewijn group: only in the German Halewijn form is the lady's climbing up into the tree suggested (as the first one of the three choices of deaths she is offered in the German versions); only in

German *J* do we find parallels to the ruse of the Hungarian lady ('Ich kann nicht klimmen den Lindenbaum').

Thus we may conclude that the Hungarian ballad comes from the German, and more particularly from a German version which contains elements 1-7 of the Ulinger group, and also has the passage of the lady's climbing into the tree from the German *E–J* Halewijn group. According to the motifs common to the Hungarian and German ballads we may hypothetically reconstruct the source of the Hungarian ballad in the following:

arrival at the tree
the knight's wish to rest
the delousing scene
the lady observes the previous victims and comes to her conclusions
she weeps
the villain's questions: why she is weeping
the lady's answers
you shall be the [nth] *victim*
the villain announces his intentions in offering three choices of deaths, including the
 climbing into the tree passage
the lady's answer: she cannot climb
her ruse

Thus we may fit the Hungarian ballad into Nygard's diagram of the interrelations of the German ballads as follows:

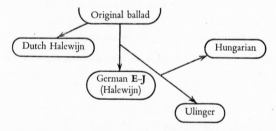

In order to explain the considerable difference between the *lady's ruse* in the Hungarian ballad and in the German *E–J* versions, we have to bear two things in mind: (1) the Hungarian ballad is akin to the German *E–J* in that the lady comes to her own realisation of what is in store for her, by looking at the murderer's tree (a trait also preserved in the Ulinger form, and analogously in the Danish group II, by looking at the grave which the villain begins to prepare for her). From this point of view, writes Nygard, the Dutch-German (Danish and, we may add, Hungarian) narrative is a more effective and satisfactory one than the British or French songs, in which the villain states outright that she is to be drowned. (2) However, in the Dutch-German as well as in the Danish ballads the villain *eventually admits* his real plans to the maid: he offers her the choices of death, and tells her that she will be the *n*th victim. The special feature of the Hungarian ballad is that it carries the original idea to the extreme: *the villain does not, at any stage, announce his real intentions to the lady.*

The difference between the lady's ruse in the German *E–J* versions and in the Hungarian ballad derives, I believe, from this different concept:

(*a*) In the German *E–J* the villain announces his intentions to the lady and offers her the choice of three means of death. The lady chooses the sword. Nygard attaches some importance to this choice, i.e. that she implies this to be the most honourable way of dying. He fails to notice, however, that this choice is already part of the lady's ruse: only by choosing death by the sword can she refer to her blood which may stain the villain's clothes, only by this excuse can she induce him to avert his attention from her to his clothes, and thereby enable her to slay him.

In the Hungarian ballad the lady has no pretext to advise the villain to remove his clothes, since she was never told of his intention. Her ruse therefore must be the exact opposite of that of the German lady in the Halewijn ballad: the success of her ruse rests on her pretence that she has not perceived the villain's plans (N.B. her evasive answers to account for her tears) and so lulls him into a false sense of security. In this way the omission of the villain's announcement concerning his real plans with the lady is exactly as important, in a negative way, in the Hungarian ballad for the success of the lady's ruse, as its presence is in the German *E–J*. In both cases the idea of the ruse is to render the villain helpless, and the first part of the original motif of the choice of death seems to have been sufficient to inspire the Hungarian minstrel with the idea of the particular ruse of the Hungarian lady.

The second problem of general interest is the delousing scene, and the lady's tears.

F. J. Child (notes to no. 4) is somewhat puzzled by this trait in the Hungarian ballad: 'Magyar A. [i.e. our **G**] is entirely peculiar. Apparently the man lays his head in the woman's lap that he may know, by the falling of her tears, when she has disobeyed his command not to look into the tree. This is like "Bluebeard", and rather subtle for a ballad.' This interpretation must have derived from a clumsy translation of this version, for both the Ulinger and the Hungarian versions show that the primary function of the delousing-motif was to enable the lady to discover the previous victims, and to be on her guard. The villain's command that she is not to look into the tree is obviously a later insertion (similar to the villain's wish in the Danish ballad that she should not deceive him while he is asleep).

The original sequence of motifs in this stage seems to have been better preserved in the Hungarian ballad than in the Ulinger versions: the delousing-scene, the lady's observing the previous victims hanging on the tree, her tears, the awakening of the villain, his questions why she is weeping, followed by her *evasive* answer. The difference between the Ulinger versions and the Hungarian ballad as far as the lady's answer is concerned is probably due to the fact that in the Ulinger version the lady's ruse is replaced by her being saved by her brother. It is therefore not important in the latter group that the lady should pretend to be unsuspecting.

Traces of the delousing-scene and the lady's tears are found in the Halewijn form as well, and both Grundtvig and Nygard believe that it was part of the original story.[1] If this was so, the Hungarian ballad seems to have preserved the most complete original form of this stage. The delousing-scene occurs in the Danish ballad as well, only there it is the lady's ruse: it is she who makes the offer to the villain, lulls him to sleep by charm, binds him, then wakes him and eventually kills him.

Already Nygard notes that the ruse in the Danish ballad appears to be 'part of the recreation of the ballad narrative'. In his opinion the change took place gradually, as the supernatural expedient disappeared from the ballad (namely, in the original form of the ballad the villain has supernatural power, his head speaks after his decapitation and requests the maid to fetch the magic salve which would heal him. The ballad singers, writes Nygard, were forced to alter the narrative and the sequence of events as they lost the supernatural import of the story; the villain's pleading had to be moved forward to a point of time before his decapitation. But if he is to plead for his life before being killed by the maid, he had in some way to be brought into her power. This was done in the Danish ballad by first putting him to sleep, then binding

---

[1] L. Vargyas in his study (*Ethnographia*, **71**, 479–502; *Acta Ethnographica*, **10**, 241–94) dealing with Hungarian ballad motifs which occur in Sibero-Turkic heroic epics, derives 'Anna Molnár' from the French versions (cp. introductory scene, defeated villain, reference to the heroine's return to her home). He puts forward the theory that the Hungarians, drawing from their own cultural heritage, enlarged the French form with the murderer's tree and the delousing scene—motifs prominent in the Sibero-Turkic heroic epics. These incidents then, in Vargyas's opinion, penetrated the western forms of the ballad from the Hungarian versions.

him. The villain's pleading for his life may thus occur when he wakes up from his sleep, and finds himself bound. That she wishes to delouse him is due to this process, in Nygard's opinion.

On the joint evidence of the Ulinger and the Hungarian versions, we may add another important reason for this change in the Danish ballad. We have seen that the original function of the delousing-scene in both the German and Hungarian ballads was to enable the heroine to discover the previous victims. In the Danish ballad the maid *does not actually see* the previous victims; she will learn of them later from the villain himself. The delousing motif has lost here its structural importance; it is no longer needed for the maid to enable her to perceive her dangerous position: the villain's digging the grave is sufficient for this. Thus the delousing motif is employed in a different function: it becomes the maid's ruse.

The third problem concerns the original supernatural aspects of the story. In the Hungarian ballad the villain appears to be similar to that of the later French versions: a suitor, who lures the lady away for a walk; he is introduced directly, stripped of all the marvellous. On closer examination, however, we find certain faint vestiges of the original supernatural quality of the villain in the Hungarian versions.

(*a*) In version **A** he promises the lady to take her to a wonderland, which flows with milk and honey. This motif is characteristic of the Scandinavian form of the ballad. Although this trait occurs in only one version of 'Anna Molnár', we find it again in 'Beautiful Kate Bán', a ballad which has sprung from the confluence of 'Anna Molnár' and 'The Cruel Mother'. Its beginning follows closely the story of 'Anna Molnár': it has the solicitation (the villain here is a Turk as in our version **F**), the lady's reluctance to go, the journey through the wood, the delousing motif, the lady's tears, the Turk's questions and the lady's evasive answer.

This ballad has been preserved in one version and a fragment, both of which have a solicitation similar to our version **A**.

Examples:

        (*b*) 'Come with me, come with me Beautiful Kate Bán
           To my country,—
           Twice does the wheat ripen, thrice comes the vintage,
           Thrice does every sort of flower bloom.'

        (*a*) 'Come now, come now, Beautiful Kate Bán,
           To our country, to lovely Turkey.'
        'I will not go, I will not go, Black Peter Rác,

For I have a son, a little toddling son,
A daughter who still has to be carried, and a dear wedded
   husband!'
'Do not worry about them!
Come now, come now, Beautiful Kate Bán,
To our country, to lovely Turkey.
Even dogs do not bark in the same way in lovely Turkey
As in Hungary!'
'I will not go...' etc.
'Come now, come now, Beautiful Kate Bán,
To our country, to lovely Turkey,
For two hundred silver coins, for sixty thalers,
For three hundred pieces of gold.'

Since this wonderland does not occur in any other Hungarian ballad, and since the beginning of 'Beautiful Kate Bán' agrees with 'Anna Molnár' in so many details, we may take it for granted that the wonderland motif of the former ballad was borrowed from 'Anna Molnár' at a time when this was a more prominent motif in the latter ballad. The wonderland motif has gradually faded away from the Hungarian ballad. Version (b) of 'Beautiful Kate Bán' may be described with Nygard's comments on a Norwegian version, in which the villain has a nobleman's estate that is as green in the autumn as it is in the spring. 'This reference to a fabulous vegetation', writes Nygard, 'in addition to the prevalence of the gold which takes the place of sand (cp. the Hungarian land of milk and honey) brings to mind the earlier wonderland motif, but now it serves in the rationalised context of a man making grand but credible offers to his lady'.

The very presence of this motif in the Hungarian ballad would suggest that some reference to the wonderland was probably included in the original German versions as well.

(b) The villain's name in the Hungarian ballad is also suggestive. The original name was probably 'Martin Sajgó'. 'Sajog, salyog' meant in old Hungarian 'glitter, shine, dazzle'. This has become 'Martin Jajgó'; 'jaj!' is an exclamation when feeling pain, i.e. 'alas!' This change has taken place probably for two reasons: the modern meaning of the word 'sajog' is 'it hurts, it aches', which is a synonym for 'jaj', 'Ouch!' and was adapted probably in view of the sinister plans of the villain. 'Martin Ajgó' is due to the loss of the first sound of his name, it has no meaning; 'Zajgó' means 'noisy, troublesome'. All these derivative forms of the name are rather sinister, but 'Sajgó', in the original sense, has also a supernatural air about it.

(c) Version **E** resembles the Halewijn form in that the villain's head speaks after it has been cut off. It would be very convenient to link the Hungarian ballad to the original Dutch Halewijn group through this link, and to point out that of all the other national forms of the ballad only the Hungarian has preserved this important motif, if only in one version. Unfortunately this cannot be done with a clear conscience. The words uttered by the villain's head in the Hungarian **E** version are the first part of the stereotyped complaint often uttered by orphans in Hungarian ballads, and I suspect that it slipped into this version from a corrupted form of 'Anna Betlen'. In the latter ballad we also have the speaking of the head and the words of the orphans' complaint, and its presence there comes undoubtedly from the misplacement of the complaint after the heroine's death. (Cf. discussion of 'Anna Betlen'.)

Finally, there is the question of the ending of the Hungarian ballad from the point of view of the heroic stature of the heroine.

In the original concept of the international story, the maid is celebrated as a heroine (Dutch Halewijn group). This feature of the original story has gradually faded from the various international versions. It may still be perceived in those versions in which she defeats the villain through her own wits (also in the versions in which she kills the villain's robber-brothers, etc.). In the Ulinger versions she is already incapable of saving herself, and the disappearance of this feature is complete in the Nicolai and Ulrich forms, in which she dies.

In the Hungarian ballad we may also follow this process of the disappearance of her heroic stature although in no versions do we find this motif as emphatically expressed as in the Dutch versions.

Already in the ruse-stage we may make a distinction between three groups:

(a) The heroine snatches the villain's sword as he is climbing into the tree. This is a 'heroic' action: she is saved *only* by her own wits, and by the success of her ruse.

(b) The villain *drops* his sword accidentally as he is climbing into the tree, she throws it up in such a way that it hews his head off at once. Here chance and luck come to the help of the heroine.

(c) And finally the small group of versions (**U–Y**) in which she kills the sleeping villain without any ruse or even apparent reason.

But even in versions which belong to group (a), the emphasis of the narrative is not on the success of her ruse or on the celebration of her bravery, but on the next stage: her reconciliation with her husband. In the recently recorded versions the multiple-murder motif tends to be omitted from the narrative, and almost the entire story concentrates on her returning home. The reconciliation with the husband is obviously a later trait in the tradition. It is peculiar to the Hungarian ballad, but, in its effect of shifting the story from the supernatural to the everyday events, in its depriving the heroine of heroic stature, it expresses the general rationalising tendency in the later international ballad tradition.

'KATE KÁDÁR'

When one mentions ballads, it is 'Kate Kádár' (together with 'Clement Mason') that will be remembered first by the average Hungarian, just as it is 'Sir Patrick Spens' that will be remembered first by a Scottish or English reader.

Version **A**

1 'Mother, mother, my mother!
Lady Gyulai, my mother!
I shall marry Kate Kádár,
The fair daughter of our serf.'

2 'I will not let you, my son
Martin Gyula,
Marry instead a lord's
fair daughter!'

3 'I do not want a lord's
fair daughter,
I only want Kate Kádár,
The fair daughter of our serf.'

4 'Then away with you, my son
Martin Gyula;
I disown you, you are no son of mine
Not now, nor ever.'

5 'My footman, my footman,
the one I hold more dear,
Drag forth my coach,
Place the horses between the shafts!'

6 The horses were placed between the shafts
They took the road.
Kate Kádár gave him a scarf:
'When its colour will turn to red
then my life too (take note of this)
will be changing.'

7 Martin Gyula goes
   Over hill and dale,
   All at once he sees a change
   on the embroidered scarf.

8 'My footman, my footman, the one I hold more dear,
   The land is God's and the horse is for the dogs,[1]
   Let us turn back, for the scarf has turned to red,
   So Kate Kádár too has long met her end.'

9 The swineherd was at the end of the village.
   'Hi, good swineherd, what is the news with you?'

10 'Our news is good, but there is ill news for you,
   For Kate Kádár has met her end.
   Your mother has had her taken away,
   She has had her thrown into a bottomless lake.'

11 'Good swineherd, show me where is that lake,
   And all my gold, my horse, my coach are yours!'

12 So they went to the shore of the lake.
   'Kate Kádár, my soul,[2] speak one word, are you there?'
   Kate Kádár spoke to him from the lake,
   Quickly Martin Gyula jumped after her.

13 His mother sent divers,
   They took them out dead, the girl in his arms,
   One of them was buried in front of the altar,
   The other was buried behind the altar.

14 Two chapel-flowers[3] sprang up out of the two,
   They intertwined on the top of the altar.
   Their mother[4] went there, she tore them off,
   The chapel flower spoke to her thus:

15 'May you be cursed, may you be cursed,
   My mother, Lady Gyulai,
   You have been cruel when I was alive,
   And even now you have murdered me!'

---

[1] 'The horse is for the dogs', i.e. it is expendable, the coachman should not spare it but drive it as fast as possible.

[2] 'My soul'—a common term of endearment in Hungarian.

[3] 'Chapel-flower' does not refer to a particular flower, and is used here, probably, to indicate that the flowers in question sprang up in the chapel where the two lovers were buried.

[4] 'Their mother'—she is regarded now as Kate's mother as well; i.e. they are regarded as married.

Versions

Thirteen versions and a fragment have been recorded from Transylvania, two recently from Moldavia.

A Csanádi-Vargyas, *Röpülj*, no. 1; =Ortutay, *Magyar Népköltészet*, II, no. 9 *a*; =*MNGY*, XI, p. 11; =Kriza, *Vadrószák*, no. 1; =Kriza (1956), no. 1 **B** Kriza, *Vadrószák*, no. 2; =Kriza (1956), no. 2 **C** Ortutay, Gy., *Magyar Népköltészet*, II, no. 9 *b* **D** Csanádi-Vargyas, *Röpülj*, no. 2; =Bartalus, *Magyar Népdalok*, III, no. 7 **E** Csanádi-Vargyas, *Röpülj*, no. 3; =Bartók-Kodály, *SZNd*, no. 127; =Kodály-Vargyas, *MNpt*, no. 119 **F** Csanádi-Vargyas, *Röpülj*, no. 4; =Bartók-Kodály, *SZNd*, no. 113; =Kodály-Vargyas, *MNpt*, no. 13 **G** Faragó-Jagamas, *MCSNN*, no. 1 *a* **H** Faragó-Jagamas, *MCSNN*, no. 1 *b* **I** *Ethnographia* (1908), 48 **J** *Ethnographia* (1908), 49 **K** *Ethnographia* (1908), 49 **L** *Ethnographia* (1912), 50 **M** *MNGY*, III, no. 38 **N** *MNGY*, III, no. 39 **O** Schram, *Magyar Népballadák*, no. 1 **P** *MNGY*, I, no. 91

Description of the ballad

I. Martin Gyula asks his mother's permission to marry fair Kate Kádár, the daughter of their serf.

B young master Nicholas; **C** clerk Martin; **E** the youngest son of Lady Gyulai; **D, G** the daughter of mistress Kádár; **H** Kate Kádár.

II. The mother does not give her consent.

A–D, L, M she bids him to marry instead some girl of noble stock from the village; **I** in a folk-tale vein: *Here in the village you can find princess and peeress*; **A, M** when her son persists in his plan the mother disowns him; **E, G, J, K, O** the mother threatens to enlist her son into the army; **F, N, P** she would rather have Kate thrown into a bottomless lake.

III. The son decides to leave home.

B–D, F, N he orders his servant to saddle his horse; **A, M**—his horse and coach; **E, J–L, O** he saddles it himself; **I** he sets off by foot; **G, H** he sets off for the army.

IV. He bids farewell to Kate. She gives him a scarf which will become red should anything happen to her.

B gives him a scarf and a bunch of flowers. The scarf will lather with blood and the flowers will wither to indicate that she is in danger; **C, D** a white scarf is given to him, which will become bloody if she dies; **E–K, N–P** the life-token is missing; **F** his horse jumps with a single leap to Kate's gate. Lady Gyulai has both of them arrested and has them thrown into a bottomless lake.

V. Amidst his wanderings Martin suddenly observes that the life-token signals danger. He turns back immediately.

(This motif occurs in **A–D, M** only; **A, M** he orders his servant, *Earth belongs to God, the horse is for the dogs, turn back, for the scarf has become red!*)

VI. At the fringe of the village he meets the swineherd.

C, D wine-herd (probably a contamination); **B, H** miller; **E, K, L** a Wallachian lad; **J, O** a Hungarian lad; **N** a little shepherd; **G** a man called Valentine Molnár; **I** called John Gál.

He questions the swineherd about the news in the village, and the man answers him.

A, M, P *Our news is good, but yours is bad* | *For your mother had Kate Kádár taken and had her thrown into a bottomless lake*; **C, D** It is no bad news about us, but there is ill news for you; **B, D, E, G, I, L, N** Nothing else, but Kate Kádár had been murdered; **C, H** she had thrown herself into a bottomless lake; **G** no bad news, no good news, but...; **J, K, O** nothing else is bad, but...; **M** three times she managed to swim ashore, three times was she forced back into the water by three executioners; **E, H–L, N, O, P** he meets accidentally the man who conveys him the sad news; **H** which ends here, adds *His bitch mother did not leave her even there, she had her buried in front of the church.*

VII. Martin asks the man to lead him to the place where his beloved was thrown into the water. For this service he offers him his gold, his coach and his bay horse.

B his bay horse and his embroidered clothes; **C, D, I** his bay horse; **E** his horse, his silken saddle and his strap; **K** his bay horse, his silken saddle, his strap and his halter; **N** his bay horse with all its equipment; **L** his bay horse and his saddle; **G** his clothes.

VIII. Having arrived at the lake, Martin asks Kate to speak to him and she answers from the lake.

E, G, I, J, L, N, O *Are you alive or are you dead, or are you thinking of me?* | *—I am neither alive, nor am I dead, all I do is to think of you;* **B** *Are you alive, my soul, my Kate?* | *—Without you I am hardly alive;* **D, K** Kate answers: *I am here dying;* **D, M** agree with **A**; **C, F, H, K** the dialogue does not occur.

IX. Martin Gyula throws himself after Kate into the lake.

I, K, O he crosses himself; **L** the Wallachian lad tries to prevent him committing suicide; **B** a geranium and a rosemary spring up from their bodies over the water, they fall in love and embrace each other.

X. Lady Gyulai sends divers to take both of them out of the lake.

I, J, O she has them taken out by iron hooks; **A, M, N** they find the lovers dead, in each other's arms; **L** ends here.

XI. Lady Gyulai has them placed in red and white marble coffins and has them buried, one of them in front of the altar, the other behind it.

A, F, I, M no coffins; **D** white and yellow marble coffins; **G** stone and marble; **J, O** two stone ones; **I, J** one of the lovers is buried by the left, the other by the right side of the altar; **M** only Kate is buried in front of the church.

XII. Two flowers spring up from the two graves and they embrace each other above the altar.

A, M two chapel-flowers; **B** white and red marble lilies; **C, F** rosemary and tulip, **C** without leaves; **D** carnation without stem, rosemary without leaves; **E, K** white and red gillyflowers; **G** two lilies; **I** two sprigs of rosemary; **J** rosemary and white gillyflower; **N** white and red marble saplings; **O** white lily and white rosemary.

XIII. Lady Gyulai plucks the flowers.

B she grinds them under her sole and places them on a thorn-bush; **E, J, K, O** and makes them wither in her bosom; **F, G** grinds them under her sole. In **G** XII–XIII appear in place of IX; **I** she has them cut off from their roots; **N** she takes them home and plants them on her window.

XIV. The flowers cast a curse on her.

A quoted; **H** like **A**. **B** *You had persecuted us during our life, | You have not let us in peace after our death. | Therefore may God not grant you any good, | May you be given a spouse who does not love you, | May you find yourself without any bread, | May nobody take pity on you. || **C** My mother, you did not leave me in peace when I was alive | And do you now not leave me in peace after my death? | May the road slope upwards in front of you, | May it turn to dust behind you, | The water you wash yourself in, | May that water turn to blood! | The towel you rub yourself with, | May that towel go up in flames! | May your bread turn to stone. | May your red knife twist in your hands, | May it injure your heart. | Wine, wheat may you not produce, | May your field not be green, | May your bread turn to stone, | May there be no blessing on you from Heaven. || **D** May you be cursed mother! | You did not leave us in peace when we were alive, | You do not leave us in peace when we are dead. | May the water swell in front of you, | May mud spring behind you, | May there be no blessing on you from Heaven, | May your bread turn to stone, | May the water you wash yourself in turn to blood, | May your towel go up in flames, | May it set your face on fire. || **E** Lady Gyulai, my mother, | You did not leave us in peace when we were alive, | And now you do not leave us in peace after our death. | May your bread turn to stone, | May your knife break in two in it, | May the water you wash yourself in turn to blood, | May your hemp turn to hackle, | And the footbridge you want to go through | May it go up in flames. || **F** Mother, Lady Gyulai, | You have not left me in peace | Either in my life or in my death, | May the devils carry you away, | May they carry you away from one branch to another. || **G** Mother, mother, my mother, | I do not wish you a greater curse | Than the one I can think of now, | The table you eat at, | May that table break into pieces, | And the bread you eat of, | May it turn to stone in front of you, | The knife with which you cut it, | May that knife break into pieces, | The towel you rub yourself with | May that towel be covered with flames. || **I** Mother, Lady Gyulai, | You are a famous witch, | May God turn you to stone, | Or, if not to stone, to a rock. || **J, K** Mother, Lady Gyulai, | You are a famous old witch, | I do not wish you any other ill | May your bread turn to stone, | May your knife break into it, | May the water you wash yourself in turn to blood, | May the footbridge you want to cross go up in flames. || **O** Mother, Lady Gyulai, | You are a famous old witch, | May your bread turn to stone, | May your knife break into it. || **N** May Lord of Heaven punish | her, who interferes with love, | Mother, mother, my murderer, | You did not leave me in peace when I was alive, | You do not leave me in peace now, when I am dead. ||* **L, P** the sympathetic plants and the curse-motif are missing.

International ballad-tree versions

The *Rumanian* 'The Ring and the Veil' (Alecsandri, *Poesii populare*, p. 20; transl. Stanley, *Rouman Anthology*, pp. 16, 193) is similar to the Hungarian ballad in many of its details.

A prince marries a serf-girl, the father opposes the marriage and sends his son to the war. The lovers exchange a ring and a veil. When their former owners die, the ring becomes rusty and the gold melts from the embroidered veil. The girl is drowned in a lake, the prince jumps in after her and they are found dead, in each other's arms. From their common grave sympathetic plants spring up.

Both the Rumanian and the Hungarian ballads show some resemblance to the popular Bavarian legend 'Agnes Bernauer', about which many popular songs and ballads were composed and circulated even in the eighteenth century. One of these songs was taken down in Transylvania also, sung by the Saxons. (*Korrespondez des Vereins für Siebenbürgerische Landskunde*, 1898.) These songs hark back much further than the date when they were recorded. The Bavarian chronicler in the fifteenth century remarks when mentioning 'Agnes Bernauer', 'de qua cantatur adhuc hodie pulchrum carmen'. References to the Bernauer story were pointed out in Gy. Király, *Nyugat* (1917), pp. 48–60. Király derives the story from Boccaccio, Bandello and Straparola who, according to his theory, drew their material from an unknown common source. Boccaccio's and Straparola's stories, however, have little in common with our ballad (the opposed love, and sending the hero abroad) while important motifs of 'Kate Kádár' (the murdering of the girl, the magic life-token, the sympathetic plants) do not occur in them at all. Besides, the crucial point in Boccaccio's and Straparola's stories is entirely different from the Hungarian ballad. In the Italian stories the girl is forced to marry someone else, her lover commits suicide in her bed on his return, and it is the girl who follows him into death.

The story related by Bandello has even less to do with our ballad. There the son of a rich merchant elopes with a girl. His mother is against their marriage. The girl is sent to a nunnery and is stabbed to death by her lover, who commits suicide afterwards.

In the *Southern Slavonic* ballad, which Gy. Király considers as a transitional form between the Italian and the Hungarian stories, the mother opposes the love and compels her son to marry someone else. The boy commits suicide on his wedding night and the girl follows his example. They are buried in the same grave. Here we have the sympathetic plants, but not the motifs of drowning the girl in the lake and the life-tokens; and the story is different also in the fact that the boy's death precedes that of the girl.

Thus, though there are some resemblances between 'Kate Kádár' and both the Italian and South Slavonian ballads, these are too general in character (and form parts of too many different stories) to give sufficient support to Király's suggestion that our ballad originated in Italy and reached Hungary via South Slavonia.

The *German* ballad goes as follows: Three hangmen entice Agnes Bernauer out of her house. They tell her that she must either renounce her love for Duke Albrecht, or else she is to be drowned in the Danube. Agnes rather chooses death, so she is thrown into the Danube. She appeals to the Virgin Mary, who helps her to swim ashore. The three hangmen then ask her whether she is willing to marry one of them (the only way a woman criminal could escape the death penalty). She refuses the offer and is forced back into the water. Duke Albrecht learns the news, summons all the fishermen to find her and drag her out of the Danube. He decides to start a war against his father, who had arranged the murder of Agnes. Then comes the message about his father's death. The ballad concludes with Albrecht's order to institute an eternal mass in memory of Agnes. (Erk-Böhme, *Deutscher Liederhort*, no. 92.)

The ballad was based on a real event that happened in 1435. Albrecht, Duke of Munich, fell in love with the daughter of an Augsburg barber or bath-master, and perhaps even married her secretly. In his absence his father, Duke Ernst, had her thrown into the Danube by hangmen. She succeeded in swimming ashore, but the hangmen threw her in again, and she drowned. Albrecht, having heard the news, gathered an army against his father, and the reconciliation between them was due only to the Hungarian King Sigismund. Albrecht had Agnes taken out of the water and had a chapel erected to her memory.

Many elements of this story (transplanted into a Greek setting) are to be found in a clumsily versified Hungarian romance printed in 1578, Kolozsvár's 'The Story of King Telamon and the Terrible Death of his Son, Diomedes'. Another version is found in F. Széll, *Egy XVI. sz.-i codex históriás énekei* (Budapest, 1884), p. 32.

In the Kolozsvár story, Diomedes, the prince, loves Katarista, the daughter of a bath-master (in the Széll version, a cobbler). His father, King Telamon, strongly opposes the love and sends his son to war. Diomedes bids farewell to his love and presents her with an engagement ring. In his absence Katarista is thrown in to the river Xanthus. Diomedes, warned by a dream, returns home. He crosses himself and jumps into the Xanthus after his love. Telamon has both of them taken out from the river by the help of divers, who find the lovers in each other's arms. The king has them buried in the same grave and casts a curse upon himself.

Motifs

While their basic idea is undoubtedly the same, the verbose and moralising story of 'King Telamon' cannot be the only source of 'Kate Kádár'. Almost all components of the ballad are motifs and incidents borrowed from various romances and from pieces of the international ballad-tree.

I. Difference between the social position of the lovers and parental disapproval of their relationship as the prelude for tragedy is indeed a stock situation in ballads and romances. Such is the case in Child's nos. 17, 64, 65 (brother's opposition), 66, 72, 87, 215, 216, 233, 239 and 269.

The motif became very popular during the Renaissance, when it served as the beginning of many short stories. Cf. Boccaccio, *Decameron*, 'Silvestra'; later Bandello, 'Bargagli'; Castiglione, *Cortegiano*, III, 13; Straparola, *Le piacevoli Notti* (1550–7), IX, 2, etc.

II. Separating lovers by compelling the man to travel is a device that occurs in many romantic tales and ballads. Thus in 'Hynd Horn' (Child, no. 17) he is being sent to the sea, in Boccaccio's and Straparola's above-mentioned stories he is sent abroad.

III. Life-tokens are, again, prominent motifs of ballads and folk tales. Rings are the most common objects used for this purpose.

In 'Hynd Horn':

> Z, E He has lookt on his ring
> And it was baith black and blue
> And she is either dead or married.

In Child, no. 92:

> A But gin this ring should fade or fail
> Or the stone should change its hue
> Be sure your love is dead and gone,
> Or she has proved untrue.
>
> .   .   .   .
>
> Black and ugly was the ring
> And the stone was burst in three.

In 'Lord Dervenwater' (Child, no. 208):

> The ring from's finger burst in two
> When he mounted his steed (foreboding his
> own death).

In 'Lamkin' (Child, no. 93):

> B, Q (when the lord's wife was killed)
> The lord sat in England
> A drinking the wine
> 'I wish a' may be weel
> With my lady at hame,
> For the rings of my fingers
> They're now burst in twain'.

The motif often appears in various folk tales, cf. Gomme, *The Handbook of Folklore*, type 24; AT Types 303, 888; Thompson, E 761 (with bibliographical references).

For the ancient belief that when somebody dies flowers of certain trees wither, cf. the bibliography, Elek, *Ethnographia* (1915), p. 115.

No notice has been taken of its appearance in 'The Unquiet Grave' (Child, no. 78):

> A T'is down in yonder garden green,
> Love, where we used to walk,
> The finest flower that ere was seen
> Is withered to a stalk.

> D Mind not ye the day, Willie,
> Sin you and I did walk?
> The firstand flower that we did pu
> Was withered on the stalk.

These motifs occur in several Hungarian folk tales as well. The hero ties a white cloth or a rose to a tree, or thrusts his knife into it. If he dies or becomes injured the cloth becomes bloodstained, the knife bloodstained and rusted, and the rose withers. Alternatively, the knife has to be extracted from the tree. If milk springs forth from the incision the hero is alive and well, if blood: he is dead or in mortal danger. In other versions the hero gives a rosebush to his brother: when he leaves him it withers, when he is near his brother it is in full bloom, when he dies it shrivels up and dies. (Cf. Berze-Nagy, Type 303; similarly *ibid*. Type 315. In the latter the cruel mother sends her son to perform a perilous task. When he sets off the pear-tree withers in their courtyard, when he approaches home it is in full bloom, when he arrives it bears ripe fruit.)

IV. The sudden return on account of some alarming omen is also a stock situation in ballads. The lords in 'Lamkin' and 'Hynd Horn' return on account of the discoloration of their ring, and F. J. Child refers to a number of similar incidents in his comments on the later ballad. In other ballads the return is due to some disturbing message, as in Child, nos. 65, 66, 75, 81 and 254.

In nos. 65, 75, 81, and 254 the urgency of arriving back in time is expressed by a formula similar to our versions **A, M.**

> O saddle me the black, the black,
> Or saddle me the brown,
> O saddle me the swiftest steed
> That ever rade frae a town.

V. Parallels to the situation of the inquiring lover and the swineherd or beggar, etc., who conveys the bad news to him can be traced back as far as Homer's *Odyssey*.

It also occurs in 'Hynd Horn'.

A, B, D, F–H   What news, what news? said young Hind Horn,
> No news, no news, said the old beggar man.
> No news, said the beggar, no news at a'
> But there is a wedding in the king's ha'.

It is interesting to notice to what extent these versions agree psychologically when recording the dialogue in question. In both the English and the Hungarian ballad there is a marked indifference on the part of the beggar or swineherd towards the disaster that is threatening (or had fallen upon) their gentleman questioner. It is perhaps to convey the idea that personal tragedies cannot and do not affect the simple everyday process of life, however cruel and tragic they may seem to him who is concerned. This artistic contrast is the one we find in so many Renaissance pictures, e.g. the ploughman busy in his field while Breughel's Icarus falls into the sea.

VI. The dead lover who speaks to her (or his) beloved repeats itself in many Hungarian as well as European ballads. The idea is carried to its extreme in 'The Unquiet Grave' (Child, no. 78), where the whole ballad is a dialogue between the dead and the living lover.

VII. Suicide after a lover's death concludes the majority of Hungarian love ballads and of many romantic tales, but it figures in only five English-Scottish ballads: Child nos. 65 A, F; 73 A, B, D; 76 B; 67 and 88 C, D.

VIII. Sympathetic plants springing from the lovers' graves and intertwining in spite of the distance which separates them is one of the most favourite motifs in romances and ballads (Thompson, E 631). F. J. Child gives a number of references of its occurrence in his notes commenting 'Earl Brand' (no. 7) and also mentions 'Kate Kádár', but in only one version.

In all the Hungarian versions the lovers are buried separately, behind and in front of the altar, on the top of which the plants from the graves intertwine. While in all English and Scottish ballads where this motif appears, the plants are invariably briar and rose, or briar and birk; in the Hungarian ballad such consistency does not exist.

IX. The plucking and destroying of the sympathetic plants is met with in Child, nos. 7 B; 74 A, and IV, p. 464; and 75. It appears also in the French prose-tale of Tristan, when King Marc has the trees cut down but next morning they are flourishing again.

X. The curse, cast upon the cruel mother by the flowers, seems to be a genuine Hungarian addition to the ballad. The idea is in some respects akin to what is related in 'The Two Sisters', in which the harp that had been strung with the hair of the victim speaks against her murderess.

In his comments upon 'Earl Brand', F. J. Child refers to a Little Russian (Carpathian Russians in Hungary) ballad, the story of which agrees with 'Kate Kádár'. It also has a conclusion analogous to the lines in our versions. ('Wicked mother, you did not let us live together, let us rest together'). This ballad, however, does not have the curse and it stands solitary, while the words in question appear in several Hungarian versions of the ballad.

Summarising the evidence concerning the origin of the ballad, we can see that most probably both the Hungarian and the Rumanian ballads derived their material from a common source, the foundation of which is apparently the Bernauer story, transposed into their respective national ballad surroundings and intermingled with motifs and incidents borrowed from various popular romances, ballads and folk tales.

Folklore and customs

Taken by itself, the abundance of the motifs which can be distinguished in 'Kate Kádár' indicates already that the story is not as 'simple-minded' as Professor W. J. Entwistle suggests.

'Kate Kádár', the most quoted of Hungarian ballads, is a simple story of true love and parental opposition, of the reported death of the lady and the despair of the lover, and two graves which give soil to intertwining 'chapel-flowers'. The lines are ragged, but the ingenuous history is carried to a swift conclusion by life-like dialogue. (W. J. Entwistle, *European Balladry*, p. 276.)

This description does not take into account the most precious motifs of the ballad, those which are based on primitive folk-beliefs. The magic scarf and flowers, which embody the ancient belief that intimate objects can show the fate of their former possessors, have been preserved only in versions **A–D**, and **M**. We have dealt with their international parallels already. Although rings and scarfs are equally popular to convey such messages there is a reason why in our ballad the use of a scarf was more convenient. According to Hungarian custom, lovers have to exchange two presents when they become engaged: the bridegroom gives his ring to his bride and receives a scarf or handkerchief instead. Also when a girl gives a scarf to a boy, it is to let him know that he is loved by her. As in our ballad, the disaster happens to the girl, it is only natural that the present she gives to Martin should be a scarf.

The power of love, which enables the dead to speak, has been preserved in ten versions, probably due to the fact that it occurs in many other Hungarian ballads as well. (Cf. 'The Boy who was Murdered', 'The Dishonoured Maiden', and even in 'The Girl who was Danced to Death', which ballad was probably composed in the eighteenth century.)

The custom of burying the lovers behind and in front of the altar has been preserved in many European and Hungarian ballads and romances, but there is no current custom recorded from which we could draw conclusions considering its real significance. Was it a custom that the one who committed suicide should be buried at a special place (behind or in front) of the altar? Or, is it merely a poetic device to convey the idea that even in their graves the lovers were separated? The last stanza of version **H**—'Her bitch mother did not leave her even there, / she had her placed in front of the altar'—would suggest that being buried in front of the altar had an unfavourable significance. However, this version is fragmentary and the stanza in question may be due to corruption.

The dead lovers whose love continues in the flowers which spring from their graves embody the primitive belief in metempsychosis. The idea is clearly expressed in versions **A, M**—'You have been cruel when I was alive, / even now you have *murdered* me.' The other versions merely indicate that plucking the flowers interfered with the peace of the dead, therefore it must be punished.

The belief in the magic power of spoken words is vigorously expressed in many Hungarian ballads. The curse of Kate Kádár (repeated in 'The Dishonoured Maiden') is of special significance, as here it is the dead who cast curses upon the living. It also serves to emphasise the power of the dead. The Hungarian curse-formulas, like the incantations, always follow the same rhytmical pattern, but sometimes we have two or more formulas mixed together. The curse of 'Kate Kádár' has preserved for us a reference to one of the oldest beliefs: the magic power of a knife, to keep away the evil. (Cf. L. Kálmány, *Szeged Népe*, II, 218.)

E, J, K, O	May your bread turn to stone, May your knife break in two in it.
G	May the bread you will eat of, May it turn to stone in front of you, May the knife with which you will cut it, May it break into pieces.
C	May your bread turn to stone, May your red knife twist in your hand, May it injure your heart.
D	May your bread turn to stone.

The evil of this wish will become obvious if we remember the incident in the *Kalevala* when Kullervo breaks his knife cutting the bread of his false hostess, who has put a stone into it.

> Then the shepherd Kullerwoinen
> Drew his knife to cut his oat-loaf,
> Cut the hard and avid biscuit,
> Cuts against a stone imprisoned,
> Well imbedded in the centre,
> Breaks his ancient knife in pieces.
> When the shepherd youth Kullervo
> Saw his magic knife was broken,
> Weeping sore, he spake as follows:
> 'This, the blade that I hold sacred,
> This the one thing that I honor,
> Relic of my mother's people!
> On the stone within this oat-loaf,
> On this cheat-cake of the hostess
> I my precious knife have broken.
> How shall I repay this insult,
> How avenge this woman's malice,
> What the wages for deception?'

(*Kalevala*, XXXIII, 177, trans. J. M. Crawford, New York, 1889.)

Date

The magic scarf, magic flowers, the sympathetic plants, the speaking of the dead, the magic power of words and the motifs of the curse-formula are motifs the preservation of which already suggests an early origin of the ballad.

We have also discussed the many incidents and motifs 'Kate Kádár' shares with other European ballads and romances of medieval origin. These borrowings could have taken place only at a time when their meaning was still fresh and obvious for the audience, in the hey-day of ballad composition, which, as we have seen in the case of the magic and Christian legendary ballads, seems to have been in the sixteenth and early seventeenth centuries.

However, 'Kate Kádár' provides one of the very few instances when we are not compelled to draw conclusions only from ethnographical and aesthetic evidence. There are two dates at our disposal which we can use at least as starting-points. One of them is 1435 when the Bernauer tragedy took place in Germany; the other is 1578 when the Hungarian 'King Telamon' was printed in Kolozsvár.

The story of Telamon was well known in Hungary in the sixteenth century. B. Balassi, the sixteenth-century Hungarian poet, refers to it in a poem similar to Villon's 'Ballade de temps jadis' ('Where is the Daughter of the Bath-owner with Diomedes?'). (The poem is supposed to have been written before or in 1578.)

The authorship of Telamon and the rest of such Hungarian romances is generally attributed to the Protestant pastors of Transylvania, where the progressive Reformation movement exerted its strongest influence, and where this movement was accompanied by vigorous literary activity, Hungarian in language, and drawing its material from various humanist short stories (such as Boccaccio's) as well as from folk tales. Such Protestant pastors might well have been familiar with the Bernauer legend, as it was related in Hondorff's *Promtuarium Exemplorum* (Leipzig, 1527), whose moral tales were frequently used in Protestant sermons in Transylvania (Gy. Király, *op. cit.*).

There remains the problem of relationship between 'Kate Kádár' and 'King Telamon'. In its first part the Hungarian romance follows closely the Bernauer story: prince falls in love with daughter of a barber; it is the father who opposes the love and sends his son to the army; it is the father who has the girl drowned in a river. On the other hand, the romance affords some resemblances to our ballad which are not to be found in the Bernauer story: the heroine is called Katarista; Diomedes commits suicide, and he is found dead in the river, embracing his dead lover. However, the life-token, the dialogue between the hero and the swineherd, the sympathetic plants and the flower's curse are wanting in Telamon's story. Though the two are undoubtedly related to each other, the balance of correspondences and differences between them make it difficult to decide with certainty which one of them accounts for the other. It is possible that the ballad had existed before 'King Telamon' was composed, which then added details from the popular German story. The fact that the three hangmen and the girl's first escape do not occur in 'Telamon', while they figure in our version **M**, seems to support this theory. In this case it may be the ballad-story from which the romance borrowed the heroine's name, the hero's suicide and the lovers who are found dead embracing each other, omitting or replacing the magic elements of the ballad (e.g. Diomedes returns suddenly because of a dream). It is also possible that it was the romance, together with the original story, from which our ballad drew its material. There is, however, no doubt that the ballad must have been current roughly at the same time as the romance.

The tune of the ballad, pentatonic and recitative as it is, belongs to the oldest group of Hungarian folksongs, and together with the rhymeless lines also supports the evidence of the ethnographical and historical data, i.e. that the ballad originated in the sixteenth or early seventeenth century.

Special Hungarian elements

Taking the Bernauer story and ballad as our starting-point, it is surprising how many motifs and incidents 'Kate Kádár' added to it.

Bernauer story	'Kate Kádár'
1. Prince falls in love with a girl of much lower social position.	1. Nobleman falls in love with serf's daughter.
2. Father's opposition to love.	2. Mother's opposition to love.
3. Father sends his son to war.	3. Mother disowns her son or sends him to the army.
4. —	4. Lovers exchange life-tokens on their departure.
5. In his son's absence, father has the girl drowned.	5. In her son's absence mother has the girl drowned.
6. The girl succeeds in swimming ashore, but is thrown in again by three hangmen.	6. The girl succeeds three times in swimming ashore, but is thrown in again by three hangmen (version **M** only).

Bernauer story	'Kate Kádár'
7. Prince learns the sad news, wants to return with army against father.	7. Hero's abrupt return, prompted by the warning of the life-token.
8. —	8. Dialogue between the swineherd and the hero.
9. —	9. Hero presents his clothes, etc., to the swineherd in exchange for being led to the lake where his lover has died.
10. —	10. Hero's suicide.
11. Prince has her drawn out from the water by fishermen's help.	11. Mother has them drawn out from the water by divers.
12. —	12. Lovers found dead, embracing each other.
13. Prince has a chapel erected for her memory.	13. Lovers buried separately in a chapel, behind and in front of the altar.
14. —	14. Sympathetic plants spring from their graves and make the lovers' knot.
15. —	15. Mother's malison: she plucks the flowers.
16. —	16. The flowers speak and cast a curse upon the mother.

As we have seen, most of these additions have their parallels in European balladry and cannot be considered as specifically Hungarian elements. The merit of 'Kate Kádár' is that it has succeeded in composing from so many elements of different sources a new, original, coherent ballad of a highly dramatic nature.

The curse of the flowers is the only genuinely Hungarian motif in the ballad. This addition is most valuable for three reasons: it is interesting from the ethnographical point of view, as it preserves ancient incantation formulas and folk beliefs, it lends a special, structural importance to the sympathetic plants, and it completes the story from the ethical point of view.

Finally, the examination of 'Kate Kádár's' relationship to the Bernauer story and the 'King Telamon' romance suggests some interesting points considering the treatment of certain motifs.

In the German ballad Duke Albrecht returns home, because he learns the news about Agnes Bernauer's death.

> Es stunde kam an den dritten Tag
> Dem Herzog kam ein traurige Klag,
> Bernauerin ist ertrunken, ja ertrunken.

In 'King Telamon' Diomedes has a dream, which tells him what has happened in his absence to Katarista. There is a token in the romance, but it is only an engagement ring Diomedes gives to his love on his departure.

In the Hungarian ballad the token is a life-token, and the hero's sudden return is due to the change he observes in it.

In the 'Hynd Horn' ballad (Ch. 17), which has some parallels to our motifs 1, 2, 3, 4, 7, and 8, we can observe a somewhat similar process.

In the Scandinavian parallels there is no life-token.

In the old English gest (thirteenth century) the hero is given a magic ring, which protects him from being slain. It is a messenger who tells him the news, which incites him to return.

In the French romance (fourteenth century) the ring is effective only in case he is faithful to his lover. The reason for his return is the same as in the old English gest.

In the English romance (fourteenth century) the ring is already a life-token and it is the change in it which induces the hero to return, as is the case in the 'Hynd Horn' ballad, and in the Hungarian ballad versions which have preserved the life-token.

Similarly, the swineherd's (or beggar's) comment on the ill news, which occurs in both the Hungarian versions and the 'Hynd Horn' ballad, is omitted from the Bernauer story and ballad, as well as from the Telamon romance. In the old English gest the hero meets a palmer, they exchange clothes, but the dialogue in question does not take place. Neither does it do so in the French romance. In the English romance the beggar is revealed as an old friend of the hero.

Yet, in the versions of the 'Hynd Horn' ballad the dialogue does take place and exactly in the same way as it does in 'Kate Kádár'.

The fact that these motifs and incidents do not appear in the relevant romances (or only in their later versions) but do occur in both the English and the Hungarian ballads would suggest that these elements are particularly suitable for ballad poetry and are ready to be adopted and transplanted when a certain psychological situation has to be depicted. Their absence from the Scandinavian parallels of 'Hynd Horn' and from the German source of 'Kate Kádár' and their presence in both the English and Hungarian variants show some correspondence in taste between the English and Hungarian ballads, concerning the selection and adaptation of certain motifs in certain circumstances.

'THE DAUGHTER OF THE CRUEL¹ KING'

While we have seen that although 'Kate Kádár' shares several motifs
with medieval romances and renaissance stories, it cannot be derived
only from these sources, 'The Daughter of the Cruel King' owes its
very existence to them.

1 'My fair Julia, my fair daughter,
My tulip that has blossomed in my garden,
Do not love your serf!'
'I do not love my serf,
I only love the youth,
The bonny youth, my soul!'

2 Alas, the aged king went out,
He bade the youth be taken,
He had him put up on the ruined tower,
On the top of the ruined tower.

3 Hey, fair Julia went out,
The youth caught sight of her:
'Hey, my Julia, my fair Julia,
My fair gillyflower that blooms in a garden,
Just go in, to your father,
Fall on your knees before him,
And speak to him with these words:
"Father, father, aged king,
Have the youth brought in
From the top of the ruined tower;
Do not let him be beaten by rain,
Do not let him be blown by the cold wind,
Do not let him be burnt by the sun!"'

4 Hey, fair Julia went in,
She fell on her knees before her father,
And she spoke to him with these words:
'Father, father, aged king,
Have the youth brought in,
From the top of the ruined tower;
Do not let him be beaten by rain,
Do not let him be blown by the cold wind,
Do not let him be burnt by the sun!'

5 Alas, the aged king went out,
He bade the youth be taken down
From the top of the ruined tower,
He bade him be taken out to the flat fields,

¹ In Hungarian 'pagan' which means both cruel and pagan.

To the middle of the flat fields,
There he bade him be killed straightway,
He bade his heart, his liver be taken out,
And he sent them home, to Julia.

6 When fair Julia saw
That they had killed the youth,
She let her head hang down to the ground,
She let herself die.

7 When the aged king saw
That his Julia was on the point of death:
'Hey, my Julia, my fair daughter,
My tulip that has grown in my garden!
Had I known that this would be so,
I would have adopted him as my son,
I would have given him
All, all my kingdom, my country!'

Versions

Three versions of the ballad and a fragment have been recorded, all of them from Transylvania.

A Csanádi-Vargyas, *Röpülj*, no. 49; =Ortutay, *Magyar Népköltészet*, II, no. 8; =*MNGY*, III, p. 8; =Kriza (1956), no. 11 **B** Csanádi-Vargyas, *Röpülj*, no. 48; =Bartók-Kodály, *SZNd*, no. 70; =Kodály-Vargyas, *MNpt*, no. 340 **C** Kriza (1956), no. 10; =*MNGY*, III, p. 10 **D** *Ethnographia*, **26**, 48 (two fragmentary stanzas of version **A**)

Description of the ballad

I. A king entreats his daughter, fair Julia, not to love her serf. Fair Julia answers that she does not love him as a serf, but as a bonny youth.

B, C the daughter of the pagan king, fair or little Lilian, is strolling featly with a fair, gentle youth. The king catches sight of this.

II. The king has the youth put on the top of a ruinous tower.

B to the rampart of the castle and exposes him to the blowing of the cold wind, to the beating of the rain; **C** the youth is thrown into the deep dungeon, where frogs gnaw him and snakes bite him.

III. The youth catches sight of Julia and asks her to fall upon her knees before her father and to beg him that he (the youth) should be brought in from the top of the ruinous tower and not exposed to the blowing of the cold wind, to the beating of rain, to the burning of the sun any longer.

B, C fair Lilian strolls to the prison (**B** to the rampart) and aks the youth what he is doing there. The youth answers, *I am but as an orphan who is separated from his companion.*

IV. Fair Julia goes to her father and repeats to him word by word the youth's message.

B, C though the message is missing in III, here she says: *The fair youth has sent you the message;* **C** to be taken out from the bottom of the dungeon, where his flesh and his bones are gnawed, his red blood is sucked.

V. The aged king has the youth brought in from the ruinous tower, has him taken to the flat moor and has him killed. He orders his heart and liver to be taken out and has them sent home to Julia.

B the pagan king turns round and kicks his daughter so hard that her red skirt tears, her red blood spurts forth, and she dies a dreadful death straight away; **C** the youth is taken from the bottom of the dungeon to the rampart of the castle. Lilian strolls there again, the same dialogue occurs as in **C** III. It continues as **B** IV–V.

VI. When Julia understands that her lover was killed, she lets her head hang down to the ground and lets herself die.

B, C they begin to toll the bells for fair Lilian, the youth hears it: *For whom are the bells tolling, I wonder. Perhaps it is for my fair Lilian? Alas, if she has died for me, alas, I too, will die for her.* Thereupon he throws himself from the rampart of the castle and dies a dreadful death straight away. **C** does not end here. The king has the youth carried up, he has them stretched out beside each other. For one of them he has a white marble coffin made, for the other a red marble one. He has them buried behind and in front of the altar. A red and a white marble lily spring up from their graves, they intertwine. The king is about to pluck them when his daughter speaks to him: *Father, my father, dear, you did not leave us in peace when we were alive, would that you would leave us in peace after our death.*

International ballad-tree versions

The motif of sending the murdered lover's heart to his beloved (preserved only in **A**) relates 'The Daughter of the Pagan King' to an extensive series of ballads and tales which seem to have derived their central idea from Boccaccio's tale *Decameron*, IV, 1.[1] Our ballad, however, has no direct connection with any of these ballads. The resemblances occur only as far as they follow a common source. Taking the motifs of the ballad one by one, they are revealed as having some parallels with other ballads not necessarily belonging to this particular group.

---

[1] Cf. F. J. Child's notes (no. 269) for bibliographical references. The English 'Lady Diamond' (no. 269) has been blended with another ballad: Child, no. 100. In the Scandinavian and German-Dutch variants the story has been entangled with Boccaccio's *Decameron*, IV. 9, where a husband orders the cooking of the heart of his wife's lover (whom he murdered), has it served to her, she eats it, and then realising what she has eaten she throws herself out of a window of the castle. In the ballads in question she is the daughter of a king (as in VI. 1) but she is forced to eat the heart of her lover.

Motifs

The points of resemblance between the ballads and Boccaccio's story (IV, I) are the following:

The only daughter (Italian, English, Hungarian) of an aged (Hungarian) king falls in love with a handsome (English, Hungarian) youth of low birth (Italian, servant; Hungarian, serf; English, kitchen boy). The king has him put in prison (Italian, Danish, Hungarian C—analogously Swedish, German, Dutch—in a dark tower; Hungarian A, B on the castle rampart), and entreats his daughter to give up her love, whom he considers unworthy of her (English, Hungarian). She refuses this, asks her father for understanding (English, Hungarian). The king has the youth killed, orders his heart to be taken out and has it sent to his daughter (Italian, English, Hungarian). The golden cup, in which the youth's heart is placed and sent to his beloved, is missing from the Hungarian ballad, although it has been preserved in both the Italian and English variants). The daughter drinks poison (Italian, Danish—analogously in the Hungarian, English, Swedish, German and Dutch ballads she dies of sorrow). The king repents his cruelty (Italian, Swedish, English, Hungarian).

Some more complicated details (requirements of Renaissance short stories but not of ballads), like Ghismunda's first marriage, her clandestine meetings with Guiscardus, the secret cave, the king's hiding behind the curtain in his daughter's room, are left out in the ballads. Ghismunda's logical argumentation with her father in the vein of Renaissance morality, her comments on esteeming people for their virtues and not for their social rank, can be traced, though in a very limited form, in version A, where Julia tells her father (making a distinction which appears strange in a ballad) that it is not the servile position of her lover which she loves, but it is his good looks.

The motif of the angry father who imprisons his daughter's lover repeats itself in various ballads (thus in Child, no. 53 C, M; 'Sir Cauline' in Percy, I, 50. It is not explicit in the English ballad, nor is the form of the imprisonment emphasized in Boccaccio's story), and the dialogue between the lovers through prison walls is equally popular in ballads which usually conclude with the heroine's releasing the prisoner and eloping with him (cf. Child, nos. 9, 53, also the Hungarian 'Szilágyi and Hagymási').

The inaugural dialogue between the father and his daughter has a very close parallel in the French 'La fille du Roi Loys' (Th. Gerold, *Chansons populaires des XVe et XVIe siècles*, Strasbourg, no. 2).

'Ma fill' n'aimez jamais Deon,
Car c'est un chevalier felon,
C'est le plus povre chevalier
Qui n'a pas vaillant six deniers.'

'J'aime Deon, je l'aimerai,
J'aime Deon pour sa beaute,
Plus que ma mere et mes parens,
Et vous mon per' qui m'aimez tant.'

Similar dialogues are also to be found in 'La belle se siet au piet de la tour' (Th. Gerold, no. 1) and in 'La Pernette' (*ibid.*), but in the further development of all these stories there is no likeness to our ballad. 'La fille due Roi Loys' is compared by Child to no. 96. Here the heroine is imprisoned by her father, and feigns death in order to escape and to meet her lover. In 'La belle se siet...' and in 'La Pernette' it is the poor lover who is kept in prison, and the ballad consists only of the dialogue (*op. cit.*). W. J. Entwistle, when he described the Hungarian ballad as 'an offshoot of King Loys' daughter' (*European Balladry*, p. 275), did so probably without having known version **A**.

Lovers often beg for the life of their beloved in ballads, as we have seen in the French ballads cited (it also occurs in 'Sir Cauline' where it is the queen who asks her husband to take mercy on their daughter's lover), and the father's cruelty on these occasions is not unusual. For example, Child, no. 72:

> A Up and spak his twa daughters
> And they spak powerfully:
> 'Will ye grant us our twa loves' lives,
> Either for gold or fee?
> Or will ye be sae gude a man
> As grant them baith to me?'
> 'I'll no grant ye yere twa loves' lives
> Neither for gold or fee,
> Nor will I be sae gude a man
> As grant their lives to thee;
> Before the morn at twelve o'clock
> Ye'll see them hangit hie!'

> B Then out bespak the clerk's fader
> An a sorry man was he:
> 'Gae till your bowers, ye lillie-flowers,
> For a' this winna dee';
> Then out bespak the aul base mayr
> An an angry man was he:
> 'Gar to your bowers, ye wile base whores,
> Ye'll see them hangit hie!'

Here the contrast between the father of the youths and the mayor in addressing the girls clearly indicates the ballad's assessment of the father's behaviour.

Sending the murdered lover's heart (cf. Thompson, Q 478.1) to his beloved is the central motif of the original story,[1] as preserved in the Italian, English and Hungarian **A** versions. However, the motif of sending a part of the victim's body to his beloved occurs in ballads which relate completely different stories, e.g. Child, no. 83 and no. 178 *A*, where it is the head and tongue, respectively, which are cut off. The original motif has a remarkable affinity for blending with the motif of the lover, who is made to eat the heart of her sweetheart. Another similar motif is discussed in the notes of 'Anna Betlen'.

Sorrow has caused the death of many a ballad heroine in English and Scottish ballads (e.g. Child, nos. 7, 26, 70, 72, 74, 75, 84, 85, 87, 214 *B*, 235, 256, 262, 269). In Hungarian ballads, however, this romantic and placid death does not often occur. The reason for this may be that death from sorrow is a rather feminine way of dying, and while in English and Scottish ballads it is usually preceded by the violent death of the hero, in the Hungarian ballads it is usually the heroine who meets a violent death in the first place, and for a hero suicide is a more becoming and more man-like death than death from sorrow.

The sympathetic plants, which talk (version **C**) are borrowed word by word from 'Kate Kádár', without bringing in the curse-motif. They also appear in the Scandinavian versions of the ballad.

Folklore and customs; date

The Hungarian ballad was probably composed in the sixteenth or early seventeenth century, and appears to have drawn its material from the original story of Boccaccio. George Enyedi (1551–97), a Unitarian bishop in Transylvania, translated the tale in question. It was printed first in 1557 in Debrecen, then again in 1582 in Kolozsvár, so the story must have been fairly popular in Transylvania where the ballad has been recorded. The fact that those motifs of the ballad for which Boccaccio's tale cannot account (i.e. the rampart of the castle, the dialogue between the lovers, the development in **B**, **C**) are not to be found

---

[1] The surprising and rather senseless twist in the story related in versions **B** and **C**, where the daughter's death is followed by the lover's suicide, would appear to be a corruption. One is led to suspect that a ballad-monger remembered only the first half of the tale, forgot the climactic motif of the gift of the lover's heart and could invent nothing better to finish the tale than a double death, or it may be that the full force of the gift or presentation of our lover's heart was not universally felt, it being a courtly motif in poetry and paintings.

in any of the particular international variants which belong to this set of ballads also suggests that the Hungarian ballad was inspired by a specifically Hungarian tradition based on Boccaccio's tale, popularised through Enyedi's translation.

The rhymeless octosyllabic lines, the frequent parallelisms and re-petitions together with the old pentatonic tune support also a sixteenth-century or early seventeenth-century origin of the ballad.

Special Hungarian elements

Although the royal father in the Hungarian ballad kicks his daughter to death, just as any angry peasant would do, he is more than just a cruel father. The 'Daughter of the Cruel King' has preserved the original princely setting of the story. Yet, neither the 'proud porters' nor any 'merry men' of the king interfere with the events; the tragedy is enacted within the narrow group of the king, the princess and her lover. The individuality of Boccaccio's characters is lost in the Hungarian ballad, especially that of the heroine, who changes from a brave, proud, resolute and very Renaissance-morality-conscious woman to a gentle but rather helpless creature similar to so many Hungarian ballad heroines, such as Kate Kádár, the wife of the great mountain robber, the dishonoured maiden, or the girl who was sold.

'My tulip', as the royal father addresses his daughter at the beginning of version **A**, is a specifically Hungarian term of endearment, the tulip being one of the most popular flowers, the one which figures most often in Hungarian peasant ornamental art. It was traditional to have in almost every peasant house a chest painted with tulips ('tulipántos láda') in which the daughter of the house kept her trousseau. Chairs and tables and other products of peasant craftsmen are also decorated with stylized tulips, and it is the main motif of peasant embroidery.

The 'flat field' is a traditional Hungarian scene of execution and occurs also in the ballad of 'Ladislav Fehér'.

'THE MAID WHO WAS SOLD'

This most pathetic and beautiful ballad is still a favourite all over Hungary. The kernel of the ballad, that a maid is sold in marriage against her will, remains the same in all versions, but according to the further development of the story the versions divide into four well-marked classes:

Class 1. (embracing versions **A–F**) 'The Maid who was Sold and Dragged to Death';
Class 2. (including versions **G–M**) 'The Maid who was Sold and Died on her Way to the Wedding';
Class 3. (the Moldavian **N** only) 'The Maid who was Sold to Poland'—here the death of the heroine is replaced by her father's subsequent protest against taking her away; Class 4. (versions **O–Z**) 'The Maid who was Sold and was Found Dead by the Bridegroom'.

As there is considerable diversity between the versions belonging to different classes, I give the full translation of four versions representing the four classes and shall deal with these classes separately when giving the description of the ballad.

Versions

Some twenty versions and six fragments have been recorded. With the exception of **S, V** (Transylvania) and **N** (Moldavia) the versions come from the Lowland. (There are several fragments of the ballad embedded in prose-tales. Those are given in the Appendix.)

1. **A** Csanádi-Vargyas, *Röpülj*, no. 30; = Ortutay, *Magyar Népköltészet*, II, no. 7 d; = Kodály-Vargyas, *MNpt*, no. 494 **B** Csanádi-Vargyas, *Röpülj*, no. 31; = *MNGY*, VIII, p. 177 (improved from EA record 3639) **C** *MNGY*, VIII, p. 555; = *MNYr*, **16**, 479 **D** *MNGY*, VIII, p. 178; = *MNYr*, **13**, 239 **E** *Ethnographia*, **21**, 207 **F** Ortutay, *Magyar Népköltészet*, II, no. 15; = *MNYr*, **32**, 459

2. **G** Csanádi-Vargyas, *Röpülj*, no. 32; = Pap Gy., *Palóc Népköltemények*, no. 1 **H** Csanádi-Vargyas, *Röpülj*, no. 33; = Kálmány, *Koszorúk*, I, p. 18 **I** Kálmány, *Szeged Népe*, III, pp. 213–14 **J** Kálmány, *Koszorúk*, II, no. 2 **K** Kálmány, *Szeged Népe*, II, no. 4 **L** Kálmány, *Hagyaték*, II, no. 1 a **M** Kálmány, *Koszorúk*, II, no. 1

3. **N** Csanádi-Vargyas, *Röpülj*, no. 34; = Domokos, *Moldvai Magyarság*, no. 24

4. **O** Csanádi-Vargyas, *Röpülj*, no. 35; = *Ethnographia* (1907), p. 127 **P** Csanádi-Vargyas, *Röpülj*, no. 36; = Ortutay, *Magyar Népköltészet*, II, no. 7 b; = *MNGY*, I, p. 180 **Q** Csanádi-Vargyas, *Röpülj*, no. 37; = *MNGY*, XIV, p. 263 **R** Csanádi-Vargyas, *Röpülj*, no. 38; = Ortutay, *Magyar Népköltészet*, II, no. 7 a; = *MNGY*, III, p. 3; = Kriza (1956), no. 21 **S** *MNGY*, VII, no. 6 **T** Domokos, P. P., *Moldvai Magyarság* (1934), no. 50 **U** Csanádi-Vargyas, *Röpülj*, no. 39; = *MNGY*, I, p. 148; = Kriza (1956), no. 20 **V** Kálmány, *Hagyaték*, II, no. 1 b **W** *MNGY*, XIV, p. 23 **X** *Ethnographia*, **21**, 208 **Y** *MNYr*, **3**, 383 **Z** *MNGY*, XIV, no. 3

1. *' The Maid who was Sold and Dragged to Death' (version **A**)*

1 In the Rákóci-inn the wine costs two pennies,
   The poor widow is going that way, she is going that way.

2 —Come in, come in, poor widow,
   Drink a glass of wine, or, if you wish, drink even two,

3 Neither for your own money, nor for your son's money,
   But for your daughter, for Catherine Bodor!

4 —Daughter, my sweet daughter, Catherine Bodor,
   I have sold you in the Rákóci-inn
   To young master Rákóci.

5 —Mother, dear mother who bore me and nursed me,
  Why have you given me to a murderer, to the young
    master Rákóci,
  Who by day sleeps, who by night murders?

6 Mother, my dear mother, who bore me and nursed me,
  What army is that black army?
  They are coming from the East, they are going West!

7 —Daughter, my sweet daughter, Catherine Bodor,
  It is coming for you, that black army!

8 —Good day, good day, my dear mother-in-law!
  —Welcome to the husband of my dear daughter!

9 —Where is she, where is she, my betrothed bride?
  —She is adorning herself in the front chamber.

10 —Good day, good day, *my betrothed bride!*
  —Welcome to you, *young master Rákóci!*

11 Then he snatches her up, ties her to his horse's tail,
  Trails her through bushes, through thorns upon thorns.

12 —Go slowly, go slowly, *young master Rákóci,*
  Already my red shoes are swimming in blood up to the heels!

13 Then he snatches her up, shortens his stirrup,
  Trails her through bushes, through thorns upon thorns.

14 —Go slowly, go slowly, *young master Rákóci,*
  Already my fine silk dress is swimming half in blood!

15 Then he snatches her up, shortens his stirrup,
  Trails her through bushes, through thorns upon thorns.

16 —Go slowly, go slowly, *my betrothed bridegroom,*
  Already my golden wreath is swimming in blood!

17 Then he snatches her up, clasps her to his heart:
  —What would you eat, what would you drink, my
    betrothed bride?

18 —I do not want to eat, I do not want to drink, all I want
    is to lie down on my bed,
  I do not want to eat, I do not want to drink, all I want
    is to lie down on my bed.

19 —What would you eat, what would you drink, my
    betrothed bride?
  —The wing of a jay from my mother's table,
  I want to drink good white wine from my father's window.

20 Open, mother, open your leafy gate,
  Make, mother, make my gay death-bed!

Description of the ballad: class 1

I. Young master Rákóci invites Catherine's mother for a drink in exchange for her daughter.

B, D, E this introductory scene, describing the actual bargain, is missing. The hero's name is: **B, D** Ladislav Borosfai, the son of Paul Vidrai; **E** the son of Paul Vidrai; **F** John Szalontai. The heroine's surname is: **A** Bodor; **B** Fodor; **D** Fodori; **E** Gyöngyvári; **F** Fair Ilona Horváth; **C** does not give her name. **F** is contaminated with other ballads. Instead of I–IV we have: *Yonder there is a castle, with three hundred windows, | There are two rooms in it. | Fair Ilona Horváth lives in one of them, | John Szalontai lives in the other.*

II. The mother informs her daughter that she has sold her.

A, B for the price of a glass of wine. Catherine resents the suitor. **A** *who sleeps by day-time, who murders by night;* **B, D** *I am not going to marry him, you yourself should marry him! | —You have to marry him, even if it kills you* answers the mother; **E** *My daughter, my dear daughter, | Go to your little garden, | Say good-bye to your flowers, | To the flower-buds! || —Mother, dear mother, | Why should I say good-bye to them? | I myself planted them, | I myself watered them! || —My daughter, my dear daughter, | Go into you chamber, | change your dress, | Put on your death-clothes! || —Mother, dear mother, | Why should I change my dress? | I myself cut it, | I myself sewed it! || —My daughter, my daughter, | Open your gate, | They are coming to take you away, | With six horses, by coach! || —Mother, dear mother, | Who is coming with six horses by coach | To take me away? | —The son of Paul Vidrai, | Your dear betrothed! || —He is the devil's betrothed | But not mine! ||* **A** adds—Catherine asks her mother what sort of black army is approaching the house and is told that it is coming to take her away; **C, F** do not have incident II at all.

III. The bridegroom arrives, asks where Catherine is and is told that she is dressing in her chamber.

B, D she is in a hidden chamber, putting on her death-clothes; **D** has a stanza previous to this: *—Lady Fodori, my dear mother-in-law, | Cook a good supper! | Kate Fodori, my dear bride, | Sit down to table! | She sat down to table, she threw down her fork. | Ladislav Borosfai wanted to pick it up, | Kate Fodori bent down for it, | She spied his cloven-hoof, | She went out from the table, | She burst out crying: | —Mother, my mother, you have killed me! ||* **E, F** do not have incident III.

IV. The bridegroom greets Catherine as his dear bride; she, how-ever, refuses to greet him as her betrothed, and greets him calling him by his name instead.

E cf. above; **C** adds *Alas, mother, you have killed me, | You have taken my life!* **B, D** he asks her to open her door for her bridegroom; she answers: *You are not the bridegroom to whom I am pledged, you are the murderer who slays me!* **F** *I would rather call you a watch-dog seven times | Than to call you my husband, or my betrothed bride once!*

V. The angry bridegroom fastens her to the tail of his horse and drags her thus through thorns and bushes in order to break her will.

B, D, E it is the mother who advises him to do so, until she calls him her betrothed. **F** he orders his coachmen to place the horses between the shafts, to prepare his coach to fasten Ilona to his horses' tail, *to harrow the street with her.*

VI. Twice Catherine asks him to go more slowly, because her red shoes are swimming in blood, her silk dress is swimming half in blood. He refuses to listen to her (**A, C** he drives her even faster; **D** it is the mother who encourages him to drive faster) until for the third time, when her golden wreath is swimming half in blood, she finally calls him *my dear betrothed* at last.

D she asks him to go more slowly when her boots are full of blood, when her fair hair is swimming half in blood, when a mist has fallen upon her two black eyes; **B** she calls him twice, both times because her round skirt is full of blood, and a mist has fallen upon her two black eyes; **E** is corrupted here, she calls only once: *Go more slowly, my coachman, my dear messenger* [?], *my flapping crimson blouse is full of my tears, my two red little shoes are full of blood;* **D** she calls him four times: when her beautiful white stockings are covered with blood up to her knees, when her fine dress is covered with blood up to her waist, when her fine red ribbons are covered with blood up to her neck, but on the fourth occasion, when she calls him her betrothed bridegroom, she is already unable to give her reasons, and just asks him to go more slowly. **F** she begs him to stop when she has almost lost half an arm and half a leg, when she has almost lost the other half of her arm and leg. Each time the man asks her to call him her husband or her betrothed bridegroom. She gives him the same answer as in IV. When she calls him for the third time, at the point of death, she calls him her dear betrothed bridegroom.

VII. Having broken her will, the bridegroom stops at once, asks Catherine what she wants to eat and drink. She just wants to lie on her bed, then she asks for the wing of a jay to eat.

A she also asks for good white wine from her father's house; **C** the bridegroom says: *Had you greeted me like this before I would have taken pity on you,* then he carries her to her bed, and she asks for a roasted sparrow to eat. **F** he and his coachman carry Ilona to her bed. She asks for the leg of a daw, and for the beak of a stork.

VIII. The bridegroom snatches his gun, goes to the forest to shoot the bird but by the time he arrives with it Catherine is already laid out on her deathbed.

F *That I cannot bring to you,* | *I cannot fulfil your wish.* | *My Ilona, my Ilona what will you leave for me?* | *—I will leave you nothing else but the gallows-tree, the grasp of the hangman.* | *May God not save you from the gallows, from the grasp of the hangman.* || **A** cf. main version; **E** has an ending similar to 'The Dishonoured Maid' and probably borrowed from one of its versions: when the bridegroom is on his way home with the jay, *He hears the death-bell.* | *—Children, children, for whom is the bell tolling?* | *—For Kate Fodori, for your betrothed!* | *—It is impossible, it is impossible!* | *Women, women, for whom are you sewing this?* | *—For Kate Fodori, your for betrothed!* | *—It is impossible, it is impossible!* | *—Men, men, for whom are you carving this?* | *—For Kate Fodori, for your betrothed!* || The son of Paul Vidrai tumbles down from his chair: *—May the mother be cursed, and the father as well,* | *Who gives away his daughter to foreign land!* | *Men, men, dig such a grave* | *In which there is place for both of us!* | *Let my and her blood run together in one stream,* | *Let my and her soul adore the same God together!* | *Masters, masters, compose such a song* | *In which a vine grows on my grave,* | *In which a tulip grows on her grave!* || **D** *The carpenters are carving a coffin made of walnut tree,* | *Lady Fodori is bringing there her wreath* | *Not for the bride, but for the fair dead maid.* | *—Kate Fodori, my dear, sweet daughter,* | *Sorrow will not leave my embittered heart,* | *The pain will kill me, please forgive me the crime I have committed!* | *—Take your wreath away, mother, take it away!* | *May the earth in which I am buried be cursed,* | *May grass not grow on it, may flowers wither in it!* | *I do not forgive you, how could I forgive* | *That you had made me to fall victim to the Devil!* || *Lady Fodori plants a lily,* | *A white lily on her daughter's grave:* | *—Kate Fodori, my dear, sweet daughter,* | *Sorrow will not leave my embittered heart,* | *The pain will kill me, please forgive me the crime I have committed!* | *May my blood and your blood run together in one stream,* | *May my soul and your soul adore the same God together,* | *May they live in the middle of Heaven forever!* ||

2. *'The Maid who was Sold and Died on Her Way to the Wedding'*
(version **G**)

1 —I have sold you in marriage, fair, rosy Elisabeth,
     to a fair, white lad,
  His face is as white as the white swan,
  Even whiter than that: like lambswool!

2 Away goes Elisabeth to the churchyard-chamber,
  She hastily fills her pockets with countless small coins,
  She goes in and out of the poorhouse.

3 —Poor, poor, you poor of God,
  Beg God to take me to Him!
  When I go to take the oath: may I shiver with cold!
  When I take the oath: may the shivering master me
     altogether!

4 —My coachman, my coachman, my head coachman,
  Whip that horse that it may jump thrice!
  My coachman, my coachman, my head coachman,
  Give me a glass of water, I am dying in agony of thirst!
  —But it is not water I give you, on the contrary,
     I give you red wine
  —Mikula, Mikula, my German Mikula,
  Give me a glass of water, I am dying in agony of thirst!
  —But it is not water I give you, on the contrary,
     I give you red wine.

5 —My son, my sweet son, my German Mikula,
What bride have you brought that does not speak to me?
She does not give her hand, nor does she speak a word,
Nor does she move her foot.
My daughter-in-law, my sweet daughter-in-law, fair
    rosy Elisabeth,
I have not known you, yet I have loved you,
You have my many fine guests put into mourning,
You have made my son and me bitter.

Description of the ballad: class 2

I. Fair, rosy Elisabeth's mother informs her daughter that she had sold her to a man whose face is as white as the swan, as white as lambswool.

H adds *and as white as a white pigeon;* I adds *as gentle dew;* G, H later in the ballad it is revealed that he is German; K the mother is the wife of the judge of Szeged town, her daughter's name is Tess, and the bridegroom's name is young John Turk; L does not give the girl's name, but gives the mother's name instead as the wife of fair rosy Stephen; the hero is called John the Turk. Neither J, K, nor L mention the whiteness of his face, but these versions have introductory stanzas similar to class 1, describing how the daughter is sold for a glass of wine and for a kind greeting. In K the mother tries to deny that she has a daughter to sell: K *I do not have such a daughter, | I have only one, whom I rock in the cradle! | —Yes, you do have a daughter, | A rosy, curly daughter, | She sold apples | At the market of Szeged, | I even bought some of them, | I even tasted some of them, | I have fallen in love indeed | With your daughter Tess. || J* the girl's name is fair rosy Elisabeth, the mother is the wife of a fair rosy Stephen. The suitor's name is referred to only once, curiously as fair rosy Steve. The mother sends out Elisabeth three times to stand on a stone bench (as in class 4) and to look around at what she can see. Twice all the girl can see is *a black army;* for the third time, however, she is able to distinguish three glass coaches and a silver flag. The mother informs her that they are coming to fetch her; M has several motifs which belong to class 4. It has a prose introduction: *Elisabeth Bátori was a widow. She had an only daughter, called Ilona. The mother sold Ilona to the son of the Turkish Emperor for a sack of gold. [They lived between Turkey and Hungary.] The girl did not know that she had been sold. When the mother thought that they will be coming to fetch her daughter, she called her...* From here onward it continues in verse. The mother sends her out to stand on the (rubbish) hill and to look in the direction of Hungary. Ilona reports to her that she could not see anything coming from Hungary, but she saw three gold coaches and nine golden flags approaching from Turkey. The mother informs her that they are coming to get her, and Ilona begins to cry. The suitor's name is John Turk. I her name is fair Elisabeth, the suitor's name is not given.

II. The girl dresses in green, puts countless coins into her pockets, goes to the poorhouse and asks the poor to pray for her that she may die; may she shiver with cold when she goes to take the oath, may the shivering master her altogether when she takes the oath.

H may she shiver with cold when they come to fetch her, may it shake her frightfully when they seat her in the coach, may it kill her off straight away when they reach the region where the bridegroom lives; **K** she does not dress in green, and instead of going to the poorhouse she asks her girl friends to pray for her; may she shiver with cold when they come to fetch her, may it shake her frightfully when they are half way, may she be laid out by the time they arrive. She curses her parents: *Cursed be the father, and cursed be the mother for a hundred times more, who drinks her daughter away at the inn!* The girl glances through the glass window: —*Look, mother, look, mother, what can I see! | I see a black cloud, | I see a raven with yellow feet | In the centre of it! | —The black cloud, | The black raven, | The raven with the yellow feet: | It is the golden coach! | Perhaps they are coming to take you away! ||* **J**, **L** have a curse similar to **K**, but: **L** *Who drinks her away at the inn, and sells her to the Turks!* These versions do not have the green dress or the poorhouse; she prays herself: may she shiver with cold when they come to fetch her, may it shake her with death when: **L** they carry her through her gate; **J** when they put her into the coach; may she be laid out when: **L** they take her to the wedding; **J** when they are half-way. **I** she does not dress in green and she does not take money with her when she goes to the poor. Like in many versions of class 4 she asks her clothes to fall down from the nails and her flowers to wither so that her mother can see that they are mourning for her. Then she observes the three glass coaches and the nine golden flags approaching.

III. The bridegroom arrives, they set off for the wedding, but by the time they arrive the bride is dead. Here all the versions are different:

L young John Turk sets off to fetch the bride with six flower-decked horses, when she beholds him she shivers with cold, when they set off it shakes her with death, when they arrive at the church she dies; **K** *Up and cries the brides-woman | —Drive more slowly, drive more slowly | Young John Turk, | Because our bride is faint! || Up and cries the bridesmaid for the second time: | —Drive more slowly, drive more slowly | Young John Turk, | Because our bride is going to die! || Up and cries the bridesmaid for the third time: | —Drive more slowly, drive more slowly | Young John Turk, | Because our bride is dead in any case! ||* **G** the bridegroom, the German Mikula, orders his coachman to drive fast, the bride feels that she is going to die with thirst and asks first the coachman, then her bridegroom for a glass of water, but they promise her red wine instead of water and they do not stop; **H**, **I** and, less explicitly, **J**, present an ingenious situation here: when the bride beholds the bridegroom she falls in love with him, asks the poor to pray for her again that she may not die (**J** she prays herself), but it is too late, the curse she had invoked upon herself takes its effect: **H** *Mother, dear mother, who bore me and nursed me, | He is not such, he is not such as you had said! | Mother, mother, dear mother, | Give me, just give me countless small coins | That I may give a gift to the poor of God, | That they may pray that I may not die! | When they come to fetch me, may I not shiver with cold, | When they seat me in the coach, may it not shake me frightfully, | For he is not such as you had said. | When they went to fetch her she was shivering with cold, | When they seated her in the coach, it shook her frightfully. ||* In this version, as in **G**, she asks her bridegroom for a drop of water and receives the same answer as is given in **G**. She asks him how far they are from the bounds of Wienerneustadt, casts up her eyes and beholds it, but when she beholds the gate of the bridegroom's house, she dies. The bridegroom orders the best man to take his bay steed out of the shafts, to have the gate of Wienerneustadt opened, to call the deacon of Győr town and to tell him that they were not bringing a bride, but a dead woman. **J** there are three exclamations, we are not told by whom: *Stop, coachman, our bride is on the point of fainting* is repeated twice, and for the third time: *Stop, coachman, our bride has fainted.* **I** she addresses her bridegroom as *white little pigeon, gentle little dew* (my pigeon—galambom—is a common term for endearment in Hungarian) and asks him three times for a glass of water. He calls her *little pigeon, little dew* and promises red wine instead. For the third time, however, he is willing to get her some water: *I shall give you some water, my little pigeon, | I shall give you some water, my little dew, | In my golden cup | From that stream yonder there. ||* This version ends here in prose: *When the bridegroom descended to get some water the bride died.* **M** the bridegroom, John Turk, arrives, and as in class 3 asks the mother three times to open her iron gate, and to hand over her fair daughter. The mother's answers: she is putting on her fine silken dress; she is putting on her gold embroidered shoes and saying goodbye to her silken dresses; she is saying goodbye to her flowers. The girl asks her silk dresses to fall from their nails, to mourn and weep for her after her mother's second answer to the bridegroom. After the mother's third reply she plucks three flowers, and asks them to wither and to collapse on the ground, to weep for her. The mother then asks her daughter three times when she will return home. The girl replies: *When blue violets will grow in your window[pane], and you know it well, this will never happen; When red roses will grow on your table, and you know it well, this will never happen; When parsley will grow in your kitchen, and you know it well, this will never happen.* When they reach a little stream the bride asks John Turk to stop and allow her to drink from the stream. As in version **I**, he himself will fetch some water for her in his golden cup. Someone exclaims: '*Stop, coachman, stop, | The bride is ill!*' | '*Perhaps she is just sad.*' | '*Stop, coachman, stop, | The bride has died!*' | '*Perhaps she is just asleep.*' || Version **M** ends here in prose: *When they arrived at his home, John Turk had a coffin made of gold; he placed this into a coffin made of glass, and he placed that on the top of a tree. It is here that the son of the Turkish Emperor used to go to mourn for her.* The bridegroom arrives home, his mother asks him what is the reason that the bride does not talk to her, does not shake hands with her, does not move, and laments for her daughter-in-law whom she had loved even before she had seen her, who brought sorrow upon her, her son and their guests. **K** the bridegroom orders his coachmen to go with the swiftest horse to his mother: *Tell my mother: | They should not prepare | For a wedding-feast, | But she should come | For a funeral-feast! |* When they arrive home she starts lamenting for her: *—My daughter-in-law, my sweet daughter-in-law, | Had you behaved well | I would have given you honey, | Had you behaved badly | I would have given you poison!* Her mother arrives, she starts lamenting for her: *—My son-in-law, my dear son-in-law, | Will you have a coffin made for her of walnut-tree? | —I will have a marble coffin made for her, mother. | —Will you have the bells tolled for her? | —I will have all the sixteen bells tolled for her, mother. | —Will you have her buried at the corner of the cemetery? | —I will have her buried at the corner of the rosegarden, mother. | —Will you lament for her when nobody watches you? | —I will lament for her when everybody watches me, mother. | —Will you escort her to the gate of the porch? | —I will escort her up to her grave, mother. ||* **J, L** the bridegroom sends for her mother, but, as in **K**, warns her that it is not the wedding but the burial of her daughter she is asked for, (**L** the mother arrives, has a coffin made of walnut tree and dresses in mourning; **J** the bridegroom laments: *My God, my God, | If only once I could have seen | The jumping of your feet, | The glance of your eyes, | The smile of your lips*). A dialogue follows between mother-in-law and the bridegroom, as in versions which belong to class 4 (cp. version **K**): walnut coffin—marble coffin; marble cross on the grave—diamond cross on the grave; coffin studded with tiny nails—coffin studded with gold nails; will you have the bell of the village toll for her—the bell of the county; coffin covered with black veil—coffin covered with silver veil; lament for her where no one can see him— lament for her where a hundred people can see him; escort her to the corner of his gate—to the corner of the cemetery.

3. *'The Maid who was Sold to Poland'* (version **N**)

1 So she cries, so she laments, Barbara Seprődi,
In her round courtyard, in her downy bed.
Barbara Seprődi was sewing at her window
And she was sewing her mourning dress.

2 She was making her stitches with black silk thread,
She was embroidering the embroidery with her heavy tears.
—Why are you crying, why are you lamenting,
    Barbara Seprődi?
—How should I not cry, how should I not lament?

3 My father has given me away to Poland,
To Poland, to the mighty king of Poland,
Not even to him, but to the son he has in his house,
Not even to him, but to the son he has in his house.

4 So they are coming, so they are coming with six horses, by coach
With sixty soldiers and with a ragged servant,
And they are having their drums beat a dance measure,
And they are making their horses tread a dance measure.

5 And they have reached John Seprődi's house,
The tied-up gate of John Seprődi's house.
—Do you hear, do you hear, Master John Seprődi!
Hand over your fair daughter, Barbara Seprődi!

6 —I will not hand you over Barbara Seprődi,
Mightier lords used to visit my father's house,
I had not bowed low before them, nor will I bow low before you!
I had not bowed low before them, nor will I bow low before you!

7 —Do you hear, do you hear, Master John Seprődi!
Hand over your fair daughter, Barbara Seprődi!
If you do not hand her over, indeed we will lay on you,
Indeed we will lay on you the tax of the Emperor!

8 Aye, he had to hand her over, there was nothing else he
could do.
There was nothing else Master John Seprődi could do.
So they carry, so they carry Barbara Seprődi,
Barbara Seprődi, with six horses, by coach.

9 With six horses, by coach, with sixty soldiers,
With sixty soldiers, with a ragged servant,
And they are having their drums beat a dance measure,
And they are making their horses tread a dance measure.

Description of the ballad: class 3

Barbara Seprődi sits in her window sewing her mourning dress and
weeping, because her father had given her away to the son of the king
of Poland.

With gay music sixty soldiers and a ragged servant arrive by coach
with six horses to take Barbara away.

They ask John Seprődi to hand over his daughter. The father refuses
to do so, but when they threaten him with laying on him the heavy
tax of the Emperor he gives way.

With gay music the delegation takes Barbara away.

4. ' The Maid who was Sold and was Found Dead by the Bridegroom'
(version O)

1 A beautiful young damsel is sitting yonder there on the balcony.
—Three golden rings have spun round into my lap,
Three white pigeons have flown upon my shoulders:
Oh, mother, Oh, mother, what is the meaning of that?
—Oh, my daughter, Oh, my daughter, it means this:
I have given you away to three young Turkish lords!
—Oh, mother, Oh, mother, it would have been better if you
had given me
To three turkey-herds,
Than to have given me to those three young Turkish lords!
Go up, my coachman, stand up on the bench,
Look round, what can you see in the direction of Turkey?
—I can see nothing, I can see nothing else
But three young Turkish lords coming nearer and nearer!

2 —My God, my God the Father, grant me my wish:
By the time they arrive in the big dining-room,
By the time they arrive, may I be laid out!

3 —Good day, good day, unknown mother!
Where is she, where is your daughter Elisabeth?
—I do not know, I do not know,
Perhaps she is in the little garden, tying flowers into bunches,
To place them on the hats of the young Turkish lords.

4 They went to the little garden.
—Good day, good day, unknown little garden!
Where is she, where is young damsel Elisabeth?
—We do not know where she is, we are mourning for her
     so very much,
We have shrivelled entirely with mourning and sorrow.

5 They went to the mother.
—Good day, good day, unknown mother!
Where is she, where is your daughter Elisabeth?
—I do not know where she is,
Perhaps she has gone to the brook to wash handkerchiefs
To place in the pockets of the young Turkish lords.

6 They went to the brook.
—Good day, good day, unknown brook!
Where is she, where is young damsel Elisabeth?
—I do not know where she is, I have been mourning for her
     for such a long time,
I have dried up entirely with mourning and sorrow.

7 They went to her father.
—Good day, good day, unknown father!
Where is she, where is your daughter Elisabeth?

8 —Why do I struggle to deny it, I have to confess now:
She is laid out in the big dining room.
Will you have the bells tolled for her?
—I will have all the sixteen bells tolled for her, father.
—Will you lament for her a little, will you lament for her
     a little?
Will you have some sort of coffin made for her?
—I will have a coffin made for her of gold and of silver, father.
—Will you have it studded with some sort of nails?
—I will have it studded with diamonds and with silver, father.
—Will you escort her up to the threshold?
—I will escort her up to her grave, father.

Description of the ballad: class 4

I. The beginning of the versions belonging to this class follow different traits when describing how the maid learns that she had been sold:

(*a*) **O, P** young damsel Elisabeth is sitting outside (**O** on the balcony; **P** in a golden chair, sewing a golden chemise) when three golden rings clink into her lap (**P** and three white pigeons fly upon her shoulders). She asks her mother to explain those, and is told that she is sold (**O** to three young Turkish lords; **P** to a young heir; 'heir' is an obvious corruption, as it is 'örökös' in Hungarian and differs in one letter only from 'török', 'törökös' = 'Turkish', 'Turkish-like').

(*b*) **Q, S, U, V, Z** have more or less the same beginning: **Q** *Clara Bátori, my dear, sweet daughter,* | *Stand up on the stone bench, stand up on the stone bench,* || *Look out of the window; is there anybody coming?* | *—There is not anybody coming, there is not anybody coming!* || *—And for the second time I say: Clara Bátori,* | *Stand up on the stone bench, stand up on the stone-bench,* || *Look out of the window: is there anybody coming?* | *—There is not anybody coming, there is not anybody coming!* || *—And for the third time I say: Clara Bátori, Stand up on the stone bench, stand up on the stone bench,* | *Look out of the window: is there anybody coming?* | *Is there anybody coming? Is there anybody coming?* || *—I see three glass coaches coming there,* | *I see three red flags, three red flags...* || *Lady Francis Bátori, my dear, sweet mother,* | *For whom are they coming? For whom are they coming?* || *—It would be no use denying it, my dear, sweet daughter:* | *They are coming for you, they are coming for you!* || **Z** she sees three golden coaches and three red flags; **V** the mother asks her to look out of the window only once, she sees three red flags coming from the direction of Turkey; **S** the mother sends Helen to go out to the gate, there she sees twelve young men from St Miklós village coming with twelve flags; **U** she sees three glass coaches and nine golden flags; this version does not give the girl's name, but has two introductory lines: *Barbara, Barbara, we have come to take your fair daughter away,* | *Hand over your fair daughter into the hands of the Turk!*

(*c*) The rest of the versions start differently: **R** *Stephen Fogarasi is leaning on his elbow on the window,* | *His sister is leaning on her elbow beside him.* | *—Have you heard news of it, my sister dear:* | *I have promised you away into Turkey,* | *As a betrothed bride of the mighty Turkish Emperor.* || **T** *Prepare yourself, my daughter, prepare yourself because I have sold you!* | *—To whom, mother, to whom?* | *—To the great mountain robber!* || **Y** is corrupted here, cf. below in II; **W** starts at incident III.

II. The desperate girl reproaches her mother for having sold her, and prays to God that she may be laid out by the time her bridegroom arrives to fetch her.

U, V *Well, had not Your Honour one piece of bread,* | *One piece of bread, one glass of wine,* | *That you gave me into the hands of the Turk?* || **Q, Z** *Lady Bátori, my mother dear,* | *So you have sold me, so you have sold me!* || *Then expect me home when on your fireplace* | *Rosemary grows, rosemary grows!* || *When on your roof grows grass ready for mowing—* | *And it never grows, and it never grows!* || **X** *I thank you, mother dear,* | *That you have brought me up,* | *Your many counsels.* | *But I do not thank you* | *That you have given me into marriage.* | *You did not give me* | *To him whom I have loved for a long time,* | *But you gave me to him,* | *Whom I have been hating* | *For a long time.* | *I have fallen apart* | *From him whom I have loved,* | *I have fallen into bed* | *With him, whom I hate!* || **O, P** she says that she would rather marry a turkey-herd and sends her coachman up to the tower, which is on the mountain, to inform her what he can see; **R** she asks: '*May God give me rather one gay dinner,* | *After the gay dinner a light illness,* | *And may I pass away with the fair rosy dawn!*' | *God granted her wish:* | *God gave her a gay dinner,* | *After the gay* dinner a light illness. | With the fair, rosy dawn she passed away. || **T** When they set off: may I be laid on my sick-bed, | By the time they are half-way may I be laid out on my bier, | By the time they arrive, may I be buried in the bottom of the earth! || **Z** it is the mother who says: When they take you away, my dear, sweet daughter, | May your heart break, may you die straightaway! || **Y** is corrupted and confused with a folksong: A white tower can be seen in Black town, | I see my sweetheart playing with someone else, | I do not dare to call her, to make her heart sad, | To estrange her heart from my heart. || In Black town a maid got married, | And love was the cause of her death: | When I left her she was shivering with cold, | When I returned she already was dead. || **U, V, Q, S, Z** She goes out to the garden, she throws herself down on the grass: | She cries out weeping: | —My flowers, my flowers, wither on your roots, | Dry on the ground, | So that everybody can see that you are mourning for me! | She goes into the house, throws herself down on to her bed, | She cries out weeping: | —My clothes, my clothes, fall down from nails, | Rot away on the ground, | So that my stepmother can see that you are mourning for me! || **P** she asks her clothes to fall down from the nails and weep over her, and adds: My turkeys, my turkeys bred by my hands, | Fling yourselves down on the ground, weep over me! || **Q** My clothes, my clothes, fall down from the nails, | Go into mourning, go into mourning! | My flowers, my flowers, wither and collapse on the ground, | Weep over me, weep over me! || **V, Z** like **Q**, but mother instead of stepmother; **S** Mother, dear mother, | Only give me leave | To go into my garden, | To look at my flowers! || My flowers, my flowers, | Are you too tired of me? | When they will take me away | Wither all of you, || Dry on your stalk, dry on your stalk, | Dry to dust, | So that my mother should see | That you too pity me! || Mother, dear mother, | Only give me leave | To go into my room, | To look at my clothes! || My clothes, my clothes, | Are you too tired of me? | Fall down from your nails, | Throw yourselves down on the ground, | Rot away to dust, | So that my mother should see | That you too pity me! || Mother, dear mother, | Only give me leave | To go into my room, | To write a letter! || Take it, my dear swallow, | If you find him asleep | Place it on his coverlet, | If you find him walking in his room, | Put it on his window. (The last two stanzas are borrowed from 'The Dishonoured Maiden'.) **V** adds: Will you escort me, mother, up to the corner of the gate? | —I will escort you, my daughter, up to your grave. || **Q, S, U, X, Z** end here.

III. The bridegroom arrives, asks the mother where he can find his bride, and the mother gives evasive answers: she is in the garden tying flowers into bunches, she is at the brook, washing handkerchiefs for the bridegroom. The bridegroom cannot find her in the garden or at the brook; finally he is told that she is laid out in her chamber.

O it is the father who confesses the truth finally; the dialogue with the garden and with the brook occurs in this version only; **R** Stephen Fogarasi tells the bridegroom that she is in the garden; he finds that all the flowers have withered away, but cannot find the bride; then Stephen Fogarasi tells him that she is in the house of the maidens, dressing herself. The bridegroom goes in and finds that all the girls are dressed in mourning and his bride is laid out; **Y** she is in the inn setting tables and drying plates; she has gone to the mountain to collect pearls for her wreath; she is in the inner chamber, her six girl friends are sitting around her and the clothes of death hang above her; **T** first the bridegroom sends in his smallest servant; the mother tells him that she is on her sick-bed, then he sends in his next servant: she is laid out on her bier; then he goes in himself: she is buried in the bottom of the earth; **W** (the fragment consists of this incident only)—the bridegroom asks Lady Francis Bátori to open her iron gate and to hand over her daughter; the mother asks him to wait till she helps her daughter to put on her last skirt, her last scarf, her last pair of shoes, and the daughter cries out, *Lady Francis Bátori, my dear mother, so you have sold me!* The fragment ends here.

IV. The versions end differently:

P like **O**, only the dialogue is between the dead bride and the bridegroom: *Will you have some sort of coffin made for me?* | *—I will have a marble coffin made for you, my rose.* | *—Will you have it covered with some sort of linen?* | *—I will have it covered with a black veil, my rose.* || *—Will you have it studded with some sort of nails?* | *—I will have it studded with silver and gold, my rose.* | *—Will you have me carried out by some sort of gipsy?* | *—I will have you carried out by princes, my rose.* || *—Will you have the three bells tolled for me?* | *—I will have all the sixteen bells tolled for you, my rose.* | *—Will you escort me if only up to the gate, my rose?* | *—I will escort you to your grave, my rose.* || **R** *Give her to me, give her to me, brother-in-law, Fogarasi,* | *Give to me my betrothed to whom I have given my ring,* | *I will have a marble coffin made for her,* | *I will have it covered with black cloth reaching to the ground,* | *I will have it studded with gold-headed nails,* | *I will have her mourned by sixty soldiers!* || *—I will not give her to you, I will not give her to you, mighty Turkish Emperor,* | *I too will have a marble coffin made for her,* | *I will have it also covered with black cloth reaching to the ground* | *I will have her also mourned by sixty soldiers* | *Let her rest here with her father and mother,* | *With her father and mother in her native-earth!* || **T** *The bridegroom crossed himself and died straightaway.* **Y** (borrowed from 'The Dishonoured Maid'): *He goes into the room,* | *Throws himself on her breast,* | *Snatches up his big knife,* | *Points it at his heart:* | *—May my blood and your blood run together in one stream,* | *May my body and your body rest together in one grave,* | *May my soul and your soul adore together the same God!*

International parallels

The well-marked differences between the four classes of 'The Maid who was Sold' make it difficult to establish the cognation of this ballad to any particular piece of the European ballad-tree.

The task is made more complicated by the fact that 'The Maid who was Sold' shares several motifs, incidents and phrases with other Hungarian ballads and it is difficult to tell with certainty which was the ballad in which those elements occurred in the first place.

Csanádi and Vargyas state (*op. cit.* pp. 463–4) that 'our ballad has only very remote international parallels, and those only in German language territory'. Further they point out that the German ballad in question ('Graf Friedrich' [Erk-Böhme, *Deutscher Liederhort*, I, no. 107], discussed under class 2) cannot account for the Hungarian ballad on the whole, as the resemblance between them obtains for class 2 and class 2 only.

Csanádi and Vargyas arrive at the conclusion that originally a genuine Hungarian ballad was composed, based on the idea that a maid was sold against her will, and then various ballad-motifs and folk-tale elements exerted their influence on the different classes of the ballad.

This seems indeed to be the case, as we shall see after having collated the motifs of the different classes, but we have to challenge Csanádi's and Vargyas's statement on one point, namely, their reducing the international correspondences of the Hungarian ballad exclusively to the German language territory.

L. Vargyas (*Ethnographia*, **71**, 172–4) draws attention to the occurrence of motifs IV and VIII (see below) in the French ballad 'Les Anneaux de Marianson', and derives therefore class 1 from this French ballad. The motifs in question appear, however, in other international ballads (cf. Grundtvig, *DGF*, II, no. 83; Child, no. 15) and the story of the French ballad belongs to an entirely different group of ballads: 'The Twa Knights' type.

Examining the motifs of 'The Maid who was Sold', we shall deal with the four classes successively, making it clear which are the motifs which occur in different classes simultaneously, which are genuine Hungarian motifs, and which are those paralleled in international balladry.

Motifs: class 1

Before analysing the motifs of this class, we have to draw attention to its hitherto unnoticed resemblance to the Scottish 'Prince Heathen' (Child, no. 104):

Here Lady Margaret sits in her bower sewing at her silken seam, when Prince Heathen appears and gives her a 'gay gold ring'. She sends him away telling him that she does not love him, but Prince Heathen swears that he will make her 'greet', i.e. weep. She also swears that she will not, and refuses to do so. ('O bonny may winna ye greet now? —Ye heathenish dog, nae yet for you!') He takes her maidenhood, yet she will not greet for him. He tells her that he has killed her entire family, still she will not weep. He puts her in a vault of stone 'where five and thirty locks hing on', yet she gives the same answer. He visits her in the prison, being attended by his armed men: 'O bonny may, what do ye now? —Ye heathenish dog, dying for you!' He takes her out to the green, where she is not to see any women but only him and his young men till she gives birth to a child. She asks for a drink—'not a drop till she rolls up a son'. She gives birth to a son and he gives his horse's sheet to her, to wrap it around the baby. Now, at last she bursts out crying: 'O bonny may, ye do greet now! —Ye heathenish dog, but nae for you / But a' is for my bonny young son: Your sheets are rough to row him in!' Having broken her will, he loves her well:

163

Ye'll row my young son in the silk,
An ye will wash him wi the milk,
An lay my lady very saft
That I may see her very aft!
When hearts are broken, bands will bow;
Sae well he loved his lady now.

We shall proceed by commenting on the motifs of class 1, and comparing them with 'Prince Heathen' simultaneously.

'The Maid who was Dragged to Death'	'Prince Heathen'
I. Mother sells her daughter.	I. A lady sits in her bower sewing at her silken seam.
This motif is the central motif in classes 2 and 4, in class 3 it is not explicit, and it is the father who promises her away. She sells her for a glass of wine: occurs in **A**, **B**, **C**, also in class 2 (**J**, **K**, **L**), and is referred to in class 4 (**U**, **V**) where the girl asks her mother whether she did not have one piece of bread, one glass of wine, i.e. whether she was in vital need to sell her.	This is met with in class 3 and class 4, but as it is a favourite international commonplace for opening ballads (cf. Child, nos. 28, 52 A, B, 77 C, etc.) this connection should not be insisted upon.
II. The daughter resents the idea and the person to whom she was sold—a prominent motif in all classes; class 1 stands alone in stressing the *personal* dislike involved.	II. The unwelcomed appearance of Prince Heathen and the lady's declaration that she did not love him. (For the ring, cf. class 4.)
III. The bride refuses to greet the man as her 'betrothed', his annoyance and determination to force her to do so.	III. The lady refuses to 'greet' for Prince Heathen, his annoyance and determination to force her to do so.
IV. The cruel treatment she receives (being trailed at a horse's tail).	IV. The cruel treatment she receives (putting her in prison, etc.).

Fastening someone to a horse's tail and thus having him/her dragged to death—a popular punishment for criminals in the Dark Ages—occurs in the French ballad: 'The Ring of Marianson'; and in the Danish 'Hildebrand og Hille'.[1] Examples for the incremental repetition when describing the girl's sufferings (VI, 32) have a particularly close parallel in 'The Girl who was Danced to Death'. English-Scottish repetitions of this kind given in 'Clement Mason'.

(The lady's asking for a drink; cf. class 2.)

V. Her consequent refusal to call him her betrothed even when in pain under tortures.

V. Her consequent refusal to weep for him even when in pain and agony of thirst, etc.

VI. Her final consent—at the point of death.

VI. Her final tears—for the sake of her child.

VII. The bridegroom's appeasement after having broken her will.

VII. Prince Heathen's appeasement after having broken his lady's will.

VIII. The bride asks for the wing of a jay, for the leg of a daw, or for a sparrow to eat at the point of dying (**A** also for a glass of wine from her father's house); the bridegroom goes away to hunt for the bird, but by the time he arrives with it the bride is dead.

This motif is better understood if we compare it to the Scottish and Scandinavian versions of 'Leesome Brand' (Child, no. 15):

In the Scandinavian versions the lady asks for water when in childbirth, partly for thirst, partly for wish of privacy, and in both the Scottish and Scandinavian versions she 'dismisses the knight (to hunt)'—again to secure privacy.[2] Although there is no question of childbirth in the Hungarian ballad, this motif precedes *the heroine's death*

---

[1] Grundtvig, *DGF*, no. 83 A, stanzas 27–31: 27. 'Mynn broder thog meg wed huiden hand: / hand band meg med en saadelbandtt. // 28. Hand thog meg y gulle lock: / hand band meg till syn saadell-knap. // 29. Hand red icke offuer saa liden en quest: / hun thog io hudenn aff mitt brøst. // 30. Hand red ike offuer saa lidell en gren: / hun tog io hudenn aff mitt byen. // 31. Hand red icke offuer saa lidenn en rod: / hun stuod y blod y myn fuod.'

[2] In interpreting and wording the motifs common to the Hungarian ballad and 'Leesome Brand' here, and further, we use the terms of H. M. Shire, *Poems from Panmure House* (Cambridge, 1960), pp. 8–9, 20.

in both the Hungarian and the Scottish-Scandinavian ballad and is well suited for adaptation in our class 1, apparently to express our heroine's wish to be left alone when dying. The cruelty of the bridegroom furthermore would indeed justify such a wish in our ballad, and this can probably account for the particular Hungarian device in adapting the motif into the ballad: the bride has to use a pretext for dismissing the man and asks for the wing of a jay, etc., knowing well that he will have to go to hunt for the bird.

IX. The commonplace 'Open, mother, open your gate,[1] / Make, mother, make my gay deathbed' figures also in 'The Maid who was Danced to Death'; the second line is often used in English and Scottish ballads (cp. Child, nos. 7, 12, 42, 52, 84, 243).

X. *Class 2.* The girl's prayer that she may die and the fulfilment of her wish is a central motif in both class 2 and class 4, and it is not paralleled in international balladry.

Although it is presented as a Christian motif in the ballad (the wish is expressed as a prayer, and it is God who grants it), it calls up the primitive belief in the magic power of the spoken word. This is especially so in versions **H, I,** and **J** where the girl is incapable of neutralising her wish once it had been expressed: it works as a curse which she had cast upon herself.[2]

Before discussing motifs XI–XII, we have to recur to 'Graf Friedrich':

In this German ballad the bridegroom wounds his bride with his sword by mischance when on their way to the wedding. She asks him to bid his men to drive more slowly, and he orders them to do so. When they arrive in his house, his mother greets them, and is surprised by the paleness of the bride, who will not eat, will not drink, but wants to lie down instead. Graf Friedrich explains to his mother that his bride is mortally wounded, and indeed she dies the same night. Her father kills Graf Friedrich, who was responsible for his daughter's death.

Since the Scottish 'The Cruel Brother' (Child, no. 11) and 'Leesome Brand' are also relevant when collating the motifs common to 'Graf Friedrich' and to our class 2, we shall compare the motifs in question to 'Graf Friedrich' and those Scottish ballads simultaneously.

---

[1] 'Gate' in Hungarian *leveles kapu*—a kind of farm-gate, constructed of broad horizontal planks joined by narrow vertical and diagonal struts.

[2] The concept of the magic power of the spoken word, as expressed in version **G**, brings to one's mind the Semele story (Ovid, *Metamorphoses*, Book III, lines 287–98). *Talibus ignaram Juno Cadmeïa dictis | formarat: rogat illa Jovem sine nomine munus. | cui deus 'Elige!' ait 'nullam patiere repulsam; | quoque magis credas, Stygii quoque conscia sunto | numina torrentis: timor et deus ille deorum est.' | laeta malo nimiumque potens perituraque amantis | obsequio Semele 'qualem Saturnia' dixit | 'te solet amplecti, Veneris cum foedus initis, | da mihi te talem!' voluit deus ora loquentis | opprimere: exierat iam vox properata sub auras. | ingemuit; neque enim non haec optasse, neque ille | non iurasse potest.*

XI. The distressful journey: the bride's strength failing:

J, K, M incremental repetition when describing the failing strength of the bride through the exclamations of the brideswoman; **G, H, I, M** her thirst (**H** her impatience to arrive at the bridegroom's lands).

'Graf Friedrich' has the distressful journey, and the bride's strength failing:

Graf Friedrich, edler Herre, | Ja bitt ich euch so sehre, | Sprecht ihr zu eurem Hofgesind, | Und sie mählig reiten thund! | Sprecht ihr zu euren Leuten, | Und das sie gemachsam reiten! | Ich leid' gross Schmerzen und gross Klag, | Und das ich nimmer reiten mag' | Graf Friedrich ruft sein Herren: | —Ihr sollt nicht reiten sehre, | Mein Liebe Braut ist mir verwundt, | O reicher Gott, mach mirs gesund!

'The Cruel Brother' offers here closer resemblance to our class 2 than the German ballad—it has the same incremental repetition as our versions **J, K, M**; it also has the bride's thirst, and her impatience to arrive: e.g.

B 'Ride up, ride up', said the foremost man, | 'I think our bride comes hooly on!' | 'Ride up, ride up', said the second man, | 'I think our bride looks pale and wan!' | Up than cam the gay bridegroom, | And straucht unto the bride he cam: | 'Does your side-saddle sit awry?...| —The rain runs not in my glove, | Nor will I e'er chuse anither love, | But O and I war at Saint Evron's well | There I wad licht and drink my fill! | Oh an I war at Saint Evron's closs, | There I wad licht and bait my horse!' | When she cam to Saint Evron's well | She dought na licht to drink her fill, | When she cam to Saint Evron's closs, | The bonny bride fell aff her horse.

'Leesome Brand' has also the distressful journey, and the lady's failing strength, but for a different reason: childbirth.

But they hadna ridden a mile but twa, | Till on the horse she was like to fa' | They hadna ridden a mile but three, | Till on the horse she was like to dee. (G. Greig, *Last Leaves* [Aberdeen, 1925], no. IX).

XII. The bridegroom arrives with the dead bride (**K, L** he sends a message to his mother about the sad news; **G, H** his mother's surprise at the bride who does not move, etc.); the happy preparations for the wedding turned to the sad preparation for the funeral.

'Graf Friedrich' has the surprise of the mother-in-law, although there she arrives while still alive:

Wie ist dein liebe Braut so bleich | Als obs ein Kindlein hab bezeight! | Wie ist also inniglei, | Als obs eins Kindeschwanger sei! | —Ei, schweig du's Mutter tille, | Und thus durch meinen Wille: | Sie ist Kinds halben nicht ungesund, | Sie ist bis in den Tod verwundt! | ... | Sie mocht weder trinken noch essen, | Ihrs Unmuths konnt sie nicht vergessen. | Sie sprach: —Ich wollt, es wär die Zeit, | Da mir das Bett schier wurd bereit! | Das höret die übel Schwieger, | Sie redt gar bald hinwider: | —Hab ich mein Tag das nie erhört, | Das ein Jungfrau zu Bett begehrt!

'Leesome Brand' has a situation somewhat similar to our class 2—
the knight arrives home after his lady's death; his sad words set against
the mother's happy preparations for welcoming him home:

A '*Get minstrels for to play,' she said, | 'And dancers to dance in my room, | For here comes
my son, Leesome Brand, | And he comes merilie to the town!' || 'Seek none minstrels to
play, mother, | Nor dancers to dance in your room, | But tho your son comes, Leesome Brand, |
Yet he comes sorry to the town!'*

XIII. The dialogue at the end of versions **J**, **K**, **L** is repeated in class
4 (**O**, **P**, partly in **V**, analogously in **R**) and in other Hungarian ballads
(cp. 'The Dead Boy'). Its elements are discussed under *Folklore and
custom.*

XIV. *Class 3.* The spectacular arrival of the wedding-procession is
particularly emphasised in class 3, but it figures in all classes of the
ballad.

Class 1: **A** there is a black army coming from the east, going to the west. **E** the
bridegroom arrives with six horses, by coach.

Class 2: **K** with a golden coach; **L** six flower-decked horses; **I**, **M** three glass
coaches, nine golden flags; **J** a black army in the distance, three glass coaches and a
silver flag on closer examination.

Class 3: with six horses, by coach, with one servant and with sixty soldiers, with gay
music.

Class 4: **Q** a glass coach, three red flags; **Z** a golden coach, three red flags; **V**
twelve young men, twelve flags; **U** like **I**, **M**, class 2; **X** coach, six golden horses.

Wedding-processions are described in Child, nos. 66, 91:

No. 66   Nor to the kirk she wud ne gae
         Nor til't she wud'n ride,
         Till four and twunty men she gat her before
         An twunty on ilka side,
         An four and twunty milk-white dows
         To flee aboon her head.

No. 91   Wi four and twenty buirdlie men
         Atween ye and the wun,
         And four and twenty bonnie mays
         Atween ye and the sun.
         Four and twenty milk-white geese
         Stretching their wings sae wide
         Blawing the dust aff the high way,
         That Mild Mary may ride.

In the Hungarian ballad we do not have such fanciful things in the
wedding procession as in the Scottish ones (geese, pigeons); in most of
the versions six horses, coaches (golden or glass), and some flags convey
all the atmosphere of extravagance.

XV. The father's refusal to hand his daughter over is met with in class 4 also (version **R**):

One would think that sixty soldiers carry enough power to take the girl away by force (as it happens in many Scottish girl-stealing ballads, esp. Child, no. 233). Their more sophisticated method—threatening by the heavy tax of the Emperor—is a special feature of the Moldavian version. (See also discussion of the *Date*.)

XVI. *Class 4*. The folk-tale elements at the beginning of versions **O, P** (the miraculous appearance of three white pigeons, three golden rings in the girl's lap) are explained in the version given in Appendix 1, p. 338, where the king of Turkey sends those tokens to his bride as a signal that he has set off for the journey to fetch her.

The golden chair in version **P** is also a folk-tale touch in its effort to make everyday articles appear in a light of splendour which belongs to the fairy world. Its resemblance to the golden chair which figures in Scottish and Scandinavian ballads (e.g. 'Lishen Brand') and serves the purpose of detecting virginity is incidental.

XVII. We have already discussed the international stereotype for introducing ballads, which occurs in versions **N, O**. In Scottish ballads it goes:

> Lady...was sitting in her window,
> Sewing at her silken seam,
> She lookt out o the bower window...

The last line is paralleled in the introductory formula in our versions **M, O, Q, R, V**, where the mother bids her daughter to look out of the window, and report to her what she sees outside.

XVIII. Paraphrases for 'never', so popular in Scottish and German ballads (cp. Child, nos. 12, 49, 51) are comparatively rare in Hungarian ballads, although they are often used in Hungarian folksongs: E.g.

> I would like to know
> When will you come back!
> —When I see roses in blossom
> On your fireplace,
> When two grains of wheat grow ten stocks,
> When two bunches of grape make ten bucketful of wine,
> And you know, my sweetheart, that it will never happen.
>
> (Kodály, *Magyar Népzene*, no. 171; also *ibid.* no. 316;
> Ortutay, *Magyar Népköltészet*, I, p. 273.)

> Can you see that dead poplar
> Yonder there, my rose?
> I will come back to you
> When it will turn green. (*Magyar Népköltési Gyüjt*, I, no. 32.)

It also occurs in a more recent ballad of infanticide:

> My daughter, my dear daughter,
> Flower of my garden,
> Will you ever come back?

She answers with the paraphrase of the grape and wheat, and adds somewhat curiously for a folk-ballad:

> When wild-geese
> Will start speaking in Greek
> And this, you know well,
> Will never happen.   (*Ethnographia*, 1936, p. 130.)

XIX. The girl's saying good-bye to her flowers, to her turkeys and to her clothes is a special (Hungarian) feature of class 4.

(The motif appears also in version **E**, class 1; and in **I**, **M**, class 2. We shall comment on it under *Folklore and custom*.)

XX. The bridegroom's searching for his bride and the mother's evasive answers will be discussed in 'The Dishonoured Maiden'.

Here we have to draw attention to a group of Scandinavian ballads ('Sir Olaf', cf. Child, no. 42, notes) where a similar situation occurs: the bridegroom dies before his bride has arrived, and his relatives try to conceal his death from the bride when she arrives.

XXI. The speeches by the garden and the brook in version **O** add a motif prominent in folk tales, both Hungarian and international. (Thompson, F 932.12; D 1610.35.)

Summarising the evidence obtained by collating the motifs of 'The Maid who was Sold' to international balladry, we agree with Csanádi and Vargyas in arriving at the conclusion that there is no particular piece of international balladry which could account for the Hungarian ballad as a whole.

Class 1 and class 2 share a sequence of motifs with 'Prince Heathen' and 'Graf Friedrich', respectively, but the resemblance is rather in detail than in general character.

'The Maid who was Sold and Dragged to Death' (class 1) is essentially a tragic ballad. It is a story of compulsory marriage, of helpless hatred and murderous cruelty. 'Prince Heathen', the story of which—according to Child—'reads like an old one, extremely corrupted and not too intelligible even in the longer form', is not a ballad with a tragic conclusion. As it stands, it is a tale of seduction, a tale of a determined suitor who wants to break his proud lady's will, the trials of the lady being relieved at the end of the ballad by the birth of a child.

These trials are not a great deal harder than those which serve to prove the lady's love for the knight in several international ballads (the best of this type being 'Child Waters', Child, no. 63), many of which also end with the lady's giving birth to a child and being well loved and compensated afterwards. The basic difference between the Scottish and Hungarian ballads in their central idea and in their conclusion make a direct connection between those two ballads unlikely; their resemblance in detail would suggest rather a common source that included the proud lady, her repeated refusal to comply with her suitor's will, his insistence in enforcing her to do so, her trials, her final break, and which probably ended with the suitor's appeasement.

The Scottish ballad, which recalls the love-trial ballads in its conclusion, has preserved more of what would seem to be the original, less tragic nature of these motifs, whereas in the Hungarian ballad they are employed to motivate a story of tragic issue.

The correspondence between our class 2 and 'Graf Friedrich' unquestionably demands notice, yet we cannot agree with Gy. Ortutay who, basing his view on these resemblances and on the evidence of the popularity of German 'Spielmannstoffe' in contemporary Hungary, takes it for granted that 'The Maid who was Sold' derives entirely from the German ballad (cf. Gy. Ortutay, *Székely Népballadák*, p. 284).

The opinion of Csanádi and Vargyas is more plausible. As we have mentioned already, they point out that only certain motifs of 'Graf Friedrich' occur in the Hungarian ballad, and those only in versions which belong to class 2, whereas there is no trace of those elements in the rest of the Hungarian versions. Consequently, while permitting the supposition of direct connection between the German and the Hungarian ballads, they believe that 'Graf Friedrich' cannot account for the Hungarian ballads, only certain motifs from it might have been borrowed into the already existing story of the maid who was sold against her will.

The logic of Csanádi's and Vargyas's conclusion becomes more obvious when one notices the definite difference even between 'Graf Friedrich' and class 2 in their underlying ballad-motivation: in the German ballad the crucial point, the death of the bride, is accidental (a tragedy of Fate), whereas in class 2 it is the inevitable consequence of the initial situation in which the heroine finds herself, and her consequent misguided vow. Furthermore, we have seen that those motifs which *are* common to 'Graf Friedrich' and class 2 are also encountered elsewhere in international balladry, in pieces which are not necessarily connected (e.g. 'Leesome Brand' and 'The Cruel Brother'). This points to the fact that the motifs in question have a tendency to in-sinuate themselves into various, sometimes unconnected, ballads where they are suitable for being adapted into the story, and therefore they should not be regarded as creating any unique or conclusive links which would affect the *origins* of the ballads in which they occur.

Comparing the motifs of the four classes of 'The Maid who was Sold' we have seen that each class has its individual features: class 4 is interwoven with folk-tale elements (the miraculous appearance of the rings and pigeons, the golden chair, the withering flowers, clothes falling from their nails, garden, brook speaking); class 3 emphasises the father's reluctance to give away his daughter and the fine contrast between the gay splendour of the wedding procession and the grief and frustration of the bride; class 2 is imbued with the belief in the deter-minism of primitive superstition; and class 1, which by the violence of its story lends in a certain sense an *a posteriori* justification for the reck-less vow taken by the bride in class 2 and class 4, where she prefers death rather than face a compulsory marriage.

Different as they are in developing the story, the four classes are linked closely together through their central idea: rendering the tale of a girl who was sold in marriage against her will.

This is a most personal affair: the feelings, the fate, the tragedy of a particular girl who finds herself in a particular situation. But this particular tragedy was only too naturally understood and felt by any member of its audience; it was a vital contemporary problem, any one girl could suddenly find herself in the same position.

Folklore and customs

To be sold in marriage was a practice so general that marriageable daughters are still called 'eladó-lány'—'a girl-to-be-sold'—in Hungary. Indeed, some elements of present-day Hungarian marriage customs represent a symbolic adherence to this tradition.[1]

---

[1] At Kalotaszeg when a young man reached an eligible age, his father gave him a thaler, symbolising his ability to go out and procure a bride for himself. He then goes to the spinning-room and shows it to the girl whom he had chosen. The *móringolás*—'arranging the finances'—which takes place after the proposal and is discussed between the future bridegroom and the bride's family, is such a serious matter that at some places in Hungary neither food nor drink is served till the question of how much money (cattle, etc.) the bridegroom is to pay for the bride is finally settled; there are several humorous scenes of bargaining on the day of the wedding: the bargain about the *ágypénz* ('price of the bed') when the bridegroom's representatives go to fetch it in order to take it to the bride's new home; the *csókpénz* ('price of the kiss') which the wedding

'The Maid who was Sold' has preserved several references to internationally held folk-beliefs, superstitions and customs.

The belief that green is an unlucky colour is expressed in Scottish and Danish ballads (cp. Child, nos. 73 D, F; also II, p. 512; Child even quotes a Danish proverb: 'They that marry in green, Their sorrow is soon seen').

In versions **G** and **H**, where the girl dresses in green immediately after having learned that she had been sold, this colour has the same foreboding significance. It figures in the same context in 'The Girl who was Danced to Death'; and we may add to the many international references a Hungarian children's game-song, in which the devil is dressed in green:

> Come up, you rascal, to knock
> On a golden carriage,
> Come up, George Lengyel, to wave your sword
> On a silver carriage,
> *Lo, there comes the Devil in his green gown,*
> From his copper tuft of hair
> The soot is dripping down!

> (A. Kiss, *op. cit.* p. 265. He remarks that this song is sung
> with mock dread and abhorrence.)

G, **H**, and **I** versions have also preserved an interesting account of the special importance of the poor as mediators between ordinary people

---

guests have to pay when the bride kisses them one by one after the wedding-feast; and the collection for the privilege of dancing with the bride. This *menyasszony-tánc* ('dance with the bride') takes place late at night after the wedding feast. The best man leads the bride, whose hair-style has just been changed to suit her new status as a wife (i.e. into a bun), into the room and announces: 'The bride is for sale!' Then, whoever wants to dance with her has to cry out: 'I buy the bride!' and pay some money to the best man, who sells the bride for the dance. Present-day Hungarian wedding customs have also preserved traces of an earlier practice in arranging marriage, namely, the bride's abduction. One of these traces (the bride's parents do not lead forth the bride at once when the bridegroom's best man and his company arrive to fetch her in order to take her to the wedding; they pretend that they do not know the bride they are looking for and produce an old woman, a gipsy, or somebody in grotesque clothes before they bring forth the real bride) would seem to be referred to in version **K**, in which the mother denies that she has a daughter to sell. The passage in question is repeated in numerous Hungarian children's singing-dancing games. For example, 'Now they are carrying her away, | They are carrying away | Lady Cucumber's daughter, | In purple, in velvet, | In golden trousers. | —Alas, I have not got, Alas, I have not got | Any fair daughters to sell! | —Ay, do not deny it, Ay, do not deny it, | I saw her in Vienna, | She sold red apples, | I even bought some of them, | But I did not taste them'...etc. (A. Kiss, *Gyermekjáték Gyüjtemény*, Budapest, 1841, p. 348.) Other examples: Z. Kodály, *Magyar Népzene Tára*, I, Gyermekjátékok, nos. 87, 435, 492, 686, 693, 354, 496, 498, 504–7, 585–6, 694, 746 (apple as love-symbol, cp. 'Fair Maid Julia').

The fact that version **K** stands alone in having this passage and that it does not form an integral part of that version but occurs at its beginning only (quite irrelevantly) would suggest that version **K** affiliated this passage from one of these children-songs, although the children-song might have been part of a song similar to our ballad-story at one point.

and God. It is in this same capacity that they are invited for funerals and funeral-feasts in many European countries as well as in Hungary. This is called 'koldus-etetés'—'feeding the beggar'—in Hungary, and a very interesting custom of a similar type is reported by John Brand in his *Popular Antiquities of Great Britain* (edited by W. C. Hazlitt, London, 1870, II, 198).

Bells ringing for the dead is a custom which is mentioned in various Hungarian and Scottish ballads (cf. 'Clement Mason', 'Bátori', 'The Dead Boy'; also Child, nos. 69, 64). The idea that *not* having bells rung for mourning is shameful (conveyed through the anxious questions of the bride or the bride's mother in the final dialogue of versions **J, K, O**, and analogously **R**) is expressed also in Child, no. 64 *B, E, G*:

Out and spak her ain bridegroom,
And an angry man was he:
—This day she has gien me the gecks,
Yet she must bear the scorn:
There's not a bell in merry Linkum
Shall ring for her the morn.

Out an spake then Sweet William,
And a sorry man was he:
—Altho she has gien you the gecks
She will not bear the scorn:
There's not a bell in merry Linkum
But shall ring for her the morn!

We have already discussed the common occurrence of coffins made of the walnut tree in 'Clement Mason', the more luxurious coffin which is made of silver and gold (or studded with silver and golden nails) in versions **O, R**, and **J**, also paralleled in Scottish ballads: e.g. Child, nos. 96 and 25 *E*, where one-half of the coffin 'was gude red goud, the other siller clear'.

The girl's request to her clothes to fall down from their nails and go in mourning over her (versions **E, I, M, P, Q, S, U, V, Z**) embodies the ancient folk-belief that objects intimately connected with a person can show the fate of their possessors. Life-tokens expressing the same belief figure commonly in international balladry (cf. references in 'Kate Kádár', motif III). Usually the object changes colour (is broken, etc.) in order to signal the death or life-danger of its (former) owner (similarly the withering flowers: cf. *ibid.* in 'Kate Kádár'). In our ballad it occurs in a more unusual context: instead of indicating a *factual event*, it indicates the *emotional state*, the grief and despair of its owner. In Scottish ballads from among the many occasions when buttons leap from breast, flee from coat, as an omen of some ill event, there is only one instance when this happens in order to express the sorrowful emotions of its owner, similar to the Hungarian ballad (Child, no. 204 *I*: 15):

> When she came to her father's lands
> The tenants a' came her to see,
> Never a word she could speak to them,
> But the buttons off her clothes did flee.

Date

For dating the ballad it is important to decide who the bridegroom was to whom the girl was sold in the original versions of the ballad.

The fact that in version **D** it is the devil to whom she is sold, together with the references in versions **G**, **H**, and **I** to the extraordinarily white face of the bridegroom, led some Hungarian scholars to suggest that 'The Maid who was Sold' is closely connected with, if not originated from, the 'Daemon-lover'-'Lenore' type of ballads. It is true that there are several Hungarian fragments (mostly embedded in prose-tales) describing the story of the girl who was ravished by the devil who often appears disguised as a lover (cf. Appendix to the 'Ballads of Magic'); in the 'Anna' ballad (cf. Appendix to our ballad), as in various international folk tales she was promised away to mysterious suitors— apparently to the devil—before she was even born. This latter ballad resembles our ballad in one detail: the girl's saying good-bye to her clothes and flowers in the same fashion as in our class 4. However, apart from this one detail, neither the Hungarian nor the international versions of the Lenore-ballad have anything in common with our ballad, except for such very general traits as the girl's hatred and abhorrence towards the bridegroom, and that, as in the 'Daemon-lover', she is finally killed by him.

There is much more evidence to point to the fact that in the original versions of 'The Maid who was Sold' the mother sold her daughter to a Turk. This is explicit throughout in class 4 (and the many folk-tale elements and preservation of ancient folk-beliefs is a guarantee of age for this class); it is also elucidated in version **L**. The rest of the versions contain unmistakable references to this state of affairs: in versions **K**, **M** 'Turk' became an adjective, i.e. the hero is called John Turk; in version **A** a black army comes from the east to fetch the girl; the red Turkish flag occurs in most of the versions, and L. Kálmány recorded various folk-tales from the Lowland relating how mothers sold their daughters to Turkey (e.g. Gabriel Bátori and Clara Bátori; cf. Appendix).

One of these tales, 'Bey, the Pasha of Buda' (cf. Appendix), which follows the story of our class 1, shows clearly the process, how the memory of the cruel Turks who occupied Hungary for one hundred and fifty years became confused and involved with stories about the cruelty of the devil, as in version **D**. (The resemblance between 'The Maid who was Sold', class 1, and 'The Maid who was Danced to Death', in which latter ballad the devil figures in several versions, should also be considered when accounting for its appearance in version **D**. This seems to answer for the devil-bridegroom in version **D**. As to the reference to his swan-white face in versions **G**, **H**, and **I**, although it recalls the deadly paleness of revenants, there is no precedent in Hungarian folk tradition for attributing a white face to the devil; it might as well have conveyed the mother's effort in describing the man to whom she had sold her daughter as being attractive.

Later, it would seem, the Turkish bridegroom was replaced by a German one (the next rulers of Hungary) in some of the versions (**G**, **H**), the last stage in this development of altering the suitor's identity according to the changing circumstances of the audiences being represented in class 1, which is concerned only with the personal disagreeableness of the bridegroom.

Taking it now for granted that in the original Hungarian ballad it was a Turk to whom the maiden was sold, we may assume that the ballad belongs to the time of Turkish occupation of Hungary, i.e. between 1526 and 1710.

Taking the central idea of 'The Maid who was Sold' into consideration, we may go one step further, and suggest that it was composed at a time when the Turks had already established themselves in Hungary, and so instead of abducting girls for their harems practised the slightly less barbaric custom of purchasing them. This would indicate an origin not earlier than the end of the sixteenth century.

The daughter's attitude towards her mother (or brother) who had sold her, and the mother's (brother's; in **N**, father's) part in the bargain, throws an interesting light on the epoch in which the ballad was sung. Some versions indicate that the mother was compelled to sell the girl because she was so poor that she had no other choice (**A**, **V**) or, as in **N**, **R**, that the father or brother was forced to do so; in other versions the mother is depicted as being unnaturally cruel (cp. **B**, **D**, where it is she who advises the bridegroom to fasten her daughter to a horse's tail). The girl's attitude varies too in different versions. In **R**, **G**, **H**, **S**, she does not reproach the mother (brother, etc.) who sold her because she knows that she (he) could not save her from the powerful suitors even if she wanted to; in **A, I, O, P, U, W**, although the news that she has been sold is unexpected, the fact that it could happen does not surprise her. On the other hand, in versions **D, J, L, K**, the daughter casts a curse upon the mother who sold her.

This disparity of the versions in dealing with the moral aspect of the story would suggest that the ballad was composed at a time when the general attitude towards such bargains was no longer uniform or stable: when in some localities selling daughters into marriage was still regarded as a sad but normal event, while elsewhere it was considered as something deplorable, something against which one ought to protest, something to be condemned. This changing attitude was probably characteristic of the time when we suggest that the ballad was composed.

The rhymeless lines with the frequent alliteration—a feature characteristic of the most ancient Hungarian verses (e.g. '*h*intóba ültetnek, *h*ideg ki is rázzon, *h*atárjába érnek, szörnyű *h*alált *h*aljon'; 'Adjon Isten nekem inkább *v*íg *v*acsorát, *v*íg *v*acsora után...*v*ilágból kimúlást', etc.), the incremental repetition in all the four classes, together with the tune of the ballad, which belongs to the oldest, pentaton-recitative tunes of Hungarian folk-tunes also warrant dating the ballad in the late sixteenth or early seventeenth century.

Such dating is implied by ethnographical evidence as well: references to customs practised in those centuries (fastening someone to a horse's tail; the bride's asking the poor to pray for her), the various folk-beliefs which have been preserved in the ballad (motifs X, XIX, XXI; and others discussed in *Folklore and customs*).

Linguistic evidences (to which we have already referred when discussing 'Clement Mason', cf. *Date* above) also support a late sixteenth- or early seventeenth-century origin of the ballad, when in Hungary surnames were not yet finally established. As we have mentioned in 'Clement Mason', at the first stage adjectives for the person's profession or nationality were used for that purpose (cp. John the Turk in version **L**—John Turk in version **M**—where he is explicitly a Turk, while in version **K** his name is John Turk, without any reference to his being a Turk); adjectives for personal characteristics (cp. 'Catherina Bodor'— 'Catherine Curly'), and adjectives made up from the name of the village or town where the person lived (cp. 'Fogaras-Fogarasi'—this name is first recorded in 1602) served also as temporary surnames. At this early stage the surname, which described accidental and individual characteristics of the bearer, was very often dropped by the descendants of the person in question, who took other names according to their own qualities or circumstances, and sometimes kept their father's name as well, as a matter of closer identification (cp. **E, B, D**—Ladislav Borosfai, the son of Paul Vidrai). Three names were also used in the sixteenth–seventeenth century (cp. the wife of Stephen Rosy, Fair) for the same reason. (Cf. Benkő, *A régi magyar személynévadás*, Budapest, Néptudományi Intézet kiadása, 1949.)

Special Hungarian elements

Summarizing the conclusions of our discussion of the international parallels, the motifs and the date, we may say that 'The Maid who was Sold' appears to be a genuine Hungarian ballad, composed some time between the end of the sixteenth and the middle of the seventeenth century. Originally it related a tale of a girl who was sold to a Turk against her will, and eventually, by affiliating several motifs from international balladry, and by emphasizing different aspects of the story, it branched into four well-marked classes.

The central theme of the ballad, the compulsory marriage and the bride's resentment of it, is often dealt with in international balladry (e.g. Child, nos. 64, 65, 66; also nos. 223, 224, 225, 296). The Hungarian ballad stands alone in (1) carrying her resentment as far as (a) protesting against her bridegroom up to the point when she is dying in class 1— a protest well justified by the brutality of the man to whom she was sold, and (b) casting a curse upon herself wishing to die—class 2 and class 4; and (2) in underlying her eventual death by the primitive belief in determinism, i.e. the belief in the magic power of spoken words (a motivation not immediately apparent in the ballad as the wish is expressed in the form of a prayer and it is God who grants its fulfilment).

Class 3, consisting of one ballad only, which does not have the death of the girl, is nonetheless original and unparalleled in international balladry; this is the most lyrical of all the versions; it is not the event itself, but the emotional effect of the event it is concerned with, expressing the bride's grief and the father's helplessness in trying to protest.

'The Maid who was Sold', being a genuine Hungarian ballad, instead of commenting on the special Hungarian elements in the details, here we have dealt with them when comparing the motifs to international variants.

'THE DISHONOURED MAIDEN'

This ballad is often cited in arguments concerning the provenance of the classical Hungarian tragic ballads. Its history appears to contradict the belief that such ballads existed only in Transylvania. Although some (mostly fragmentary) portions of it have been recorded in Transylvanian villages, the full versions all come from the Lowland from the northeastern parts of Hungary, and from the Baranya comitat, where it was a great favourite.

I shall here give the full translation of two of its versions: version **A**, which represents the ballad as it has been preserved in most of the Hungarian versions; and version **I**, which is important when comparing the Hungarian ballad with international variants.

Version **A**

1 Barbara Angoli had a little skirt made,
   It grew shorter in the front, longer at the back,

2 It grew shorter in the front, longer at the back,
   Her fine, slender waist grew fatter and fatter.

3 —My daughter, my daughter, my daughter, Barbara Angoli,
   What does it mean that the round-hemmed skirt

4 Is growing shorter in the front, longer at the back,
   That your fine, slender waist is growing fatter and fatter?

5 —The tailor did not cut it well, the sempstress did not sew
      it well,
   This chambermaid has not put it straight on me.

6 —My daughter, my daughter, my daughter Barbara Angoli,
   What does it mean that the round-hemmed skirt

7 Is growing shorter in the front, longer at the back,
   That your fine, slender waist is growing fatter and fatter?

8 —Mother, mother, mother, Kate Vándorvári,
   I have drunk river-water, that has made me fatter.

9 —My daughter, my daughter, my daughter, Barbara Angoli,
   What does it mean that the round-hemmed skirt

10 Is growing shorter in the front, longer at the back,
   That your fine, slender waist is growing so much fatter?

11 —Why do I struggle to deny it, I have to confess now:
   I am growing fatter by young Master Gyöngyvári.

12 —Constables, come, seize her, take her,
   Seize her, take her, put her in prison!

13 For thirteen days not to eat, not to drink,
   Neither to eat, nor drink, nor to sleep!

14 On the thirteenth day her mother comes forth:
   —Are you eating, or drinking, or are you sleeping indeed?

15 —I neither eat, nor drink, nor do I sleep,
   Give me only one hour that I might write my letter,

16 That I might write my letter to young Master Gyöngyvári,
   To young Master Gyöngyvári, to my dear pigeon.

17 —Good evening, good evening, my unknown mother,
   Where is she, where is my dear sweetheart?

18 —She is out in the little garden, picking lilies of the valley,
   Tying them into a sad chaplet, putting it on her head.

19 —She is not there, she is not there, my unknown mother,
   Tell me, where is my dear sweetheart?

20 —Why do I struggle to deny it, I have to confess now:
   She is in the room, on the black-coloured bier.

21 The bridegroom goes in quickly, he goes in quickly,
   He takes his big knife, points it at his heart:

22 —Let my blood and your blood make one stream together,
   Let my heart and your heart rest together in one grave,

23 Let my heart and your heart rest together in one grave,
   Let my soul and your soul worship the same God together.

Version I

1 —Daughter, my dear daughter, Catherine Fodor,
  What has happened to your skirt?
  It is growing short in the front,
  It is growing long at the back.

2 —Mother, my mother, the tailor did not cut it well,
  The tailor did not cut it well,
  The sempstress did not sew it well,
  The sempstress did not sew it well.

3 —Daughter, my dear daughter, yes, the tailor cut it well,
  Yes, the tailor cut it well,
  Yes, the sempstress sewed it well,
  Yes, the sempstress sewed it well!

4 —Mother, my mother, why do I struggle to deny it,
   Why do I struggle to deny it,
   I have to confess at last,
   I have to confess at last:

5 It is that I have an eight months' burden
   From John Gyöngyvári, from John Gyöngyvári,
   I have an eight months' burden
   From John Gyöngyvári.

6 —Seize her, put her in the bottom of the prison,
   In the bottom of the prison,
   For fifteen days
   Put her into hard irons!

7 On the fifteenth day her elder brother went,
   Her elder brother went
   To the gate of the prison,
   To the gate of the prison:

8 —My younger sister, my dear younger sister, Catherine Fodor,
   Are you alive, or are you dead?
   My younger sister, my dear younger sister,
   Are you alive or are you dead?

9 —My elder brother, my dear elder brother, I am neither
        alive, nor dead,
   I am neither alive, nor dead,
   All I do is to languish here,
   All I do is to languish here.

10 —My younger sister, my dear younger sister, Catherine Fodor,
   Write your letter
   To John Gyöngyvári,
   To your dear sweetheart.

11 —My elder brother, my dear elder brother, but I have not
        even a pen,
   But I have not even a pen!
   —Let the tip of your fingers
   Be your pen!

12 —My elder brother, my dear elder brother, but I still
        have no ink,
   But I still have no ink!
   —Let your heavy tears
   Be your ink!

13 —My elder brother, my dear elder brother, but I still
        have no messenger,
   But I still have no messenger!
   —Let the chattering swallow
   Be your messenger!

14 —My elder brother, my dear elder brother,
   I am writing my letter
   To John Gyöngyvári,
   To my dear sweetheart.

15 —My God, my God, they are taking me to the place of
      execution,
   They are taking me to the place of execution,
   To the field of Simeon,
   To the field of Simeon!

16 My swallow, my dear swallow, take my letter,
   Take my letter
   To John Gyöngyvári,
   To my dear sweetheart!

17 If you arrive in the morning, fly on his bedstead,
   Fly on his bedstead!
   If you arrive at noon,
   Fly on his plate!

18 If you arrive in the evening, if you arrive in the evening,
   Fly on his table,
   If you arrive in the evening
   Fly on his table!

19 It arrived at noon,
   It flew on his plate,
   John Gyöngyvári,
   Dropped his spoon.

20 John Gyöngyvári mounted his horse straightaway,
   He mounted his horse straightaway,
   He rode straightaway
   To the field of Simeon.

21 There he waved his Viennese scarf,
   There he waved it,
   Thus he saved
   His dear sweetheart.

22 —Catherine Fodor, fair love of my heart,
   Come closer now,
   Come closer now!
   I will embrace you to my heart!

23 He went to her, took her in his arms,
   Took her in his arms,
   The beautiful loving pair
   Lost their lives.

24 One of them was buried in front of the altar,
In front of the altar,
The other was buried
Behind the altar.

25 Two fair sprigs of rosemary grew on their graves,
Two fair sprigs of rosemary,
Even they intertwined,
Even they intertwined.

26 Her mother went there, her mother went there,
To keen over her daughter,
Her mother went there
To keen over her daughter.

27 She tore a branch from the rosemary,
She tore a branch,
Thereupon a drop of blood
Poured straightaway out of it.

28 —Daughter, my dear daughter, Catherine Fodor,
Rise from your grave,
Rise, my dear daughter,
Rise from your grave!

29 —Mother, my mother, leave me in peace in my death,
Leave me in peace in my death,
If you did not let me live,
Leave me in peace in my death!

Versions

Twenty-seven versions and some sixteen fragments of the ballad have
been published. (There are several pieces connected to our ballad as
well as to 'The Maid who was Sold', through some motifs and formulas, but which cannot be regarded as versions of either of these ballads.
We shall deal with them when discussing the motifs of the ballad.)

A Csanádi-Vargyas, *Röpülj*, no. 59; =Bartók, *Das Ungarische Volkslied*, no. 34 *a*; =Kodály-
Vargyas, *MNpt*, no. 495 **B** F. Schram, *Magyar Népballadák*, no. 14 **C** Csanádi-Vargyas, *Röpülj*,
no. 60; =Ortutay, *Magyar Népköltészet*, II, no. 12 *b*; =*Ethnographia* (1907), 41 **D** *MNGY*, I,
no. 15 **E** Csanádi-Vargyas, *Röpülj*, no. 61; =*MNGY*, II, p. 3 **F** Csanádi-Vargyas, *Röpülj*,
no. 62; =*Ethnographia* (1907), 38 **G** Kálmány, *Szeged Népe*, II, no. 7 **H** Csanádi-Vargyas,
Röpülj, no. 63; =Berze-Nagy, *BMNh*, I, no. 21 **I** Csanádi-Vargyas, *Röpülj*, no. 64; =Ortutay,
Magyar Népköltészet, II, no. 12 *d*; =Berze-Nagy, *BMNh*, I, no. 22 **J** Ortutay, *Magyar Népköltészet*, II, no. 12 *a*; =Kriza (1956), no. 30; =*MNGY*, III, p. 419 **K** *MNGY*, I, no. 13 **L** *MNGY*,
I, no.17 **M** *Ethnographia*, **12**, 155 **N** *Ethnographia*, **18**, 40 **O** Kálmány, *Szeged Népe*, II, no.
8 **P** *Ethnographia*, **18**, 108 **Q** *Ethnographia*, **18**, 109 **R** *MNYr*, **15**, 191 **S** Bartók, *Das
Ungarische Volkslied*, no. 161 **T** Berze-Nagy, *BMNh*, I, no. 37 **U** Kálmány, *Hagyaték*, II, no.
2 *a* **V** Kálmány, *Koszorúk*, II, no. 6 **W** Kálmány, *Koszorúk*, II, no. 5 **X** Berze-Nagy,
BMNh, I, no. 38 **Y** Berze-Nagy, *BMNh*, I, no. 36 **Z** Berze-Nagy, *BMNh*, I, no. 39 **AA**

Berze-Nagy, *BMNh*, I, no. 40   **BB** Kálmány, *Szeged Népe*, III, no. 2   **CC** Kálmány, *Hagyaték*, II, no. 2 *b* fragm.   **DD** *MNGY*, I, no. 14   **EE** *Ethnographia*, **18**, 39   **FF** *Ethnographia*, **23**, 355   **GG** *Ethnographia*, **26**, 310   **HH** *Ethnographia*, **13**, 273   **II** *MNGY*, I, no. 16   **JJ** *Ethnographia*, **22**, 50   **KK** Bartók, *Das Ungarische Volkslied*, no. 165   **LL** Kálmány, *Hagyaték*, II, no. 3 *c*   **MM** *Ethnographia*, **30**, 75   **NN** *Ethnographia*, **18**, 40   **OO** Domokos, *Moldvai Magyarság*, no. 100; =Domokos-Rajeczky, *Csángó Népzene*, no. 7   **PP** Domokos-Rajeczky, *Csángó Népzene*, II, no. 19 (2 fragments)   **QQ** Domokos-Rajeczky, *Csángó Népzene*, II, no. 28

Description of the ballad

I. The suspicious mother asks her daughter to explain why her skirt has become shorter in the front, longer at the back, why her slender waist has grown stout.

S, T, Y her green silk skirt; **X, OO** blue (silk) skirt; **FF** her apron; **J, AA** her shift has grown tighter; **DD** the mother addresses her daughter *you rascal daughter*. Some versions have passages previous to the mother's question: **E, CC, PP, QQ** *My God, my God, what can be the matter with me? | Three ells of ribbon is not enough to girdle me! | Hitherto I used to take only one: I used to tie it with a bow, | Now I have taken three: I still could not tie it with a bow* (**PP, QQ** this passage is followed by formulas from 'The Great Mountain Robber' similar to its **B**, stanzas 12–13, and they end here). **U, V** *Kate, Kate, | Kate Szegvári, | I will have a round-hemmed skirt | Made for you, | A round-hemmed skirt, | And a pair of high-heeled boots* (**B, D, G, L, O** also have the idea that the skirt has just been made for her). **M** *Lady Landorvári had twelve daughters, | The twelfth daughter was Dora Landorvári; ||* **P, Q, S, T, Z** like **M**, but **P** Lady Undorvári; **Q** Lady Andorvári; **T, Z** Londonvári; **S** a widow...the twelfth daughter was Helen Landorvári; **N** *A king had twelve daughters, | The thirteenth was Dora Landorvári; ||* **R** like **N**, but *a queen had...;* **X–Z, FF–HH** have an obviously modern addition before the mother's question: *Good evening, brown-haired girl, | Whatever is the matter with you? | Perhaps the supper was not to your taste? | I have brought some wine with me, | Do drink some of it, | Console your sad heart with it; ||* **FF** adds *I will not drink your wine, | You yourself should drink it, | Since you did not spare | My fair maidenhood; ||* The daughter's name is: **G, O** Kate; **F, H, I, EE, NN** Catherine Fodor; **E, CC** Kate Gyöngyvári; **L, DD** Kate Hédervári; **BB** Kate Szedervári; **LL** Kate Édervári; **U–W** Kate Szegvári; **B** Barbara; **A** Barbara Angoli; **C** Barbara Hangoli; **D** Susan; **J, JJ** Susan Homlódi; **II** Susan Hollódi; **KK** Susan Homródi; **K, X** Dora; **M, N, R** Dora Landorvári; **Y** Dora Landervári; **T** Dora Londonvári; **Q** Dora Andorvári; **P** Dora Undorvári; **S** Helen Landorvár; **Z** Helen Londonvári; **OO** Sweet Lisbeth; **FF–HH** do not mention her name. **AA** has borrowed the introductory stanzas together with the heroine's name from another ballad: 'Mary Szücs' (Mary Furrier). *It is evening, it is evening, seven o'clock, | Every virgin maid hurries to the spinning-room. || Poor Mary Szücs | She would have gone too, | Had the sky not clouded | Above her. || It clouded, it clouded, | Darkness descended: | The last evening | of poor Mary Szücs. ||* The fragmentary **JJ–MM** start at incident VI.

II. At first the girl prevaricates: the tailor did not cut the skirt well, the dressmaker did not sew it well. However, when the mother repeats the question, she confesses that she is pregnant.

184

R when the mother repeats the question she adds: *Why are your tender breasts grown so rounded?* **G, M, O, T, A, V** the daughter elaborates the excuse: **U** *The scissors did not cut it well, | The thread did not sew it well, | Had gathered it unevenly; || **G** The needle did not pierce it well; **V** like the first two lines of* **U** *and* **G**; **A** *The chambermaid did not put it straight on me;* **O** *There was no servant to hold it straight;* **Y** *Small Nicholas King ruined it;* **S** she adds: *Alas, how he [the tailor] ruined it, may God punish him!* **Y, GG** are more subtle: the girl's words *May God punish him, who ruined it* can refer either to the lover or to the tailor; **A, K, N, P** the question is repeated three times, the daughter's second evasive answer being: **N** she has drunk cold water; **A** she has drunk river-water; **K, P** she has drunk of the Danube's water; **P** she has swallowed a water-insect; In several versions the mother guesses the truth before (**B, E, I, K, L, Q, V, BB, CC**) or without (**C, H, O, R, S, EE–HH, OO**) the daughter's confession; **H, I, L, Q, T, W, BB, EE–GG, OO** the mother answers: *Yes, the tailor cut it well, | Yes, the sempstress sewed it well! || **F** adds *May God punish him, who ruined it!* **V** the mother contradicts her daughter's excuses one by one: **B** *I was there myself, I myself had it cut round;* **K** *I did not ask you who cut it, who sewed it, | All I asked, what is the reason for...!* etc. | I did not ask you what you have eaten, what you have drunk, | All I asked was, what is the reason for...!* etc. || **E, CC** before her confession, the mother tells her daughter: *May God punish your wicked-self!* **GG, HH** *Your lover alone has caused the trouble;* **E, M, N, CC, DD** she has a seven months' burden from he who had asked her in marriage seven times (**CC** twice; **E, CC** during the Holy Week; **N, DD** during Carnival-time); **F, G** she has a seven months' burden; **I** eight months' burden; **B** thirteen weeks' burden; **W** two months' burden; **U, V** *I fell in love with John Ármádi | In the little flower garden, | Under the apple-tree; || **K, Q** *I prepared a green bed | For small Nicholas King, | I fell in love; || **BB** *I was walking in my garden, | I fell in love | With John Gyöngyvári, | My dear beloved. ||* She is made pregnant by: **A–C, L** young master Gyöngyvári; **G, I, BB, DD, EE** John Gyöngyvári; **E** John Árkádi; **U, V** John Ármádi; **W** John Ármándi; **D, H** young master Váradi; **O** John Váradi; **K, P, Q, S, T, Y** Small Nicholas King; **Z** as a result of a corruption from 'király' ('king') into 'Károly' ('Charles'): Small Charles Nicholas; **M, N, R** Small Prince Nicholas; **V, X, AA, CC** Prince Nicholas; **F** he has two names: George Hédervári and John György-vári; **J, FF–LL, NN** do not give his name; **OO** ends here.

III. The girl's reluctance in admitting the real state of affairs is indeed justified by her mother's reaction to it; she orders her to be put in prison or has her taken straight to the place of execution.

E, CC before the mother has her daughter taken away, she exclaims: *Daughter, my dear daughter, what a monstrous bitch have you grown into, | You have brought shame on me in my house! || **A, B** the mother summons constables to take her daughter away; **G** she asks her maids to take her away; **W** her servants; **L, S, T, X, Z, AA, BB, FF, GG** she summons headsmen; **U, V** the headsmen of Gyula; **E** soldiers; **EE** her own soldiers; **H, J, M, N, O–R, DD** she asks her coachman to place the horses between the shafts in order to take her daughter away; **N** place the eight horses between the shafts; **H** prepare the coach; **J** the mourning coach; **DD** the glass-coach; **M** the golden coach; **C** *take her, devils...;* **F, I, K, T** it is not explicit to whom the mother is giving the orders; **A, B, E–I, L, O, U, W, DD–FF, HH** the mother bids her daughter to be in prison (**G, I, H** in the bottom of the prison; **G** in the dark prison; **DD, EE** in the dark bottom of the prison; **FF, HH**, in the darkest prison; **L** in the deepest prison; **E, T** in the bottom of her own dark prison); **A, B, F, G, W, DD** she is not to eat, not to drink, and not to sleep (**G** till 10 o'clock on the following day; **A, B, F, W, DD** for thirteen days); **F** the mother adds: *On the thirteenth day I myself will go, I myself will go to witness her death;* **B** *on the thirteenth day | May she be beheaded; || **I** she is to be put into hard irons for fifteen days; **C, K, M, N, P–R** the mother has her daughter taken to the *beheading-bridge;*[1] **K, N, P–R** *to the beheading bridge, | to the rose-decked foot-bridge; || **J** to the rose-meadow, | to the place of execution; || **U, V** Take my daughter | In the condemned cell, | From the condemned cell | To the gallows-tree; || **BB** to the condemned cell; **S, T, V, X, AA** take her to the gallows-tree; **GG** *headsmen, take my daughter, cut off her head;* **D** the mother orders her coachman to bring the headsman to her house so that her daughter may be beheaded; **Q** the mother herself goes with the coachman to take her daughter to the beheading-bridge; **Y** does not have incident III.

IV. From the prison (**A, B, E–I, L, EE**) or before being taken to the place of execution (**C, D, K, M, N, P–V, X, Z, BB**) or before the prison (**W**), the girl writes a message to her love. She entreats a bird (in most cases a swallow) to take it to him, giving also some instructions how the letter ought to be delivered.

A, B, E–G, CC, DD her mother goes to the prison; **O** her father; **I, DD** her brother; **H** her sister; **A, B, O, DD** thirteen days later; **A, B, F, H, I, O, DD** a dialogue follows, according to the formula: **A, B** *Are you eating, or drinking, or are you sleeping, indeed ? | —I neither eat, nor drink, nor do I sleep, | Give me only one hour . . . etc. || **B** adds after the first two lines: *You did not take pity on my life, | do not care for my death; || **F, H, I, DD** the question is: *Are you alive, or are you dead?* the answer: **F** *Mother, dear mother, I am neither alive, nor dead, | All I do is to worship God; || **H** *I am still alive, by favour of God;* **I** cf. quoted above, p. 181; **DD** *I am alive as I am, in great misery;* **O** the father says: *Are you alive, my daughter, Kate? | I am speaking after your death. | —I am neither alive, nor dead, | All I do is to feel sorrow; || **E, F, G, CC** the girl has a dream in the prison, which is explained by her mother. **E, CC** *Daughter, dear daughter, my Kate Gyöngyvári, | Whatever did you dream during this long night? | —My yellow gloves were on my hands, | My red shoes were on my feet! || —Daughter, dear daughter, my Kate Gyöngyvári, | Your yellow glove: it is your passing, | Your red shoe: it is the shedding of your blood; || **CC** the version ends before the mother's explanation. **F** *I dreamt a dream last night, I dreamt: | I had a gown on me that was red up to the knees, || My yellow shoes were on my feet, | A two-tailed little whip was in my hands! || —Daughter, dear daughter, Catherine Fodor, | Your red gown: it is your red blood, || Your yellow shoe: it is your yellow colour, | Your two-tailed little whip: it is your two headsmen! || **G** *What did you dream, my daughter, | My dear daughter, Kate? || —I had a dream, mother: | I put my red boots on my feet, || I fastened my short coat lined with fox-fur | On my neck. || —Your red boot: | It is the headsman's sword, | Your short coat lined with fox-fur: | It is the gallows-tree! || —Stretch out, my mother, stretch out | Your right hand to me, | So that I may thank you | For your goodwill! || —I will not stretch out, | I will not stretch out, | My right hand! || —You were*

---

[1] 'Beheading-bridge' in Hungarian *fővevő híd; híd* is 'bridge' meaning both structure carrying road or path across a stream, etc., and 'scaffold or block'. I kept 'bridge' instead of 'scaffold' in order to convey the peculiar connotations of the Hungarian expression.

fortunate | *Not to have stretched out your hand to me,* | *I would have branded you* | *With the brand-mark of the town!* || —[*My*] *maids, seize her, take her* | *To the execution-bridge!* || **AA** she asks her mother to wait while she says goodbye to her flowers and asks her flowers to wither, to weep for her on the following morning at 8 o'clock; **A–C, E, K, M, N, P, Q, S, T, W, X** she asks her mother's permission to write a letter to her love; **A–C, K, P** she asks her to wait for an hour till she finishes her letter; **W** for one-half hour; **S, T** for half an hour or for a minute; **X** for an hour, for half an hour, or for a minute; **G** she asks her mother's maids, who are taking her to the place of execution, to slow down, so that she may write her letter; **I, DD** it is her brother who advises her to write; **H** her sister; **I** cf. quoted above on p. 181—she says she had no pen, no ink and no messenger; the brother answers: let her fingertips be her pen, her heavy tears her ink, the swallow her messenger; **DD** she has no ink, and no pen: let her red blood be her ink, let her tiny white nails be her pen, her fine tears her ink, and her fine palm (!) her letter; **E** she herself says it: *My thumb will be my pen,* | *My tears will be my ink!* || **F, EE** she prays to God that he may send one of his angels to her in the shape of a little bird, so that she may send her letter by it; **F, K, M, N, P, Q, R, W, BB, EE** she sends the letter by 'a bird'; **A, C, E, G–I, L, O, S, T, X, Y, Z, AA, DD** by a swallow; **V** by a stork; **E** *My raven, my dear raven, take my letter* | *To my pigeon, to John Árkádi!* || —*Do not send it by the raven, for the raven is such:* | *Wherever it finds a carrion, there it settles every time.* || —*My magpie, my dear magpie, take my letter* | *To my pigeon, to John Árkádi!* || —*Do not send it by the magpie either, for the magpie is a chatterer,* | *It will not keep very secret your secret verses!* || —*My swallow, my swallow, take my letter...etc.* **G, H, L, DD** are analogous to **E**, but ont in the form of a dialogue: **H** she will not send it by the magpie, for it is a chatterer and may blurt it out, neither will she send it by the crow, for it may find a carrion and leave the letter behind there, but the swallow is a swift bird, she will ask the swallow; **DD** she will not send it by the magpie, for it settles every time when it finds a carrion; **L** the magpie is a chatterer; **G** she will not send it by the stork, for it settles every time when it finds some bones; **B** she will not send it by the swallow, for it may blurt out her secret sins, but she will send it by the raven; **U** *Write* [?] *a letter, my stork, take it...;* **D** she sends it by her coachman.

There is a slight difference between the versions as far as the delivery of the letter is concerned: **C, H** if the bird arrives at noon, it should place the letter on the plate of her love; if in the evening, it should place it on his pillow; **C, W** add *I know when he will read it he will soak it with tears;* **I** in the morning, on his bedstead; at noon, on his plate; in the evening, on his table; **D** in the morning, in his window; at noon, on his plate; **K** if he is having his lunch, on his plate; if he is having his dinner, in his window; **S** at lunch, on his table; at dinner, on his plate; **M, P–R** if he is having his breakfast, in his cup; if lunch, on his plate; **R** adds: if dinner, on his table; **N** if breakfast, on his table; if lunch, on his plate; **B** if he is eating, on his plate; if he is drinking, in his glass; **DD** if he is in bed, on his pillow; if he is walking, on his right shoulder; if he is having his lunch, on his plate (this version ends here); **O** at lunch, on his plate; if he is walking, on his right shoulder; if he is lying, on his face; **E** if he is walking, on his shoulder; if he is at home, on his plate; **G** if he is walking, just let it drop in front of him; if he is having his lunch, on his plate; **L** at lunch, on his plate; if he is asleep, sit down on his right arm; **U** if he is walking, on his window; if he is lying, on his pillow; **V** if he is walking, on his window; sleeping, on his pillow; eating, on his plate; **W** in the morning, on his pillow; at lunch, on his plate; **X, Z** at lunch, on his plate; at dinner, on his pillow; **AA** in bed, on his pillow; at lunch, on his plate; **Y** sleeping, on his pillow; at lunch, on his plate; **F** *when you arrive, fly on his window, place it on his plate;* **T** at lunch, on his plate; **A, BB** do not have the instructions. **FF–HH** have substituted a passage from 'The Maid who was Sold' for incident IV: the girl asks her mother to give her leave to see once more her clothes and her flowers, she asks her clothes to drop on the ground, her flowers to wither, etc. (cf. 'The Maid who was Sold', motif XIX). These three fragments end here. **FF** ends with a stanza borrowed from a folk-song: *My courtyard, my courtyard,* | *My two tender arms* | *Shall sweep you no more!* | *In the middle of my courtyard* | *There is a golden apple-tree,* | *In the middle* [?] *of it* | *There is golden colt,* | *Let us mount on it,* | *Let us wander away on it* (Gy. Ortutay, *Magyar Népköltészet*, I, 270) || **J, II– NN** do not have incident IV.

V. Having received the message from his love, the young man orders his coachman to harness his horses, and set off at once, anxious to arrive before it is too late.

B, D, G–I, K, M, O, P, Q, V, Z describe the scene when he receives the letter: **G–I, K, P, O** the swallow arrives at noon, places the letter on his plate; **M, Q** it arrives when he is having his breakfast, and places the letter on his plate; **B** it finds him asleep, and places it on his pillow; **O, M, Q** the bird reports that it has fulfilled the errand, though it is not explicit that it flies back to the girl in order to tell her this: e.g. **Q** *I reached him, when he was having his breakfast,* | *I placed it on his plate,* | *I greeted becomingly* | *Small Nicholas King* || **G–I** when he receives her letter, he lets his spoon drop; **H** adds: the tears start running from his eyes; **O** he cannot see it properly for tears; **L** the bird placed it on his shoulder, he read it with sorrow, he lamented bitterly; **D** *'Good day, good day,* | *Young Master Váradi,'* | *—Welcome to you, welcome* | *The servant of my love!* | *—Quickly, but quickly,* | *For her death!* || **D** before he orders his coachman to harness his horses, he exclaims: *It would be impossible* | *For the sky to look like this,* | *If my Susanne* | *Were lying dead!* || **C** *My coachman, my coachman, my swiftest coachman,* | *Place the six horses, the best ones, between the shafts,* | *Do you be a thunderbolt, and I the speeding light,* | *[So that] we may reach Barbara Hangoli alive!* || **F, W, N, S, R, BB** have six horses; like in **C** he does not care what happens to the horses, all he wants is to find her alive; **AA** his six swiftest horses; **N** adds, as an explanation to the coachman: her mother has just sent her to the execution bridge; **S, T, X, Z** add *Let us drive as fast as the wind, or as thought;* **E** he aids his coachman to place the horses between the shafts of the black mourning coach, for his love is just being taken to her *death-hour;* **K, P, Q** he orders his eight horses to be placed between the shafts, in order *to fetch* his love; **G, W, Z** he orders his swiftest steed to be prepared for him; **Z** his best horse, with golden bridle and silver halter; **H** he asks his coachman to take him to his beloved, to *the young Viennese damsel*, and the reciter adds in prose that he took a great deal of gold with him; **I, O** he rides alone to his love; **L** after he had ordered his coachman to place the horses between the shafts, he says: *May I rest in the dust under the gallows-tree;* **U, V** *The Master is walking, he is walking* [*up and down*] | *In his room,* | *His heart almost breaks* | *In his sad sorrow.* || *—My cook, my cook,* | *My dear cook,* | *Do not cook for myself any more,* | *But cook for yourself,* | *And for my coachman!* || *—My coachman, my coachman,* | *My dear coachman,* | *Harness the six horses* | *To the glass coach* | *In black and scarlet,* | *In silver harness!* || *My coachman, my coachman,* | *Drive on, my dear coachman,* | *The six horses will be yours,* | *And the silver harness!* ||

Z he also asks the cook not to cook for him; **V** instead of the last stanza of **U**, he asks his coachman to drive because he cannot see for his sorrow. Two horses die by the time they arrive; **A, B, J, M, II, JJ–NN** do not have the man's orders to prepare his horses; **Y** does not have incident V; **W** ends here.

VI. He goes straight to his sweetheart's house, and after greeting the mother demands to see her daughter. Now it is the mother's turn to palter with the truth (her daughter is in the garden, at the neighbours, etc.); ultimately, however, on the urging of the young man who could not find his beloved at any of these places, she has to confess the truth: she had just sent her daughter to the place of execution.

The evasive answers are:

A, B she is out in the little garden picking lilies of the valley, tying them into a sad chaplet, putting it on her head; **C** she is at the river Tisza washing handkerchiefs, she is picking lilies, she is laying the table in the room; **K** she is next door saying good-bye to her girl friends; she is in the garden picking roses, putting them into a silken scarf; **M** like the second answer in **K**; **R** like **M**, but it is a white scarf; **H** here the mother is a duches; there is a repetition of: *Good day, good day, Lady Duchess, | Do not return the greeting of the young Master of Váradi! ||* and at the end: *Return the greeting...etc.* The mother's answers in this version: *I have just sent her to the big gilded garden to the small gilded well, to the big gilded well;* **D** the mother is a duchess, as in **H**; she says that her daughter is in the top-chamber adorning herself, she is enjoying herself in the flower garden; **G** she is preparing the guest-bed; **P** she is next door saying good-bye to the neighbours; **Q** she is at the rose-decked footbridge picking flowers and tying them into a bunch, she is in the other room cleaning herself; **MM** she is in the wood picking lilies of the valley and tying them into a bunch, she is in the church at mass, she is in the inn to lay the table; **U, V** she is under the apple-tree sewing a coverlet for the baby; **LL** she is under the gold bush sewing a gold cushion; **J** the mother has just sent her to the rose garden to look at the flowers and enjoy herself, she has just sent her to the sea-shore to catch golden fish; **KK, II** like **J**, but **II** instead of golden fish, big fish; **KK** instead of sea, Danube; **JJ** she has just sent her to the bank of the Maros to catch golden fish and enjoy herself; **S, T, Z** she is at the river washing her feet and consoling herself; in the little garden picking flowers and tying them into a chaplet; next door with her girl-friends; **Y** like the first two answers of **S, T, Z**; **AA** she is in the little garden, watering flowers; she is at the little well washing her white feet, at the river washing her white feet; she is in the wood picking lilies of the valley to console herself.

In **J, II, KK** there is a dialogue between the young man and the little gardener-boy and sailor-boy: **J** *Good day, good day, you little gardener-boy! | Where is she, where is Susanne Homlodi? | —I do not know, I have not seen her, yesterday, Ai! | she was still here! || ...—Good day, good day, you little sailor-boy! | Where is she, where is Susanne Homlodi? | —I do not know, I have not seen her, yesterday, Ai! | she was still here! ||* **JJ** like **J**, but the first question is put to the mother, and it is she who answers: *I have not seen her, yesterday she was still here, weeding the garden.* The mother's admission of the truth: **II, J** she has just sent her to the rose meadow, to the place of execution; **M, Q**, she has just sent her to the *beheading-bridge*; **K, P** she is at the *beheading-bridge* on the little rose-decked foot-bridge; **G** they are just taking her to the execution-hill; **KK** she has just been taken to the flower-meadow, to the headsman, so that they may bury her in the black earth; **H** she has just sent her to the headsman; **LL** she has just been taken to the beheading-chair; **JJ** she has just sent her to the headsman, so that he may take her blood into the lime-bucket (cp. 'Clement Mason'); **Z** she is in the cellar, swimming in blood; **Y**, **AA** in her room, in the black coffin; **A**, **B** she is in the room, on the black bier; **MM** lying in the room on the black bed; **S** she is laid out in the room on a green silken cushion; **D**, **R**, **U**, **V** the mother's evasive answers are not followed by her admitting the truth; **C**, **T** she does not say explicitly that her daughter is dead: *She is sleeping in her room, resting in her bed;* **T** she is in her room, in her bed; **J** the young man exclaims after the mother's confession: *Oh, you pagan mother, why have you had her beheaded? | You have buried my body in the same grave as hers! ||* The formula: *Why do I struggle to deny it* etc. occurs in **A–C, J, K, M, P, Q, S, T, Y, Z, AA, KK, LL, MM; E, F, I, L, O, N, U, W, BB** he does not go to the mother's house; **X** there is no dialogue between him and the mother.

VII. The young man goes to the place of execution, and with these words: *Let my blood and your blood run together in one stream, | Let my body and your body rest together in one grave; | Let my soul and your soul worship together the same God ||* he kills himself next to his beloved.

F, **U**, **V** on his way to the place of execution, he beholds a crowd: **F** *My dear good friends, what sort of crowd is this? | What sort of crowd is this dark crowd? | —They are just taking Catherine Fodor to kill her! | —Mother, mother dear, Mistress Peter Sár-Fodor, | You have had your daughter killed, and me after her! ||* **U**, **V** *Good morning, good morning, my dear good man,* [**V** *my dear old man*] *| What crowd is there | Beyond the city? | —A girl is being executed: | Kate Szegvári! || —My coachman, my coachman, | Drive on, my dear coachman! | The six horses will be yours, | So will be the glass coach, | And the silver harness! | By the time they arrived | They had only two horses left alive. ||* **W** they meet an old man: *For whom are the bells tolling? | —For your beloved, Kate Szegvári; ||* **BB** when they arrive she has just been executed. He kills himself. **G**, **LL** he orders his coachman to drive to the place of execution; **J**, **Q**, **II–KK** he greets the headsman: e.g. **J** *Good day, good day, you beheading headsman, | Where is she, where is Susan Homlódi? ||* **A**, **II–KK** he addresses him as *you little headsman-boy,* continuing the repetition of *you little gardener-boy* and *you little sailor-boy;* **J**, **Q**, **KK** the headsman answers: **J** *Here is she, here rests she, she sleeps peacefully;* **Q** *Why do I struggle to deny it? Her throat, I cut, her self: I buried;* here he answers the headsman: *Cut my throat as well, bury me as well;* **KK** *Hang me as well;* **H** has a similar passage, but the words are addressed to the mother: *Which headsman had her beheaded? | —The one from Sopron. | —If he had her beheaded, | Let him have me beheaded as well; ||* **N**, **R** *Lords, and young Masters, | Stay the sentence, | That harsh sentence; ||* **R** adds: *Let me repeat three Lord's Prayer | One for myself, | The other for my Dora, | The third for our little child; ||* **O** *'Wait, headsman, wait!' | The headsman did not wait, | He cut her throat; ||* **G** he asks the chambermaids to be more slow when performing the execution; **I** cf. quoted above, p. 182; **A–C, S, T, X, Y, AA, MM** according to incident VI, he does not go to the place of execution, but in the room, where his beloved lies dead: *He goes into the room, | Snatches up his big knife, | Points it against his heart; ||* **B** *He encircled her for the first time:*

he embraced her, He encircled her for the second time: he kissed her, He encircled her for the third time: he thrust his knife into himself; **L** has the same incremental repetition as **B**, but it is not made clear whether he is at her bedside, or at the place of execution.

The formula: *Let my blood and your blood...* etc. occurs in versions **A–E, G, H, J, K, L, N–R, T, U–X, AA, BB, II, JJ, KK, MM**; in **J, H, N, Q, II, KK** the wish is expressed to the headsman, and instead of *my...your* they have *my...her*.

Instead of *may my soul and your soul worship together the same God:* **H** *may serve the same God;* **U** *may my soul and your soul ascend to Heaven;* **Y** is corrupt: bodies in the same Heaven, souls in the same grave; **B, E, J, T, X, AA, II, KK** do not have this line; **J, II, KK** *Bury my body together with hers in the same grave, let my blood and her blood...* etc.; **KK** has *red blood*.

Instead of *let my body and her body:* **A** *may my heart and your heart;* **R** *let my heart interlock with your heart;* **G, N, Q** do not have this line; but **Q, N** add: *may our child ascend to Heaven;* **JJ** *Let my blood and her blood* etc. *Let my tears and her tears be covered by the same soil;* **AA** has instead of bodies *resting* together, bodies *withering* together; **D** *Flowers, flowers, fling yourself upon us, mourn over us!* | *My body to your body,* | *My blood to your blood,* | *May my soul and your soul* | *Rejoice in Heaven,* | *May the Lady Duchess* | *Be burnt in Hell.* || **O, T, G, V** add [the three latter in prose]: *Thereupon he fell on his sword, and died;* **C** adds *Have me buried in the front* [part] *of the church, Have Barbara Angoli buried in the middle part of the church, Have our little child buried on the top of the altar!* **K** the last line only; **M** like **C**, but *have me buried in the corner of the church;* **N** like **C**, but *I pray to God, may he give permission, that our child may be buried in front of the altar;* **P, R** like **C**, but *...our child in front of the altar;* **MM** adds *The bells are tolling,* | *But not for midday-meal time,* | *Now the faithful couple is being taken* | *To the big cemetery;* || **T, X** the mother laments that she has to bury two bodies and has to forget three; **W** before he kills himself, he casts a curse on the mother: *May God punish* | *That long street,* | *May God set the house of Lady Szegvári* | *On fire,* | *Because she had* | *her daughter Kate killed.* | *May the water in which she washes* | *Turn to blood,* | *May her towel* | *Go up in red flames,* | *May her knife with the white handle* | *May it injure her heart.* || **Z** has a unique ending: he kills the mother. *You wicked* [woman] *you thought that you had only one person killed* | *But you have murdered four, including yourself.* | *Your blood and my blood are running together in one stream* | *Your soul and my soul are departing together for eternal damnation;* || **A–E, G, J, L–N, P–Y, AA, II, JJ, KK, MM** end here.

VIII. The rest of the versions end with the sympathetic plants that spring from the lovers' grave, and by cursing the mother.

I as quoted above, has two sprigs of rosemary spring from their grave, the mother plucks a branch, whereupon a drop of blood pours out from the plant. She asks her daughter to rise from the grave, and hears her saying the conventional answer for such occasions: *Leave me in peace in my death, if you did not let me live, leave me in peace in my death;* **H** (the first two lines in prose): Two flowers sprang from the grave. The woman managed to pluck her son-in-law's, but she could not pluck her daughter's: *Out with you, pagan, out with you from the house of God!* | *—I have a home and a well laid table in Heaven!* | *—But yes, indeed, you have; of sharp razors and of iron filings* | *In the depths of hell!* | **K** Three sprigs of rosemary sprang up from the grave; the mother goes there to pluck them: *Go away you cursed mother,* | *You had not only one person killed,* | *You had murdered three;* || **LL** *They are taking the old mother,* | *She weeps over her* *daughter.* | *—Do not weep over her* | *You cursed mother...etc.,* like in **K**; **NN** *One of them was buried in front of the small altar,* | *The other was buried in front of the big altar.* | *A fair ivy and fair black grapes.* | *They start talking to her: —Go away, go away,* | *Do not pick me,* | *Do not mourn over me;* || **F** *One of them was buried towards East,* | *The other was buried towards West.* | *Two sprigs of rosemary sprang from the grave of one of them,* | *Two pairs of turtle-doves hatched out on the grave of the other;* || **O** *One of them was buried towards East,* | *The other was buried towards West.* | *They did not place* | *A cross on Kate's grave,* | *But they thrust a dead acacia-tree into it;* | *The tree came into leaf,* | *Her mother went that way,* | *She kept on folding* | *The leaves of the acacia-tree.* | *—Do not hurt, mother, do not hurt* | *This green acacia tree,* | *For you are damned,* | *But I have found salvation!* || **BB** *A little white pigeon* | *was hatched on one [of the graves],* | *A little white cock* | *was hatched on the man's grave.* || *The little white pigeon* | *keeps on cooing* | 'May the mother be cursed, be cursed,* | *Who does not give her daughter away* | *When she is asked for.*' || *The little white cock* | *crows:* | *May the mother be cursed, may the father be cursed,* | *Who do not let* | *Her sweetheart know about this.* || (The singer explained the last two lines in prose: had the parents let him know about her pregnancy, the wedding would have taken place.)

International variants

Detailed investigation into the motifs of the Hungarian ballad and its connection with international balladry has not yet been made.

Gy. Ortutay lists a number of international variants in his *Székely Népballadák* (p. 217) without committing himself to any suggestion concerning the dissemination of the ballad. E. Dános in *Magyar Népballadák* (p. 121) proposes that it reached Hungary through German transmission. The only grounds on which she bases this theory is the verbal similarity between lines 6–7 in the Hungarian version **A** (repeated in all versions except the fragmentary **BB–EE**), and the following lines in the German 'Ritter und Magd':

> Dein Röcklein ist von hinten, so lang,
> So kurz ist dirs von vorne.[1]

From among the many ballads dealing with the story of the fallen maiden, we shall examine only those which, to our mind, are in genetic relationship with the Hungarian ballad. There are two ballads which are of immediate interest to our purpose: 1. The Romance versions of 'Conde Claros de Montalvan'; 2. The German versions of 'Der König von Mailand'. The Scottish 'Lady Maisry' (Child, no. 65) will only be

---

[1] E. Dános' suggestion is somewhat ambiguous, since she quotes Gy. Ortutay's list of international variants which mentions two different German ballads ('Ritter und Magd' and 'Der König von Mailand'), but she writes: 'It seems that the ballad reached Hungary through German transmission, this is indicated by the close resemblance between certain lines of the Hungarian and *the* German ballad.' Then she quotes the lines printed above. These lines, however, occur in 'Ritter und Magd' only. For the description of the latter ballad, cf. our p. 195.

taken into consideration because of its tragic conclusion, which is found only in the Hungarian ballad, and in view of its relationship with the ballads mentioned above.

Romance versions of 'Conde Claros de Montalvan'

Romance versions: F. Wolf-C. Hofmann, *Primavera y Flor de Romances Castellanos* (Berlin, 1856), pp. 372 f., no. 191 (*W*); A. Garrett, *Romanceiro*, I (Livraria, 1949), no. 12 (*G*); F. P. Briz, *Cansons de la terra, cants populars catalans* (Barcelona-Paris, 1874), p. 39 (two versions), B_1, B_2; V. E. Hardung, *Romanceiro Portuguez*, I (Leipzig, 1877), no. 12 (five versions), H_1, H_2, H_3, H_4, H_5.

The beginning is variable (a bet, boasting, occasionally a love-tryst). The father (usually a King *W*, the king of France) notices (seldom: is informed) that his daughter is pregnant. The girl says that her dress was not well cut (B_1, H_3 she has drunk river water which made her swollen). The dressmakers (seldom: doctors, ladies-in-waiting, mid-wives) are summoned, they declare that there is nothing wrong with the dress, the lady is pregnant. She is put in prison (and is made to stand there in water up to her waist *W*, B_{1-2}), later to be burnt (seldom: to be killed H_2; beheaded H_3). She learns the news from ladies and gentle-men (H_2 from a young cousin; *G*, H_1 the father tells her) who visit her in the prison. She asks for a messenger to go to her beloved with a letter; she does not pity herself but the royal blood under her heart. (B_2 nuns give her paper and pen, she writes with the blood of her tongue.) A page (or a bird B_2, H_2; seldom: a young cousin H_3) takes the letter (B_2, $H_{1,4}$ she gives instructions concerning the delivery of the letter) and runs a great distance in a short time. As her beloved reads the letter he weeps (*G* his tears blind him; B_1 he weeps blood) and orders his horse to be saddled ($H_{1,4}$ his best horse; B_1 the one which flies). He puts on a monk's habit (occasionally on his mother's advice $H_{2,3}$) in a cloister where he prepares himself. (*G* on his arrival in the cloister he hears bells tolling, asks the monks for whom they toll, and is informed that it is for his beloved.) He stops the procession or the process of the execution and asks permission as a confessor to go to the girl. He asks her with whom she had sinned, she tells his own name only. He asks for a kiss under the secrecy of the confession; she will kiss no one else but her beloved. At this point he allows himself to be recognised, and rides away with her (*W* not before killing the knight to whom she had been promised away, in a duel).

'Der König von Mailand'

Version S. V. Schimurski, 'Die Ballade vom König von Mailand in den Wolga-Kolonien', *Jahr-buch f. Volksliedforschung* (1928), I, 160. (This is the version Schimurski publishes in full text, and marks as version *W*. To avoid confusion with the Romance version *W*, I refer to it as *S*.)

Version *A* Erk-Böhme, *Deutscher Liederhort* (Leipzig, 1894), no. 97.
Version *B* Swiss version: Stutz, *Gemälde aus dem Volksleben in zürcherischer Mundart*, III (Zürich, 1878), 24–8.
V. Schimurski gives a detailed description and analysis of the 'König von Mailand' in the article cited above; he also describes the Romance versions. I have adopted his description in both cases, inserting references which are significant from the Hungarian ballad's point of view.

There is a long exposition (a Prince, or the King of Milan, a Knight from Milan visits another Prince, and falls in love with his daughter, whose beauty is duly described; a nocturnal rendezvous follows, and the Prince's promise to return to her in forty weeks' time).

The girl becomes pregnant (*A* she tells her brother about it, and both brother and sister offer assistance). She gives birth to a son. The mother learns the news (*B* both parents hear the child crying; *A* the mother overhears a conversation between two women about the beauty of the child, but reports to the father that the child is ugly and looks like the devil).

The mother orders her daughter to be hung by Friday (*A* the misinformed father asks his neighbours' help in building the gallows: the daughter will be hung and the child will be drowned; *B* the father will have his daughter beheaded and her son sunk in the sea).

The brother informs her (not in *B*) about the cruel decision. The girl asks for a messenger who would bring her letter to the King of Milan (*S* it is the brother who advises her to write; *A* she asks for ink and pen; *S*, *B* there is no ink, she cuts her finger and writes with blood). The brother offers himself to take the letter (*B* a quick messenger takes it), and delivers it after some complications (*S* he meets the Prince halfway, but is not recognised at first; *A* a servant withholds him from entering the Palace). When the Prince reads the letter he cries (*B* he becomes pale), orders his horse to be saddled (not in *S*) and sets off for the journey. On Friday (*B* on the third day) they lead the girl to the gallows together with her child (*A* the child is going to be drowned). *W* she asks her father, mother, sister, brother, everybody present, to save her child, but it is the mother who answers every request, ordering the hangman to hang them both. (*A* she asks the hangman to wait a little because she hears a rider coming quickly, perhaps it is her lover; the hangman waits till he arrives; *B* she sees a rider on the high road). The Prince arrives, he greets everybody present, takes the girl and the child and rides away with them. (*A* he kills the mother with his sword, and would heartily kill the father as well; *S* he curses the mother, to go to Hell, he wishes the father to ascend in Heaven, and everlasting happiness for his brother-in-law. *A*, *B* have an epilogue: *A* half a year later the king gives a feast, he would like to invite the girl's father, his wife advises him against it, but he thinks that the angry father should be forgiven; *B* after seven years a beggar comes to their house, is recognised as her father, and she forgives him.)

'Ritter und Magd'

Versions *A-E*, Erk-Böhme, *Deutscher Liederhort* (Leipzig, 1894), no. 110.

A Count seduces a maid at night, in the morning she weeps. The Count offers her a bridegroom and some money; she refuses, all she wants is to go home to her mother. On her arrival the mother greets her, and asks her what has happened to her skirt (cf. p. 83, the lines in question occur in all versions except *D*). The maid admits at once that she had 'played' with a nobleman, and is expecting a child. The mother advises her to keep this in secret, when the child is born they will drown it in the Rhine. She does not agree: they will write a letter to the Count instead. They offer her food and drink, she cannot eat or drink, she wants to lie in bed. During the night she dies in childbirth. The Count has a dream that she has died, orders his horse to be saddled, and sets off immediately to see her. On his arrival in the town, he hears the bells tolling and wonders what it can mean. (**E** he also sees men digging a grave in the churchyard and asks them for whom it is being made); as he proceeds he meets men in black carrying a bier. He stops them and asks them to uncover it; his beloved is lying there. He draws his sword, points it against his heart, and dies with the following words:

> Hab ich dir geben Angst und Pein,
> So will ich leiden Schmerzen.

(*B, C* he asks the men to bury him in the same grave with her.) Lilies spring up from their grave.

The following table relates the motifs and incidents of these international versions to the Hungarian ballad.

Hungarian	Romance versions		'Der König von Mailand'	'Ritter und Magd'
—	(expository stanzas)		yes	yes
Suspicion-Discovery				
1. Mother's suspicion aroused by the odd looks of her daughter's dress	1. yes (father's)	1.	—	1. yes 'verbal' similarity
2. The girl's evasive answers	2. yes	2.	—	2. —

Hungarian	Romance versions	'Der König von Mailand'	'Ritter und Magd'
Suspicion–Discovery (cont.)			
(a) the tailors did not cut it well	(a) yes		
(b) she drank river-water	(b) yes		
3. Her avowal: she is expecting a child	3. (tailors, etc., declare that she is with child)	3. (she confides in her brother and sister and asks for help. The baby is born; parents hear the child crying, etc.)	3. yes
Punishment			
1. Prison	1. yes	1. —	1. —
2. Later to be	2. (a) (W yes)	2. (a) (B yes)	2. —
(a) beheaded	(b) —	(b) yes	(for the sake of secrecy the child is going to be drowned: a suggestion)
(b) hung	(to be burnt)		
Message			
1. (Visitors in the prison):	1. yes	1. (brother goes to see her, but not in prison)	1. —
(a) (brother/sister's sympathy)	(a) (relatives', friends')	(a) (yes)	
(b) (brother advises her to write to her beloved)	(b) —	(b) (yes)	
(c) (mother's visit, her interpretation of the daughter's dream)	(c) —	(c) —	
2. There is no ink, no pen, she writes with blood or tears	2. (B_2 yes)	2. yes	2. —
3. Letter sent	3.	3.	3. —
(a) by bird	(a) (B_2, H_2 yes)	(a) —	(she intends to write)
(b) by a page	(b) yes	(b) (B yes) (brother takes it)	
4. Choice between the birds	4. —	4. —	4. —
5. Detailed instructions for the delivery of the letter	5. (yes)	5. —	5. —
Delivery of the letter			
1. (Reference to the instructions given in *Message*, 5)	1. (yes)	1. — (complications in delivering it)	1. —

	Hungarian	Romance versions	'Der König von Mailand'	'Ritter und Magd'

Delivery of the letter (cont.)

Hungarian	Romance versions	'Der König von Mailand'	'Ritter und Magd'
2. When the beloved reads the letter he cries	2. yes	2. yes	2. —
(a) (tears blind him)	(a) yes	(a) yes	
(b) (he lets his spoon drop)	(b) —	(b) —	
3. He orders his horse to be saddled and sets off at once	3. yes	3. yes	3. yes (he sets off on account of a premonitory dream)

Before his arrival at the place of execution

Hungarian	Romance versions	'Der König von Mailand'	'Ritter und Magd'
1. He goes to the mother's house	1. — (he disguises himself as a monk)	1. —	1. —
2. Mother's evasive answers	2. —	2. —	2. —
3. Mother's confession	3. —	3. —	3. —
4. (His anxiety increases when he sees a crowd from afar; he makes inquiries and is told that his beloved is being executed; **W** hears bells tolling)	4. (G hears bells tolling)	4. —	4. He hears bells tolling (sees men digging a grave), meets men carrying her bier

At the place of execution

Hungarian	Romance versions	'Der König von Mailand'	'Ritter und Magd'
1. (a) he greets the headsman, and asks where his beloved is	1. (a) —	1. (a) yes — (he greets everybody present)	1. (a) (stops the men who carry the bier)
(b) he asks him to stay sentence	(b) yes	(b) —	(b) —
2. He arrives too late, and cannot save her	2. — (he saves her)	2. (she asks the hangman to wait—he waits; he saves her)	2. He arrives too late; she is dead
3. He stabs himself to death with his knife	3. —	3. —	3. yes (with his sword)
4. The formula for dying	4. —	4. —	4. (a different formula)

Epilogue

Hungarian	Romance versions	'Der König von Mailand'	'Ritter und Magd'
1. Sympathetic plants, etc.	1. —	1. —	1. yes
2. Cursing the mother	2. —	2. yes (**A** killing her)	2. —

Placing these four sets of ballads side by side it is apparent that the Romance versions of 'Conde Claros' resemble most closely the Hungarian ballad:

1. Up to 'Before his arrival at the place of execution' the Romance ballad follows a similar structural pattern:

Parent's suspicion
Girl's evasive answer
Exposure/confession
Imprisonment and orders to put her to death
Visitors in the prison (only in three Hungarian versions)
Message to the beloved
His hasty preparations for the journey to rescue her on receiving her letter

2. It shares several motifs and details with the Hungarian ballad:

A. Motifs which do not occur in either of the German ballads:
Evasive answers: tailors, water
Letter sent by bird (only in two Romance versions)
Instructions for the delivery of the letter
The letter arrives when the Count is dining (one Romance version only)
His asking the executioners to 'stay the sentence' (two Romance and two Hungarian versions only)
B. Motifs which occur in the German ballads as well:
Suspicion aroused by the odd appearance of the girl's dress
When the beloved reads the letter he cries
He orders his (best) horse to be saddled

Motifs

Let us consider the more general traits in these agreements first.

I. The initial problem of the heroine's pregnancy, its discovery, her parent's order to put her to death, is so widespread, and is found in so many different types of international ballads—moreover, it is such a natural subject for ballads—that in order to trace the origin of 'The Dishonoured Maiden' we have to narrow the field of our investigations to those ballads which, *in addition* to these traits, have more individual connections with our ballad.

Of the three international ballads described above, 'Ritter und Magd' deals with a different situation (seduction, pregnancy, death in childbirth), so we may concentrate on 'Conde Claros' and on 'Der König von Mailand'.

II. The S.O.S. message to the beloved in desperate circumstances, his tears when reading the appeal to be rescued, his immediate orders to have his horse saddled, and his quick departure are also stock situations in ballads concerned with the lapse of the heroine, but are found in ballads belonging to other classes as well (e.g. Child, nos. 65, 66—letter to the parents, nos. 72, 91; 75, 87, 99, 221, 222, 240, 254 A). Again, this should warn us not to regard parallels to this sequence as decisive factors.

In view of the facts, however, that (a) it occurs in no other Hungarian ballad, and (b) that it is present in both 'Conde Claros' and 'Der König von Mailand', which are related to 'The Dishonoured Maiden' through several other motifs, it seems plausible that the Hungarian ballad adapted this pattern from one of these two ballads.

Furthermore, if we consider that the Romance versions share the most important structural points with the Hungarian ballad preceding this pattern, while in 'Der König von Mailand' there is no suspicion, no evasive answers and no imprisonment (also note, the child is born!), we may concede that the adaptation was made from the Romance ballad.

This is borne out if we turn our attention to the first item in the table, *Suspicion–Discovery*.

III. The first part of the Hungarian formula introducing the suspicion motif by the mother's reference to the odd appearance of the girl's dress is, as we have seen, closely paralleled in 'Ritter und Magd'. This 'verbal' resemblance may be incidental, since similar passages occur in numerous international ballads (cf. Child's list in the notes to no. 101). Besides, in 'The Dishonoured Maiden' it is in most versions accompanied by a second part of the stereotype 'Your fine, slender waist is growing fatter and fatter', which does not occur in 'Ritter und Magd'.

But even if we accept Dános' suggestion that the first part of the formula was borrowed from the latter ballad, we can, on no account, agree with her in regarding this correspondence as satisfactory evidence proving that 'Ritter und Magd' was the direct source of the Hungarian ballad. The small resemblance and the great difference between these two ballads is apparent. As we have mentioned before, 'Ritter und Magd' deals with a completely different situation (seduction-pregnancy-death in childbirth, seducer's suicide motivated by bad conscience). Although it shares certain 'wandering motifs' (lover's request to be buried in the same grave with the beloved, sympathetic plants) with 'The Dishonoured Maiden', neither the characters nor the incidents of these ballads are in any genuine sense alike. The mother's question concerning the girl's dress fails to evoke dramatic tension and has no further significance in the narrative of 'Ritter und Magd'.

On the other hand, the passage in question has a particular structural importance in the development of the Romance ballad: the reference to her dress prompts the girl to give an evasive answer blaming the tailors, who are summoned and declare that she is pregnant. Such treatment of this otherwise common motif is paralleled in the Hungarian ballad only, in which the question concerning the girl's dress is followed by her blaming the tailors (in twenty-eight versions), her final confession being substituted for the summoning of the tailors and her exposure by them. (Parallels to the tailor's announcement in 'Conde Claros' that there is nothing wrong with the dress can be found in the Hungarian versions **B, H, I, L, Q, W, X, Y,** in the mother's answer to her daughter's excuse.) This substitution was no doubt facilitated by the natural tendency of ballad tradition: in the Hungarian ballad the mother's repeated questions and the girl's evasive answers follow the pattern of triplicate incremental repetition, the third member providing for her climatic confession (cp. 'Edward', 'The Two Brothers', etc.).

IV. This brings us to the question of the girl's second evasive answer (preserved in four Hungarian versions) which figures in two versions of 'Conde Claros': she has drunk river-water which made her swollen. The full implications of this seemingly insignificant motif can be understood only if we turn our attention to another ballad of the Romance tradition, 'Dona Aldonca' (V. E. Hardung, *op. cit.* no. 12).

At the door of Dona Aldonca there is a stream of clean water. She, who drinks of it, becomes pregnant. Dona Aldonca sits at the table, her father expresses his suspicion that she is pregnant. Her answer is that the maids did not arrange her petticoat properly when they dressed her, whereupon the father orders her to burn the petticoat without delay. In the further development of the story there is no likeness to our class; 'Dona Aldonca' really belongs to another group, in which magic herbs, magic rivers, cause pregnancy. (Cf. 'Dona Ausenda', Hardung, *op. cit.* p. 180.)

In 'Dona Aldonca' the river is not used as an excuse, but it is treated as tragic reality, and the girl's words about the maids express rather genuine incredulity searching for a natural explanation than the concealment of guilt.

Since both 'Dona Aldonca' and 'Conde Claros' tell the tale of the heroine's pregnancy, it is not surprising that the river-motif found its way into the latter ballad. In version H_5 we have such a contaminated telling:

In Coimbra there is a clear fountain, she who drinks of it becomes pregnant. Dona Areira has drunk of it, her father makes the usual remark at the table about her dress, she blames the tailors, who, on their turn, declare her pregnancy. She is to be burnt, exclaims that all she cares for is the noble lineage in her womb, sends a letter to Don Carlos, etc.

Here the reference to the river is evidently incongruous with the rest of the story.

Versions B_1 and H_3 represent the next stage of the infiltration of the magic river motif into our class, where the motif is already fitted into the love story, being reduced to form part of the girl's evasive answers. To adapt this motif for her excuse was appropriate in the Romance versions of 'Conde Claros', since for the audience of 'Dona Aldonca', although the allusion to having drunk of a river did not actually disprove her pregnancy, at least it might have suggested her innocence of incontinence.

On the evidence of version H_5 (which leaves no doubt about the process of contamination with 'Dona Aldonca'), and bearing in mind that (1) from among the international parallels reference to the drinking water appears only in 'Conde Claros' and 'The Dishonoured Maiden', and (2) that the image of such magic river has no trace whatsoever in any other form of Hungarian traditional poetry (and without light from the Romance tradition the excuse is senseless and irrelevant in 'The Dishonoured Maiden'), we need not hesitate to grant that the Hungarian ballad affiliated this motif from 'Conde Claros', more particularly from versions similar to B_1 and H_3, where the motif was already reduced to form part of the girl's evasive answers.

The Hungarian version **A** is of special interest in supporting this evidence, and indicating that such contaminated versions of 'Conde Claros' must have existed in several forms and stages in the Romance tradition: it has the same excuse of having drunk river-water as B_1 and H_3 of 'Conde Claros', but it also has Dona Aldonca's reply to her father ('the chamber-maid has not put the dress straight on her')—a stage in the process of contamination which, to my knowledge, has not been preserved in the recorded Romance versions of 'Conde Claros'.

V. The rest of the motifs common to 'Conde Claros' and 'The Dishonoured Maiden' must also be set against the background of Hungarian oral tradition.

Thus, message sent by bird does not warrant necessary connection with the Romance ballad, as it is common ballad property, and is particularly popular in Hungarian folksongs and prisoner-ballads in which birds (usually a swallow or a raven) are invariably chosen to carry letters to the beloved (cf. Csanádi-Vargyas, *op. cit.* nos. 85, 87, 155; Gy. Ortutay, *Magyar Népköltészet*, I, pp. 216, 217, 219–27, 230, 234; II, pp. 151, 167, 168, 325).

It is remarkable how—probably owing to its popularity in folksongs

—the bird-messenger motif tends to introduce lyric elements into the ballads. In the prisoner ballads it is followed by the prisoner's lamentation, in our case by the fine passage of the girl's meditation to choose a suitable messenger from among the birds.[1]

VI. On the other hand, instructions for the delivery of the letter figure in twenty-six versions of 'The Dishonoured Maiden' but nowhere else in Hungarian balladry or folksongs, which indicates that parallels in 'Conde Claros' should be seriously taken into consideration. It occurs in two Romance versions, with the elements; if he is asleep, wake him up; if he is eating, do not let him finish it (H_1); and if you find him asleep, wake him up; if you find him at his window, give it to him (H_4).

> H_1 Se elle estiver a dormir
> Facam—no logo acordar,
> Se elle estiver a comer
> Nao o deixem acabar

> H_4 Se o achares a dormir
> Dexa—o primeiro acordar
> Se o achares a janella
> Cartas che vas entregar

It is not impossible that the original form of the fragmentary Romance B_2 also had a similar passage. This may be assumed by comparing the lines 'Quan de va arrivar alli, / Troba al compte que dinava' ('when [the bird] arrived it found the Count dining') to the Hungarian **G–I, K, P, O** (analogously **B, M, Q**) in which the equivalent passage (the bird arrived at noon, etc.) repeats word by word the instructions given to the bird in the preceding stanza.

Although the message is not sent from the prison in 'Der König von

---

[1] This trait might have much deeper roots in Hungarian tradition than meets the eye. There is an interesting resemblance between this motif as it occurs in a Hungarian folksong and in a passage from the Chinese 'Hang P'eng', a story told in prose with a great deal of rhymes (A. Waley, *Ballads and Stories from Tun-huang*, London, 1960, p. 57). 'She thought of giving it [her letter] to a man to take; but she was afraid of men's gossip. She thought of giving it to a bird, but the birds flew too high. She thought of giving it to the wind, but the wind was in empty space. "Letter" she said, "if my feelings have power, go straight to Han P'eng; but if they have not power, fall down amid the grass". Her feelings had power, and the letter went straight to Han P'eng.'

Hungarian folksong (Gy. Ortutay, *ibid.* I, p. 155): 'I would send it by my thrush, but it is a chatterer, / So it cannot take care of my secret lament. // I would send it by my bee, but it might find a field, / It might settle upon a flower to the liking of its heart, // It imbibes honey, the poor one, death pursues it, / Thus my secret sorrow might be left with it forever. // Blow away, good wind, blow away my sorrow, / Make you easier my woeful days, / Carry it where the wind blows, where the river flows below, / Carry it to the glass window of my beloved. // Even further blow it onto her bosom, / Onto her bosom, so that she may die with it...' // Further comparisons would be possible, but lie outside my competence.

Mailand' two incidents from the table (*Message* section) relate the latter to 'The Dishonoured Maiden'.

VII. The brother's (sister's) sympathy figures in three Hungarian versions. In **I, DD** the brother, in **H** the sister visits the girl in prison offering his/her sympathy; in **I, DD** the brother, in **H** the sister advises her to write to her beloved.

This motif obviously belongs to 'Der König von Mailand', in which the brother plays an important role: the girl confides in her brother and sister, asks for their help which is granted; it is her brother who informs her of their parents' decision to put her to death; he himself delivers the letter; and in version **S** it is the brother who advises her to write.

The structural conditions of the Hungarian ballad were suitable for the assimilation of this motif (imprisonment, visitors in prison, letter to the beloved); in fact, it is suggested in 'Conde Claros' as well (visitors' sympathy, H_3 her youngest cousin takes the letter). Since both ballads have the same theme and thus are particularly susceptible to contamination, moreover, as we have seen, they agree in the succeeding traits characteristic of this class (cf. II), the adaptation of this motif is readily understandable.

VIII. Writing the letter with blood (**DD**; or tears **E, H, I**), since there is no ink, is also a motif typical of 'Der König von Mailand':

S *Und als sie nach Feder und Tinte gritt,* | *Da fürwahr die Tinte nicht.* | *Sie schnitt sich in Finger, nein, ob's weh auch tut,* | *Und schrieb mit ihrem eignen Blut.* || *B Es haut sich in Finger und schrybt mit Blut.* (*A* has just 'Es heischt Dinte und Federe her'.)

Though this trait appears in one of the Romance versions as well (*B*₂ nuns give her paper and pen, she writes with the blood of her tongue), we find several reasons to believe that it was taken from the German ballad: (1) it occurs in all the three versions of 'The Dishonoured Maiden' which bring in the brother/sister on the influence of 'Der König von Mailand'; (2) with the exception of **E**, which does not have motif VII, these two motifs are closely connected in the Hungarian versions, as it is the brother (**H** sister) who advises her to write with blood or tears; (3) in the German ballad she cuts her *finger* and writes with blood; in all the four Hungarian versions reference is made to her finger, thumb, fingernails to be used for pen.

To write with tears instead of blood is a slight modification of the motif, probably due to the parallel situations in Hungarian *prisoner-songs* and ballads, in which tears are indispensable stage-property.

Stylistic evidence: (1) the sentimental style of this passage in the

German S version which Schimurski regards as the oldest of the German class; (2) its irrelevant occurrence in the Romance B_2 version with the incongruous reference to the nuns; (3) its prosaic treatment in the Hungarian versions (**H** 'Let your fine palms be your letter' has a particularly gruesome, Tom-Lehrerian quality) points to the fact that it was a subsequent insertion into the ballad. Since in three cases out of four this motif occurs together with the brother/sister's appearance in the Hungarian versions, we may presume that the adaptation of both of these motifs took place simultaneously, and at a later stage in the history of the Hungarian tradition. The facts that only four versions of 'The Dishonoured Maiden' bear marks of the influence of 'Der König von Mailand' and that neither of its motifs have any significance in the development of the Hungarian ballad also support this conclusion.

Considering the structural importance of the motifs common to the Hungarian ballad and 'Conde Claros', the frequency of these motifs in the Hungarian versions and their deep connections with the Romance tradition, compared with the absence of these motifs in the German ballads and the general or episodic nature of the motifs which they share with 'The Dishonoured Maiden', we may safely conclude that (1) the ballad could not have reached Hungary through German transmission, (2) the primary source of the Hungarian ballad was one of the Romance versions of 'Conde Claros' which (3) according to the structural and stylistic evidence was later influenced by the German ballad of 'Der König von Mailand' in certain variants.

There are, however, two characteristic differences between 'The Dishonoured Maiden' and both 'Conde Claros' and 'Der König von Mailand':

1. The Hungarian ballad starts 'in medias res', contrary to the lengthy exposition of 'Der König von Mailand' and 'Conde Claros'.

2. Both of these international versions differ sharply from 'The Dishonoured Maiden' in their happy ending and in the development of the story from the 'Before his arrival at the place of execution' section of our table onwards.

IX. *Other motifs.* Before proceeding to the further developments of the Hungarian ballad, we have to deal with yet another motif which belongs to the parts we have been discussing but does not occur in the international versions.

The mother's visit to the prison and the interpretation of her daughter's dream figure in **E, F, G, CC**. It is interesting to compare this motif with its presentation in Hungarian prisoner-songs.

In those songs as well as in the later Betyár-ballads, the visit of the prisoner's mother, her grief and anxiety for her son's life, expressed in dialogues, are indeed prominent motifs (cf., for example, Gy. Ortutay, *Magyar Népköltészet*, II, nos. 75 *b*, *c*, *h*, *l*; 107, 120, 123; also 155, 182–5, 191, 192; and Kálmány, *Hagyaték*, II, nos. 24, 32 *a*, 33).

A dream similar to our versions occurs in one of the older fragments of this type.

Mother, mother, mother, | My dear mother, | What a dream I had | In my last night's dream: | There were two ells of red cord | Around my neck, | There were two black ravens | Above my head! | —Confound, my son, | That dream of yours! | The two ells of red cord: | It is your red blood, | The two black ravens: | They are your two headsmen! (Csanádi-Vargyas, *op. cit.* no. 82.)

In the above song there is a reasonably close relationship between the factual report of the dream and the interpretation of it given by the mother. On the other hand, when one compares in **E–G**, **CC** the dream-descriptions with the mother's interpretations, one sees that the relationships are rather unreasonable (**E**, **CC** 'Your yellow gloves: it is your passing, your red shoes: the shedding of your blood'), and in the case of **G** quite absurd ('Your red boots: it is the headsman's sword, your short coat lined with fox-fur: it is the gallows-tree'). The reasons for these corruptions, I believe, are to be found within the context of the ballads themselves, that is, in the prisoner-song we have the picture of a compassionate mother visiting her son, and both son and mother are distressed by the ominous dream; in 'The Dishonoured Maiden' the mother's traditional visit to the prison happens under quite different circumstances. Here they are antagonists, the mother herself has ordered the imprisonment of her daughter, and in interpreting the girl's dream the mother seeks to confront her daughter with her already formed decision to have her executed. The importance of the scene rests here on the further manifestation of malice in the mother's character, in her gloating over her daughter, rather than on the superstitious aspects of the symbolic dream, so that the *actual* dream-content becomes less and less significant in comparison with the interpretation of the vengeful mother. This is supported by the fact that in the prisoner-song it is the prisoner, whereas in our versions **E**, **G**, **CC** it is the mother who introduces the question of the dream ('Daughter, my dear daughter, whatever did you dream', etc.).

It is not surprising therefore that the insignificance of the dream and the relative importance of the interpretation have ultimately led to a corruption of the dream-motifs and a consequent loss of coherence in their relationship. Version **F** seems to have preserved the original form of the dream; in the other three versions only its disconnected fragments occur with confused interpretation.

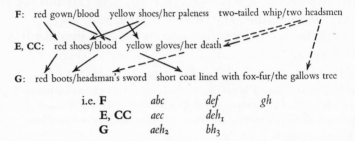

i.e.
F	*abc*	*def*	*gh*
E, CC	*aec*	*deh*$_1$	
G	*aeh*$_2$	*bh*$_3$	

Whether the incident was part of the original ballad, or was a later insertion is difficult to decide. The fact that it is not to be found in other ballads than 'The Dishonoured Maiden' would indicate that it was part of the original form of the ballad. On the other hand, bearing in mind that it has been preserved in four versions only and in most cases in a very corrupted fashion, and that contrary to the ballad tradition, the ominous dream has been deprived of its significance and serves merely to emphasise the mother's relation to her daughter, I am inclined to believe that it was a later insertion on the influence of prisoner-songs similar to the one quoted above. The lack of further evidence for the popularity of this motif (apart from the fragmentary prisoner-song) makes it impossible however to justify a decision in this matter.

X. In proceeding to discuss the progress of our ballad from the point of 'Before his arrival at the place of execution' of our table onwards, we are immediately confronted with a much involved case of local horizontal transmission.

The motifs of the lover's searching for his beloved and the mother's evasive answers do not figure in the international versions of this class, but this incident is also characteristic of class 4, of 'The Maid who was Sold'. Although this correspondence is constantly referred to in Hungarian ballad-scholarship, no attempt has previously been made to decide with which of these two ballads the motif was primarily associated.

The difficulties lie in the fact that it appears to be equally appropriate to both themes: in 'The Maid who was Sold' the evasive answers are given because the mother is afraid to admit to the mighty suitor that her daughter, whom she had sold to him as a bride, is dead; in 'The Dishonoured Maiden' the answers are given because the mother fears the revenge of the lover whose beloved she has just sent away to be executed.

The most important indication concerning the original place of this motif is to be sought, I believe, in the relationship of the *actual* evasive answers to the situation in which they occur in the two ballads, respectively.

In 'The Dishonoured Maiden' they seem to have been chosen entirely at random (e.g. she is enjoying herself in the garden, she is at the river washing her feet, she is laying the table, she is next door with her girl friends, etc.), whereas in 'The Maid who was Sold' (**O**, **P**, **R**, **Y**, similarly **M**) the answers, without exception, are strictly relevant to the situation: they all refer to the bride's presumed preparations for the wedding, and are in accordance with the traditional Hungarian wedding customs. They can be classified into four groups:

'The Maid who was Sold'

(*a*) **O**, **P**, **R** she is in the garden tying flowers into bunches to place them on the hat of the bridegroom or to present him with them. [It is customary for the bridegroom to wear flowers on his hat or in his buttonhole for the wedding]; **Y** she has gone to the mountain to collect pearls for her wreath; **M** she is saying good-bye to her flowers (cp. motif XIX of 'The Maid who was Sold').

(*b*) **O**, **P** she is at the river or brook, washing handkerchiefs to give to the bridegroom. (This refers to the custom of giving an embroidered scarf or handkerchief to the bridegroom, usually in exchange for the wedding or engagement ring; cf. 'Kate Kádár').

(*c*) **R**, **M** she is dressing herself in the house of the maidens (i.e. for the wedding); **M** and saying good-bye to her dresses and shoes (reference to the bride's leave-taking).

(*d*) **Y** she is preparing tables, drying plates at the inn (referring to the more recent custom of holding the wedding-feast at the local inn).

The relevance of these answers to the given situation in 'The Maid who was Sold' and the apparent arbitrariness of them in 'The Dishonoured Maiden' already suggests that the motif belongs to the former ballad originally. To test the validity of this conclusion we may re-examine the evasive answers of the latter ballad.

We find that taking as a starting-point the four elements of the answers in 'The Maid who was Sold', we can now easily classify the evasive answers of 'The Dishonoured Maiden':

(*a*) She is in the *garden* picking *flowers*, tying them into a *bunch*. **C** she is in the garden picking flowers, tying them into a bunch; **S**, **T**, **Y**, **Z** she is in the garden picking flowers, tying them into a chaplet; **A**, **B** she is in the garden picking lilies of the valley tying them into a sad chaplet; **AA**, **MM** she is in the wood picking lilies of the valley tying them into a bunch; **Q** she is at the rose-decked footbridge (!) tying roses into bunches; **K, M, R** she is in the garden picking roses into a silk scarf; **II** she is in the rose meadow (!) picking roses, enjoying herself; **J** she is in the garden looking at the roses, enjoying herself; **AA** she is in the garden watering the flowers; **H** she is in the golden garden; **U, V** she is in the garden under the apple-tree, sewing a coverlet for the baby; **LL** she is under the golden bush sewing a golden pillow.

(b) She is at the *river* or brook, *washing handkerchiefs*. **C** she is at the river washing handkerchiefs; **S, T, Y, Z, AA** she is at the river washing her feet; **AA** adds at the well washing her feet; **J, KK, JJ, II** she is at the sea-shore to catch a golden fish (or big fish); **H** she is at the golden well (big, small).

(c) She is *dressing* herself in the *house* of *maidens*. **D** she is in the top chamber adorning herself; **Q** she is in the other room cleaning herself; **K, P, S, T, Z** she is next door saying good-bye to her girl friends (**P** neighbours).

(d) She is *preparing* tables at the *inn*. **C** she is preparing the table; **MM** she is at the inn laying the table; **G** she is preparing the guest-bed.

In accordance with the story of our ballad, explicit references to the heroine's preparations for her wedding, which are the basis of the evasive answers of 'The Maid who was Sold', are naturally omitted. In 'The Dishonoured Maiden' the mother's evasive answers contain *only* the *scenes* of the preparation (e.g. garden, river) or the *actions* (picking flowers, washing) of those of the bride in 'The Maid who was Sold'; these scenes and actions evoke then new associations in 'The Dishonoured Maiden' which have no longer a bearing on Hungarian wedding customs.

Thus, e.g., the original garden/flowers/presenting them to the bridegroom becomes garden/flowers/enjoyment; the original river/washing handkershiefs/presenting them to the bridegroom becomes river/washing her feet, or river/[water]/well, or river/[enjoyment]/gold fish, gold fish/golden well/golden garden, etc.

Versions **A, B, S, Y, AA, MM**, analogously **C, T**, leave no doubt of the influence of 'The Maid who was Sold', since the mother's final confession (her daughter is lying dead in the other room) is in accordance with the latter ballad but is definitely incompatible with 'The Dishonoured Maiden' in which she has been sent away to be executed.

Some other considerations also support the conclusion that the evasive answers belonged to 'The Maid who was Sold' primarily. In this ballad the bridegroom's appearance in the mother's house is perfectly well accounted for by the fact that he goes there in order to fetch his bride. In 'The Dishonoured Maiden' it is not inevitable for the young man to search for his beloved in the mother's house, since her letter was supposed to inform him that she was either kept in prison or had been taken to the place of execution. Consequently, reason should direct him not to the mother's house but rather to the place of execution, as it actually does in versions **E, F, I, L, O, N, U, BB**, as well as in 'Conde Claros' and 'Der König von Mailand'.

Psychological factors should also be remembered: the mother's evasive answers (especially since those refer to her daughter's preparations for the wedding) may sound plausible for a bridegroom who is merely impatient to fetch his bride but not suspecting her death, whereas in 'The Dishonoured Maiden' it is rather unconvincing that the young man, who has wasted no time in hastening to rescue his beloved on receiving her desperate message and who is anxious for her very life, should believe the answers of the mother who pretends that there is nothing out of order with her daughter or with her relationship with her (e.g. 'I have just sent her to the rose garden to look at the flowers', or 'to the sea-shore to catch a gold fish'), and that he should be tricked into going to search for her at various places where she is supposed to 'enjoy' herself.[1]

XI. The passage in our versions **U, V**, in which the lover wishes to know the reason why a crowd has gathered beyond the city and is told that it is for the execution of his beloved, is inserted into the description of the lover's ride to the place of execution and is part of the sequence discussed in motif II.[2] It may be compared to the motif of the ominous sound of bells, which serves to heighten the suspense in many international ballads (e.g. Child, nos. 75, 76, 84, 85). The question: for whom they are tolling, and the answer: for the beloved (**F, U, V, W**), are characteristic of ballads which belong to Child, no. 75, and to those in which the lover feigns death (cf. Child, notes to nos. 75, 25, with references to the international parallels). This motif occurs also in 'The

---

[1] The contamination of the 'The Dishonoured Maiden' with 'The Maid who was Sold' at this point of the ballad can probably account for the further infusion of details/motifs from one ballad to the other. Thus, (1) the *heroine's name*: cp. Catherine Fodor, Fodori, Bodor in 'The Maid who was Sold', **B, D, A**, and Catherine Fodor in 'The Dishonoured Maiden', **F, H, I, EE, NN**; Catherine Gyöngyvári in 'The Maid who was Sold', **E,** and 'The Dishonoured Maiden', **E, CC**; the *hero's name*: Gyöngyvári in 'The Dishonoured Maiden', **A–C, G, I, L, BB, DD, EE**; Barbara (with different surnames) in 'The Maid who was Sold', **N, U**, and in our ballad **A, B, C**; (2) the motif characteristic to 'The Maid who was Sold', motif IV (i.e. the heroine saying good-bye to her flowers, garden, etc.), occurs in our ballad, versions **AA, FF, GG, HH**; (3) the motif of the sympathetic plants, the curse, and the suicide-formula appears in 'The Maid who was Sold', version **D**, although in a corrupted form: the mother *plants* lilies on her daughter's grave, but it is not the plant that speaks, and the suicide-formula occurs without the suicide; version **Y** of 'The Maid who was Sold' has the suicide-formula and the suicide.

[2] The succeeding passage in versions **U, V** (the promising of the horses, the coach, and the silver harness to the coachman if he drives fast) is taken from 'Kate Kádár'. The last two lines of this stanza in **U, V** ('By the time they arrived, they had only two horses left') is paralleled in 'Lady Maisry', *B, C, E, F*, in which the knight exhausts three horses in order to arrive at the place of execution in good time: e.g. *F*: 'It's first he burst the bonny black, an syne the bonny broun, but the dapple-grey rade still away, till he cam to the toun.'

Maid who was Sold', version **E**; 'The Daughter of the Cruel King'; in 'Conde Claros', version *G*; and in 'Ritter und Magd'.

XII. The rest of the ballad follows the conventional ballad pattern of the lover who arrives only to find his beloved dead or dying, and commits suicide next to her body.

A similarity in details is to be noticed between both 'Conde Claros' and 'Der König von Mailand' and our ballad in the scene of the lover's arrival at the place of execution, in his addressing/greeting the execu-tioner. This similarity, as well as the close resemblance between the passage in our versions **N**, **R** and 'Conde Claros' *G*, *H*₁ (Hungarian 'Stay the sentence, that bad sentence'; Romance *'Parem lá os da Justica, Justica de mao pezar'*) appear to be incidental, due to the parallel situation.

We have commented on the frequent suicide motif in Hungarian ballads (compared to the popular death from sorrow in English and Scottish ballads) in the discussion of 'The Daughter of the Cruel King' and 'Kate Kádár'. The tragic conclusion of 'The Dishonoured Maiden' is paralleled only in the Scottish 'Lady Maisry' from among this class. In the Scottish ballad the knight threatens with burning all those who were accomplices to the burning of his beloved, and is determined to throw himself into the flames in *A*, *F*.

XIII. The suicide-formula occurs in twenty-eight versions of 'The Dishonoured Maiden'. J. Berze-Nagy has drawn attention to the fact that close parallels to this formula are repeated in those heroic epics and sagas which W. Radloff recorded at the end of the nineteenth century among a Turcic tribe the so-called 'Abakan'. (J. Berze-Nagy, *BMNh*, I, 219; Dr W. Radloff, *Proben der Volksliteratur der Türkischen Stämme Süd-Sibiriens*, St Petersburg, 1868, II. I am greatly indebted to Professor Resid Rahmeti Arat, Professor of Turcology at the University of Istanbul, who supplied me with the exact translation of the passages quoted from Radloff.) In these heroic epics the equivalent passages occur as stereotypes for the solemn oath-of-friendship pacts.

Examples:

1. When he dies let his soul be together with mine,
   When it flows let his blood flow together with mine.

   (Radloff, op. cit. nos. 2, II: 757–9)

2. When he dies let his bones be together with mine,
   When it flows let his blood flow together with mine.   (*Ibid.* no. 5, II: 1195–6)

3. When he dies our bones will be together,
   When it flows let our blood flow together.   (*Ibid.* no. 6, II: 434–5)

4. When I am in trouble you come to me,
    When you are in trouble I come to you.
    Let our dead bones together make a mountain,
    Let our shed blood flow together and make a river.   (*Ibid.* no. 19, 11: 1416–19)

5. When we die let our bones together make a mountain,
    When our blood flows let it flow together and make a river.

(*Ibid.* no. 21, 11: 739–40)

Elements of the formula in the 'Abakan' sagas:

(*a*) Let blood flow together (exx. 1–5) and make a river (exx. 4, 5);
(*b*) Let bones be together (exx. 2–5) and make a mountain (exx. 4, 5);
(*c*) Let souls be together (ex. 1).

Elements of the formula in 'The Dishonoured Maiden':

(*a*) Idea of blood flowing together as one stream: **A–E, G, H, J–L, N–R, T–X, Z★, AA, BB, II–KK, MM.**

(*b*) *Let my body and your body rest together in one grave:* **A★–E, H, J–L, O, P, R★, T–Y★, AA★, BB, II, KK, MM.**

(*c*) *Let my soul and your soul worship the same God together:* **A, C, D★, E, G, H★, K, L, N, O–R, U★, V, W, Y★, Z★, BB.**

(*d*) *Let my tears and her tears be covered by the same soil:* **JJ.**

★Variations: (*a*) **Z★** cf. p. 191. (*b*) **A★** *Let my heart and your heart...;* **R★** *Let my heart and your heart interlock;* **AA★** *wither* instead of *rest;* **Y★** corrupt: bodies in heaven, souls in grave. (*c*) **H★** *serve* instead of *worship;* **U★, Y,★ D★** ascend to heaven; **Z★** cf. (*a*); **Y** cf. (*b*).

The close agreement between the Hungarian and the 'Abakan' stereotypes indicate a common source, both are probably part of a common Turcic heritage. This would imply that in the formula of 'The Dishonoured Maiden' we have a relic of Hungarian oral tradition which may be dated back to the ninth century, before and during which period (according to ethnological and linguistic evidence) Hungarians were closely associated with Turcic tribes.

In the Hungarian formula the wording of (*b*) and (*c*) is fairly homogeneous and straightforward throughout the versions, whereas it is somewhat involved in (*a*).

With the exception of **D**, which has just 'My blood to your blood', all versions represent the idea of blood flowing together as one stream. In the versions of 'The Dishonoured Maiden' I have examined, this idea is presented in six different wordings (for **Z**, cf. p. 191), and there are some difficulties in rendering these accurately into English because the emphasis and the exact meaning of the Hungarian text is often ambiguous.

Thus:

1. *Vérem a véreddel egy patakot mosson* (**A, C, G, N, O, Q, U, V, W, BB**)
   'Let my blood and your blood make one stream [together]'
2. *Vérem a véreddel egy patakot folyjon* (**E**)
   'Let my blood and your blood run to make one stream [together]'
3. *Vérem a véreddel egy patakon folyjon* (**H, R**) ...*egy patakban*... (**K**)
   'Let my blood and your blood run together as one stream'
4. *Vérem a véreddel egy patakba folyjon* (**B, L, P, T, X, AA**) ...*patakba fusson* (**MM**)
   'Let my blood join the stream of your blood'
5. *Véremet vérével egy patak mossa el* (**I, II, JJ**)
   'Let the same stream bear my blood as her blood'
6. *Hogy a patak mossa mi piros vérünket* (**KK**)
   'So that the stream may wash away both our red blood'

We may observe that characteristic to the Hungarian formula is the association of blood with a running stream. From among the different wordings in the Hungarian versions 'Vérem a véreddel egy patakot mosson' (1) seems to have preserved the original idea: blood running together to *make* one stream, similar to the idea expressed in the 'Abakan' examples 4 and 5.

The ambiguity of our (5) is due to the unusual use of the verb *mos* in the Hungarian (1). *Mos*, literally 'wash', is employed there in the sense of *kimos, kiváj* = 'erode' (i.e. erode/make a stream-bed for itself). The singer of (5) must have remembered the original phrasing of (1) but could not make sense of the unusual employment of the verb *mos*, and so interpreted it as *elmos*,—'bear, bear away', leaving it ambiguous in the context whether the stream which is supposed to bear the hero's blood is the stream which was made by the running of his beloved's blood, or whether there was a stream nearby which should bear away both their blood. Version **KK** (6) has the verb *mos* in the sense of 'wash, wash away'. Here the divergence from the general idea of two streams of blood joining together is not even ambiguous, the stream which is to wash away the blood is definitely not identical with the stream of the lovers' blood.

Most probably the archetype of the Hungarian stereotype resembled the 'Abakan' parallels even more than the recorded passages of 'The Dishonoured Maiden'. The Hungarian formula must have lingered for centuries on the periphery of oral tradition till it was included in the ballad. During this time some of the original words and ideas were lost or faded in transmission, became imbued with new meaning according to the changes of the cultural environment, and were finally subjected to the influence of ballad tradition in order to suit the context of 'The Dishonoured Maiden'.

Examples:

'Let our soul worship the same God together' has definitely a Christian overtone in the context of our ballad, especially when placed alongside references to ascending, rejoicing in Heaven, obtaining salvation, etc.

The idea of blood flowing together and making one stream appears to be almost identical with the 'Abakan' 'Let our shed blood flow together and make a river', or 'When our blood flows let it flow together and make a river'. Yet, when examined in the context, it is revealed that there is a difference between the ideas behind them.

In the 'Abakan' sagas these are the words of a solemn oath. When translating them, Professor Arat emphasised that the bones are not supposed to make only a hill or a mound but explicitly a big mountain; the blood flowing together should not make merely a brook or stream, but a big river. This is deliberate, poetic exaggeration: the death of the heroes, the shedding of their blood is but an eventuality, the formula is to be taken as a metaphor to convey the magnificence and power of friendship and loyalty. In the Hungarian ballad the formula has no metaphorical quality: the words are uttered by the young lover before he commits suicide over the dead body of his beloved, death and the streams of running blood is reality, his words are meant to be taken literally. In this context 'stream' is appropriate, and 'river' would be out of place. In this way we find 'let...*bodies* rest together...' in the Hungarian formula, instead of the 'Abakan': 'let *bones* be together'. In the formation of this phrasing in the Hungarian formula we may also assume the influence of the prominent motif in international balladry: the lover's request to be buried in the same grave as the beloved.[1]

With respect to the possible original form of this element it deserves mentioning that a recently recorded version of our ballad has, according to L. Vargyas, the following formula: 'My blood to your blood / My bones to your bones' (*Ethnographia*, **71**, 4, p. 502).

XIV. The general features of the motifs of the lovers buried behind

---

[1] This request, however, remains unfulfilled in Hungarian balladry, in which lovers are always buried separately. Versions **C, M, N, P, R**, in which it is the young man's own wish to be buried in front of the church, etc., while his beloved should be placed in the middle of the church, is obviously a corruption due to this pattern. This passage is in contradiction with the suicide-formula (to be buried in the same grave) in **C, P, R**. Versions **N** and **R** get around this inconsistency: **N** has no second element of the formula, and **R** replaces it by 'may our hearts interlock'. The corruption of this passage is also shown by the additional line: 'Our little child [should be buried] on the top of the altar', a wish clearly incompatible with the story. This additional line (also present in **K**) has probably derived from the passage in **K, DD**: 'You had not only one [person] killed, / You had murdered three.'

and in front of the altar, sympathetic plants that spring up from their grave and intertwine, the mother's malice in plucking them and the curse of the flowers, were discussed in 'Kate Kádár'.

In 'The Dishonoured Maiden' another aspect of the curse-motif is revealed: compared to the international parallels it is substituted for the fearful revenge in 'Lady Maisry' and for the punishment of the mother (stabbing her to death) in version *A* of 'Der König von Mailand', and in our version **Z**.

The power of the curse, and the impression made by the speaking of the plant, is conveyed by the circumstance that it interrupts, and in most cases prevents, the mother from destroying the flowers. There are only two versions in which she manages to pluck them, and even in these versions she succeeds only partially (**I** she plucks one branch; **H** she plucks one of the plants).

The motif of the two pairs of turtle-doves that hatch out from the grave (version **F**), or a white pigeon and a white cock (**BB**), is popular in Romance ballads (cf. Child, notes to no. 7). L. Vargyas (*Ethnographia*, **71**, 2–3, p. 259) refers to another version of our ballad which has the same motif, in which two sprigs of rosemary spring up on one grave, on the other there is a sad turtle-dove. This motif occurs nowhere else in Hungarian balladry.

Folklore and custom

The primitive belief in metempsychosis manifests itself beyond the appearance of the sympathetic plants that speak and the birds on the grave in version **I**: when the mother hurts the plant, it starts bleeding.[1]

Version **O** refers to the belief familiar from the Tannhäuser-legend: dead tree comes into leaf as a sign of absolution. This belief was still current in Hungary at the time when the ballad was recorded. L. Kálmány, who discovered this version, notes that he was told of the case of an old sinful beggar who was not absolved. He thrust a dead branch into the mountain Radna, and watered it with the water of the river Maros, which he carried to the tree on his knees till it came into leaf as a sign of his absolution.[2]

---

[1] For a beautiful combination of the ideas and beliefs expressed in the suicide-formula, the sympathetic plants, the attempt to destroy them, the bleeding of the plant, birds on the grave, and the punishment of the wicked one who caused the lovers' death, see the passage of a Chinese folktale of 'Han P'eng' (A. Waley, *op. cit.* pp. 64–5).

[2] Also it was said that after 1849 they thrust a dead branch into the soil at Radna with the idea that when it came to leaf then Hungary would have a King. The tree came into leaf in the year of the coronation. The peasants waited for the return of Lajos Kossuth in the same fashion. The tree came into leaf, but he never returned. (L. Kálmány, *Szeged Népe*, II, p. 172.)

In our version this belief was blended with the motif of the sympathetic plants: the dead branch that has come into leaf has not sprung up from the girl's grave but was thrust into it instead of a grave-post; however, when the mother fumbles with its leaves, it is her dead daughter who talks to her.

The rather absurd passage in version **G** ('You were fortunate not to have stretched out your hand to me, I would have branded you with the brand-mark of the town') refers to the punishment current in the Middle Ages and later. The first Hungarian date for this punishment is to be found in St Stephen's (1000–38) first codification of Hungarian law, which decrees the branding of witches with the red-hot key of the church. The custom of the branding of criminals with the seal-mark of the county was recorded in Hungary as late as the end of the seventeenth century. (Data from 1678 in M. Kertész, *Szokás-mondás*, Budapest, 1922, p. 230.)

The connection with roses (rose meadow, rose gardens, etc.) with death occur in several Hungarian ballads. Thus, in the 'Great Mountain Robber', similar to our ballad, the place of execution is in the 'rose meadow'; in 'Balthasar Bátori' it is at the 'rose market'; in 'The Daughter-in-law who was Burnt to Death' the remnants of her body are hidden in the rose meadow, or rose garden; in 'Anna Bíró', the heroine is killed under a rose bush; 'Anna Betlen', when mortally wounded, claims to have received her wounds by the thorns of roses in the rose garden.

For want of historical or folkloristic data for roses being actually connected with the place (or a place) of execution in Hungary, we are restricted to make conjectures based on general folk-beliefs in order to explain this conception.

First of all we must bear in mind that the term 'rose' covers not only garden roses, but also briar or dog roses, etc., in folk tradition. Thus 'rose meadow', that is, a meadow in the outskirts of the village (the mother has to send the girl there by coach) full of wild-rose bushes, is indeed a likely place for executions (cp. 'Rosenlund' in Danish ballads).[1] Similarly, the scaffold itself, if not just a temporary one, could have been overgrown, 'rose-decked', with dog roses and the like. 'Rózsás *pallag*' ('rose-decked foot bridge') comes probably from

---

[1] Cp. 'Rosenlund' in Danish ballads: 'Her Thønne rider y rossens-lundt, / handt *bieder* den vilde hindt: / der møder hannem dvergens datter, / hun hviller sig under en lindt.' (*DGF*, ii, no. 34; also cf. *DGF*, ii, p. 106, st. 1; ii, p. 415, st. 15; *Danske Viser*, ed. Abrahamson, Nyerup, Rahbek, Kopenhague, 1812, iii, p. 363, st. 17; iv, p. 92, st. 52.)

the analogous association of 'pallag' with 'fővevő-híd' ('beheading-bridge', 'híd' there in the sense of 'scaffold'), 'pallag' being a synonym for 'híd' (in the sense of structure forming road or path over streams, rivers, etc.). This is suggested by the circumstance that the expression 'rózsás (kis) pallag' occurs in the text *always* after the expression 'fővevő-híd'. 'Pallag' may also come from 'parlag' ('parlag-pallag') as the result of the association with 'híd' as described above, 'parlag' being synonymous with 'mező' ('meadow') and meaning 'unculti-vated, unploughed land'—again an appropriate place for executions. Markets were also used for this purpose (cp. 'rose market' in 'Balthasar Bátori').

Furthermore, we must also consider the symbolic aspects of the con-nection between roses and death. In this respect, the motif is not speci-fically Hungarian. According to E. L. Backman (*Religious Dances in the Christian Church and in Popular Medicine*, London, 1952, p. 189), both in pagan and early Christian Germany roses had a symbolic connection with death. Roses were planted on both heathen and Christian graves; pre-Christian graves, churches and churchyards were known as 'rose gardens', and in Carinthia, Silesia and Styria this euphemism was preserved right up to the nineteenth century.

'During the Middle Ages', writes Backman, 'the symbolism of the rose became more and more associated with the Virgin Mary, who, enthroned in Paradise, was said to be sitting in a rose garden; in Renaissance pictures of the Madonna this is frequently her setting. The rose garden remained, however, simultaneously a symbol of the churchyard, of death and of the paradise achieved through death.' (Cp. the wish to rejoice in Heaven, and the Tannhäuser-motif in the Hungarian ballad.)

In one version of the 'Great Mountain Robber' we find 'meadow of blood' instead of 'rose meadow' as the place of execution. This substitution recalls the well known symbolism of roses springing up from the blood of slain victims (cf. Thompson, E. 631. o. 3. 1; also roses from the blood of the slain in the Wars of the Roses, A. 2656. 2).

Whether it was the symbolic implication of roses in connection with blood and death, or whether it was simply a descriptive passage to be taken literally, or else, the combination of both of these factors to which Hungarian ballads owe the 'rose meadow', 'rose garden', '(little) rose-decked footbridge' as the scene of execution, for the modern reader the effect is mainly one of a contrast between violent death and the implied beauty and peace of the surroundings—a feeling that inspired one of the earliest Spanish folksongs admired so much by F. G. Lorca:

Dentro del vergel | moriré, | dentro del rosal | matar ma han. | Yo me iba, mi madre, | las rosas coger, | hallara la muerte | dentro del vergel. | Yo me iba, mi madre, | las rosas cortar, | hallara la muerte | dentro del rosal. | Dentro del vergel | moriré, | dentro del rosal | matar me han.[1]

Date

Since we have no factual evidence concerning the date of the ballad, and since none of its motifs or incidents point to a definite historical period, we have to rely entirely on stylistic evidence, and on the conclusions we have drawn from comparing 'The Dishonoured Maiden' with the international parallels.

The pentatonic, recitative tunes of 'The Dishonoured Maiden' belong to the oldest group of Hungarian folksongs. Most of the versions are composed of rhymeless dodecasyllables. Parallelism ('the dressmaker did not cut it well, the sempstress did not sew it well'; instructions given to the bird, etc.) as well as the frequent use of incremental repetition (the girl's and mother's evasive answers and confession; choice of the bird messenger, etc.) are characteristic of most Hungarian ballads of the sixteenth and seventeenth centuries.

Another feature of 'The Dishonoured Maiden' also points to this date. In the Scottish ballad all members of the girl's family are responsible for burning her to death. In 'Conde Claros' it is the father who orders her to be burnt (a circumstance determined by the royal setting of the ballad); in 'Der König von Mailand' the girl's execution is ordered by both father and mother, but it is the mother who is to blame; in the Hungarian ballad it is solely the mother who is responsible for the heroine's death. The portrayal of the power of the mother is a characteristic feature of most Hungarian ballads dating from the sixteenth–seventeenth century (cp. 'Kate Kádár', 'The Maid who was Sold', 'The Maid who had been Cursed', 'The Daughter-in-law who was Burnt to Death', and also 'The Miraculous Dead', 'Fair Maid Julia', 'Ilona Budai', 'Lady Albert Nagy-Bihal', and 'The Poisoned John'.

Its contamination with 'The Maid who was Sold' would suggest

---

[1] Translated into prose by J. L. Gili, *Lorca* (The Penguin Poets, 1960), p. 135; included in Lorca's essay on the 'Duenda'. 'In the garden I shall die, in the rose-bush I shall be killed. I was going, dear mother, to pick some roses, I found death in the garden. I was going, dear mother, to cut some roses, I found death in the rose-bush. In the garden I shall die, in the rose-bush I shall be killed.'

that at the time 'The Dishonoured Maiden' became popular, the former ballad was already well known in Hungary.[1]

The international currency of ballads dealing with the story of a fallen maiden, the discovery of her pregnancy and her parents' order to put her to death, suggests that it belonged to the traditional stock of medieval minstrelsy. Their telling probably included certain stock situations and stylistic devices which occur also in ballads belonging to different classes, but which are characteristic of our class as well: that is, formulas referring to the odd appearance of the dress worn by the pregnant girl; letter sent to the beloved (by messenger or by bird); his tears when reading the letter; his immediate orders to have his horses saddled; his quick departure for the rescue; and his arrival at the place of execution.

Beyond these general traits, the international parallels of the Hungarian ballad have very little in common. The stories seem to have developed independently, according to the local Scottish, German, and Romance oral tradition, respectively. Each has some specific features not to be found among the versions of the other nations.

Thus, the Scottish ballad is distinct as regards the unanimous hatred of the girl's family against the 'English lord' whom she has chosen to marry, their preparation of the fire, burning her to death and the final threat of forthcoming blood-feud. The German ballad is distinct mainly in the circumstance that the child is born, and also in the motifs of the mother's intrigue against the child (i.e. 'Flore et Blanchfleur'-motif), the sympathy and active part of the girl's brother, her appeal to the members of her family and to the onlookers at the place of execution to save her child, and the happy ending due to the lover's arrival. The Romance ballads are distinct from the others in the motifs of the evasive answers given by the girl, the summoning of the tailors, the imprisonment of the girl, in the motifs of the lover's device to save her by disguising himself as a monk, his 'confessing' the girl, the test of her faithfulness, and the happy ending due to his ingenuity.

'The Dishonoured Maiden' contains all the elements which occur

---

[1] It is rather unfortunate that we have no linguistic data concerning the expression *fővevő-híd*, or any extensive study as regards the development of the customs and methods of execution in Hungary. All we know is that beheading was a customary punishment even in the middle of the eighteenth century (cf. the sentence of beheading at a witch-trial in 1755. A. Komáromy, *Magyarországi Boszorkányperek*, 1910, Budapest, p. 567). There is no recorded Hungarian law which empowers parents to have their children executed. According to Dr K. Demkó (*A felsőmagyarországi városok életéről a XV. és XVII. században*, Budapest, 1840, pp. 181–2) authorities put themselves willingly at the disposal of parents who wanted to have their children punished in the fifteenth to seventeenth centuries, but he gives no further references to this statement.

simultaneously in the international parallels. We have pointed out that beyond these general traits the Hungarian ballad follows a structural pattern similar to 'Conde Claros', and agrees with the Romance ballad in several details. Since there are no traces of the features common to the 'Conde Claros' and 'The Dishonoured Maiden' in any other international versions of this class (i.e. the girl's evasive answers, her excuse of having drunk river-water, the blaming of the tailors, her imprisonment; also the instructions given to the bird concerning the delivery of the letter) we have submitted that the original source of the Hungarian ballad is to be sought in one of the Romance versions of 'Conde Claros'.

The fact that in the further development of the story (following the lover's ride to the beloved) there is no resemblance between 'Conde Claros' and 'The Dishonoured Maiden' does not contradict the assumption of the genetic relationship between them.

The developments of the Hungarian ballad from this point onwards *bear no resemblance to any* of the international parallels, except for the very general agreement with the Scottish ballad in respect to the tragic ending. The concluding part of 'The Dishonoured Maiden' was assembled from different motifs gathered from three *Hungarian* sources: (1) dialogue between mother and the young man, mother's evasive answers, his searching for the girl: 'The Maid who was Sold'; (2) suicide-formula: ancient oral tradition; (3) lovers buried separately, sympathetic plants, etc.: 'Kate Kádár'. (With respect to this process, 'The Dishonoured Maiden' is not different from the international parallels: we have seen that all of the international versions have developed a conclusion of their own.)

Since the close agreement between 'Conde Claros' and our ballad (up to the point of the lover's disguise) leaves very little doubt about the Romance ballad being the source of 'The Dishonoured Maiden', we are left with two possible explanations. It could be that the Romance ending of the ballad did not become popular in Hungary, the lover's disguise, his testing the girl's loyalty being too fanciful and episodic, and altogether alien from Hungarian balladry. Alternatively, the ballad could have reached Hungary already in a truncated form. In both cases a substitution was needed for the completion of the story, which was eventually supplied by the adaptation of other Hungarian motifs as described above.

For the very reason that there are no other international versions which contain the motifs common to 'Conde Claros' and 'The Dishonoured Maiden', it is impossible to say exactly how and when the transmission of the Romance ballad took place. The ballad of 'Conde Claros' was certainly popular throughout Castilia, Catalonia and Portugal by the middle of the sixteenth century, and probably before that.

In lack of any further evidence we must be content to say that the ballad could have reached Hungary any time after this (i.e. after the middle of the sixteenth century) and (according to the evidence of the tune and the indications of the style, etc.) probably before the end of the seventeenth century.

Special Hungarian elements

The most important difference between 'The Dishonoured Maiden' and the international versions of this class concerns the beginning and the ending of the ballad.

The Hungarian ballad opens at the dramatic moment when the mother's suspicion is aroused. There is no exposition to relate the love affair which has led up to the situation (as in 'Conde Claros' and in 'Der König von Mailand').

Versions **E, M, N, CC, DD, BB** give some hints to the preceding events, that is, the father of the child has asked the girl in marriage several times. This, however, is included in the passage of the girl's confession, and it serves rather as a 'mitigating circumstance' for the lapse of the heroine than as a descriptive part.

Nevertheless, in some versions there are traces of the exposition of the international versions. In the introductory part of both 'Conde Claros' and 'Der König von Mailand' we are given a picture of a royal setting. In 'Conde Claros' the affair takes place in the house of the Emperor, in the German ballad the father is a Prince, and in both cases the beloved is usually a Prince himself or a King.

In 'The Dishonoured Maiden' the original royal setting has faded, but traces of it can be found in different parts of the ballad. Thus, in **N** the father of the girl is a king; in **R** her mother is a Queen; in **D, H** her mother is a Duchess; the name of the beloved is Small Nicholas King in versions **K, P, Q, S, T, Y**, or Small Prince Nicholas in versions **M, N, R**, Prince Nicholas in **V, X, AA, CC**, and he is referred to as 'the Prince' in **X, BB**, and as 'a Count' in **T**.

We have seen that, in the concluding part of the ballad, 'The Dishonoured Maiden' has no analogies in the international versions. It has been composed from several elements taken from different sources of Hungarian oral tradition. Some of these traits are motifs which occur in international balladry, although not in our class, for example, the lover's wish to be buried in the same grave as the beloved (in the suicide formula); lovers buried separately, sympathetic plants; attempt to destroy them. The rest of these motifs are specifically Hungarian: lover's questions, mother's evasive answers; his search for the girl; 'rose meadow' as the place of execution, etc.; suicide-formula (affected by the international motif, cf. preceding paragraph).

There are two incidents in the middle part of the ballad which are not to be found among the international tellings: the mother's visit in the prison, the girl's dream and its interpretation; and the lyric passage of the choice of the bird-messenger. The unusual employment of the traditional ominous dream-motif and its interpretation could also be described as a Hungarian element.

A characteristic feature of 'The Dishonoured Maiden' is the prominent use of threefold incremental repetitions:[1]

1. Mother's questions repeated three times; girl's evasive answers, her confession following the third question. (Parallelism [threefold repetitions] in the first answer: *The tailor did not cut it well,* | *The sempstress did not sew it well,* | *The needle did not pierce it well.*)

2. Three elements of the dream.

3. Incremental repetition of the writing of the letter with blood or tears (no ink, no paper, no pen).

4. Incremental repetition of the choice of the bird-messenger.

5. Instructions given to the bird (evening, noon, morning; or eating, sleeping, walking).

6. Mother's evasive answers and confession. (Thus sharp questions/evasive answers occur at two points of the ballad: at first in the dialogue between the mother and her daughter, when the mother is the questioner; secondly, between mother and the daughter's beloved when it is the mother who gives the evasive answers. It is interesting to note that despite the difference of source of the two sections, the eventual effect—in the *complete* ballad—of this reversal of the mother's role heightens the air of condemnation with which the mother's cruelty is regarded.) The young man's search for the girl at different places. Dialogue with the gardener, the sailor-boy, the executioner.

7. Threefold repetition in the suicide-formula. (**B, L** the additional stanza before the formula: *he encircled her at first, at second,* etc.).

8. Wish to be buried separately, behind and in front of the church, child on the top of the altar in some versions.

Some of these traits occur in the international parallels as well, but

---

[1] It was probably this feature of 'The Dishonoured Maiden' which misled W. J. Entwistle into regarding the Hungarian ballad as 'the Magyar representative of the Schlangenköchin' (*op. cit.* p. 276), i.e. the German version of 'Lord Randal'. The Hungarian ballad which is in fact related to 'Lord Randall' and to 'Schlangenköchin' is: 'The Poisoned John'.

only in the Hungarian ballad are they treated as parts of threefold incremental repetitions; thus:

1. The evasive answers occur in 'Conde Claros' but are not followed by the girl's confession; also the father's suspicion is not expressed in repetitions.

3. The motif occurs in 'Conde Claros' and in 'Der König von Mailand' but not as incremental repetition.

5. The repetition occurs in 'Conde Claros' but is not threefold.

7. Suicide-formula: elements in the 'Abakan' sagas, but there the formula consists of two elements.

The pressure of parallelism can be seen in (3) and (8), in which the elaboration of the motifs into a threefold repetition produces rather absurd (3) or incompatible (8) passages.

Here we have to draw attention to a group of six ballads recorded in the Lowland, which are composed entirely of elements taken from both 'The Maid who was Sold' and 'The Dishonoured Maiden' and are arranged under separate heading in Kálmány, *Hagyaték*, II (nos. 3 *a*, *b*, *c*, *d*, *e*, *f*). They consist merely of the dialogue between a young man searching for his beloved at her mother's house, the mother's evasive answers and final admission that she is dead, and the suicide with the suicide-formula of 'The Dishonoured Maiden'. They cannot be regarded as fragments of either the latter ballad or 'The Maid who was Sold' because the motifs are contaminated to such an extent that it is impossible to separate them.

The contamination can be summarised in the following:

1. The young man's appearance at the mother's house and his searching for the girl (both ballads).

2. He refers to the girl as *my bride* in 3 *c*, *d*, *f*; he is referred to as *the bridegroom* in 3 *e* ('Maid who was Sold').

3. On the other hand, it is clear that he *knows* and loves the girl, and that this affection was mutual ('Dishonoured Maiden').

4. The answers given by the mother: (*a*) she is in the garden/forest/next village picking flowers/roses/lilies of the valley/gilly-flowers tying them into a chaplet/sad chaplet in 3 *a*, *b*, *c*, *d*, *e* (both ballads); bunch for the bride in 3 *d* ('Maid who was Sold'). (*b*) she is in the kitchen/next village drying plates/laying tables (mostly 'Maid who was Sold').

5. Admission of the truth: she is lying dead in the other room/on her bed ('Maid who was Sold').

6. Suicide with the suicide-formula ('Dishonoured Maiden').[1]

---

[1] The suicide formula in these versions: 3 *a*—'My blood belongs to your blood, my heart belongs to your heart, so I take my leave now'; 3 *b*—like our **C**; 3 *c*—'Let my body and your body rest together in one grave, let my blood and your blood run together as one stream, let my soul and your soul ascend to Heaven together'; 3 *d*—'Let my blood and your blood make one

Occasionally a modernised explanation is added to the dialogue and suicide-formula in prose:

3 a—parents object to the marriage of the young lovers, they decide to commit suicide, the girl falls ill in her sorrow, the boy visits her, then the dialogue;

3 d—'Fair Mary left her fiancé because she found a wealthier suitor, this was the reason for the *murder*';

in verse:

3 f—(from the same folksong which was borrowed in version **U** of 'The Maid who was Sold'): *A white tower is seen | Of the black town, | There I can see my beloved, | Playing in the lap of someone else.*

In this way these six ballads exemplify a process which might be described as a sequence of motifs derived from the contamination of two ballads becoming a commonplace and as such serving as several independent ballads.

'ANNA BETLEN'

The tragic story of Anna Betlen, who loved the coachman of her brother's friend and had to pay with her life for it, is a semi-historical ballad. The particular importance of this ballad lies in the circumstance that it is the only piece in Hungarian balladry in which brother kills sister for unchastity—a practice which serves as a common theme for many English-Scottish as well as Scandinavian ballads.

Version **A**

Michael Sárosi, John Betlen
Were sitting at the same table,
They were eating, drinking together,
They were talking to each other.
Up and speaks[1] Michael Sárosi:
'Listen, my dear fellow,
Punish your young sister[2]
That she should not go to my stable
At night time,
She makes love with my coachman

---

stream together, let my body...', etc.; 3 e—'Let my blood join the stream of your blood, let my heart and your heart worship the same God together'; 3 f—'Let my blood flow away at the same time as your blood, let my soul fly away at the same time as your soul, let my body and your body...', etc.

[1] 'Up and speaks' literally means 'with words he says'; I have adapted the Scottish formula.

[2] 'Your young sister': *hugát*, i.e. 'the sister who is younger than you'. In Hungarian there are four distinct words for younger brother/sister—older brother/sister respectively.

And keeps waking my faithful steed.'
'Listen, my dear fellow,
My young sister is a chaste girl!'
Up and speaks Michael Sárosi:
'I will demonstrate to you her chastity
With the strength of my two arms,
With the blade of my bright sword.'
He hears the creaking of the gate,
The patter of high horseshoes,
The rustle of silk skirt.
At once he went to the stable,
To the stable-door.
Up and speaks he to the coachman:
'Open your door coachman!'
'I cannot open it, my dear master,
My faithful steed is loose,
If I opened the door
I know I could not catch it ever again.'
He gave such a kick to the door
It fell in two pieces straightaway.
Now there she was, Anna Betlen.
He hooked his sword into her,
The silk skirt was ripped,
Her red blood spurted forth.
Anna Betlen went home,
She lay down on her bed.
In the morning came her sister-in-law:
'What has happened, what has happened to you,
    Anna Betlen'
'Oh, what has happened, my dear sister-in-law!
I stepped into my paved garden,
I got caught in a rose bush,
The silk skirt was ripped,
The blood spurted forth at once,
I am covered with clotted blood from head to foot,
I myself am dying!'
'Listen you, Anna Betlen!
Stand out into your courtyard,
Pray to God
To forgive your sins.'
'My sister-in-law, my sister-in-law, my dear
    sister-in-law,
Let them wash me in sweet wine,
Let them cover me with soft cambric,
Let them send me to Kolozsvár,
Let it be an example for everyone
What is the fate of an orphan.

Versions

'Anna Betlen' is a very rare ballad; it has been preserved in three versions only, all from Transylvania.

A Csanádi-Vargyas, *Röpülj*, no. 28; = Ortutay, *Magyar Népköltészet*, II, no. 20; = *MNGy*, III, p. 18; = Kriza (1956), no. 31   **B** *Magyar Nyelvőr*, **34**, 110   **C** *Erdélyi Műzeum*, **23**, 49–51

Description of the ballad

I. John Betlen is asked by Michael Sárosi (**B** Michael Bíró; **C** Samuel Sárdi) to castigate his young sister who loves Sárosi's coachman, visits him at night in his stable and keeps disturbing Sárosi's steed. John Betlen does not believe Sárosi's accusation, and he offers him to prove the truth of his words with the 'strength of his two arms and with the blade of his sword'. (**B, C** these words are said by John Betlen; in these versions he does not doubt the truth of the other's words; **C** Betlen says he would punish his sister on the following morning.)

II. At night Sárosi hears the creaking of the gate, the patter of high horseshoes and the rustle of a silk skirt. He goes to his stable, asks his coachman to open the door. The coachman refuses to open the door on the pretext that the steed is loose, if he opened the door it would be impossible to catch the horse again. Sárosi kicks the door open, finds Anna Betlen in his stable: with his sword he tears her skirt and wounds her so that her blood spurts forth.

B we are not told whether he hears Anna approaching or not, the excuse of the coachman is: *I will open it straightaway, only let me put my trousers on;* instead of using his sword, we have: *He hit Anna Betlen so hard | That her tender skin was torn, | Her red blood spurted forth.* || In version **C** we have a somewhat different course of events: it is John Betlen himself who investigates the matter, it is he who hears *the patter of red slippers, the swishing of a silk-skirt,* he speaks to the coachman in the person of his master, the coachman gives the same answer as in **A**. John Betlen kicks the door open, and, similar to **B**, he does not use his sword: *He beat Anna Betlen so hard, | That her yellow hair was torn out, | Her red blood spurted forth, | The red skirt was ripped.*

III. Anna goes home and lies down on her bed. When her sister-in-law questions her she gives an evasive answer: she got caught in a rose bush, that is the reason for her blood and for her torn skirt.

C this is elaborated: —*Anna, Anna, Anna Betlen, | Whatever has happened to you, Anna Betlen? | Are you accustomed to get up early in the morning | And walk in your rose garden? || —I am accustomed to get up early in the morning | And walk in my rose garden, | But the rose has injured me so much | That now I am lying in blood up to my knees. || I was walking in my rose garden, | I could not find the key of my chest, | I bent down to pick it up, | The* *rose bush caught me,* | *My yellow hair was torn out,* | *My red blood spurted forth,* | *The silk skirt was ripped.* || **B** her brother questions her as well, she repeats the answer given to her sister-in-law.

IV. Anna's excuse is, however, not much use. John Betlen bids his sister to go out into her courtyard (**C** in the middle of her courtyard where she should kneel down; **B** in front of her door), beg God to forgive her sins (**B** to beg God not to forsake her), then he cuts her head off (**B** he draws his sword and cuts her head off there and then). In version **A** we are not told explicitly that she is going to be beheaded. After John Betlen has asked her to go out into her courtyard and pray, she begs her sister-in-law to let her be washed in sweet wine, let her be covered with soft cambric, and send her to Kolozsvár, so that her case might be an example to everyone of an orphan's fate.

This motif occurs in version **C** as well, but after she has been beheaded. In this version it is her head that speaks:

Up and speaks her head: | —*Maidens, maidens, my maiden friends,* | *Take up my head,* | *Cover it with soft cambric,* | *Send it to Kolozsvár,* | *Place it up on the tower,* | *So that I may be an example for maidens!*

International variants

In its initial situation, central theme as well as in certain motifs and incidents 'Anna Betlen' represents a very general pattern. Nevertheless, the sequence of events, as narrated in 'Anna Betlen' is, as far as my knowledge goes, not found elsewhere in international balladry.

Motifs

I. Ballads with the central theme of sister killed by brother for unchastity have a world-wide currency (cf. Child, bibliography and notes to no. 64, for German and Scandinavian ballads; Child, no. 65, sisters killed by brothers and daughters, by parents for the same reason). In English and Scottish ballads, however, it is more common for the brothers to kill or wound to death their sister's beloved and thereby cause her death by sorrow (e.g. Child, nos. 7, 69, 214).

II. The introductory scene (brother/parents informed of maiden's unchastity, the brother's incredulity and his arrangements to investigate the matter) is a stock situation in balladry, especially in ballads dealing with a heroine who has just given birth to a child (Child, notes to no. 64); usually the informer is of lower rank. In Hungarian balladry, however, these traits do not occur elsewhere.

The introduction (sitting, drinking together) may be compared with the beginning of many English and Scottish ballads, e.g. Child, no. 88:

B *Young Johnstone and the young Colonel | Sat drinking at the wine, | 'O gin ye wad marry my sister | It's I wad marry thine.' ||* (Cp. also Child, nos. 58, 60, 72, 97, 214, 246.)

III. Delay in opening doors on some pretext is a stock situation in Hungarian ballads. It is found also in 'Barcsai', 'The Great Mountain Robber'.

IV. Man wounds girl found being unchaste so that girl's brother should recognise she is the girl in question is not paralleled in international balladry (except in very vague resemblances, as in 'The Twa Knights', Child, no. 268, and its parallels: seducer cuts off lady's finger to prove that he had won her).

V. Evasive answers given by wounded girl are met with in the Scottish 'The King's dochter Lady Jean' (Child, no. 52). *Examples:*

A: O sister, sister, mak my bed, | O the clean sheets and strae, | O sister, sister, mak my bed | Down in the parlour below! || Her father he came tripping down the stairs, | His steps they were fu slow: | 'I think, I think, Lady Jean,' he said | 'Ye're lying far ower low.' || O late yestreen, as I came hame | Down by yon castil wa, | O heavy, heavy was the stane | That on my brest did fa! || also in *B: When I came by the high churchyard | Heavy was the stain that bruised my heel, | ...that bruised my heart, | I'm afraid it shall neer heal.*

VI. The testament of the girl, wishing to have her body/head washed in sweet wine and covered with soft cambric, to be displayed on the tower, occurs in 'The Great Mountain Robber' and in 'The Three Orphans'. We have commented on it in the discussion of the latter ballad (only there it is her heart, or heart and liver, which is to be treated like this).

The head that speaks after being cut off in version **C** is probably the result of a misplacement of the formula. (It figures, however, in the German and Dutch versions of 'Heer Halewijn'.)

Folklore and custom

The particular tower of Kolozsvár mentioned in our ballad **C** was an especially appropriate place for displaying such tokens, because it was used as a prison for condemned criminals in the sixteenth–seventeenth century.

Date

According to P. Gyulai (*MNGy*, III, p. 430), the ballad dates from the reign of Michael Apafi, Prince of Transylvania (1662–90). F. Kanyaró (*Erdélyi Múzeum*, XXIII, pp. 49–51) agrees with Gyulai, and suggests that it was composed in the atmosphere of denominational dispute. He points out that the names Sárosi, Sárdi, Bíró belong to well established old Unitarian families in Transylvania, and submits that John Betlen in the ballad is identical with John Bethlen the historian (1613–78) known as Sallustius, the author of *Rerum Transylvanicarum libri quatuor* (1629–63), an ardent Catholic, a most influential baron in Transylvania, made Chancellor by Apafi. In Kanyaró's opinion, the ballad of 'Anna Betlen' was composed by Unitarian minstrels in order to ridicule John Bethlen, their most eminent, erudite opponent, by the spreading of this story, and in order to denounce the licentious life of the Catholic barons in power. He finds support for his assumption in the fact that the girl wishes to have her body/head displayed in Kolozsvár, the headquarters of Unitarians.

There are no definite data to establish Kanyaró's conclusions (not even for the existence of Anna Bethlen, or indeed of any sisters of John Bethlen Sallustius). Nevertheless, the historical names which occur in the ballad date the ballad at the suggested time, when the families in question were sufficiently well known in Transylvania to figure as main characters in the story.

The tune of 'Anna Betlen' has not been preserved .The lines are irregular octosyllables, with occasional suffix-rhymes. In the first stanza of version **A** (also in the second line of version **C**) we see certain traces of the stylistic devices characteristic of sixteenth–seventeenth century Hungarian minstrel literature, which, we might assume, was probably the original form of the ballad:

A stanza 1:

> Sárosi Mihály, Betlen János
> Egy asztalnál ülnek *vala*,
> Együtt esznek, isznak *vala*,
> Együtt beszélgetnek *vala*.

The monotonous repetition of the word *vala* ('was', 'had been') employed at the end of subsequent lines to substitute for rhymes, was typical of the rhymed chronicles composed by known authors, such as Sebastian Tinódi (d. 1556) and his contemporary Péter Ilosvai Selymes. This coincidence would also bear out giving the ballad an early date.

Special Hungarian elements

There are traces in 'Anna Betlen' which point to the individual minstrel-composer, whose personality is seldom felt in balladry. The personal touch is manifested in the developing of the story: even in ballads which are very much blended with folk-tale elements we do not find outsiders interfering with family matters in the fashion Michael Sárosi does in 'Anna Betlen'. It is also felt in details: whether or not the author was a Unitarian, he certainly couched Sárosi's complaint in terms calculated to ridicule the John Betlen of the ballad.

His complaint also reveals the character of Sárosi/Sárdi: it is not a malicious intrigue against the heroine (as would be natural in ballads) nor is it motivated by moral indignation (as Kanyaró would have us believe); the girl is infinitely less important for Sárosi than his love and care for his horse which is 'disturbed' or 'frightened' by her nightly visits. This attitude of treating the girl as an object with which one may do what one pleases (culminating in the stable-scene—N.B. the coachman remains unhurt) is not typical of traditional balladry, but it throws an interesting light on the attitude of barons at the time the ballad was composed. It was probably the tragic outcome of the story which appealed to the more humble audience that was to preserve it in oral tradition for centuries.

'Anna Betlen' is therefore particularly interesting, since, while the original minstrel composition is still to be perceived in both style and content, we may follow the process of the story being stamped with traditional ballad marks during the course of oral transmission: the *vala*s disappear after the introductory stanza to give place to dialogues and evasive answers and typical ballad-devices (delay in opening the door, etc.) are employed to illustrate the sequence of events.

Similarly, version **C** gets rid of the interference of Sárdi; it is the brother himself who takes the matter in hand, who finds and beats his sister in the stable. (This change, however, results in what is generally known as 'Zersingen': by keeping the original dialogue of version **A**, that is, between master and coachman, but putting it into the mouth of John Betlen, it produces the unwitting effect of introducing a new motif in the ballad: John Betlen appears to speak in the person of Samuel Sárdi.)

The traditional ballad-view of love being its own excuse, and the condemnation of anyone who interferes with it, is conveyed by the annexing of the testament-formula of desperate orphans and of those innocently murdered (cp. 'The Three Orphans' and 'The Great Mountain Robber', respectively). In 'Anna Betlen' the inclusion of this formula evokes a feeling of pity and concern for the girl—a sentiment not otherwise present in the story as we have seen—and it is added even at the cost of irrelevancy, as in version C the speaking of the head, and as in version A which ends: 'Let it be an example for everyone what is the fate of an *orphan*.'

'BARCSAI'

The ballads of thwarted love and forced marriage provide an interesting background to those dealing with tragedies in married life.

'Barcsai', a story of adultery, frenzy and murder, is equalled only by 'Clement Mason' in its dramatic intensity.

Version A

1 —Go my husband, go, ay, out to Kolozsvár,
Ay, out to Kolozsvár, to my father's courtyard,
Fetch from there, fetch from there the big rolls of linen,
The big rolls of linen, the cambric that was given free.
—Do not go father, do not go, ay, do not go out from home,
My lady mother loves Barcsai, truly she does!
—Do you hear, wife, do you, what the child is stammering?
—Do not believe it my husband dear, that child is raving.

2 Thereupon he set off, harkening to the word of his wife,
To the word of his wife, ay, out to Kolozsvár;
When he had travelled half-way
He remembered the word of his smaller child.
There and then he turned back, started for home,
He started for home, he reached home.

3 —Open the door, open the door, my woman wife!
—I will open straightaway, I will open straightaway my sweet,
gentle husband!
Only let me throw my working skirt over my shoulder,
Only let me tie my apron before me!
—Open the door, open the door, my woman wife!
—I will open straightaway, I will open straightway, my sweet,
gentle husband!
Only let me put my newly soled boots on my feet,
Only let me put my working scarf upon my head!
—Open the door, open the door, my woman wife!
...Ay, what else could she do, she had to open the door.

4 —Give forth, give forth the key of the big chest!
—I shall not give, I shall not give the key of the big chest:
I have been next door, I went through the garden,
I dropped the key of the big chest there,
But we shall find it in the fair, rosy dawn,
In the fair, rosy dawn, at bright daybreak!

5 There and then he broke his brightly coloured chest with a kick,
He ripped one side of it right off:
Barcsai just rolled out of it,
Ay, he snatched up his sword, cut off Barcsai's head with it.

6 —Do you hear, my wife, do you hear, my wife, do you hear:
Which one do you choose from among three deaths?
Either you choose that I cut your head off,
Or else you choose that I sweep out the house with your silken hair,
Or else you choose that you keep vigil till morning,
That you hold a candle gaily for seven tablefuls of guests?
—I choose from among the three deaths
That I will hold a candle gaily for seven tablefuls of guests...

7 —My servant, my servant, my smallest servant,
Bring forth, bring forth the big churn of pitch,
Bring forth, bring forth the big rolls of linen,
The big rolls of linen, the cambric that was given free,
Start at her head, roll her up to the soles of her feet,
Tie the pile of cambric that was given free on her head,
Start at her head, cover her with pitch to the soles of her feet,
Start at her soles, set fire to her all the way along!

8 I will set a Wallachian pipe-player at her head,
I will set a gipsy fiddler at her feet,
Play, gipsy, play on the gipsy fiddle,
Blow to all the four winds, play the tune at once,
Now let the heart of my wife be gay!

Versions

'Barcsai' is known only in Transylvania. It has been preserved in five versions (one of them in a very imperfect form) and in a fragment.

A Csanádi-Vargyas, *Röpülj*, no. 20; =Ortutay, *Magyar Népköltészet*, II, no. 18 (reference mistakenly given here to *MNGY*, I, p. 194 instead of p. 149); =*MNGY*, I, p. 149; =Kriza (1956), no. 15 B Csanádi-Vargyas, *Röpülj*, no. 21; =Bartók-Kodály, *SZNd*, no. 34; =Kodály-Vargyas, *MNpt*, no. 339; =*Ethnographia*, **23**, 229 C Csanádi-Vargyas, *Röpülj*, no. 22; =Kriza, *Vadrózsák*, no. 381; =Kriza (1956), no. 14 D *MNGY*, I, p. 151 E *MNGY*, VII, p. 21 F Bartók-Kodály, *SZNd*, no. 85; =Kodály-Vargyas, *MNpt*, no. 177

Description of the ballad

I. A lady sends her husband to Kolozsvár in order to fetch some cambric from her father's house. Their child warns the father (**A** not to go) that the mother loves Barcsai. The lady assures her husband that the child is only raving, and he sets out for the journey.

B–D, F start with the child's warning; **F** consists only of this stanza, it ends with the husband's warning the wife: *Do not let the child's words become true;* he sets out for Kolozsvár in **A, C; B** he travels the country; **D** he sets out and goes to a *great old road;* the fragmentary **E** starts with incident III.

II. He returns after he has travelled half-way (**A** because he remembers the child's words) and asks his wife to open her door for him. The woman tries to gain time, and asks her husband to wait till she puts on her working skirt, her apron, her newly soled boots, and her working scarf.

B when the husband returns he stands by his windows—presumably to find out what is going on inside; the excuses of the wife: **B** she wants to put on her gold-embroidered[1] skirt and her red iron-studded boots; **C** gold-embroidered skirt, crimson apron, veil of net and fine red boots; **D** black boots, black skirt, white veil; the husband's demand for the door to be opened treated as incremental repetition occurs only in version **A**.

III. The husband loses his temper, opens the door with a kick (**A** he is let in eventually), bids his wife to hand over the key of their big chest. Once more she tries to evade: she has lost the key in her garden when she went to see her neighbours. The husband breaks the chest with another kick, finds Barcsai and cuts his head off with his sword.

D when he kicks the door, it falls into the middle of the house. There is an additional stanza here describing the house: *The floor of the house is painted, its table is made of sheet-iron, it has fine glass windows and an oven made of tiles.* (The stanza in question was borrowed from folksongs which might be fragments of a lost ballad. Gy. Ortutay, *Magyar Népköltészet,* I, pp. 149–50; J. Kriza (1956), p. 160). In this version the excuse is that she has lost the key in the church and we are not informed whether the husband kills Barcsai or not; **B, E** have additional episodes: **B** *What are we having to eat, wife, what are we having to eat, wife?* | —*As it happens, there is even some peppered sucking-pig-meat in the window.* | —*I do not want, I do not want anybody's leavings,* | *I want only some walnuts and hazelnuts from the big chest!* | —*My heart, my gentle husband, I have been*

---

[1] 'Gold-embroidered skirt' in Hungarian 'vont arany szoknya'. Vont arany is difficult. It has several interpretations: (1) Czuczor-Fogarasi, *Dictionary:* 'skirt made of gold thread'; (2) Csanádi-Vargyas, *Röpülj,* Glossary: 'heavy silk interwoven with gold thread'; (3) F. Schramm, *Néprajzi Közlemények,* I, p. 90; 'silk skirt embroidered with golden trimming, fashionable in the sixteenth and seventeenth centuries.' I have adapted interpretation (3).

bustling about in the kitchen, | I have lost, I have lost the key of the big chest. || In this version the husband does not kill Barcsai at once: *He seized his hair, dragged him to the threshold, | Dragged him to the threshold, cut through his neck. ||* **E** starts with this incident: the husband arrives, tells his wife that he has just come from Torda-County, and has grown very hungry. His wife offers him bread that is on the table, he refuses to eat anybody's leavings, or nut-cakes. In the following part, **E** is corrupted by 'The Great Mountain Robber': *My husband, my gentle husband, I would go down to the cellar | But its key has been lost or mislaid. | —See, here is my axe, and sure I am that...I will cut to pieces | The cellar-door. | My wife, my wife, my dear wife, | Why are you weeping? | —My husband, my gentle husband, | I have been feeding the fire in a bad kitchen, | I have been burning oak-wood, | The wicked smoke of the wood | Has got into my eyes.*

IV. The husband, after having killed Barcsai, allows his wife the choice of three modes of death: she may be beheaded, or he would sweep the house with her silken hair, or else she would hold a candle gaily for seven tablefuls of guests.

B, E twelve tablefuls; all versions agree as far as the third punishment is concerned, but they differ in respect to the two other possibilities: **B** she may choose to be a chopping block, or a block for cutting wood; **C** like **A**, but instead of the silken hair, *or I put a bullet through your head;* **D** to be beheaded or to be killed [?]; **E** is corrupted: *Go up, go up [i.e. from the cellar] you wicked one! | What shall become of you? | Will you be my woodcutter? | —I will not be your woodcutter, | I will be your wedded wife. | —Go up, go up, you wicked one! | Will you be my still? | —I will not be your still, | I will be your wedded wife. | —Go up, go up, my bitch wife! | Will you be a great candlestick for twelve persons? | That I will be my gentle husband. ||* Woodcutter and still do not make any more sense in Hungarian than in English. The finding of Barcsai is missing in this version.

V. The wife chooses the third punishment. Her husband orders his servants to bring forth big rolls of linen (**B** oilcloth) and a big churn of pitch (**D** ten ells of linen, two churns of pitch), bids them to roll his wife up with the linen (**A** and with the cambric that was given free,[1] to cover her then with pitch, starting at her head to the soles of her feet, and to set fire to her, starting with her soles, all way along (**D** the other way around).

B the husband himself takes part in the burning of his wife: *Let us start with her legs, we will roll her up to her head, | We will set fire to her head, we will burn her gaily.* **E** the husband asks twelve young men to come in to his house, to roll his wife up with the linen, then he asks them to light twelve matches and set her on fire; there is no mention of pitch in this version.

---

[1] This fine trait, which recalls the wife's words at the beginning of the ballad, and so serves to illustrate the turning of the tables, is inconsistent here. When he was half-way to his destination we were told that the husband turned back, so he could not have fetched the 'cambric' that was given free from his father-in-law's house.

Some of the versions have a few additional lines:

A quoted above; **D** *My wife, my dear wife, this is what you have chosen | From among three deaths.* **B** *Let this serve an example to everybody: | Of what happens to a bitch. || **C** My God, my God, what have I done! | I have killed Barcsai and my dear wife!*

International versions

Apart from a Rumanian ballad of questionable authenticity[1] 'Barcsai' has no close international parallels. This is to say only that its motifs and incidents are not found elsewhere in the same conjunction, and not that its theme is particularly original.

Motifs

On the contrary, the theme is too general, and the sequence of events is too simple to be located in any one country.

Several of the motifs and incidents feature in so many tales that we may ascribe them to the common stock of European romance and it will be sufficient to refer to their occurrence in Boccaccio's *Decameron*.

(*a*) Adulteress entertaining her paramour when husband is known to be occupied elsewhere (III. 3; IV. 10; VI. 7; V. 10; VII. 2, 3, 6; VIII. 1, 2), or when he has been sent away on some pretext (III. 4; VII. 5, 7).

(*b*) His unexpected return (V. 10; VI. 7; VII. 1, 2, 3, 6).

(*c*) Reference to the feast she has prepared for her lover (our versions **V**, **E** 'I do not want anybody's leavings') (V. 10; VII. 1).

(*d*) Lover hidden in a chest (IV. 10; VIII. 8; in a chicken-coop, V. 10; in a tub, VII. 2).

(*e*) Her delay in opening her door for the husband (V. 10; VII. 3).

Some of these traits figure already in the stories told in the *Gesta Romanorum*: no. 123 has (*a*), (*b*), (*c*), (*e*); no. 122 has (*a*), (*b*), (*e*)—in both of these stories the lover is hidden under the bed; no. 117 has (*e*), but there it is the betrothed who is unfaithful.

The husband discovering his wife and lover and killing them is too common a motif to need illustration.

---

[1] Rumanian version: *Ethnographia*, **8**, 184–92 (transl.). Bogdán's wife invites the handsome Jenesel to her house, knowing that Bogdán is fighting in the mountains. Jenesel accepts the invitation, but does not commit any sin, for 'he does not feel like it'. Bogdán arrives unexpectedly, and asks his wife to let him in. She hides Jenesel in a chest; meanwhile Bogdán forces the door open. Questions similar to the ones in 'Our Goodman' (Child, no. 274) follow his entrance; whose is that horse, those boots, etc. The wife tells him that Jenesel visited her, but being drunk he left his horse, his boots, etc., behind. Bogdán asks for the key of the chest for he wants to count his money. His wife bends the key with a stone before giving it to him, blaming their children for it. Bogdán forces the chest open, finds Jenesel. Jenesel rebukes Bogdán's wife for having invited him in the house, tells the husband that he committed no sin. Bogdán believes him, offers him some wine, but binds his wife with ropes and iron, wraps her in tow, and burns her. Thus she provides the light for their supper. Then Jenesel and Bogdán set off together for Wallachia.

A set of Spanish ballads (cf. E. Geibel and A. F. Schack, *Romanzero der Spanier und Portugiesen*, Stuttgart, 1860, no. 350; J. M. de Cossio, and T. M. Solano, *Romancero popular de Montana*, Santander, 1933–4, I, nos. 120–9) has the motifs of the wife's entertaining her gallant (this is described in a lengthy exposition: the Emperor/a soldier asks for the lady's favour, she lets him in, tells him that her husband is away hunting, they say a malediction, or curse, so that he will not come home); the husband's unexpected return at night, his knocking at the door asking to be let in, the lady's delay in opening the door, her excuse: she has lost the key of the door, or of the new corridor (where she has hidden her lover). These ballads continue with the dialogue characteristic to 'Our Goodman': whose is that horse, that hat, that sword? etc. In some versions the wife herself asks her husband to kill her when she realises that she has been found out but he merely takes her back to her parents; in other versions she dies of fright.

There is another Spanish ballad which tells the story of an adulterous love, but in which wife and lover are killed by the husband. Here the husband is warned by someone that his wife is deceiving him. He arrives home unexpectedly, knocks at the door, gets no answer, and forces it open with a kick. He sees candles burning, wonders whether someone has died, or his wife has a lover, goes up into his bedroom, finds the lovers there, and kills them.

Motifs which occur fairly generally, but which have a certain characteristic Hungarian element in them, are:

I. Husband being warned about his wife's infidelity figures in several ballads (e.g. Child, nos. 80, 81; also cf. preceding paragraph), but the disclosure of mother's infidelity by her son seems to be a special Hungarian element. There is a general tendency in Hungarian ballads which deal with husband-wife relationships to introduce the child into the story (cp. 'Anna Molnár', 'Balthasar Bátori', and 'The Great Mountain Robber').

II. The wife's delay in opening the door figures, as we have seen, in Boccaccio's tales, and it is elaborated in the Spanish ballad which has the excuse of the lost key. The lady's dressing herself as an excuse for the delay is not paralleled elsewhere in international balladry, but it has become a formula in Hungarian ballads (cf. 'Balthasar Bátori', 'The Great Mountain Robber', and some versions of 'The Maid who was Sold').

III. The choice of different means of death offered to the victim occurs in several international ballads (cp. 'Halewijn': Dutch, Low-

German, some Danish, French and English versions). Burning is included in the choice of the means of death offered to treacherous women in several Bulgarian and Serbian ballads (cf. L. Vargyas's list in *Ethnographia*, **71**, 306), and in these the burning is often accomplished in the fashion described in our ballad: covering her with pitch or with rugs, and then setting her on fire. The riddle-quality of the presentation of the third means of death (i.e. 'to hold a candle' instead of 'burning') is a motif entirely peculiar to 'Barcsai'.

Date

L. Vargyas attempts to trace back the ballad to the ninth century and even earlier (*op. cit.* pp. 504–7; *Ethnographia*, **71**, 504–7; *Acta Ethnographica*, **10**, 276–81). He suggests that the story related in 'Barcsai' derives from Hungarian heroic epics current at the time of the Conquest of Hungary (896?). According to him, the present form of 'Barcsai' was acquired by the amalgamation of elements of those heroic epics with elements taken from ballads similar to the Spanish ballad we described in the text (which, he assumes, is of French origin). His entire justification for such a derivation is based upon a comparison he draws between 'Barcsai' and a Mongolian saga, in which he claims to recognise the presence of all the motifs contained in the Hungarian ballad. However, the connection with the Mongolian saga seems far too tenuous and unsubstantiated to be worth further elaboration.

The Mongolian saga goes as follows:

The hero's mother and sister send him away to fetch the heart of a magic snake which is supposed to cure his sick mother. Their real motivation for sending him away is that they have allied themselves with the hero's enemy, and hope that either the hero will not return, or if he does, they can supply his enemy with the snake's heart, which will empower him to kill the hero in a fight. The hero returns after many adventures with the heart, the women give it to his rival secretly, but he is still too weak to fight. Next the women send the hero to fetch surf from the sea. He returns successfully, and in the meantime his magic horse informs him of the women's intention. He fights with his opponent, but neither of them succeeds in killing the other. The mother and sister hide the rival in their chest. One day the hero returns from hunting, he is hungry, and asks for his father's cup. His mother and sister tell him that it is in the chest, he opens it, his rival springs up, and with the women's help kills the hero. His magic horse and his dog, however, succeed in resuscitating him, and now the hero kills his rival. After the victory he offers the women the choice of punishments: they may choose between filling eighty canals with water and milking eighty mares. The women choose the second punishment, and they are trampled to death by the wild horses.

According to Vargyas, the epic and the ballad present the following common motifs: the women (in 'Barcsai' the wife) get rid of the hero on some pretext; he learns their real motivation from his magic horse (in 'Barcsai' from his child); the two fights are omitted from 'Barcsai', but we find the motifs of his asking for food, finding his enemy in the chest, finally his killing the rival, and choice of punishments offered to the women. Even if we accept these parallels they are of no significance, since these motifs, as they occur in 'Barcsai', are with one exception commonplaces. (The one exception is the motif of asking for food, which in the Hungarian ballad is prompted by the husband's knowledge of the lover's whereabouts; in the Mongolian saga, it is due to hunger.)

The second part of Vargyas's suggestion is much more plausible, that is, that both the Spanish and the Hungarian ballads drew their material from a common source (which did not contain the contamination with the 'Our Goodman' motifs). However, we cannot establish even that much with certainty, owing to the very general and 'commonplace' nature of the motifs which 'Barcsai' shares with the Spanish ballads.

Whether there existed an early connection between these ballads or not, there is no linguistic or folkloristic evidence which would indicate that 'Barcsai' was composed before the sixteenth–seventeenth century. The ferocity of the punishment could suggest any dating, presumably before the end of the seventeenth century. Husbands had the right to kill adulterous wives according to Werbőczi's legislation in 1514, and this right was still in force in the eighteenth century (cf. Werbőczi's *Tripartitum*, Part I, Titulus 105, paragraph 1. For the eighteenth century: Decree 11 from the legislation of 1723: 'Adulter in privato etiam occidi potest' [L. Kubinyi, *Enchiridion*, Posonii, 1798, p. 28, quoted by E. Dános, *op. cit.* p. 20]). It is also possible that the Hungarian ballad borrowed the motifs of the choice of deaths and the method of burning from Serbian-Bulgarian sources in which these are very common motifs, and this borrowing could have taken place at any time. Stylistic evidence, however, helps us to date 'Barcsai' rather in the sixteenth than in the seventeenth century. The lines are the rhymeless dodecasyllables characteristic of the ballads of both these centuries, but the repetition of half-lines is a feature typical of the earlier ballads of the sixteenth century (cf. 'Clement Mason', 'Fair Maid Julia'). The tune of 'Barcsai' belongs to the old pentatonic group of Hungarian folksongs.

Special Hungarian elements

The reason why 'Barcsai' is ranked among the best Hungarian ballads in spite of its simple story is the highly dramatic terseness with which it presents the sequence of events. Stylistically dramatic tension is achieved by the circumstance that the entire ballad is told in dialogue. Psychologically it is achieved by the concentration on one single situation told from a particular point of view.

This method is completely different from, for example, the English-Scottish ballad which deals with the same theme. In 'Little Musgrave and Lady Barnard' (Child, no. 81), the interest is evoked by the description of the love scene between the paramours, and suspense is aroused by the simultaneous portrayal of the lovers' dialogue in the lady's chamber and the husband's ride home. We are allowed to look at the situation from four different points of view. There is the lady, who is oblivious of everything but her love for Little Musgrave; the lover, who visits the lady but who is nervously aware of his dangerous situation; the little footpage, who would not accept the lover's bribes but runs to inform the husband in spite of the lover's threat; and finally, there is the husband, whose first reaction of bitterness toward his rival, but self-restrained courtesy in offering him a duel, changes into frantic cruelty when he turns to his wife. The effect is created by placing these four different attitudes side by side, and contrasting them with each other.

'Barcsai', on the other hand, is interested only in the husband, in his personality, and in his reaction. The suspense is built up gradually: his suspicion, his return, his impatience when his wife delays in opening the door, his discovery of the lover, and his frantic anger culminating in the brutality of the murder.

This concentration of the husband's personality is made clear right from the beginning: the circumstance that it is the child who warns the father about the mother's infidelity puts us immediately against the wife. From his point of view, it is natural that the lover's personality is treated as being absolutely insignificant as well as the wife's relationship with him: there is no dialogue between wife and lover; Barcsai does not utter a single word throughout the ballad.

The brutality of the murder is enhanced by the husband's final gloating over his wife, the bringing of musicians, and the deliberate cunning which enables the husband to disguise the most painful and vile of the three deaths in such a way that she seizes upon it as the *least* severe of the punishments lends an added air of sadism to the action. Here we must appreciate the actual phrasing of the third punishment; although the husband makes it clear that all three punishments mean death, the words 'to keep vigil', 'to hold candles', and 'gaily' suggest the actions of someone still alive. (We may draw attention, however, to version

C, which ends with the husband's regret. This is paralleled in 'Little Musgrave', versions **A, B, G, L**.)

The motif of the lady's dressing herself is particularly interesting, since it gives us an insight into the process of a certain motif becoming a formula.

In 'Barcsai' the lady's excuse serves a practical purpose: she is delay-in the opening of the door because she has to gain time in order to hide her lover, and also, in the particular context, the excuse itself (that she is dressing herself) may be literally true. In 'Balthasar Bátori' and 'The Great Mountain Robber' this excuse serves no practical purpose, it merely illustrates *a state of mind* similar to that of the lady in 'Barcsai': she is too frightened of her husband to open the door for him.

In version **W** of 'The Maid who was Sold' the phrase is slightly recomposed: There the bridegroom demands that the door be opened for him, for he has come to fetch the bride who was sold to him in marriage; the mother answers:

> Wait a little, wait a little, wait a little,
> While I put her last (!) dress upon her,
> ...While I put her last scarf upon her,
> ...While I put her last pair of shoes on her!

(This version of the ballad is fragmentary; it ends after the mother's answers are followed by the girl's exclamation: 'Lady Ferenc Bátori, my dear mother, so you have sold me!') The fact that the answers are given by the mother, and the inclusion of the word 'last' convey a situation completely different from both 'Barcsai' and 'Bátori', etc. They imply the girl's reluctance to put on the bridal dress, her wish to die, and the mother's determination to give her daughter away against her will. In short, they summarise the complete story of 'The Maid who was Sold'.

The different significance of the formula in the given contexts seems to illustrate clearly what A. B. Lord writes in *The Singer of Tales* (Oxford, 1961, p. 4), that 'formulas are not ossified clichés which they have the reputation of being, but that they are capable of change and are indeed frequently highly productive of other and new formulas'.

'BALTHASAR BÁTORI'

The fine ballad of 'Balthasar Bátori' is the only other classical Hungarian ballad which deals with adultery, and here the theme is treated in a most ingenious fashion.

Version **A**

1 Delicate lady[1] Judith was sitting at her table,
 She was rocking a fine golden cradle with her feet:
 'Hush-a-bye, hush-a-bye my fair toddling son,[2]
 For your father is not Balthasar Bátori,
 Aye, that other one is your father, that Transylvanian captain,
 Who gave you your fine golden cradle,
 The four golden bracelets for its horns,
 And the cap from Pozsony to put on your head.'

2 Now, Balthasar Bátori is listening at the door:
 'Do not deny, lady, the words you have just uttered.'

3 'Indeed I do not deny them, my soul, my gentle husband:
 I am scolding the maids, the bad maids,
 They plucked the best of my flowers before these had opened,
 Tied them into bunches and gave them to young men!'

4 'So you have denied lady, the words you have just uttered!
 Open the door, open the door, my lady wife!'

5 'I will open it straightaway, I will open it straightaway, my soul,
     my gentle husband,
 Let me just put my carmine boots[3] upon my feet,
 Let me just throw my gold-embroidered skirt over my
     shoulder!'

6 But he could not bear to wait, he opened the door with a kick,
 'Prepare yourself, lady, prepare yourself for noon sharp[4]
     tomorrow
 For the rose market, for the place of beheading!'

7 'Where are you my sweet servant, my favourite postillon,
 Make ready for me my six horses, my coach!'

8 They have got ready, and they have set out,
 They have set out, and they have arrived there.

9 'Wait a little, wait a little, you black headsman,
 For the knell is rung three times for the dead,
 Behold, it is not ringing even once for my hapless self!'

---

 [1] 'Lady'—literally 'woman, wife'.
 [2] 'Toddling son'—a typical example of an epithet being used without being adjusted to the context, i.e. to the son in the cradle. The epithet occurs also in 'Clement Mason' and 'The Cruel Mother'.
 [3] 'Carmine' in Hungarian *karmazsin*—originally 'of carmine colour', later used for felt, satin, coloured or colourless leather imported from Turkey.
 [4] 'Sharp noon' in Hungarian *álló dél*—literally, 'standing, static noon'. This is a Hungarian idiom, embodying the folk-belief that at noon sharp (i.e. twelve o'clock) the sun arrests its course in the sky for a little while. The expression occurs in several ballads. I have translated it 'sharp noon' consistently.

10 At this moment the Transylvanian captain arrived,
He turned her round once, he kissed her twice,
He turned her round twice, he kissed her a hundred times:
'You are mine, not another's, you woman-thing.'

Versions

This ballad has been preserved only in Transylvania. It exists in three versions and two fragments.

A Csanádi-Vargyas, *Röpülj*, no. 26; =Ortutay, *Magyar Népköltészet*, II, no. 19 *a*; =Kriza, *Vadrózsák*, no. 3; =Kriza (1956), no. 12 **B** Csanádi-Vargyas, *Röpülj*, no. 27; =Bartók-Kodály, *SZNd*, no. 84; =Ortutay, *Magyar Népköltészet*, II, no. 19 *b*; =Kodály-Vargyas, *MNpt*, no. 318 **C** Kriza (1956), no. 13; =*MNGY*, III, p. 17 **D** *MNGY*, I, p. 233 (fragment of **C**) **E** Csanádi-Vargyas, *Röpülj*, p. 452 (fragmentary, reference given only for the ending of the ballad)

Description of the ballad

I. The wife of Balthasar Bátori (**C, D** John Mónusi) is sitting at her table, rocking her son in the cradle (**A** golden cradle). She is singing a lullaby to her son, in which she tells him that his father is not her husband but a Transylvanian captain, who gave him his golden cradle, the four golden bracelets for its horns, and his cap from Pozsony.

B like **A**, but instead of the golden bracelets: *his fluttering crimson shirt;* **C, D** are different: **C** *Lady John Mónusi is leaning on her elbow in the window,* / *There she is embroidering with black silk thread,* / *Where her silk does not reach, she fills [the gap] with her tears.* / *She is rocking her little toddling son at her feet:* / *—Hush-a-bye, my son, hush-a-bye, Sammy Mónusi,* / *If God lets you reach manhood* / *Do not call John Mónusi 'father',* / *But give the name 'father' to the sheriff of Ders;* // **D** like **C**, but *the sheriff of Dézs.*

II. Her husband overhears this strange lullaby through the door and demands of her not to deny what she has said. She prevaricates: she was scolding the maids for plucking her finest flowers before those were in full blossom, tying them into bunches and giving them to young men.

A, C he demands that she open her door, she delays in doing so, and he forces it open with a kick; **A** before he forces the door open, she asks him to wait while she puts on her golden-embroidered skirt, her carmine boots; **C** her explaining the words she said in her lullaby occurs after he has forced the door open; the excuse is that she was calling for the maid. **D** incident II is missing altogether.

III. Henceforth all the versions are different.

A the husband bids her prepare herself, for at noon on the following day she has to be at the rose market, at the place of execution. She calls for her coachman, and asks him to prepare the six horses and the coach for her, and they set out for the place of execution; **C, D** the husband is willing to spare her life on condition that she never again mentions her beloved. This she refuses: **D**, **C** *Lady, you have denied your words, have you not! | I will spare your life if you will never mention | The sheriff of Ders; but if you mention him | I will have him beheaded and you as well! | —But of course I will mention him, I will not forget him, | Never, never will I cast him out of my mind, | Let my head fall into the same hole as his head, | Let my blood and his blood make one stream together, | Let my soul stand before God together with his soul!* // The fragmentary **D** ends here. **B** has a new incident included, but traits of **A** are clearly discernible: '*Prepare yourself, lady, prepare your coach and six, // Your coach and six, and your handsomest servant, | To go to the town, to Pozsony, to a great wedding! // Prepare yourself lady, prepare yourself for noon sharp tomorrow!' | They set out, indeed, they arrived there. // The Transylvanian captain just started to dance, | Twice the Transylvanian captain | Turned the delicate lady Judith round, twice he kissed her, | Balthasar Bátori kept an eye on them. // 'Prepare yourself, lady, prepare yourself for noon sharp tomorrow, | For noon sharp tomorrow, for the place of beheading! // Your head has been played with, your head will be cut off!'*

IV. The conclusion of the ballad is also varied.

B *The Transylvanian captain just drew his sword, | He just drew his sword, he let himself fall on it: | 'You have died for me, I will die for you!' // **C** And John Mónusi blazed into anger, | He summoned the sheriff of Ders at once, | As soon as the sheriff of Ders arrived | He made the two kneel down together, | And he had both their heads chopped off, | And he had them both put in the same hole. // **A** cf. in full translation.* The fragmentary **E** quoted by Csanádi-Vargyas ends thus: *Wait a little, wait a little, you black headsman, | For indeed you will not drink of my red blood. //* (The singer added in prose: *Then he took her away and they did not find out who he was.*)

International versions. Motifs

The ballad has no international parallels to my knowledge. Its motifs are linked mostly with other Hungarian ballads, although some of them may be compared to international ballad-devices.

I. The introductory stanza of **C**, **D** contains three elements:

(*a*) Lady leans on her elbow in the window; (*b*) and she is sewing at her seam with black silk thread; (*c*) where her silk does not reach, she fills the gap with tears. (*a*) taken by itself is a formula for opening Hungarian ballads. It occurs in 'The Maid who was Sold', 'The Cruel Mother', and 'The Clever Unfaithful Wife'.

(*b*) is found in 'The Maid who was Sold' (**L**), and is a popular formula for introducing Scottish ballads (e.g. Child, nos. 4 *A*, 39 *D*, *G*, 41 *A*, 52 *A*, *B*, 77 *C*, *D*, 104).

(*c*) figures in 'The Maid who was Sold' (**J**), which contains all the three elements. It is interesting to discover (*a*), (*b*), (*c*) together in a fragmentary Scottish ballad—Child, no. 28: *Burd Ellen sits in her bower windowe, | With a double laddy double, and for the double dow | Twisting the red silk and the blue. | With the double rose and the May-hay // And whiles she twisted, and whiles she twan, | And whiles the tears fell down amang.*

II. Secrets revealed in a song (lyrical lament, etc.) and overheard constitute a motif more characteristic of folk tales and of romantic stories than of ballads, although it figures in ballads occasionally: cf. Child, no. 36 (sung by enchanted maiden); no. 62 (sung by forsaken mistress); no. 271 (sung by betrayed Lord). In these ballads the song reveals the unjust mistreatment of the singer. In this context the motif figures in 'The Great Mountain Robber' and in 'The Mother of the Rich Woman'. The expression for overhearing the complaint/song ('he/she listens at the door') appears in these latter ballads as well.

The special features of the 'Bátori-motif'—as we may call it since it has no parallels in international balladry—are:

(a) The secret is revealed in a lullaby, sung by mother to baby child.
(b) The secret disclosed in the song compromises the singer herself.
(c) The nature of the secret: child born of an adulterous relationship.
(d) The song is overheard by the wronged husband.

Traits of the 'Bátori-motif' are met with in Scottish traditional pieces, but there are no examples in which all four elements occur together. Thus, elements (a), (b), and partly (c), occur in a Scottish song (K. Elliot and H. M. Shire (eds.), *Music of Scotland*, London, 1951, no. 69): a mother tells her son in a lullaby about his father, a courtier who seduced and betrayed her, now he is dead, and the child should not follow his father's way. In 'Queen Eleanor's Confession' (Child, no. 156), the wife reveals her infidelity to her husband unwittingly, but that is a different motif: the husband disguised as a confessor pries into his wife's secrets deliberately.

III. Evasions are occasionally used in balladry in order to explain away compromising words. The discreditable words are usually messages, and the way of escaping the awkward situation caused by them is either to give a false interpretation to the message (e.g. in Nygard's Ulinger-versions 16, 24, 27 of 'Halewijn', a bird warns the maid against seduction, she asks the villain to explain what the bird says, he answers her that it is complaining about its red feet which have gone bare in the winter) or to deny that the message was addressed to the right person (e.g. Ulinger-versions 20, 23, 40, 44: the villain says that the bird is lying and that it has taken him for someone else; in Child, no. 83, the message from Child Maurice is not meant to be addressed to the lady of the house, but to the nurse).

The evasion in 'Balthasar Bátori' is similar to our first example in respect to the complete falsification of the original words, but is made entirely different by the circumstance that the lady utters the compromising words herself, and thus when she has recourse to evasion, it is her own words that she falsifies. This trait also recalls Boccaccio's cunning ladies and we find no ballad-parallels to it.

IV. Similarly, the husband's cunning in version **B** (taking his wife to a wedding in order to get proof of her infidelity) recalls the elaborate plots of Renaissance tales.

V. The motifs of the husband's demand that the door be opened, the lady's dressing used as an excuse for her delay in opening, the husband's forcing the door open with a kick come from 'Barcsai' and they will reappear in 'The Great Mountain Robber' as well.

VI. The motifs of ordering the coachman to prepare the coach and six to take the lady to the place of execution, and the 'rose market' as the place of execution appear in 'The Dishonoured Maiden' and in 'The Great Mountain Robber'. The formula in version **A**, 'For the knell is rung three times for the dead', etc., figures in 'Clement Mason'.

VII. Lovers are often confronted with the alternative of either suffering death or renouncing their beloved. Our lady in **C**, **D** replies to her husband according to the ballad code of honour: she would rather die than forsake her beloved. The same attitude is portrayed in Child, nos. 65 *A*, *D*, *H*, *I*; 81, and 298.

Examples:

> Child, no. 65 *I*   If you will not that Englishman forsake,...
> O I will burn you at a stake!
> —I will not that Englishman forsake...
> Tho' you should burn me at a stake.

Child, no. 81—similar to our ballad, the dialogue takes place between husband and unfaithful wife. She declares her love for her paramour and repeats it, being well aware that she will have to pay for it with her life.

> Child, no. 81 *G*   'Oh weel I like his cheeks,' she said,
> And weel I like his chin;
> And weel I like his fair bodie,
> That there's nae life within!'
>
> 'Repeat these words, my fair ladie,
> Repeat them ower agane,
> And into a basin of pure silver
> I'll gar your heart's bluid rin!'
>
> 'Oh weel I like his cheeks,' she said,
> 'And weel I like his chin'...etc.
>
> Syne he took up his gude braid sword,
> That was baith sharp and fine,
> And into a basin of pure silver
> Her heart's bluid he gart rin.

VIII. The lover's suicide in **B** is related according to the traditional formulas which are found in Hungarian as well as in international ballads:

(a) 'He lets himself fall on his sword' occurs in 'Anna Bíró' and 'The Dishonoured Maiden'; also cp. Child, no. 88 *C*—

> William having his two-edged sword,
> He leaned it quite low to the ground,
> And he has given his own bodie
> A deep and deadly wound.

(b) 'You have died for me, I will die for you' figures in 'Anna Bíró' and in 'The Daughter of the Cruel King', as well as in several Scottish ballads; e.g. Child, no. 84—

> Since my love died for me today,
> I'll die for him tomorrow;

also Child, nos. 64 *C*, 73, 75 *B*, 76, 88, 222.

The ending of version **A** has been subject to discussion. A. Greguss (*A balladáról*, Budapest, 1865) interprets it as a tragic ending: 'When the captain arrives she has already died, and the captain kisses her body with the bitter consolation: "You are mine, not another's..."' On the other hand, according to P. Gyulai (*Magyar Népköltési Gyüjtemény*, XII, p. 428) the captain arrives in time to save her:

The captain arrives with the greatest possible speed, rushes to the place of execution, seizes his beloved, once he turns her round as if he wanted to ascertain that she was alive, he embraces her and covers her with kisses. Then, as if he did not give credit to his eyes he turns her round once more, kisses her, and, as if he found words only at this moment, he exclaims with passion, joy, and with a feeling of triumph: *You are mine*, etc.

Both Greguss and Gyulai employ the *a posteriori* interpretation which was fashionable at the time when ballads were discussed from the romantic point of view.

To me, the present form of version **A** reads like a happy ending. There remains, however, the problem: which was the original ending of the ballad? The difficulties in answering this question lie in the circumstance that not only are we presented with the alternative of a happy or a tragic ending in the few versions which have been preserved, but even those versions which have a tragic conclusion differ from each other in their final development of the story: in **B** the lady's death is implied only by the words of her lover before he commits suicide, and by the husband's threat; in **C** both lovers are killed by the husband; in short, as many endings as there are versions.

It is impossible to decide with certainty which was the original ending of the ballad. The suggestions I offer are merely speculative. I am inclined to believe that originally the story had a tragic ending, and that it contained the lady's death and the lover's suicide. This would be suggested by the fact that all versions (except the fragmentary **E**) have preserved traditional suicide formulas, or traits of these:

B has the actual suicide, and the suicide formula: *You have died for me...;* **D** ends with the suicide formula of 'The Dishonoured Maiden': *Let my blood and your blood...etc.* **C** has the suicide formula, *Let my blood... etc.*, but it is followed by the husband's killing both his wife and her lover. This would also be an appropriate ending of the ballad, and would agree with the ending of 'Barcsai'. The stylistic evidence, however, makes us suspect that this version of the ballad has been tampered with, in the last part: (*a*) superfluous lines are introduced: *Never, never will I cast him out of my mind* is a glaring literary insertion (N.B.: this line is missing from version **D** which follows **C** word by word); (*b*) in true ballad tradition, emotions are never described in the narrative. *John Mónusi flared up in anger* appears to be inserted merely for the sake of rhyme; (*c*) contrary to the previous rhymeless lines of this version, suddenly rhymes are introduced; (*d*) up to this point the story has been told in dialogues, now it is changed into narration, and therefore the last part, which ought to be the climax of the ballad, lacks all dramatic tension. On the whole, this last part seems to be a 'rounding off' of the story by the collector, which he annexed to the ballad.

A in its present form reads like a happy ending, but in the lines immediately preceding the exclamation *You are mine* we may recognize a third suicide formula. *At this moment the Transylvanian captain arrived, | He turned her round once, he kissed her twice, | He turned her round twice, he kissed her a hundred times. ||* In 'The Dishonoured Maiden' this is the description of the lover's suicide next to the dead body of his beloved: **C, L** *When he arrived | First he embraced her, | He encircled her for the second time, | Then he kissed her, | He encircled her for the third time, | Then he thrust his knife into himself. ||* If we substitute *turn round* for *encircle*, we get a very similar formula to the one in our version **A** (of course, without the third member).

Here we must note that the two words *kerül, megkerül* (encircle) and *fordul, fordít, megfordít* (turn round, turn somebody round) are used together idiomatically: *kerül-fordul*, i.e. 'be out and be back', 'come and go', and thus they are particularly susceptible to exchange. In fact, we have both *kerül* and *fordul* in the formula as it occurs in 'Gabriel Bátori and Clare Bátori' (cf. Appendix to 'The Maid who was Sold'). Here the mother advises her son how to mourn over his dead bride:

> Valahányszor *fordulsz*, mindig megcsókolod,
> Valahányszor *kerülsz*, mindig megsiratod.

('Whenever you will turn round, you will kiss her, whenever you will turn back you will mourn over her.')

We may draw attention to the fact that part of the formula, as it is represented in **A**, occurs also in version **B** (which has the actual suicide), although in a different place: it is included in the dancing scene. (*Twice he turned her round, twice he kissed her.*) If we bear in mind that *fordít, megfordít* may refer to 'turn round *in a dance*', it is not impossible that the entire dancing-incident of **B** was inspired by the modified formula of **A**. **A** and **B** agree almost word by word up to this incident. If we assume that the individual singer of **B** remembered that the story ended with the lover's suicide, but heard version **A** sung, in which the original suicide-formula has lost its third member, and thus, for him, was senseless, it is feasible that the actual wording 'turned round... kissed...embraced...' suggested to him the inclusion of a dancing-scene. Thus he employed part of this formula of **A** in this sense, thereby creating a new incident in the ballad. This would seem to be the case if we compare the text of **B** to **A**: the dance-scene is told with words identical to **A**, and the new description is contained in just four lines.

Date

The existence of so few versions and the great divergence between them as far as the conclusion of the story is concerned suggest an early ballad which has been partly forgotten and then eked out with motifs and incidents borrowed from other ballads. Its theme, and the historical names of the characters (John Mónusi, Balthasar Bátori),[1] suggest that it was composed at the same time as 'Anna Betlen' and 'Barcsai'. Its tune belongs to the old pentatonic group of Hungarian folksongs, the lines are rhymeless dodecasyllables characteristic of most ballads of the sixteenth–seventeenth century. For lack of any further evidence, we are unable to date 'Bátori' more precisely.

Special Hungarian elements

It is unfortunate that the developments of the original narrative cannot be established satisfactorily. In its present form its most characteristic feature is the expository situation, which we have called the 'Bátori-motif'. This has been preserved in all the fuller versions of the ballad, and it was certainly the most ingenious part of the ballad, otherwise it would have been forgotten like the rest of the story.

It is interesting to compare the two Hungarian ballads which deal with adultery. 'Barcsai' concentrates solely on the action as it takes place in the present. 'Bátori', on the other hand, encompasses both the past and the present with its reference, in the lullaby, to the earlier adultery of the heroine. Even in her excuse she is still unburdening her heart of the grief of someone who was married off against her will (the bunching of flowers implying wedding; the unripe flower implying unreadiness for wedding), and thus very subtly giving the cause of adultery.

---

[1] The Mónusi—old, established Transylvanian family; Balthasar Bátory—the nephew of Sigismund Báthory (prince of Transylvania, 1581–97), himself Prince of Transylvania for a fortnight in 1594.

'Barcsai' is interested mostly in the husband: it tells the story from his point of view, his suspicion, his reaction to the discovery of his betrayal. In 'Bátori' the situation is much more complex, and the main interest is focused on the woman who lives in a loveless marriage, on her reactions, and it seems to create a certain atmosphere of pity and concern toward her. This effect might have been intended by the ballad singer, or it may be the reverberation of our response to other ballads which tell the tale of unfortunate heroines, and with which 'Bátori' shares several motifs (e.g. 'The Maid who was Sold', 'The Dishonoured Maiden', 'The Great Mountain Robber'). To a person familiar with these other ballads, the recognition of the common motifs evokes not only a feeling of sympathy and understanding toward the heroine, but also a feeling of continuity: as if these other ballads were the background or the antecedents of our ballad, and as if 'Bátori' was just the final tableau of the cyclodrama of love and marriage as presented in Hungarian ballads on the whole: thwarted love, the maid sold in marriage, adultery, almost as a natural consequence of a loveless marriage, and finally being murdered by the husband.

THE DISCUSSION OF
THE MAIN HUNGARIAN
CLASSICAL BALLADS

PART II*

---

* In Part II we shall give a brief review of ballads which fall into the
categories 1–4, as discussed in chapter 1, p. 7.

6

BALLADS OF LOVE AND INTRIGUE
(*continued*)

'THE ASP'

This piece is included among those few traditional songs and ballads which were recorded by Ádám Pálóczi Horváth before 1813 (*Ötöd-félszáz Énekek*, no. 292).

It has been preserved in numerous versions, throughout the Hungarian language territory. F. J. Child refers to it in the discussion of 'The Maid Freed from the Gallows' (no. 95). E. Pohl discusses it in his extensive study of the German ballad group ('Die deutsche Volksballade von der "Losgekauften" ', Helsinki, 1934, *FF.C.* no. 105). In Ortutay's opinion the ballad reached Hungary from South Slavonia (cf. *Székely Népballadák*, p. 300). In the South Slavonian versions the lover who is willing to pluck the snake from his beloved's breast often finds gold there instead of the snake, as in some of the Hungarian versions. Here I give one of the most typical versions of the Hungarian form of this ballad.

Text: Gy. Ortutay, *Magyar Népköltészet*, II, no. 35*b*

= Kálmány, *Hagyaték*, II, no. 6*a*

1 I went to be in service
In the *puszta*[1] of Kecskemét,
I tended oxen
By the water Sási,[2]
I bent my head
Under a briar,
A poisonous asp
Has sneaked in upon my breast.
It is sucking my red blood,
It is saddening my heart,
It is almost tearing through
My slender waist:

---

[1] *Puszta* meaning 'bleak, bare, deserted region'.
[2] 'By the water Sási' in Hungarian *Sási vize mellett*. *Sási* may stand for the name of the river, stream, etc., or it may simply mean 'by a water surrounded by *sás*', i.e. sedge.

2 Good day, good evening to you,
   My dear father!
   I was in service
   Down at the *puszta* of Kecskemét,
   I bent my head
   Under a briar,
   A poisonous asp
   Has sneaked in upon my breast,
   It is sucking my red blood,
   It is saddening my heart,
   Take it out, take it out, take it out,
   My dear father!

3 —Indeed I will not take it out,
   My dear sweet daughter,
   I will rather be left
   Without a fair daughter of mine,
   Without a fair daughter of mine.
   Go to your mother,
   Perhaps she will take it out.

4 —Good day, good evening to you,
   My dear mother!
   I was in service
   Down at the *puszta* of Kecskemét,
   I bent my head
   Under a briar,
   A poisonous asp
   Has sneaked in upon my breast,
   It is sucking my red blood,
   It is saddening my heart,
   Take it out, take it out, take it out,
   My dear mother,
   If you are true to me!

5 —Indeed I will not take it out,
   My dear sweet daughter,
   I will rather be left
   Without a fair daughter of mine,
   Without a fair daughter of mine,
   Than without a half hand of mine.
   Go to your elder brother,
   Perhaps he will take it out.

6 —Good day, good evening to you,
   My dear elder brother!
   I was in service
   Down at the *puszta* of Kecskemét,

I bent my head
Under a briar,
A poisonous asp
Has sneaked in upon my breast,
It is sucking my red blood,
It is saddening my heart,
It is almost tearing through
My slender waist.
Take it out, take it out, take it out,
My dear, sweet brother!
Take it out, my sweet brother,
If you are true to me!

7 —Indeed I will not take it out,
My dear sweet younger sister,
I will rather be left
Without a fair younger sister of mine,
Without a fair younger sister of mine,
Than to be left without a half hand of mine.
Go to your elder sister,
Perhaps she will take it out.

8 —Good day, good evening to you,
My dear elder sister!
I was in service
Down at the *puszta* of Kecskemét,
I bent my head
Under a briar,
A poisonous asp
Has sneaked in upon my breast,
It is sucking my red blood,
It is saddening my heart,
It is almost tearing through
My slender waist!
Take it out, take it out, take it out,
My dear elder sister,
Take it out, my sweet elder sister,
If you are true to me!

9 —Indeed I will not take it out,
My dear sweet younger sister,
I will rather be left
Without a fair younger sister of mine,
Without a fair younger sister of mine,
Than to be left without a half hand of mine.
Go to your betrothed,
Perhaps he will take it out.

10 —Good day, good evening to you,
My dear sweet betrothed!
I was in service
Down at the *puszta* of Kecskemét,
I bent my head
Under a briar,
A poisonous asp
Has sneaked in upon my breast,
It is sucking my red blood,
It is saddening my heart,
It is almost tearing through
My slender waist.
Take it out, take it out, take it out,
My dear sweet betrothed,
Take it out, my dear betrothed,
If you are true to me.

11 —Indeed I will take it out,
My dear sweet betrothed,
I will rather be left
Without a half hand of mine,
Than to be left
Without my fair betrothed!

12 He rolled up the sleeves of his shirt,
He put his hand in her breast,
He took out the asp,
It became transformed to a bag of gold;
'My father has no heart,
Neither have my mother and my elder brother,
Nor my elder sister,
Only my beloved has a heart!'

(This version adds in prose: 'She did not invite any of them to her wedding, neither her sister and brother, nor her father and mother. From this time onwards when a child gets married, it leaves its parents.')

Other versions

Csanádi-Vargyas, *Röpülj*, no. 118; = *MNYr*, **11**, 240; = *Ethnographia*, **19**, 50 Csanádi-Vargyas, *Röpülj*, no. 119; = Bartók, *Magyar Népdal*, no. 157; = Kodály-Vargyas, *MNpt*, no. 353 Ortutay, *Magyar Népköltészet*, **11**, no. 35 *a*; = Pálóczi Horváth, no. 292 Kálmány, *Szeged Népe*, **11**, nos. 10, 11 *Ethnographia*, **18**, 112; **42**, 140 Kálmány, *Koszorúk*, **1**, no. 2; **11**, no. 7 Domokos, *Moldvai Magyarság*, nos. 7, 8, 9 Faragó-Jagamas, *MCSNN*, nos. 6 *a*, 6 *b*, 6 *c* Bartók-Kodály, *SZNd*, no. 102 Kálmány, *Hagyaték*, **11**, 6 *b* Kodály-Vargyas, *MNpt*, no. 51

'THE MAID AND HER GOOSE'
(or 'Fair Helen')

This seems to be one of the oldest Hungarian humorous ballads. The earliest version has come down to us from a MS song-book of the eighteenth century. Since then it has been recorded throughout Hungary and is still popular. For bibliographical references to other versions, cf. Kálmány, *Hagyaték*, II, p. 240, compiled by Gy. Ortutay. The comical effect is achieved by the maid's pretence, the literal references to the goose—a symbol of virginity in Hungarian folk-songs (Csanádi-Vargyas, *Röpülj*, p. 512).

Text: Kriza (1956), no. 38 = *MNGY*, III, p. 13

1 'Good day, honoured sheriff, in your house!'
'Welcome, fair Helen, in my house.
Why are you weeping, why are you weeping, fair Helen,
      in my house?'
'I drove out my geese to the fair green lawn,
The sheriff's son came to drive them in,
Your son slew my fine goose!'

2 'Do not weep, do not weep, fair Helen, for your fine goose,
I shall pay for your fine goose, tell me how much it was worth.'
'For each of its smallest feathers: a piece of gold,
For its tail which was fanning behind: a golden fan,
For its wing, for its two wings: two golden plates,
For its foot, for its two feet: two golden corns of wheat,
For its neck, for its fine neck: six ells of ribbon,
For its head, for its fine head: a golden apple,
For the two eyes burning in it: two burning candles,
For its throat that heralded the daybreak: a golden trumpet,
For the expense it had cost me: six pounds of rice,
For its gizzard, for its liver: six heads of cabbage.'

3 Fair Helen has numerous demands,
The place for the sheriff's son is the gallows tree!
'Let the gallows be like two open roses,
Let my two arms be its two arms, [let them be] his gallows-tree!'

'SZILÁGYI AND HAGYMÁSI'

This ballad has been preserved in one version and a verbose fragment (for the latter: *MNGY*, I, 158), both from Transylvania. Two Hungarian codexes and a recently discovered fragment have preserved the literary treatment of the story, which might have been the source of the ballad.

The *Csoma* codex (compiled in 1636, published by F. Toldy, *A magyar költészet kézikönyve*, Budapest, 1876, 2nd ed., I, p. 49) has preserved a piece composed in 1571 by a youth from the castle of Szendrő. The 'Anonymous of Szendrő', as he is referred to in Hungarian histories of literature, admits that he borrowed his song from 'the poems of a poet'. The second text has been preserved in the *Vasady* codex which has 1561 as the date instead of 1571 (published by A. Szilády, *Régi magyar költők tára*, VII, Budapest, 1912, pp. 169–74). The third text was discovered by J. Varga (see *Irodalomtörténeti Közlemények = ITK*, 1958, pp. 526–9) and bears 1560 as its date.

There are some differences between the work of the 'Anonymous of Szendrő' and the ballad. In the literary version Szilágyi's Christian name is Mihály (Michael); the Sultan's daughter falls in love with Szilágyi and asks him whether he will marry her if she helps him to escape; the Turkish pursuers catch up with the escapees on an island; the princess hides in a forest while the two Hungarian knights fight the Turks; the two knights duel for the princess, and Hagymási (the one who is married) loses an arm in the duel.

The names involved are historical names: Michael Szilágyi was King Matthias's uncle, a most influential Hungarian baron. As a result of the investigations of J. Thury (*ITK*, 1893, p. 293) it appears that Michael Szilágyi and Ladislav Hagymási/Hajmási (the administrative head of Temes comitat) were actually good friends and they owned neighbouring lands. Thury discovered another interesting circumstance: a Turkish princess had land close to theirs, and she married one of Szilágyi's men. Michael Szilágyi was actually captured by the Turks but he was set free after himself paying the required ransom.

There are various theories as to the origin of the story (J. Honti, 'A Szilágyi és Hagymási monda rokonai és eredetkérdése', *Ethnographia*, **41**, 25–37; J. Honti, 'A Szilágyi és Hagymási monda szövegtörténete', *ITK*, **40**, 304–21; R. Gragger, *Ungarische Balladen*, Berlin, 1926, pp. 172–4; B. Korompay, 'Szilágyi és Hagymási históriája a szlovéneknél és a magyar monda eredetkérdése', *ITK*, **57**, 218–26). The ballad shares several motifs with romances and heroic epics: the elopment, fight with the pursuers followed by a dual between friends, their reconciliation, appear in Waltharius (M. D. Larned, *The Saga of Walter of Aquitane*, Baltimore, 1892) and in South Slavic traditional epics (see J. Honti, *Ethnographia, loc. cit.*, Korompay, *op. cit.*); the conversation between lovers through prison walls, the overheard lament, the lady's stealing the key to the prison, and her father's horses (*MNGY*, I, 159) appear in

Child, nos. 9, 53; the knight's allowing one person to leave the battle-field alive in order to 'carry the tidings home' appears in Child, nos. 8, 15.

L. Vargyas (*Ethnographia*, **71**, 214) has drawn attention to Portuguese, Italian, and French parallels to the stock phrase referring to the state of the prisoner in our stanza 1, who had not seen the sun and the moon for seven years. The curious passage about the one or two bunches of grapes is repeated in Kodály-Vargyas, *MNpt*, no. 173, and Kriza (1956) no. 19. The origin of 'Szilágyi and Hagymási' is probably to be sought among Serbian heroic epics, which often have Szilágyi as their hero (under the name of Svilojevic Mihajloban). This opinion was voiced recently by B. Korompay (*op. cit.*) according to whom the duel be-tween the friends for the lady is of secondary importance, the core of the ballad being the popular theme: a prisoner accepts the love of the lady who aids his escape, but is unable to reciprocate her affection or to fulfil her hopes: he is already married.

Text: Csanádi-Vargyas, *Röpülj*, no. 74 = MNGY, I, 160

1 My friend, my friend, my good friend,
It is seven years now since we were captured
[And put] in the Sultan's prison for two bunches of grapes!
In all that time we have not seen the course of the sun,
The changing course of the moon and the stars...

2 The Sultan's fair daughter listened at the door.
Up and speaks the Sultan's fair daughter:
'Hark to my words, you two young Hungarian masters,
Young men who have escaped from my father's prison [*sic!*],
If I will release you from there, will you pledge yourself
To take me to the country of Hungary?'
Great Nicholas Szilágyi answers these words:
'Indeed we will pledge ourselves, Sultan's fair daughter!'

3 The Sultan's fair daughter went straightaway
To her father's house,
She took the keys of the prison in her hands,
She put her few pieces of gold in her pocket,
She went in haste and opened the door [of the prison].

4 They set off to leave in great haste.
While they were on their way, the Sultan's fair daughter
Kept on looking back.
'Harken to my words, you two young Hungarian masters,
Young men who have escaped from my father's prison:
Behold, there comes, behold there comes my father's host,

Alas, if they catch up with us, they will slay you,
And they will take me back!'
'Do not be at all afraid, do not be afraid, Sultan's fair
    daughter,
Neither will they slay us, if this sword does not break,
Nor will they take you back, if God will help us!'

5 Then the cruel host arrived.
'My friend, my friend, take care of the young damsel,
That I should not fail us!...'
The host reached him, he began to do battle with them.

6 Thrusting forward he carved a footpath [through them],
Returning, he slashed a cartroad [through them].
He left only one person alive from the entire camp
That he might return [to his] home, and report the news.

7 When they were at the point of leaving[1]
Thus speaks, thus speaks Ladislav Hagymási:
'My friend, my friend, let us try each other
[To see] who shall have the Sultan's fair daughter!'

8 'Harken to my words, you two young Hungarian masters,
Young men who have escaped from my father's prison:
Never should you fight over me,
But rather will I kneel, and you shall take my head!'

9 Great Nicholas Szilágyi says straightaway:
'My friend, my friend, my good friend,
I will let you have the Sultan's fair daughter,
For I have a bride, a betrothed at home,
A wedded wife to whom I have pledged faith.'

10 Upon these words the Sultan's fair daughter
Was left there for Ladislav Hagymási.
Great Nicholas Szilágyi set off for home,
And Ladislav Hagymási took the young damsel away.

(Other version: MNGY, I, 158.)

'THE MAID WHO WAS CURSED'

'The Maid who was Cursed' has been preserved in six versions, all
recorded in the Lowland. The story is the direct opposite of that related
in 'The Maid who was Sold', class 2, yet it is composed of the same
elements. Here it is the mother who resents her daughter's intention to

---

[1] 'When they were at the point of leaving' in Hungarian *Mikor az eltelék, hogy elindulának*
could stand also for 'When this [affair] has ended, on the point of their leaving'.

get married, and it is the mother who casts a curse on the girl that she may die on her wedding-day.

Version **A**

1 A widow has a fair marriageable daughter;
The girl wishes to marry, her mother does not give her leave.
The girl has not obeyed her mother's word,
The woman has cursed her daughter dreadfully:
'When you go to take the oath, may you shiver with cold.
May your soul leave your body on the evening of your
wedding!'

2 First cries out the smaller bridesman:
'Honourable Madam, dear Madam, the bride is faint!
—If she is faint let her be faint, perhaps she has grown tired,
You have brought her from afar, perhaps she is faint only
for that reason!'

3 Next cries out the elder bridesman:
'Honourable Madam, dear Madam, the bride is ill!
—If she is ill let her lie, perhaps her head is aching,
You have brought her from afar, perhaps her head is aching
only for that reason!'

4 Next cries out the bridegroom himself:
'My mother dear, the bride is dead!
—My coachmen, my coachmen, my mourning coachmen,
Go, harness the horses, fetch her mother!
But do not bring her as if for a wedding:
[Bring her] for the burial of her daughter who has a curse
upon her.
Let her bring not cake, but a winding-sheet,
Coffin and nails for her daughter who has been cursed!'

5 The bell is tolled for midday, but not for a midday-meal,
It is now they are putting my dear daughter into the ground.
Fall, leaves, and hide me, I beg you,
For I have driven my good daughter to her death.
Stars, stars, shine forth beautifully,
Show my good daughter her way.

Versions

A Csanádi-Vargyas, *Röpülj*, no. 40; =*MNGY*, xiv, p. 23 **B** Gy. Ortutay, *Magyar Népköl-
tészet*, ii, no. 14; =*Ethnographia*, **18**, 111 **C** Csanádi-Vargyas, *Röpülj*, no. 41 **D** Kálmány,
Hagyaték, ii, no. 4 *a* **E** Kálmány, *Hagyaték*, ii, no. 4 *b* **F** Kálmány, *Hagyaték*, ii, no. 4 *c* **G**
Berze Nagy, *BMNh*, i, pp. 228–9 **H** *Ethnographia*, **40**, 149 **I** *Ethnographia*, **13**, 272

Description of the ballad

I. A maid gets married against her mother's will. The mother casts a curse upon her: 'When you go to take the oath, may you shiver with cold, / May your soul leave your body on the evening of your wedding!'

F the mother is a widow, the girl is her only daughter; E, F the mother's objection is that there is no hurry for the girl to marry and to leave her by herself; H that she cannot cook; D the mother has two daughters; Kálmány, who recorded this ballad, notes that 'two' (két) is a corruption from szép meaning 'fair'.

The second line of the curse: B *May you shiver to death in the middle of your evening meal;* C, D, G, H, I *In the evening at the evening meal may your soul leave your body;* E, F *May your soul leave your body at your last [?] supper.*

II. The following part, relating how the curse takes effect and how the girl dies, consists merely of a sequence of incremental repetition: first the younger bridesman cries out to the bridegroom's mother that the bride is faint; next the elder bridesman cries out that she is ill; finally, the bridegroom himself cries out that the bride is dead. His mother does not attach too much significance to the warnings of the two bridesmen; she attributes the bride's faintness, etc., to the long tiring journey.

The second warning is somewhat varied:

A, F, H she is sick; B she is growing pale; E repeats the first warning: she is faint; D the elder bridegroom cries out that the bride is dead; the bridegroom's mother answers him: *She is not dead, she is only asleep, she has come from afar, all she wants is to sleep.*

In version C, the repetition is elaborated but there are no answers to the warnings:

First cries out the bridesmaid: | —My mother dear, the bride is ill! | Next cries out the brideswoman: | —Goodwife, my friend, the bride grows pale! | Next cries out the best man himself: | —Goodwife, my friend, the bride grows pale! || Next cries out the bridegroom himself: | —My mother dear, the bride is at the point of death! || Next cries out the grooms-man himself: | —Goodwife, my friend, the bride is dead! || G, I the first two warnings are the same: the bride is ill, and are made by the younger and the elder bridesman, respectively. G the mother's answer is that she is sad because she had to travel so far. The bride's death is announced by: G the groomsman; I the best man.

III. At her own son's exclamation, his mother bids the coachmen (A, D, I the mourning coachmen) harness the horses (C to the mourning coach) and to fetch the bride's mother. They should not ask her to come for the wedding, but to come for the burial of her daughter who was cursed.

A the mother-in-law adds to the message that the bride's mother should bring a winding-sheet, a coffin and nails for her daughter; **C** she asks the coachman to fetch the bride's mother and father, not for the wedding but for the burial-feast of their daughter; **F** she orders her coachman to take the dead girl back to her mother; **G** instead of incident III, the bridegroom stabs himself to death with his knife; **H** does not have incident III.

IV. The last part of the ballad consists of the lyrical complaint of the girl's mother, who now repents her curse. This part is composed of lines borrowed from various Hungarian folk-songs.

A quoted above; **I** like the last two lines of **A**; **B** *Wherever I walk even the trees weep there,* | *Their fragile branches shed leaves,* | *Fall, leaves, and hide me,* | *For I*[1] *have cursed my only child!* | *For every bride they light the daybreak-fire,* | *But for my daughter the bell is tolled three times.* (*To light the daybreak-fire* refers to the Hungarian wedding custom of lighting a fire at dawn in front of the house of newly wedded couples.) **E** *Fall, leaves, and hide me,* | *Why have I cursed my only child!* | *Stars, stars, shine forth beautifully,* | *Show the maid, who was cursed,* her *way!* | *Show her the way to the end of the village,* | *Or to the balk amidst the thick forest.*[2] || **F** like **E**, but *stars, stars, show the way, show the way to the middle of the forest;* **C** (contaminated with a fairly recent ballad, as also 'The Dishonoured Maiden' **FF, GG, HH,** cf. description I) *Now the good* [?] *mother has arrived,* | *She has fallen on her good daughter's neck.* | *—Whatever is the matter with you, my dear daughter?* | *Perhaps the supper was not to your taste?* | *—The supper was to my taste,* | *My mother's curse reached me quickly;* || **D** the mother invites the bridegroom to come and live in her house; he answers: *I will not go, I will not go* | *To live in any-one's house,* | *A day after tomorrow, at noon* | *I shall be laid out!* || **H** ends with the mother casting a curse upon herself: *May God punish* | *the mother who cast a curse upon* | *her only daughter terribly,* | *I had only one daughter too,* | *I cast a curse upon her,* | *I caused her ruin.* || **G** the mother has been lying in the hospital of Pécs for three years, and addresses her daughter somewhat incompatibly with the story: *My sweet, good daughter, when will you come home?* | *When your threshold will be overgrown with roses,* | *Then will your cursed daughter return.* | *My daughter, my daughter, it will never happen,* | *therefore my heart is plunged in sorrow forever.*

Notes

Csanádi and Vargyas offer two explanations for the origin of the ballad (cf. Csanádi-Vargyas, *op. cit.* notes to nos. 40, 41): it is possible that it is a more recent direct adaptation from 'Graf Friedrich', since the

---

[1] There is an obvious corruption in the original recording of the ballad since it says 'for you have cursed me, my only child' (in Hungarian *megátkoztál* instead of *megátkoztam*). We have translated it according to the form corrected by Z. Kodály, who recorded this version.

[2] The motifs of which the complaint was composed are stanzas included in several different folk-songs. Examples: *Stars, stars,* | *Shine forth beautifully!* | *Show his way* | *To that lad,* | *Show his way,* | *To that lad,* | *Who cannot find the house* | *Of his beloved.* || (Gy. Ortutay, *Magyar Népköltészet,* I, p. 151.) *Wherever I walk, even the trees weep there,* | *Their fragile branches shed leaves.* | *Fall, leaves and hide me, I beg you,* | *For my beloved* | *Loves someone else, not me!* || (*Ibid.* p. 198.) (Cp. also, *ibid.* pp. 166, 174, 269, 275.)

German ballad has the motif of the bride's strength failing, and her death in the bridegroom's house. The motif of sending for the bride's mother may also come from 'Graf Friedrich', in which the bride's relatives come to see her after she has died. Alternatively, they note, it is also possible that 'The Maid who was Cursed' comes from 'The Maid who was Sold', class 2 (i.e. after the motifs of the German ballad have been adapted to suit the Hungarian story of the girl who was sold into marriage against her will), and became an independent ballad by exchanging the roles of the mother and daughter in the curse motif.

I am inclined to agree with the second alternative, since in my opinion there is no reason to believe that 'The Maid who was Cursed' adapted the motifs in question directly from 'Graf Friedrich'. This could be suggested only if 'The Maid who was Cursed' agreed more closely with the German ballad than it does with 'The Maid who was Sold', class 2, which is not the case.

It is not very plausible that 'The Maid who was Cursed' adapted the motif of the bride's strength failing directly from 'Graf Friedrich', since the treatment of this motif (i.e. through incremental repetition of exclamations by the bride's companions) is not paralleled in 'Graf Friedrich', whereas it does occur in several versions of 'The Maid who was Sold' (cp. also with 'The Cruel Brother', Child, no. 11, quoted and discussed in 'The Maid who was Sold' under this motif). In fact the incremental repetition is the most important part of 'The Maid who was Cursed' and occurs in *all* versions. (Csanádi and Vargyas have noted that the introductory lines and the ending of the ballad seem to be more recent compositions or adaptations to the ballad.)

Furthermore, the reason given for the bride's strength failing and for her eventual death could certainly not have come by direct adaptation from 'Graf Friedrich' since there the reason is entirely different: the bridegroom wounds his bride on the journey by mischance. On the other hand, it could have come perfectly easily from 'The Maid who was Sold', class 2, in which the motivation is also a curse taking effect (only there it is the girl who casts the curse upon herself, and it is expressed in the form of a prayer). The exchange of parts (i.e. that in 'The Maid who was Cursed' it is the mother who resents the marriage, and not the daughter) is a phenomenon very common to balladry (e.g. the Scottish ballad with the similar theme, 'The Mother's Malison' or 'Clyde's Waters', Child, no. 216, in which it is the young man who is turned away from the girl's house by her mother who pretends to speak in his beloved's person, while in 'The Lass of Roch Royal', Child, no. 76, from which ballad this motif seems to have been adopted, it is the girl who is turned away by the young man's mother who uses the same device).

Other motifs of 'The Maid who was Cursed' may have been adapted also from 'The Maid who was Sold', class 2: the mother-in-law plays a part in both ballads, and the motif of sending the coachman to fetch the bride's mother is encountered in 'The Maid who was Sold', versions **L** and **K**. In **L**, the bridegroom orders his coachman to fetch the bride's mother and to warn her that it is not the wedding but the burial of her daughter to which she is asked; in version **K**, he orders his coachman to go to his own mother (another example of parts exchanged) and warn her that she should not prepare a wedding-feast, but a burial-feast.

'THOMAS MAGYARÓSI'

'Thomas Magyarósi' is not a tragic ballad in its present form. It tells the story of Thomas Magyarósi, who is about to marry the daughter of the local Governor in the Transylvanian Lowland. The bride keeps on weeping on their way to the wedding. He questions her as to the reason for her distress, and learns the truth from the exclamations of the bridesmaids: she is delivering a child in the coach. He takes her back to her parents.

This is a very old ballad; it has been preserved in two versions only, both from Transylvania. We have included it here because it has traces of the incremental repetition of the bride's companions characteristic of 'The Maid who was Sold', version **K**, and 'The Maid who was Cursed'.

Versions

A Gy. Ortutay, *Magyar Népköltészet*, II, no. 21; =*MNGY*, III, 14; =Kriza (1956), no. 35
B Csanádi-Vargyas, *Röpülj páva*, no. 29; =Bartók-Kodály, *SZNd*, no. 121 =Kodály-Vargyas, *MNpt*, no. 235; =*Ethnographia*, **19**, 46

Version **A**

'From where are you taking a wife, Thomas Magyarósi?'
—I am taking my wife, aye, from Barasso,
She is the fair grown-up daughter of the old Mistress
    John Vaivode,

Her Ilona Vaivode![1]
The coach is rocking, the girl is weeping softly,
Thomas Magyarósi keeps on looking back:
'Why are you weeping, what are you grieving for, my
    fair bride?
Are you perhaps thinking that I do not possess
Twelve good oxen, a good cart bound with iron?'
'I am not thinking that; I know very well that you have.'
Up and speaks the elder bridesmaid:
'Hand over, hand over, Thomas Magyarósi,
Your soft cambric shirt for swaddling clothes!'
'I will not give, I will not give my soft cambric shirt
For swaddling-clothes to the rascally bitch!'
The coach is rocking, the girl is weeping softly,
Thomas Magyarósi keeps on looking back:
'Why are you weeping, what are you grieving for, my
    fair bride?
Are you perhaps thinking that I do not possess
Good war-horses, a good sheepfold-ful of sheep?'
'I am not thinking that; I know very well that you have!'
Up and speaks the little bridesmaid:
'Hand over, hand over, Thomas Magyarósi,
Your belt of silken cord for a swaddling-band.'
'I will not give, I will not give my belt of silken cord
For a swaddling-band to the rascally bitch!'
'My coachman, my coachman, turn back the coach,
Tell her mother—the devil take her—
If that is the way she has brought her up,
She must make do with her that way!'

Version **B** tells the same story with little variation. Thomas answers the question, '*Wherefore did you marry?*' by saying, '*For the Vaivode's lowland, for the Vaivoide's daughter, for the Vaivode's Ilona.*' The questioning of the bride as to the reason for her weeping is missing, but the bridesmaids speak up twice, following the stanzas, '*The coach is rocking, the girl is weeping softly*'. First the younger bridesmaid speaks: '*Had she no grievance she would not weep, indeed!/ but she has a grievance, believe me, therefore she is weeping.*' Next the elder bridesmaid speaks and asks for the cambric shirt, for the silk scarf of the bridegroom to be used for swaddling-clothes, and for a swaddling-band. Thomas Magyarósi speaks only at the end of the ballad:

---

[1] 'Vaivode' in Hungarian *Vajda*, i.e. local Governor' in Transylvania. I have kept 'Vaivode' in the text, in order to convey that while in version **B** the heroine is 'Ilona, the Vaivode's daughter' in version **A** she is actually *called* 'Ilona Vaivode'—as a result of a process similar to the one which we have discussed in connection with the name of 'Clement Mason', i.e. Clement, the mason, and Mason Clement.

'My servant, my servant dear, turn back my horse,
Turn back my horse, my countless wedding-guests!'
When they were going in at the gate of the Vaivode:
'Are you in, are you in, my honoured father, the Vaivode?'
'I am in, I am in, son Magyarósi.'
'Whom we had taken away, her we have brought back,
If that is the way you have brought her up,
You must make do with her that way.'

The rather abrupt ending of the ballad might suggest that originally it had a somewhat different conclusion; the absurd situation (delivering a child in a coach) and certain inconsistencies in the telling (e.g. **A** the bridegroom keeps on asking the girl why she weeps when in the previous stanzas he has already been told the reason, and has even called her 'a rascally bitch') give the impression that both versions are fragmentary.

The bridegroom's repeated questioning of the girl may be compared to the stock-phrase in 'The Cruel Brother' and in 'Leesome Brand' (as well as their Scandinavian parallels).

Does your side-saddle sit awry?
Or does your steed...
Or does the rain run in your glove,
Or Wad ye chuse anither love?
—The rain runs not in my gloves,
Nor will I e'er chuse anither love...etc.

It is not impossible that this sequence of motifs (incremental repetition in relating the bride's strength failing, expressed sometimes by the exclamations of her companions, the knight's questioning the reason for her distress, her thirst, her impatience to arrive) which occurs in certain international ballads was once altogether present in Hungarian balladry. This would seem to be suggested by the fact that although the sequence of motifs has not been preserved *as a unit* in Hungarian balladry, *all its elements* are found if we compare *simultaneously* 'The Maid who was Sold', class 2, 'The Maid who was Cursed', and 'Thomas Magyarósi' to the international sequence of motifs:

(a) the lady's strength failing	('The Maid who was Sold', class 2; 'The Maid who was Cursed')
(b) expressed through the exclamations of her companions	('The Maid who was Sold', version **K**; 'The Maid who was Cursed'; 'Thomas Magyarósi')
(c) the knight's questioning the lady as to the reason for her distress	('Thomas Magyarósi')
(d) her thirst and impatience to arrive	('The Maid who was Sold', class 2)

'THE GIRL WHO WAS RAVISHED
BY THE TURKS' (I)

This ballad is related to 'The Maid who was Sold' by its similar theme:
here the girl is not sold into marriage to a Turk, but is ravished by him,
and, similar to 'The Maid who was Sold', she prefers to die rather than
to be the bride/lady of a Turk. In 'The Maid who was Sold' (classes 2,
4) she dies as the result of her vow; in this ballad she throws herself
into the Danube. Her dialogue with the Turk, refusing his wish, recalls
the dialogue in 'The Maid who was Sold', class 1, in which the bride
refuses to 'greet' the rejected suitor. The lyrical passage at the end of the
ballad entreating the fish, and her clothes, to mourn over her is characteristic of 'The Maid who was Sold', class 4. The ballad has been
recorded in two rather divergent versions, both in the Lowland.

Versions

A *Ethnographia*, **71**, 192–3; =Csanádi-Vargyas, *Röpülj*, no. 43; =*Ethnographia* (1914), p. 36. (The
latter two versions do not have the last five lines of **A** which occur in the original MS.)
B Csanádi-Vargyas, *Röpülj*, no. 42; =Kálmány, *Szeged Népe*, II, no. 3, p. 4. (Both Csanádi-Vargyas
and Vargyas, *Ethnographia*, **71**, 193, refer to this version erroneously as *Szeged Népe*, III, instead
of II.)

Version A

The waters of Tisza and of Danube flow down—
A fine golden galley sails thereon, sails thereon,
An ugly Turkish Vaivode is therein, is therein.
A fair maiden of Komárom is going that way, is going that way,
Two jugs are on her arms, thus she is going to the Danube.
—Give me, give me some water, fair maiden of Komárom!
—How could I give you some, how could I give you some,
    you ugly Turkish Vaivode?
You are in the middle of the Danube, I am on the bank of
    the Danube.
She hands him her jug: he seizes her white arms,
He drags her onto the galley, on to the top of the galley.
—Come and embrace me, fair maiden of Komárom!
—May the devil from hell embrace you rather!
—Come and kiss me, fair maiden of Komárom!
—May the lion from the wilderness kiss you rather!
—Come and lie down beside me, fair maiden of Komárom!
—May the weapons of the Hungarians lie down beside you!

[In prose: 'He smote her in the face with an iron gauntlet. Her red blood poured
forth through her nose, through her lips.']

The bottom of Danube: the bottom of my coffin.
The two sides of Danube: the two sides of my coffin.

The waves of Danube: my shroud.
The fishes of Danube: the nails in my coffin,
The little fishes of Danube: my mourners,
The little birds in the sky: my choir.
Fishermen, fishermen, fishermen of the Danube,
Fish me out by Thursday noon,
Fish me out and bury me too!
My clothes, my clothes, my finest clothes,
Fall down from the nails, fall on each other,
So that my mother may learn that you are mourning over me!
Into the Danube she threw herself, she threw herself;
Fishermen fished her out by Thursday noon,
Her finest clothes fell down from the nails,
They fell down from the nails, they fell on each other too,
Thus did the mother learn of her daughter's death.

Version **B** is interwoven with folk-tale elements, and is not too intelligible at some points: Fair Rosy Elisabeth is washing herself in the Danube, when all of a sudden the chief Turkish pasha snatches her away. As they proceed toward Turkey, the Turk asks her whether she loves him. Three times she gives him the ambiguous answer: 'If I did not love you, you would certainly not have caught me!' They arrive; there is a great feast for the Turkish chiefs. Someone warns her not to drink of the sleeping-wine which is going to be served there, lest she fall asleep for ever. The version is rather obscure here, because the warning goes: 'You must not drink it if you love me [?]', as if it was the Turk himself who warned her. This is, however, highly improbable, since the story continues with her escape: everybody drinks of the wine and falls asleep, except her. She sets off for home, asks her mother to open her gate. No sooner has the mother let her daughter in when the Turks arrive. The mother denies having a daughter; as in 'The Maid who was Sold', version **K**. The mother's excuse links the ballad with our version **B** in which the girl drowns herself in the Danube:

Away with you, you devil, away with you, do not haunt me!
I have no daughter: I am fishing for her, dragging the Danube for her,
Nine weeks have passed since I have been looking for her,
My twelve shavings are looking for her in the Danube!

According to Kálmány, 'my twelve shavings' refers to an ancient folk-belief: a burning shaving stuck in a piece of bread is supposed to come to rest in the water above a drowned person.

The story ends in prose: 'She hid her daughter so the Turks could not find her and they went away.'

L. Kálmány and L. Vargyas have drawn attention to a similar Rumanian ballad (cf. L. Kálmány, *Ethnographia* (1914), 37; L. Vargyas, *Ethnographia*, **71**, 191–6, bibliography, for other references, including the Rumanian ballad):

A girl goes to fetch water from a well (or from the Danube, from the sea), catches sight of the Turks, and asks her mother to hide her. The mother denies having a daughter to the Turks and she even shows them her daughter's grave. Nevertheless, they find her eventually and take her off with them. When they arrive at the water the girl asks leave to drink (to wash her face) and throws herself into the water with the words: 'I would rather be eaten up by fishes and shell-fish (or frogs) than be the young wife of a Turk.'

The exact origin of the Hungarian and Rumanian ballads cannot be established, because both Hungarian versions which have been preserved are fragmentary, and we cannot tell what the original versions were like. In their present form (if we take both Hungarian versions into consideration), the Rumanian ballad is certainly the more coherent.

L. Vargyas's comparisons with French ballads and with ballads and stories of the people neighbouring on Hungary are not very convincing. He relates the Hungarian ballad to French ballads in which a girl is abducted or enticed onto a boat and commits suicide (with a dagger, or by throwing herself into the sea) rather than be dishonoured. Vargyas attaches great importance to the circumstance that in these French ballads as well as in our version **A**, the heroine commits suicide *on a boat*. This comparison seems to be somewhat far-fetched if we take into consideration the fact that thousands of prisoners were taken to Constantinople by boat during the years of Turkish occupation, and so suicide by throwing themselves overboard must have been a very obvious desire for those who could not face the prospect of being taken to Turkey as prisoners. Stories and ballads dealing with prisoners, especially girls who drowned themselves rather than be taken to Turkish harems, have a wide circulation in those countries which were involved in the conquests by the Turks.

The other trait which serves as ground for Vargyas's comparison is the motif of the girl talking to the fish. This occurs in several Rumanian, Bulgarian, Serbian and Moravian ballads in which the heroine drowns herself. In these ballads the motivation for her suicide is often capture by the Turks, but it is sometimes completely different as well (e.g. resenting incestuous marriage, danger of being dishonoured, etc.). The stock-phrase in these ballads is either the girl's *asking the fish to eat her up*, or her saying: '*I would rather be eaten by fishes* than be in the power of Turks.'

It is certainly interesting that, as Vargyas points out, traces of this stock-phrase are found in a French ballad, in which they are said by a sailor when he throws a girl (who is not willing to fulfill his wishes) overboard: 'Chantez, chantez, grenouilles, vous avez de quoi chanter, Vous avez de l'eau à boire, et ma mie à manger.' (Cf. Doncieux, *Le romancéro populaire de la France*, Paris, 1904, no. 42.)

These comparisons are, however, not very relevant to our purpose, because in the Hungarian ballad the stock-phrase in question does not occur at all. Not only is there no mention of being eaten up by fish but the reference to the fishes in the Hungarian ballad is only part of a stanza borrowed from seventeenth–eighteenth century Hungarian songs composed by exiles and prisoners. In these songs passages like the one in our ballad are repeated in more or less the same form:

> My God, my God, my dear God,
> My hopes rest only in Thee,
> I beg Thy Majesty not to forsake me,
> My life depends only on Thee.
>
> You tiny birds, take pity on me,
> Beasts in forest, mourn over me,
> Whales of sea, bury me,
> You, that dwell in the depths of the surfy sea.
>
> (Ortutay, *Magyar Népköltészet*, I, p. 266)
>
> A young lad of noble birth lies in great Turkey,
> Guiltless and for no reason the poor [lad] is kept
>   a prisoner there.
> Up and cries: —Mother, my mother,
> You have three stone castles, ransom me with one
>   of them!
> —I will not ransom you, I will not ransom you,
>   my soul, my dear son,
> For God will give a son to replace a son,
> But God will not give me anything to replace my
>   stone castle.
> —I do not care, I do not care, my soul, my dear mother,
> For the two sea-shores will be my coffin,
> The surf of the sea will be my winding-sheet,
> I shall even have the tolling of bells, the roaring of the sea,
> Fishes will bury me in the sea,
> Birds in the sky will mourn over me,
> Birds in the sky and beasts in the forest.
>
> (Csanádi-Vargyas, *Röpülj*, no. 81)

Who knows where death will overcome me?
In a forest or in a field? or in the cold breeze?
I [may] fall ill—who will mourn over me?
I may happen to die—who will bury me?

The great sea-shore: the side of my coffin,
The depth of the sea: the bottom of my coffin,
The heavy surf of the sea will be my winding-sheet,
Fishes of the sea will be my gravediggers,
Birds in the sky will be my mourners.

(Csanádi-Vargyas, Röpülj, no. 93)

My God, my God, where will death overcome me?
In a forest or in a field? or on the sea?
If I die in a forest who will bury me?
If I die on the sea who will mourn over me?
Beasts of the forests will truly bury me,
Birds in the sky will truly mourn over me,
The great surf of the sea will be my winding-sheet,
The roaring of the sea will be the tolling of bells for me.

(Z. Kodály, Magyar Népzene, no. 178)

We may note that the passage containing the reference to the fishes in the Hungarian ballad is different from Vargyas's parallels not only in its actual wording but also in its emotional content. In the Rumanian, Serbian, etc., the stock-phrase 'being eaten up by fishes' portrays a horrible death, the fishes are also enemies, and the motif expresses the despair and courage of the heroine who is willing to choose a horrible death rather than live a miserable life. In the equivalent passage of the Hungarian ballad the emotional content of this passage is the same as in the prisoner and exile songs: the only consolation when facing a lonely death is the *sympathy of nature*: instead of family or friends it is the birds, beasts and fishes that will bury and mourn for the singer.

This emotional implication is further emphasized in the passage (contaminated with 'The Maid who was Sold') in which the girl asks her clothes to fall down from the nails and mourn over her, especially if we remember that in 'The Maid who was Sold' this is a continuation of her request to her flowers to wither, and to her animals (turkeys) to mourn her sad fate.

'THE GIRL WHO WAS RAVISHED
BY THE TURKS' (II)

Closely related to the preceding ballad in theme is the following piece. It was found in Moldavia only quite recently (1954–8) in three versions, interspersed with lyrical passages. Certain motifs (the demand to hand the maid over, the mother's denial of having a daughter, her betrayal of the girl, the girl's request to her clothes) come from 'The Maid who was Sold', and occur in class 1 also of 'The Girl who was Ravished'. Stanza 5 seems to be another link between the two otherwise rather different treatments of the theme. The heart motif is characteristic of the orphan-ballads.

Versions

A Faragó-Jagamas, *MCSNN*, no. 8. B *Néprajzi Közlemények* (1958), pp. 53–4 C *Néprajzi Közlemények* (1958) pp. 54–6.

Version **A**

1 'Mother, my mother,
   Hide me,
   Soldiers are coming
   To ravish me.

2 Mother, my mother,'
   'Where shall I hide you?
   Go into the chamber,
   Climb into the chest.'

3 Seventy-seven soldiers
   Arrived indeed,
   Seventy-seven soldiers,
   A regular company.

4 'Where is your daughter?
   Hand her over to us!
   Where is your daughter?
   Hand her over to us!'

5 'I have no daughter,
   She is dead,
   She is buried,
   We have mourned for her.'

6 'Leave your daughter,
   And we shall take you, yourself.'
   'Go into the chamber,
   There she is in the chest.'

7 'Mother, my mother,
   May God allow,
   May God allow
   That you be eaten by worms!'

Versions **B** and **C** do not have the curse. In **B** the daughter is put into prison by her ravishers, and the ballad continues with her complaint, a commonplace in Hungarian prisoner songs (cf. Csanádi–Vargyas, nos. 187, 188, 189):

> Mother, my mother,
> The nurse who has brought me up,
> The prison floor
> Is my feather-bed,
> The eyes of snakes and frogs
> Are my burning candles,
> My last hour
> Will come soon.

In **C** the mother is threatened: they will have her beheaded and her daughter as well unless she hands her over to them. When the mother reveals her daughter's hiding place and she is found, the daughter bids her clothes fall to the ground when she is beheaded. She takes leave of her mother, and leaves her lamenting. Before being taken away, she asks her mother to have her head placed on a brass plate, to send it to Kolozsvár, and to place it on the town gate, so that it may show the fate of one who is ravished.

All three versions end with stanzas borrowed from different folk-songs, sung to the same tune as our ballad.

References to the Turks, as Faragó-Jagamas point out, were kept very much alive in Moldavia by the circumstance that Rumania gained its independence in alliance with the Russians during the 1877–8 Russian-Turkish war. Some veterans of this war were still alive, in the 1950s, and the memory of the battles is so vivid still that even nowadays when children play at war the enemy is called 'the Turk' (Faragó-Jagamas, *MCSNN*, p. 27).

'THE GREAT MOUNTAIN ROBBER'

This ballad is known mainly in Transylvania, but some versions have been recorded in Transdanubia also. It is very popular among the people of the neighbouring countries, especially in Czechoslovakia, Rumania, and Poland.

The Hungarian versions are mostly lyrical: they consist mainly of the lyric complaint of the wife of a great mountain robber. In some versions the story has been dissolved into a folk tale. In order to illustrate the great variety among the various versions of this ballad, I give here the full translation of five versions.

Versions

A Ortutay, *Magyar Népköltészet*, II, no. 17 *c*; =Kriza (1956), no. 25; =*MNGY*, XI, p. 194; =Kriza, *Vadrózsák*, no. 292 **B** Csanádi-Vargyas, *Röpülj*, no. 57 **C** Csanádi-Vargyas, *Röpülj*, no. 56; =the variation offered to version C, *Ethnographia*, **19**, 107–8 **D** Ortutay, *Magyar Népköltészet*, II, no. 17 *b*; =Csanádi-Vargyas, *Röpülj*, no. 58; =*MNGY*, VIII, p. 184 **E** Ortutay, *Magyar Népköltészet*, II, no. 17 *a*; =*MNGY*, I, p. 228

Other versions

Csanádi-Vargyas, *Röpülj*, no. 55; =Bartalus, *Magyar Népdalok*, I, no. 1 *Ethnographia*, **19**, 106; **19**, 107; **19**, 107–8 (latter =Bartók-Kodály, *SZNd*, no. 125; =Kodály-Vargyas, *MNpt*, no. 357) Domokos-Rajeczky, *Csángó Népzene*, I, p. 61; II, nos. 13 (version 3), 15, 18 (fragments) Faragó-Jagamas, *MCSNN*, no. 12 *a* (=Domokos-Rajeczky, II, no. 13, versions 1–2); no. 12 *b*, no. 12 *c* *MNGY*, III, p. 88 (contaminated with 'Barcsai') *MNGY*, I, p. 195 Bartók-Kodály, *SZNd*, no. 83 *MNYr*, **4**, 567; =Kriza (1956), no. 26 Domokos, *Moldvai Magyarság*, nos. 12, 14, 15, and 13 (contaminated with 'The Maid who was Sold').

Version **A**

1 'I am not used to, I am not used to
   Getting up at dawn,
   Before rosy dawn
   Washing bloodstained clothes,

2 Soaking them in my tears,
   Beating them with groans,
   Soaking them in my tears,
   Beating them with groans.

3 Enough had I begged
   My father and mother
   Not to give me [in marriage]
   To a far-famed robber.

4 The far-famed robber
   Is even now away,
   To wait in ambush,
   To rob men,
   To lose his soul
   For a coin or two.

5 The far-famed robber
   Listens at the door
   To how his wife
   Is weeping at her own [misfortune].

6 'Open your door,
   My lady wife!'
   'It is open, it is open,
   My sweet, gentle husband.'

7 'Why were you weeping, why were you weeping,
My sweet wife?'
'I was not weeping, I was not weeping,
My sweet, gentle husband.

8 I was bustling about in the kitchen,
I was burning oak-wood,
The smoke of the oak-wood
Has brought tears to my eyes.'

9 'Why were you weeping, why were you weeping,
My sweet wife?
To-morrow at noon sharp
I will have you beheaded!'

10 The woman runs to the back,
She calls the servant:
'My Johnny, my Johnny,
My long-haired Johnny,

11 Make my coach ready for me,
Place my six horses between the shafts,
To-morrow at noon sharp
Take me to the place of beheading.

12 When I am beheaded
Wash my head in sweet wine,
In fair sweet wine,
Cover it with soft cambric,

13 Put it into my coach,
Carry it to Moldavia,
Set it on the table,
Of my father and mother,

14 That it may be a lesson
For the whole of Moldavia,
That none should give their daughter
To a robber.'

Version **B**

1 Come here Danube, come here! Come here Danube,
   come here,
By shower, by rain, and by my heavy tears

2 Sweep me away, Danube, sweep me away, sweep me away,
   Danube, sweep me away,
To my father's gate, to my father's gate,

3 Let me make him weep, let me make him weep:
Father, father dear! father, father dear,

4 To whom did you give away your daughter:
   To a far-famed robber, to a far-famed robber,

5 Who is even now away, who is even now away,
   To wait in ambush on the big roads, to wait in ambush
        on the big roads,

6 To grind knives, to grind knives,
   To kill an Armenian priest, to kill an Armenian priest!

7 Mother, mother dear! Mother, mother dear,
   When you bore me, when you bore me,

8 Would that you had rather borne, would that you had
        rather borne
   A small marble stone, a small marble stone

9 That is washed by this stream, that is washed by this
        stream...
   Mother, mother dear! mother, mother dear,

10 When you bathed me, when you bathed me,
   In soft warm water, in soft warm water

11 Would that you had rather bathed me, would that you
        had rather bathed me
   In boiling hot water, in boiling hot water.

12 When you dressed me, when you dressed me
   In soft cambric clothes, in soft cambric clothes,

13 Would that you had rather dressed me, would that you
        had rather dressed me
   In glowing embers, in glowing embers!

14 Mother, mother dear! mother, mother dear,
   When you rocked me, when you rocked me,

15 When you rocked me, when you rocked me
   In a little rocking cradle, in a little rocking cradle

16 Would that you had rather rocked me, would that you
        had rather rocked me
   Under the ground seven ells deep, under the ground
        seven ells deep.

17 My two arms are wearied, my two arms are wearied
   Of washing bloodstained clothes, of washing bloodstained
        clothes,

18 Of beating them with groans, of beating them with groans,
   Of soaking them with tears, of soaking them with tears.

19 My two ears are wearied, my two ears are wearied
   Of the rustling of the green wood, of the rustling of the
        green wood,

20 Of the singing of wild birds, of the singing of wild birds,
   Of the crackling of shotguns, of the crackling of shotguns.

Version **C**

1 My God, my God, make the water swell,
   That it might carry me along to my father's gate,
   That it might sweep me away to my mother's table,
   That I might plain my many plaints:

2 Mother, my mother, why did you sell me
   To the cold snowy mountains, to a great mountain
       robber,
   To a highwayman, to a robber,
   Who even now is away killing men?

3 For a single onion he will take a man's life,
   For a single onion he will take a man's life,
   For a coin or two, he does not shrink from bloodshed,
   For a coin or two, he does not shrink from bloodshed.

4 Amid mountains and valleys is my dwelling,
   I hear only the murmur of the calm river,
   The calm river falls asleep in winter,
   But my sorrow is never calmed.

5 My feet have become wearied by now of pressing a
       marble slab,
   Of pressing a marble slab, of washing bloodstained
       clothes,
   Of pressing a marble slab, of washing bloodstained
       clothes,
   Of draining off into the water many an innocent's blood.

6 Would that God had granted that I had not seen you,
   That I had not heard of your fame, of your name,
   Would that God had granted that I had not seen you,
   That I had not heard of your fame, of your name...

7 'Why are you weeping woman, why are you weeping?
       Have you perhaps been home to your mother,
   Or has your mother come here, or have you gone to her?'
   'I am not weeping, I am not weeping, nor have I been
       to my mother,
   I have neither gone to my mother, nor has she come here:
   I have been burning oak-wood, I have been rocking the
       child,
   The smoke of the oak-wood has brought tears to my
       eyes...'

8 He carried her down into the cellar and cut her throat.
   'Father, father, where is my mother?'

'Be silent my son, be silent my son, your mother will
    come forth,
Your mother will come forth when it is time for the
    midday meal!'

9 'Father, father dear, it is time for the midday meal,
It is time for the midday meal, my mother has not come...'
He carried him down into the cellar, he cut his throat,
He cut his throat: 'Here is your mother.'

Version D

1 'Every mother should consider well
To whom she gives her fair marriageable daughter!
I, like others, was sold by my mother
To a highwayman, to a murderer,
Who steals away from me every night,
To lie in ambush on the roads, to kill men,
Who brings to me always about midnight,
Who brings to me his bloodstained clothes:

2 "My helpmeet, my dear helpmeet, take away these clothes
To the dark cave, to the watery stream,
There open them out so that nobody may see them,
That not even the birds may speak of them,
Wash them so, wash them so, that not even their tumble
    might be heard,
That not even their tumble might be heard, that not even
    a drop of their water might be seen!
My helpmeet, my dear helpmeet, have you been weeping
    somewhere?" '
'I have not been weeping, I have not been weeping, my
    husband, my husband,
The smoke of the oak-log has come into my sloe-blue eyes,
Its flames have shot my two red cheeks.'
'My helpmeet, my dear helpmeet, why have you been
    weeping, why have you been weeping?'
'They have sent me word from my father's house that I
    should go to a wedding,
They are marrying my brother, they are giving away my
    younger sister.'
'My helpmeet, my dear helpmeet, what present will you take
    for them?'
'My husband, my dear husband, I will take a pair of wax
    candles.
That is the custom there: when a maiden is given away,
When a lad is married off, they are given wax candles.'

'My helpmeet, my dear helpmeet, why is it, why is it
That even the birds are silent in your father's wood?'
'My husband, my dear husband, that is the custom
When a maiden is sold even the birds are silent.'
'My helpmeet, my dear helpmeet, why is it, why is it
That there is nobody ploughing with a plough in your
        father's field?'
'My husband, my dear husband, that is the custom
That when a maiden is sold, they neither sow nor plough.'
'My helpmeet, my dear helpmeet, why is it, why is it,
That the bells are tolling loud in your father's town?'
'My husband, my dear husband, that is the custom
That when a maiden is sold the bells are ringing to tell
        the news.'
'My helpmeet, my dear helpmeet, why is it, why is it
That I can see many people in your father's courtyard?'
'My husband, my dear husband, that is the custom
That when a maiden is sold, a fine crowd gathers.'
'My helpmeet, my dear helpmeet, why is it, why is it
That I can hear great wailing from your father's courtyard?'
'My husband, my dear husband, that is the custom
That when a maiden is sold she is bewailed with lamentations.'
'Seize him, take him into the depths of the prison:
He killed my father, he killed my mother!
Take him, throw him into the depths of the prison:
He killed my brother, he killed my sister!'

Version E

The hollow fir-tree has three branches,
Its very first branch bends over towards Moldavia,
Its second branch bends over towards Kolozsvár,
Its third branch bends over towards little Hungary.
On the top of it there is a little bower,
In which a great mountain robber is growing.
     'My servant, my dear servant, go down to my courtyard,
Drag out my half-mourning coach,
Place my four grey foals between its shafts,
That I might go to try my fortune
To the king's court, to the princess.'
    So he went away.
He dressed himself as an emperor's son,
He went into the king's courtyard,
With the half-mourning coach,
With the four grey foals.
And he did indeed ask the princess's hand in marriage,
And he helped the princess up

Into his half-mourning coach,
He struck his grey foal,
And he went through remote parts[1]
Until he reached his little bower.
 He went up into his little bower,
And lo! he began to say:
'My wife, my wife, make me ready
That I might go to try my fortune
As a highway robber.'
 So she made him ready,
And the mountain robber went away.
His wife sat in the window,
There her tears began to fall.
 'Bird, little bird,
Take my letter
To my father.
Indeed he gave me in marriage
To a mountain robber,
Who is away even now,
To lie in ambush,
To kill men.
Would that he had given me instead
To a poor gipsy.'
 The robber listens at the door
To his wife's weeping complaint.
The mountain robber says:
'Woman, my wife, open your door!
'I will open it straightaway, my dear, gentle husband,
Let me just put on my funeral garments.
The knell is rung three times for a dead person,
Not once will it ring for me who am of noble birth.'
 The robber could not bear to wait,
He opened the door with a kick.
'Why are you weeping, my dear wife?'
'How could I not weep, my dear, gentle husband?
I have been bustling about in the kitchen, I have been
 burning oak-wood,
The smoke of the oak-wood has brought tears to my eyes.'
 'Woman, my wife, will you rather stand
Holding a candle gaily for two tablefuls of guests,
Or will you be left straightaway without a head?
 My servant, my dear servant, go down yourself
To the cellar,
Bring me up, yourself, two wooden churns of pitch
And two rolls of linen.'

---

 [1] 'Through remote parts' in Hungarian *hetedhét országon*, lit. 'in the seventh seven land':
a formula in Hungarian folk tales which serves to convey the idea of great distance.

He began at her feet, he finished at her head
Covering her with linen.
But when he started to pour the pitch on her, drop by drop,
There was no way of escape left for the robber
Because the family of the princess
Blocked all the doors and windows.
They shot at him through the doors and windows,
And soon they caught the great mountain robber.
The king had him seized,
Had him carried to his court,
He had the great mountain robber fastened
To the tails
Of four fiery foals.
And they went round the town with him indeed.
When he reached the point of death,
They had him set up at the four ends of the town,
Even there they shot him down with weapons.
By that time there was nothing that could be done
To save the princess,
All the pitch had melted on her body.
She died perforce
Within three days or so.

We may recognise several motifs and formulas which have been borrowed from other ballads: for example, the formula 'he listens at the door', the husband's demand that the door be opened, the lady's evasions come from 'Barcsai'; the 'beheading place' and the order given to the coachman were taken presumably from 'The Dishonoured Maiden'; the dialogue between father and child belongs to 'Clement Mason'; and the sending of the head comes from 'The Three Orphans'.

It is interesting to find the villain questioning the lady as to the reason for her tears, and her evasions, in this ballad since these traits belong to 'Anna Molnár', that is, the Hungarian representative of the Halewijn ballad. This agreement might suggest some connection between our ballad and the Halewijn group, especially if we bear in mind that in the German version J (cf. Nygard, op. cit.), the French and British versions as well, the villain is a robber; and that in the Nicolai-form there is no apparent reason why he should kill the maid except for the circumstance that she has been crying or complaining.

The plaint of the bride to her mother is sung at weddings, as the bride's farewell to her parents (cf. 'Fair Maid Julia'). Similar passages are very rare in English-Scottish balladry. The nearest parallel to it occurs in 'Mary Hamilton' (Child, no. 73):

Oh little did my mother think
The day she cradled me,
What lands I was to travel through,
What death I was to dee,
Oh little did my father think
The day he held up me,
What lands I was to travel through,
What death I was to dee.

The maid's wish to have died in her cradle is found also in Danish (*Dansk. Vis.* IV, p. 266, st. 28). Dialogues resembling that of version **D** appear in the 'Elveskund' type ballads (cf. bibliography to Danish, Swedish, Norwegian, Italian, Spanish, and French parallels in Child, I, pp. 375–87, notes to 'Clerk Colvill').

The implication of a visit to the wife's mother and her presumed complaint as suggested by the robber in version **C** and some other versions, followed by her death as a revenge—though unjustifiably cruel—brings to mind a not altogether clear Danish ballad in which the wife is also killed by her husband who overhears her complaint to her father (*DGF*, II, no. 110).

The reference to the Armenians suggests, in Domokos's opinion, a seventeenth-century origin of the ballad, since the Armenians appeared in Transylvania during the years 1668–9, having lived previously in Moldavia for 150 years (Domokos, *op. cit.* p. 260).

'LITTLE SOPHIE KÁLNOKI'

This fragmentary version was recorded in Transylvania, and it reads like an old piece in Hungarian ballad tradition. It tells the tale of the tragic death of Little Sophie Kálnoki, who was kicked to death by her husband. Unfortunately, the reason for this cruel treatment on the husband's part remains obscure.

Text: Gy. Ortutay, *Magyar Népköltészet*, II, no. 16

= *Ethnographia*, **71**, 253

1 'It is seven years today
And three full days
Since we have been together,
Since we have been together.
We have not eaten
One mouthful of bread together,
We have not drunk

One glass of water together.
My God, my God,
What is the reason for this,
What is the reason for this,
Valiant John Egri?'

2 'You know well, you know well,
Little Sophie Kálnoki,
The reason for it is
That I have never
Loved you,
Nor will I ever love you!'

3 Thereupon he kicked her so,
Thereupon he kicked her so:
He kicked her from the table
To the door,
He kicked her from the door
To the table.
Little Sophie Kálnoki
Up she spoke:

4 'It is enough now, enough,
Valiant John Egri,
On my left side
The sun has shone into me,
On my right side
My blood has streamed forth.'

5 Up and speaks
Valiant John Egri:
'My servant, my dear servant,
My older servant!
Lift her up in your arms,
Put her down on her bed.'

6 'My servant, my servant,
My older servant,
Let us go to chase the hare,
To chase the hare, to hunt!'

7 Up and speaks
Little Sophie Kálnoki:
'My servant, my dear servant,
My younger servant,
Drag forth, drag forth
My mourning coach,
Place my fast horses
Between the shafts, place them between the
    shafts.

8   The coach is for the fire,
The horse is for the dogs,
Drive on, drive on
As fast as you can do,
To my mother
To Mistress Paul Kálnoki,
To Mistress Paul Kálnoki,
To my mother.

9   Good day, good day,
My soul, my mother!'
'Welcome to you, my dear,
My soul, my good daughter!'
'I have not come for joy,
But I have come to die.'

10   'My servant, my dear servant,
My older servant,
Climb into this tree:
Have a look, can you see a light anywhere?'
'I cannot see a light anywhere
But at my noble lady's.'
'Come there, come there,
To my mother-in-law's.'

11   'Good evening, good evening
My dear gammer!'
'Welcome to you, my dear,
My dear son-in-law!
How have you left, how have you left
My dear daughter?'
'I have left her well, I have left her well,
I have left her in good health.'

12   So she went in
Into her little house,
Into her little house,
In a hidden chamber.
She cut off a slice of bread
From her table,
She poured out a glassful of water
From her jug:

13   'Eat this so, my son,
My dear son-in-law,
As if it were my daughter's flesh,
Drink it so, my son,
My dear son-in-law,
As if it were my daughter's blood!'

L. Vargyas draws attention to the circumstance that the image in our stanza 4 (i.e. that the sun has shone into the sides of the lady) is a characteristic of Portuguese traditional songs to convey the large size of the wound (*Ethnographia*, **71**, 255; *Acta Ethnographica*, **10**, 275–6).

'FAIR ANNA BÍRÓ'

This ballad is known only in Transylvania. The subject-matter seems to be of more recent origin than the rest of the ballads we have been dealing with.

On the other hand, the narrative technique: the frequent incremental repetitions, the use of formulas ('You have died...', etc.; 'So they go on, so they go on the big road...'; 'I will give you my grey horse') and the reference to the ominous sign (the tearing of the lady's apron) suggest an old ballad. L. Vargyas draws attention to a French ballad which was probably the source of the Hungarian ballad (*Ethnographia*, **71**, 164, with bibliography to the Hungarian, French and Italian versions; see also Vargyas, 'Rapports...', pp. 70–2). We should like to point out that 'Fair Anna Bíró' has wider affiliations with the 'Hr. Truels' Døttre'-type ballad, very popular in Scandinavia (bibl., cf. Child, notes to no. 14).

> *Text* **A**: Ortutay, *Magyar Népköltészet*, II, no. 31
> = Bartók-Kodály, *SZNd*, no. 66
> = Csanádi-Vargyas, *Röpülj*, no. 51

> Three young soldiers are drinking away, they are
>   drinking away
> At the tied-back gate of Mistress Sigismund Bíró.
> Out she strolled to them, Ai, did fair Anna Bíró:
> 'Where do you come from, three young soldiers?'
> 'From Meződebrecen and, Ai, from Barasso.'
> 'Do you happen to know Benedict Hajdú,
> Benedict Hajdú, my beloved?'
> 'Indeed we know him, he is our dear companion.'
> 'Do you mind if I go with you?'
> 'We do not mind, we feel we gain by it.'
> In she stepped quickly, Ai, fair Anna Bíró,
> 'Mother, mother, my sweet mother dear,
> Three young soldiers are drinking away, they are
>   drinking away,
> At the tied-back gate of Mistress Sigismund Bíró.
> I asked them, I did: "Where do you come from?"
> "From Meződebrecen, and, Ai, from Barasso."

"Do you happen to know Benedict Hajdú,
Benedict Hajdú, my beloved?"
Indeed they knew him, he was their dear companion.
Do you mind if I go with them?'
'Do not go away, my daughter, my fair flower;
If he does love you, he will surely come and find you.'
Up and answered her, Ai, fair Anna Bíró:
'Mother, mother, I will go with them!'
Fair Anna Bíró, Ai, set out with them.
On they go, on they go on the old highway,
On the old highway, through the snowy wilds.
Up and spoke the big young soldier:
'Let us kill, Ai, let us kill fair Anna Bíró!'
Up and answered the other young soldier:
'I do not mind, I do not mind, I feel we gain by it.'
Up and answered the smallest young soldier:
'Let us not kill the poor thing, let her come with us!'
'If you will not join us in killing her, we will kill
      you as well!'
Up and answered, did, Ai, fair Anna Bíró:
'In my right pocket there are three hundred florins,
I give those to you, only do not kill me!'
Up and answered the other young soldier:
'Your money is ours, you yourself are ours too!'
Up and answered, Ai, fair Anna Bíró:
'There are four hundred florins in my left pocket,
I will give all to you, only do not kill me!'
Up and answered the other young soldier:
'Let us kill, Ai, let us kill fair Anna Bíró!'
On they go, on they go on the old highway,
On the old highway, through the snowy wilds.
When they were passing the river Lemon,
Ai, the three of them killed fair Anna Bíró.
They forgot to take from her her many costly pearls,
Her many fine, costly pearls, and her ruffling cambric blouse.
'Go back, go back you smallest soldier,
Fetch me, fetch me her fine costly pearls,
Her fine, costly pearls and her ruffling cambric blouse!'
When he passed the river Lemon,
Ai, fair Anna Bíró was still alive then.
'Do not fear me, do not fear me, Ai, fair Anna Bíró,
What words do you send by me to Benedict Hajdú?'
'I send to Benedict Hajdú only these words:
He should not let himself be killed for the sake of a
      worthless girl.
For I let myself be killed for Benedict Hajdú.'
Presently Benedict Hajdú came [to the inn] too:

'Where did you get these, you three young soldiers?
You three young soldiers, these many fine costly clothes?'
Up and answered the big young soldier:
'We got them as winnings, we got them as winnings.'
Up and answered the other young soldier:
'One of our sisters died, they were left to us by her.'
Up and answered the smallest young soldier:
'It is not that our sister has died, or that we got her
    money:
Hey, we, the three of us, we killed fair Anna Bíró.'
'Come with me, come with me, you smallest soldier,
Show me, Ai, fair Anna Bíró,
Fair Anna Bíró, my beloved!
For I will give you my grey horse,
My grey horse and all of my gear!'
On they go, on they go, on the old highway,
On the old highway, through the snowy wilds,
When they were passing the river Lemon
He drew his pointed dagger and let himself fall on it:
'You have died for me, and I will die for you!'

Text **B**: Kriza (1956), no. 27 = *MNGY*, III, p. 20

Ai, fair Anna Bíró was sitting in the window,
She was embroidering with black silk thread,
Where the silk did not reach, she filled [the gap] with
    her tears.
At one point she glanced out of her window,
Behold, there were three young soldiers walking there.
Up and spoke, Ai, fair Anna Bíró:
'Where do you come from, you three young soldiers?'
'Ai, indeed we are from Mezőmadaras.'
'Have you heard of my beloved,
Of my beloved, of Benedict Hajdú?'
'Ai, indeed we have heard of him, he is a good friend of
    ours,
He is a good friend of ours, he is our dear companion.'
Up and speaks, Ai, fair Anna Bíró:
'If you did not mind, if you wanted also,
I would myself go to my beloved,
To my beloved, to Benedict Hajdú.'
Up and spoke the big young soldier:
'Oh, we do not mind, indeed, that is what we want!'
Ai, fair Anna Bíró dresses up straightaway:
She has thrown her fine silk skirt over her shoulder,
She has put her apron of fine net before her,
She has put her ten golden rings on her ten fingers,

She has put her three hundred gold pieces into her
    right pocket,
She has put her three hundred florins into her left pocket.
The wind did not blow it, a branch did not catch it,
Yet her apron of fine net was torn.
Up and spoke her mother dear:
'Do not go away, do not go away, my dear daughter,
For your journey will not be a fortunate one!'
Yet, Ai, fair Anna Bíró went away.
On they went in the snowy wilds,
In the snowy wilds, in vast forests.
Up and spoke, Ai, fair Anna Bíró:
'Oh, I want so much to drink that I am nearly dying!'
Up and answered the big young soldier:
'Wait a little, it will not be for long, Ai, fair Anna Bíró,
We are going, we are going to the rose meadow,
To the rose meadow, under the rose bush!'
They went on until they reached the place
And they sat down under the rose bush.
Up and spoke, Ai, fair Anna Bíró:
'Oh, I want so much to sleep that I am nearly dying!
If you do not mind, if you are willing,
I would like to sleep a little under the rose bush!'
Up and answered the big young soldier:
'Oh, we do not mind, indeed that is what we want!'
Thereupon she fell asleep in the rose bush.
Up and spoke the big young soldier:
'Let us kill, Ai, let us kill fair Anna Bíró!'
Up and answered the smaller young soldier:
'Let us not kill the poor thing, let us spare her life,
Let us spare her life, let her come with us!'
Up and answered the big young soldier:
'If we do not kill her, let us kill you [instead]!'
Yet they kill, Ai, fair Anna Bíró,
They take off her costly clothes.
On they went in the snowy wilds,
They spied Benedict Hajdú from a distance.
Up and spoke Benedict Hajdú:
'Where do you come from, you three young soldiers?'
'Ai, we have come from Mezőmadaras, indeed we have.'
'And where have you got the costly clothes?'
Up and spoke the big young soldier:
'Well, we got them indeed at the market of Barasso,
At the market of Barasso, at a sale.'
Up and answered Benedict Hajdú:
'You are lying, you are lying, for I know them well!'
He drew his sword, he let himself fall on it.

'LADISLAV FEHÉR'

This ballad is still popular throughout Hungary. In Transylvania only a few versions have been recorded.

The various versions agree in the central situation, and in the development of the story: Anna Fehér's brother, Ladislav, has stolen a horse and is therefore imprisoned. Anna wants to ransom him with gold and silver, but the judge will release him on one condition only: if Anna spends a night with him. Anna goes to Ladislav' prison door, and tells him the judge's offer. Ladislav advises her not to trust the judge's promise. Nevertheless, Anna visits the judge. She is awakened at night by the rattling of chains, the judge reassures her that his horses are being taken to the water and that is the noise she is hearing. In the morning Anna goes to the prison of her brother. The prisoners tell her that Ladislav was hanged (or shot) during the night. Anna casts a heavy curse on the judge.

The story seems to have originated in Italy, and is one of the stories that have been made 'classic' by Shakespeare ('Measure for Measure'). The traditional ballad form of the story is found only in Hungary, Italy and Spain. B. Zolnai has treated the international parallels in his study of the Hungarian ballad (*Irodalomtörténet*, 1917, pp. 405–11).

The Spanish ballad is fragmentary (see F. Wolf, *Proben portugiesischer und catalanischer Volksromanzen*, Wien, 1856, p. 143).

There are interesting Hungarian data to indicate that the story was known in Hungary in the sixteenth century. The first reference to it was made in a private letter written in Latin in 1547. The letter was written in Vienna and sent to the Hungarian town Sárvár. It introduces the story as a new and memorable one. In a town near Milan, two citizens started quarrelling, and one killed the other. The murderer was sent to prison. His wife went to appeal to the judge for her husband's life. He would grant mercy to the husband for the favours of the wife. The woman was reluctant at first, but on the persuasion of her relatives she surrendered to the request. Next day her husband was beheaded. The desperate woman appealed to Prince Ferdinand Don Gonzaga, the governor of Milan. The prince invited the false judge for dinner and rebuked him for his treachery. He made the judge pay three thousand pieces of gold and had him married to the lady. After the marriage the prince had the judge beheaded. This letter was translated from the Latin, and published by John Illésy (*Századok*, 1893, pp. 456–9). L. Kropf has published this letter in German (*Jahrbuch d. Deutschen Shakespeare-Gesellschaft*, 1894, pp. 292–3).

The other sixteenth-century Hungarian reference is to be found in Peter Bornemissza's *Postilla* (1578).

In the Italian ballad 'La povera Cecilia' (F. G. Widter and A. Wolf, *Volkslieder aus Venetien*, Wien, 1864, no. 85), the heroine is the prisoner's wife. Her husband does not object to her spending a night with one of the captains on whom his release depends. The Italian ballad has the motif of Cecilia waking up at midnight, the captain's questioning her as to the reason for her sighs; she feels her death approaching. In the morning Cecilia goes to the balcony and sees her husband hanging from the gallows. She cries, the captain offers to marry her, but she refuses.

In the various international narrations of the story the heroine is made either the wife or the sister of the prisoner. 'Ladislav Fehér' stands alone in the motif of the prisoner's advising the lady *against* making the sacrifice, and in the curse motif at the end of the ballad. The reason for Ladislav's imprisonment (i.e. that he stole a horse) is a nineteenth-century Hungarian 'couleur locale' in the telling, as a result of the influence of the *betyár* ballads.

The style of the ballad suggests a nineteenth-century composition. On the other hand, the tune which accompanies the rhymed octo-syllabic lines is one of the most ancient of Hungarian tunes.

Text: Csanádi-Vargyas, *Röpülj*, no. 70

1 Ladislav Fehér stole a horse
  At the bottom of the black hill.
  His leather whip cracked noisily,
  It was heard in the town of Gönc.

2 'Come on, come on, citizens of Gönc,
  Ladislav Fehér has been caught!'
  Anna Fehér has heard it,
  She runs down into the stable:

3 'Coachman, place the horses between the shafts,
  Put pure gold upon their backs,
  To-morrow we are going to the town,
  To release my brother...

4 Welcome to you, Your Worship,
  Welcome to you, welcome to you.
  I have brought you pure gold,
  Release my brother.'

5 'I do not want your pure gold,
  I only want you to spend a night with me.
  Spend one night with me,
  And your brother will be free by one o'clock.'

6 Thereupon Anna does not utter a word,
    She hurries along the corridor,
    From one corridor to another,
    She goes to the gate of the prison.

7 'Ladislav Fehér, my brother dear,
    Harken, what the judge has told me:
    Would I spend a night with him,
    You would be free by one o'clock.'

8 'Do not spend a night with that rascal,
    With that gallows-bird!
    He will take your maidenhood,
    He will have your brother beheaded!'

9 Thereupon Anna does not utter a word,
    She hurries along the corridor,
    From one corridor to another,
    She goes to the judge's chamber.

10 'What is rattling in your courtyard
    At one o'clock after midnight?'
    'They are taking your horse to water,
    It is the bridle in its mouth that is rattling.'

11 Thereupon Anna does not utter a word,
    She hurries along the corridor,
    From one corridor to another,
    She goes to the gate of the prison.

12 'Ladislav Fehér, my brother dear,
    Are you asleep or are you dead?'
    The rest of the prisoners answer her:
    'Do not look here for your brother,

13 But in the green wood, in the green meadow,
    At the top of the gallows-tree.'
    Thereupon Anna does not utter a word,
    She walks along the corridor weeping:

14 'Cursing is not a habit with me,
    But if it takes effect in your case, I shall not mind that:
    May the water in which you wash turn to blood,
    May your towel go up in flames,

15 May you weigh down the bottom of your bed
    For thirteen years,
    May thirteen cart-loads of hay
    Rot away in your bed,

16 May thirteen rows of medicines
    Be emptied for you,
    May you be carried to the churchyard
    At the end of the thirteenth year!'

The passage of Anna's calling to her brother in the prison ('Are you asleep, or are you dead?') is a formula in Hungarian ballads. It occurs in 'Kate Kádár' and in 'The Dishonoured Maiden' as well, with slight variations: 'Are you alive or are you dead?' and 'Are you eating, or are you drinking, or are you sleeping indeed?' It may be compared to the 'O sleep you, wake you' formula in English and Scottish ballads (cf. Child, nos. 7, 30, 69, 70, 71, 73, 77, 90, 186, 187, 203). In Hungarian ballads it is always addressed to someone dead, or to someone who is in prison.

The sequence of motif consisting of the killing at night, the lady's awakening and her suspicion, her questioning the villain, his evasive answers, and the lady's disbelief in them are paralleled in *DGF*, I, no. 4. In the Danish ballad it is the lady's brothers who are murdered by her husband (*A*, sts. 18–20).

> 'I sigger meg, her Loffmor, herre myn:
> hvor haffver y weritt om natter-thid?'
> 'Ieg war meg ude paa helde,
> Som ieg hørde dy høgge dy gieldde.'
> 'Saa lennge snackitt du om høge dynn,
> herre Gud rade well for brøder myn!'

For bibliography to the Hungarian versions, cf. Kálmány, *Hagyaték*, II, pp. 238–9, compiled by Gy. Ortutay.

An apparently old ballad, steeped in folk-tale atmosphere, is worth quoting here, since its theme belongs to the Ladislav Fehér ballad type. (For the encounter with the robbers and their captain's offer, cf. Child, no. 8.)

'THE PRINCE AND THE PRINCESS'

Text: Ortutay, *Magyar Népköltészet*, II, no. 74 *a* = *Figyelő*, I, 88

1 A king of yore had a daughter of yore,
  Her hair was like gold, her eyes like stars, she had
    no match.
  She was always clad in royal splendour,
  With silver, with gold, with clothes set with diamonds.

2 A king of yore had a son of yore,
  His sword was made of gold, his horse was silver,
  He had the sun on his forehead, the moonlight on his chest.

3 The king of yore had a son of yore,
  The other king had a fair daughter.

The beautiful prince arrived with a coach and six horses,
He asked the princess in marriage without further parley.
She was given to him, they were made one,
The wedding was celebrated for a whole week.

4 The young prince was carrying the girl lovingly
On a golden-wheeled coach with six horses.
Aye, they were passing a big forest,
Four heyduck-soldiers stood in their way.

5 'We wish good day to you, prince,
Within this hour you must die!'
'Alas, do not harm me, do not shed my blood.
I will give you my gold, my silver, my horse.'
The princess begs them: 'Four heyduck-soldiers!
Do not seek our death!'

6 'Hear it, hear it you, royal princess!
You can ransom yourself, you can help your husband:
You sleep three nights in our captain's bed,
Afterwards you may go away together with your husband
    and horse!'

7 Her husband agreed, the princess agreed,
She slept three nights in the captain's bed,
On the fourth morning the heyduck-soldiers
Chopped off her husband's head and hers.

8 'God bless you, God bless you, my sweet husband dear!
May our souls meet in the other world!'
'God bless you, God bless you, my wife dear,
May your soul come and find me in the other world!'

'THE GIRL WHO WAS DANCED TO DEATH'

This ballad, similar to 'Ladislav Fehér', is still popular in Hungary, especially in the western and in the north-eastern parts. On the evidence of the tune and of the words, this ballad should be listed among the new-style ballads. It tells the story of a girl who rejected her suitor, or loved two young men at the same time, and was therefore punished by a most cruel death: she had to dance with the suitor till she died. The ballad has been preserved in numerous versions. Sometimes the singers of the ballad comment on the story and express the view that the person who danced with the girl till she died was the devil, for no human being could have danced in the way that the man of the ballad did. Other singers added that the devil appeared in the guise of the girl's lover. The introduction of the devil into the narrative (cp.

Thompson, G 303.10.4) and the strange punishment of the girl together with the use of incremental repetition may suggest an earlier origin of the ballad than indicated by the style and tune of its present form. The significant motif of dancing till the boots are full of blood occurs in the Scandinavian 'Elveskud' type ballads (cf. Child's bibl., II, p. 374) and in 'Liden Kirstins Dans' (*Dansk. Vis.* IV, 315, st. 13). L. Vargyas compares this piece with the French 'Les tristes noces' (*Ethnographia*, 71, 126–31) and suggests that the Hungarian ballad originates from this French ballad. Most of the more than two hundred versions are still unpublished; for bibliography, cf. Kálmány, *Hagyaték*, II, pp. 237–8.

Text: Csanádi-Vargyas, *Röpülj*, no. 65

= Pap, *Palóc Népköltemények*, no. 7

1 The young men of Sár are dancing, they are dancing
In the inn of Sár,
Small Clement Darvas is among them, he is among them,
He is not eating, he is not drinking, neither takes he
  part in the dancing.

2 The young men of Sár came, they came
To the wife of the sheriff of Sár, and to Kate Sallai:
'Good day, good day to you, good wife of the sheriff of Sár,
We have come, we have come
To the wife of the sheriff of Sár, and to Kate Sallai.'

3 'Mother, mother, my rich mother,
Bring in my ball-dress for me,
My headdress with the golden top, my little skirt made
  of damask,
My boots with the narrow soles!'

4 The young men of Sár came, they came
To the inn of Sár.
'Come in for a dance, fair Kate Sallai,
The daughter of the sheriff of Sár!'
'I will not come, I will not come, Small Clement Darvas,
Your clothes are filthy, they will dirty me!'

5 'And I say for the second time: come now to dance
  [with me],
Fair Kate Sallai, the daughter of the sheriff of Sár!'
'I will not come, I will not come, Small Clement Darvas,
Your clothes are filthy, they will dirty me!'

6 'And for the third time I say: come dance with me, come,
Fair Kate Sallai!
You have made mock of me: I will make mock of you!'

7 'Mother, my mother!
Bring in now that ball-dress of mine,
My silk hat, my velvet gown,
Fill its pockets with pieces of gold and silver!'

8 'Come now to dance with me, fair Kate Sallai,
The daughter of the sheriff of Sár!
Musicians, musicians, you twelve musicians:
If you start playing [the tune] in the evening let it end
    in the morning!
If you start playing [the tune] in the morning, let it end
    in the evening!'

9 'Let me go, let me go, Small Clement Darvas!
My headdress with the golden top has cleaved to my
    head.'
'Indeed I will not let you go: seven times have I asked
    you in marriage,
If they do not give you to me, they will give you to
    nobody else!
Musicians, musicians, you twelve musicians:
If you start playing the tune in the morning, let it end
    in the evening!
If you start playing the tune in the evening, let it end
    in the morning!'

10 'Let me go, let me go, Small Clement Darvas,
My small damask skirt has cleaved to my waist.'
'Indeed I will not let you go: seven times I have asked
    you in marriage,
If they do not give you to me, they will give you to
    nobody else!
Musicians, musicians, you twelve musicians:
If you start playing the tune in the morning, let it end
    in the evening!
If you start playing the tune in the evening, let it end
    in the morning!'

11 'Let me go, let me go, Small Clement Darvas,
My boots with the thin soles are full of clotted blood.'
'Indeed I will not let you go: seven times I have asked
    you in marriage,
If they do not give you to me, they will give you to
    nobody else!
Musicians, musicians, you twelve musicians,
If you start playing the tune in the morning, let it end
    in the evening!
If you start playing the tune in the evening, let it end
    in the morning!'

294

12 'Let me go, let me go, Small Clement Darvas,
Alas, my life is gone! I shall straightaway die!
Take me, my good maiden friends,
Carry me to the wife of the sheriff of Sár,
To my mother.
Open, mother, open your gate,
Make, mother, make ready for me my bed,
Find for me, also, my burial-clothes!'

13 'Mother, my mother, for whomever are they tolling the
knells three times?'
'My son, my dear son, Small Clement Darvas:
It is for Kate Sallai, for the daughter of the sheriff of Sár.'

14 'Good day, good day to you, good wife of the sheriff of Sár,
I have come once more to the wife of the sheriff of Sár,
And to Kate Sallai.'

(The singer added prose: 'Thereupon Small Clement Darvas bent over the body of fair Kate Sallai, and died there.)

7

BALLADS OF FAMILY CONFLICT

Introduction

Different as they are in their narrative plots—mother escaping from the enemy abandons her children who are then brought up by animals ('Ilona Budai'), mother trying to test her daughter's charity imprisoned by daughter ('Lady Albert Nagybihal'), unrecognised children dying in their parents' house ('The Brother and the Sister who had been Imprisoned by the Turks'), mother-in-law murdering her daughter-in-law ('Merika'), and the 'Lord Randal'-type 'Poisoned John'—all the Hungarian ballads dealing with family conflict have two features in common:

1. All of them are significantly imbued with folk-tale elements.

2. Perhaps on account of this fact all of them leave one with the impression of incompleteness in the sense that rather too little information is provided about the background of, or antecedents to, the action of the ballad. The circumstance that most ballads which fall under this class were recorded in Transylvania and Moldavia only ('The Brother and the Sister...' has one version from the Lowland, but this does not necessarily mean that the ballad was generally known in that region) would suggest that the reason for the above characteristics may be sought in Rumanian influence, or borrowing, since the tendency to elaborate the ballad story with folk-tale elements is characteristic of the Rumanian tradition.

Since the investigation into this problem would involve an extensive study of all popular genres, especially folk tales of Rumania and of other ethnic groups neighbouring Hungary, it lies outside the scope of this work.

'ILONA BUDAI' or 'THE CRUEL MOTHER'

This ballad of the cruel mother who deserted her two children has been recorded only in Transylvania and in Moldavia.

Text: Csanádi-Vargyas, *Röpülj*, no. 15 = Ortutay, *Magyar Népköltészet*, II, no. 4 *a* = Kriza, *Vadrózsák*, no. 585 = Kriza (1956), no. 6

1 Ilona Budai was leaning on her elbows at the window,
She heard that the enemy was plundering the neighbourhood.
All at once she remembered her small treasure-chest,
And she took her small treasure-chest under her arm,
She led her little maiden daughter with her right arm,
She took her little toddling son on her left arm.

2 On she goes, on she goes, on she goes through a dense
    pine-forest,
On a deserted road, in a dark forest,
And lo! it is as if she heard the sound of horses' hooves,
And she quickly puts down her little maiden daughter.
Her little maiden daughter wept thus:
'Mother, my mother, do not leave me on the road,
May your heart be softened, do not leave me here!'
'Indeed I will leave you, my daughter, here,
For God will give a daughter to replace a daughter,
But God will not give me any gift to replace my money.'

3 On she goes, on she goes through the dense pine-forest,
On the deserted road, in a dark forest,
And lo! it is as if she heard the sound of horses' hooves,
And she quickly puts down her little toddling son.
Her little toddling son wept thus:
'Mother, my mother, do not leave me on the road,
May your heart be softened, do not leave me here!'

4 'Indeed I will leave you, my dear son, here,
For God will give a son to replace a son,
But God will not give me any gift to replace my money!'

5 On she goes, on she goes through the dense pine-forest,
On the deserted road, in the dark forest,
Until she reaches a fair, wide meadow,
Behold, a she-buffalo is coming across it:
She was carrying her new calf between her horns,
And she was calling her old calf to follow behind her.
As soon as Ilona Budai glimpsed this,
She threw herself on the ground, she wept bitterly,
She wept bitterly, she blamed herself:
'The witless beast does not leave its calf,
My God, my God, my dear God,
How could I, who have a soul, have left my child?'

6 Thereupon she turned back in the big pine-forest,
On the deserted road, in the dark forest,
Soon she reached her little son,
She stretched out her finger to him, she started to call
    him kindly.

'Indeed I will not come, for you have not been a true
   mother,
Had you been that, you would not have left me here!'

7 On she goes, on she goes in the big pine-forest,
  On the deserted road, in the dark forest,
  Soon she reached her little maiden daughter,
  She stretched her finger out to her, she started to call
    her kindly.

8 'Indeed I will not come, for you have not been a true
   mother,
  Had you been that, you would not have left me here!'

9 When she heard these words, she wept thus:
  'Here and now I have become like a tree by the side of
    the road:
  Whoever goes by, let him damage my branches,
  Let him damage my branches, and tread them into the mud.'

The versions recorded in Moldavia have added (or preserved) a
motif which is characteristic of traditional tales: wolves take care of the
children (cf. Thompson, B 535; Vargyas, *Ethnographia*, **71**, 509, =*Acta
Ethnographica*, **10**, 281–4).

Text: Gy. Ortutay, *Magyar Népköltészet*, II, no. 4 *b* = *MNYr*, **4**, p. 287

The poor, hapless woman
In order to avoid
Bitter captivity,
Captivity among the Tartars,
Took on her right arm,
Her weeping little son,
Took on her left arm
Her weeping little daughter.
'My God, my God,
My loving God,'
She began to sigh,
'Which of them should I put down.
Perhaps, after all, I shall put down
My weeping little daughter,
And take with me
My dear little son.
Sit down here, sit down here,
My weeping little pigeon,
So that I might go off too,
To pick roses,
Out of the rose meadow,
Among the rose bushes.'

She went off weeping,
Out into the rose meadow,
All at once she met
A young cow.
It had taken this year's calf
Into its mouth,
But let last year's calf
Follow behind it.
'My God, my God,
This is a cow
And I am a creature with a soul,
And yet it has not abandoned
Either of its calves,
So I will not
Abandon either of my children.'
When she got back
[Her daughter] had fallen
Into the clutches
Of three ravenous wolves;
You have something to weep over, woman.
The biggest says:
'Let us tear her into three pieces!'
The second says:
'What will we gain by it?'
The smallest says:
'Let us not tear her into three pieces.
This will be better: let us take the poor thing
Into our father's den,
Let us bring her up there
On tender meat of lambs,
Let us not fill the meadow
With innocent weeping.'
The three of them carried her away,
They brought her up,
On tender meat of lambs,
Among the howling wolves.
When she could use her brain
She began to ask:
'Father, my father,
My dear wolf-father,
Give me leave to go
And play in the forest,
Run around in the meadows,
And pick flowers!'
'Do not go out, do not go out,
My weeping little daughter,
Those who pursue game

May catch you!'
There was nothing he could do,
He had to let her go,
He could not resist the words
Of the sweet, pretty little girl.
And lo! her own mother
Spied her:
'Are you here, my little angel,
My weeping little daughter,
Come to me at last,
My weeping little daughter,
Look how well he has grown up
My sweet, bonny little son!'
'Be silent, woman, be silent,
You are not my mother,
Had you been my [true] mother,
You would not have left me!'

'Ilona Budai' has no close international parallel in balladry. 'The Cruel Mother' (Child, no. 20) has a similar theme, but there the mother kills her two children. Both the British and the Hungarian ballads share the mother's repentance, and the children's rebuke for her cruelty.

The most prominent feature of the ballad, the she-buffalo who puts the mother to shame, appears to be indigenous to Hungary.

Other versions

Domokos, *Moldvai Magyarság*, no. 26　Faragó-Jagamas, *MCSNN*, no. 5　Domokos-Rajeczky, *Csángó Népzene*, II, no. 3 (four versions)

'BEAUTIFUL KATE BÁN'

This ballad has been recorded in the Lowland and, as we have already mentioned in the discussion of 'Anna Molnár', it has derived from the confluence of the latter ballad and 'Ilona Budai'. It is interesting to observe the process of folk-tale elements being introduced into the story. (The saliva left behind by the escapee, which has the magic speech: cf. Aarne-Thompson Type 313.) We have placed in italics the passages which are told in prose.

Text: C. Kálmány, *Szeged Népe*, II, p. 169 = Csanádi-Vargyas, *Röpülj*, no. 14 = Ortutay, *Magyar Népköltészet*, II, no. 5

1　'Come now, come now, Beautiful Kate Bán,
To our country, to lovely Turkey!'

2 'I will not go, I will not go, Black Peter Rác,
  For I have a son, a little toddling son,
  A daughter who still has to be carried, and a dear wedded
      husband.'

3 'Do not worry about them!
  Come now, come now, Beautiful Kate Bán,
  To our country, to lovely Turkey,
  Even dogs do not bark in the same way in lovely Turkey
  As in Hungary!'

4 'I will not go, I will not go, Black Peter Rác,
  For I have a son, a little toddling son,
  A daughter who still has to be carried, and a dear wedded
      husband.'

5 'Come now, come now, Beautiful Kate Bán,
  To our country, to lovely Turkey,
  For two hundred silver coins, for sixty-six thalers,
  For three hundred pieces of gold!'

Then she went off with him.

6 They reached the forest, there she left her son,
  Her little toddling son, her daughter who still had to be
      carried.
  'I leave you here, by the poplar,

7 Whenever the birds are flapping their wings,
  Just imagine
  That your mother is talking to you.

8 Whenever it is raining, just imagine
  That I, your mother, am bathing you.'

She put them into the tree, and left them.

9 Eagles maul their hearts, ravens pick their eyes,
  They tear the sad hearts of the poor innocent things.

10 On they went, on the went, then they sat down,
  Kate searched in the hair of the Turk.

11 'What can it be, what can it be, Beautiful Kate Bán,
  It is not raining, nor can any clouds be seen,
  Yet my hair is dripping wet, through and through?'

12 'A black cloud passed here just now,
  And a few drops of rain fell from it.'

She had looked up, and had seen that a bird was feeding its young one, that was why she wept.

13 'Let us move on, let us move on, Beautiful Kate Bán,
  Let us move on, let us move on, for the evening will fall
      upon us!'

14 As soon as they reach the house of the Turk,
As soon as they rest in the room of the Turk,
Black Peter Rác just says to her straightaway:
'Prepare the meal now, prepare the meal, Beautiful Kate Bán.'

15 Beautiful Kate Bán went into the kitchen,
She spat spittle on the middle of the kitchen [floor].
'Now, my sweet little spittle, when the Turk will say:
—Prepare the meal, prepare the meal, Beautiful Kate Bán!—
Just answer him: 'It will be ready, now, in an instant!'

16 'Dish up, dish up now, Beautiful Kate Bán!'
'I will dish up in an instant, Black Peter Rác!'
'Dish up, dish up now, Beautiful Kate Bán!'
'I will dish up in an instant, Black Peter Rác!'
'Dish up, dish up now, Beautiful Kate Bán!'
'I will dish up in an instant, Black Peter Rác!'

17 Black Peter Rác could not bear waiting any longer,
He went into the kitchen.
He could not find Beautiful Kate Bán anywhere,
Beautiful Kate Bán had set out on a journey.

18 Black Peter Rác saddled straightaway
His best horse,
He galloped in her track through forest after forest,
Still he could not find her,
So Black Peter Rác galloped back.

By the time Beautiful Kate Bán reached the forest where she had left her children, she found
nothing there but bones. She took some of them home, to her mother's house.

19 'Open, mother, open, your locked door!
I am your daughter, your daughter Kate!'

20 'Away you go, devil, do not haunt me,
I have no daughter,
Nine weeks have passed, this is the tenth
That the fishermen have been searching for her with nets,
Nowise can they find her!'

21 'Open, mother, open your locked door!
I am your daughter, your daughter Kate!'

22 'Away you go, devil, do not haunt me,
I have no daughter,
Nine weeks have passed, this is the tenth
That the fishermen have been searching for her with nets,
They can find her nowhere!'

23 'Open, mother, open your locked door,
For if you do not open it, my heart will break!'

24 'I will not open, I will not open it, I have no daughter,
  Nine weeks have passed, this is the tenth
  That the fishermen have been searching for her with nets,
  They can find her nowhere.'

When her mother opened her door, Kate Bán was lying there—she had flung herself on her face next to the bones of her two children.

'LADY ALBERT NAGY-BIHAL' or 'THE MOTHER OF THE RICH WOMAN'

This ballad has been preserved in five versions in Transylvania. Its tune belongs to the oldest pentatonic group of Hungarian folksongs. The lines are dodecasyllables, with occasional rhymes. It tells the story of a mother, who has learned that her daughter (who married a wealthy man, often a Turk) does not help the poor. She arrives at her daughter's house in the guise of a beggar and is imprisoned, on her daughter's order. She has spent seven years in the prison, when a servant overhears her complaint and reports it to the mistress of the house. When the mother reveals her identity to her daughter, she offers many presents to compensate her mother for the years in prison. The mother refuses to accept the presents and casts a curse on her daughter.
  I give the full translation of two versions.

Text **A**: Gy. Ortutay, *Magyar Népköltészet*, II, no. 27 *b*
= Csanádi-Vargyas, *Röpülj*, no. 45 = Bartók-Kodály,
SZNd, no. 28

1 A woman had three fair daughters,
  She had given them in marriage into three countries,
  The youngest had gone away to Turkey,
  The mother heard that she was a wealthy landowner and
    did not have pity on the poor.

2 'Husband, my husband dear, I ask you this:
  Give me leave to go to Turkey,
  To visit my youngest daughter,
  To visit my youngest daughter!'

3 'Go, coachman, go, place the horses between the shafts,
  Have your Mistress taken to Turkey,
  To visit her youngest daughter,
  To visit her youngest daughter!'

4 They set out indeed [and went] into Turkey
  To visit her youngest daughter.

At the outskirts of the town the lady alighted:
'Now, you coachman go away, go away to your home,

5 In three months time come for me,
In three months time come for me!'
The lady put on beggar's dress,
She went to her daughter's gate.

6 She began repeating in her sorrow and sadness:
'Give me a little bread and a small glass of water!'
The servant heard it, he went to his Mistress:
'My Mistress, my Mistress, my honoured Mistress,

7 I place my life and death in your hands,[1]
A poor beggar-woman keeps on repeating:
"Give me a little bread and a small glass of water,
Give me a little bread and a small glass of water!"'

8 The poor beggar-woman kept on repeating the same chant.
The servant heard it, he went to his Mistress:
'My Mistress, my Mistress, my honoured Mistress,
I place my life and death in your hands,

9 The poor beggar-woman keeps on repeating:
"Give me a little bread and a small glass of water!"'
'My servant, my chamber maids, my dog and hounds,[2]
Go and put her in the dark prison!'

10 The poor beggar-woman keeps on repeating the same chant
there:
'Keep mother, keep, keep your daughter,
And have your red blood poured out of yourself,
And have your sweet milk sucked out of you,
Yet, what you deserve is that she puts you in prison,
Yet, what you deserve is that she puts you in prison!'

11 The servant heard it, he went to his Mistress:
'My Mistress, my Mistress, my honoured Mistress,
I place my life and death in your hands,
The poor beggar-woman keeps on repeating this:

12 "Keep mother, keep, keep your daughter,
And have your red blood poured out of yourself,
And have your sweet milk sucked out of you,
Yet, what you deserve, is that she puts you in prison!"'

13 'Go and clear off, for I have many things to do,
My mother, she does not come to see me!'

---

[1] 'I place my life and death in your hands' is a formula for addressing a king or a powerful person in Hungarian folk tales.
[2] 'My dog and hounds' in Hungarian *ebem s kutyájaim*. The Hungarian words are synonyms, and were used probably in order to complete the number of syllables in the line.

The poor beggar-woman keeps on repeating [the chant],
The servant heard it, he went to his Mistress:

14 'My Mistress, my Mistress, my honoured Mistress,
    I place my life and death in your hands,
    The poor beggar-woman keeps on repeating that,
    The poor beggar-woman keeps on repeating that.'

15 'Go, my servant, ahead, that I might go after you,
    That I might see what sort of a beggar-woman she is.'
    She opened the door, she beheld her mother,
    She fell on her neck, she weeped over her:

16 'Mother, my mother, why did you not speak out,
    That I should not have been able to do this to you!
    Come in mother, to my inner chamber,
    I will give you now a glass of my best wine!'

17 'May the wind of Hell throw into confusion your inner
        chamber,
    May the wind of Hell spill the glass of your best wine!
    For I have not come here in order that you should offer
        me [something]
    But I have come since I had heard what sort of a woman
        you are!'

Text **B**: Ortutay, *Magyar Népköltészet*, II, no. 27 *a*
= Kriza, *Vadrózsák*, no. 4 = Kriza (1956), no. 17
= *MNGY*, XI, no. 19

1 The poor prisoner woman is lamenting about herself:
    'It is seven years and three full days today,
    Since I have fallen into captivity, into a dreadful, heavy
        captivity:
    Where I have been able to reach my flesh, I have eaten
        my flesh,
    Where I have not been able to do so, snakes and frogs
        have gnawed me,
    Where I have been able to reach my blood, I have drunk
        my blood,
    I have often sucked the blood of my arms and legs.

2 He, who would give me the crust of his bread
    Would certainly go to Heaven,
    He, who would give me the water in his glass
    Would certainly taste the savour of Heaven.'

3 The Mistress' chambermaid listens at the door.
    'My Mistress, my Mistress, my deeply honoured Mistress,

I would say something, if you do not have me whipped
    [for it],
The poor prisoner woman is lamenting over herself:
"It is seven years and three full days today,
Since I have fallen into captivity, into a dreadful, heavy
    captivity:
Where I have been able to reach my flesh, I have eaten
    my flesh,
Where I have not been able to do so, snakes and frogs have
    gnawed me,
Where I have been able to reach my blood, I have drunk
    my blood,
I have often sucked the blood of my arms and legs,
He, who would give me the crust of his bread
Would certainly go to Heaven,
He, who would give me the water in his glass
Would certainly taste the savour of Heaven." '

4 'I would rather throw the crust of my bread to the smallest
    of my watch-dogs
Than to give it to her,
I would rather have the water in my glass sucked up by
    the ground around my palace
Than to give it away;
Seize her, take her to the place of beheading!'

5 'Wait a little, wait a little, you honoured Lady,
For the knell is rung three times for the dead,
Are they not to ring it even once for my hapless self?
Whose daughter have you been, you honoured Lady?'

6 'I have been until now, the daughter of Francis Bodrogi!'
'If you have been indeed Francis Bodrogi's daughter,
So have I been indeed Mistress Francis Bodrogi,
Mistress Francis Bodrogi, your own mother!'

7 'Come in now, I say, come in, mother,
I will bath you in milk, I will have you anointed with butter!'

8 'Do not bath me, do not have me anointed
For you have anointed me often enough in the dark prison,
May my God, my daughter, pay you for that!'

Another version (Csanádi-Vargyas, *Röpülj*, no. 44 = *MNGY*, III,
p. 16 = Kriza (1956), no. 18.) concludes with the following:

'Is it you, is it you, my soul, my mother!
Do come in, do come in, do come in quickly!
I will have good caraway-seed soup made for you,

I will give you, I will give you a snow-white cambric shift,
I will give you, I will give you my painted palace,
I will give you, I will give you my gay-coloured coach,
I will give you, I will give you my six fine horses!'

'May the dog eat your caraway-seed soup,
May a strong wind blow away your snow-white cambric shift,
May fire burn your painted palace,
May rust eat your gay-coloured coach,
May the plague knock down your six fine horses,
I do not want anything from you, not even yourself,
Keep yourself for yourself, you fair honoured Lady!'

Other versions

MNGY, III, p. 59   Csanádi-Vargyas, *Röpülj*, no. 46; =*Ethnographia*, **19**, 51

In the latter version the prisoner's lament has the motif of seven years
without seeing the sun and the moon, which occurred in 'Szilágyi and
Hagymási'.

'THE BROTHER AND THE SISTER WHO
HAD BEEN IMPRISONED BY THE TURKS'

This ballad was recorded all over Hungary, in four versions. Versions **A**
and **C** were taken down in Transylvania, **D** in the Lowland, and **B** in
Moldavia.

A Csanádi-Vargyas, *Röpülj*, no. 75; =*Ethnographia*, **19**, 43; =Ortutay, *Magyar Népköltészet*, **II**,
no. 28 *a*   **B** Faragó-Jagamas, *MCSNN*, no. 7   **C** Csanádi-Vargyas, *Röpülj*, no. 76   **D** Csanádi-
Vargyas, *Röpülj*, no. 77; =Kálmány, *Szeged Népe*, **II**, no. 2; =Ortutay, *Magyar Népköltészet*, **II**,
no. 28 *b*.

Version **A**

1 Two fair prisoners were caught
    One fair prisoner was John Bíró
    The other fair prisoner was Kate Bíró,
    The other fair prisoner was Kate Bíró.

2 'Look back, my dear younger sister,
    Are the Turks approaching?
    Are the Turks approaching,
    The Turks and the Tartars?

3 Are the Turks coming?
    Are the Turks coming?
    They will slay me,
    They will take you back.

4 Hide yourself, my younger sister, in the creek,
  Pray to God there,
  Pray to God there,
  For victory for my two arms,

5 For victory for my two arms,
  For strength for my shield,
  For victory for my two arms,
  For strength for my shield!'

6 God helped him,
  Only one was left [of the enemy] to carry the
    tidings home,
  God helped him,
  Only one was left [of the enemy] to carry the
    tidings home.

7 'Come out, my younger sister, from the creek,
  Let us set off for home,
  Come out, my younger sister, from the creek
  Let us set off for home.'

8 When they reached their father's gate,
  He up and speaks: 'Go in, my dear younger sister,
  Go in, my dear younger sister, go into our father's
    house,
  Ask for accommodation for us if only for tonight,
  If only for tonight, if only next to the door.'

9 'My lady, my lady, my honoured lady,
  Give us accommodation for tonight,
  If only for tonight, if only next to the door.

10 We have just come from Turkey,
   I am here with my older brother,
   I am here with a good older brother of mine,
   He is badly wounded!'

11 'Out with you, beggar, out with you, for I cannot
     stand,
   For I cannot stand the stinking of beggars!'

12 Thereupon the poor girl who had been imprisoned
     runs out,
   She finds her father in the courtyard.

13 'Sir, Sir, my honoured Sir,
   Grant us accommodation if only for tonight,
   If only for tonight, if only next to the door.

14 We have just come from Turkey,
   I am here with my brother,
   I am here with a good elder brother of mine,
   He is badly wounded.'

308

15 'It is all right, it is all right, you poor girl who
         had been imprisoned,
   It is all right, it is all right, you poor girl who
         had been imprisoned.'

16 'My sister, my dear younger sister, now listen to me,
   At the first cock-crow I shall fall ill,

17 At the first cock-crow I shall fall ill,
   At the second cock-crow I shall turn livid,

18 At the second cock-crow I shall turn livid,
   At the third cock-crow I shall part with this world.'

19 'My elder brother, my dear elder brother, my heart,
         my soul, my elder brother!
   We have indeed been to Turkey,
   We have indeed managed to get back to our
         father's house,

20 We have indeed managed to get back to our
         father's house,
   We have asked for accommodation from our own mother,

21 And she up and spoke: "Get out, beggar, get out,
   For I cannot stand the stinking of beggars." '

22 The elder kitchen-boy was listening to this through
         the door,
   He said to his Mistress:
   'My honoured Lady,
   I have heard weeping before, but never one like this:

23 One of the beggars has died and the other is mourning
         for him thus,
   One of the beggars has died and the other is mourning
         for him thus:

24 "My brother, my dear elder brother, my heart, my soul,
         my elder brother,
   Indeed we have been to Turkey,
   We have indeed managed to get back to our
         father's house,

25 We have indeed managed to get back to our
         father's house,
   We have asked for accommodation from our own
         mother,
   Who up and spoke: 'Get out, beggar, get out,
   For I cannot bear the stinking of beggars!' " '

26 Thereupon the lady ran indeed,
   She opened the door, and up she spoke:

27 'Had I known that you were my son and my daughter,
   Not only would I have given you accommodation next
      to the door,

28 Not only would I have given you accommodation next
      to the door,
   But I would have clasped you to my heart.'

29 Thereupon she embraced [her] and died straightaway.

Version **B** runs like **A**, but includes some explanations in prose; for example, after stanza 1: 'They had been the Turks' prisoners for thirty years, then they escaped.' During their escape John Bíró is wounded. In this version he asks Kate to bandage his right arm, which is wounded. The details of the story are elaborated by incremental repetition: the brother sends his sister in to ask for accommodation three times. Finally, their father allows them to spend the night in the barn. The lady of the house sends out three servants to listen to the girl's complaint; she does not believe the first two, but after the third report she goes out herself. At the end the singer added 'It happened at Pusztina [where this version was recorded]. When they were taken prisoners there were only two houses in Pusztina. When they returned there were thirty houses and their father did not recognise them.'

Version **C** the brother is a younger brother; he is kept in prison, while his sister is apparently enjoying more freedom, for he asks her to fetch the key to the prison, to release him and to set off for home together. The mother refuses to let them in, she is sad because she had just buried her child. Finally, she allows them to sleep in the sheep pen. The brother's illness is missing—he just asks his sister to see whether the evening star has come up. The mother, similar to the daughter in 'The Mother of the Rich Woman', tells her that she would have caraway-seed soup cooked for them, she would have dressed them in cambric shirts, had she known who they were, and the daughter replies with the curse of the latter ballad: 'May the dog eat your caraway-seed soup, may your fine cambric shirt be devoured by flames!'

Version **D** the mother is the wife of the judge of Szeged (N.B. 'Bíró' the surname means 'judge' or 'elderman' in Hungarian). It begins with the daughter's request for a slice of bread for herself and for her brother. The mother orders the servant to give her some out of the dog's food, but he takes pity on them and cuts from the servants' portion. The mother asks her daughter to leave her house. The brother then orders his sister to ask for a piece of cloth for his winding-sheet, with strict instructions against revealing her identity. The mother bids the servant to give her some of the horse's sheet, but again he takes pity on them and gives her some good cloth; then the brother sends his sister to ask for a plank of wood for his coffin—the servant gives her some decent wood in spite of the mother's order to give them some of the worst wood. Finally, the brother bids his sister to invite his mother to his funeral, this time in his own name. The mother arrives, takes her son home, puts him into bed, but as soon as he is put into bed, he dies. In this version, the mother addresses her daughter three times as 'the seductress of my servant, the slut of my soldier'.

L. Vargyas in his interesting treatment of the ballad (*Ethnographia*, **71**, 166–71; cp. Vargyas, 'Rapports...', pp. 72–9) derives it from French sources and points out Slavic parallels to the story. In the French ballad a brother and a sister return from war. Robbers are attracted by the girl's singing as they pass through a forest. Their captain demands the girl for the night. Her brother refuses, a fight follows in which the brother is wounded. The brother and the sister go to their father's house and ask for accommodation. The father refuses, he has a house full of guests, and sends them away. In one French telling the brother dies; the girl laments for him in the stable (where they had been given permission to stay) and wishes she were in her lost home, where she had white sheets which she could use for winding-sheets. The mother overhears her complaint, and recognises them.

L. Vargyas has drawn attention to a fragmentary piece (quoted by him, *Ethnographia*, **71**, 170, from Gy. Kerényi, 'Erdélyi Népzene', *Éneklő Ifjúság*, March 1944, p. 80; cp. Vargyas, 'Rapports...', pp. 76–7) which resembles the beginning of the French ballad. In this piece a knight and a lady are walking in a forest and he asks her to sing. She is reluctant, the robbers might hear her loud voice, they will ravish her, they will kill the knight. He slaps her on the face, and the lady begins to sing. The youngest robber hears her voice and says, 'I do not know what it is that I have heard: a song, a trumpet or violin-music'. The robbers stand in ambush, ravish her and kill the knight. It turns out that the youngest robber is the brother of the maid. The singer did not know the ending of the ballad.

The robber motif is paralleled in 'The Prince and the Princess', and in the Scottish 'Erlinton' (Child, no. 8). Slovenian parallels to the French ballad have the motifs of our version **C**, the brother is imprisoned, while the sister is well treated. Seven years after their capture she remembers her brother, releases him from the prison. In these versions there is no encounter with robbers (although this theme figures frequently in Slavic epic poetry) but they seek accommodation in their mother's house, and it is refused. The brother dies at cock-crow, the sister laments: why did he have to die in his mother's house, and not in Turkey. The mother's young son, or the neighbour, overhears the complaint.

All international parallels agree with the Hungarian versions in their very obscure motivation for the undisclosed identity of the brother and sister.

The many elements the ballad shares with 'Szilágyi and Hagymási' would indicate, I believe, a Slovenian rather than a directly French origin of this ballad. The elopment, the fight, the girl's noticing the pursuers, and the one person who is left alive 'to carry the tidings home', as well as verbal agreements between the texts ('They will slay me, they will take you back', etc.) are shared between the two ballads. Even more interesting is the fact that there are certain details (the girl's hiding during the fight, the wound in the right arm) which do not occur in the traditional ballad of 'Szilágyi and Hagymási' but which are represented in the work of the 'Anonymous of Szendrő' and in 'Waltharius'. The girl's lament, the complaint that is overheard by the servant who reports it to his Mistress, and the ending of our version **C** occur in 'The Mother of the Rich Woman' also. In fact, the entire ballad seems to be exactly the reverse of the latter ballad: here it is the children who are maltreated, there it is the mother. The incognito of the mother-brother-sister is equally vague in both ballad types. The mother's referring to a daughter whom she had just buried is repeated in 'The Girl who was Sold', 'The Girl who was Ravished' (in both classes), and in 'Beautiful Kate Bán'. This agreement suggests that this motif certainly belonged to ballads which deal with Turkish captivity or attempted ravishment by Turks in Hungarian ballads. Faragó-Jagamas point out that the Tartars, as the allies of the Turks, would occasionally raid Moldavia as late as the beginning of the eighteenth century, taking prisoners with them. They were forced to withdraw to the Crimean peninsula in the second half of the eighteenth century, after repeated Russian victories over the Turks.

'MERIKA' or
'THE DAUGHTER-IN-LAW WHO WAS
BURNED TO DEATH'

This ballad has been recorded only in Moldavia, among the *Csángós*. In spite of the length of the narrative the action of the mother-in-law who burns her daughter-in-law in a similar fashion to the burning of the faithless wife in 'Barcsai' is not clearly justified. The refrain would suggest that the hatred toward the young wife was national in origin (in Wallach: Merika, in Magyar: Margitka), namely, that the young Rumanian soldier (his name, Ráduj, is a Rumanian name) brought home a Hungarian wife, who was hated by his family. The riddling quality of the expository part may suggest other causes for the hatred: in version **A** it may imply a Cordelia-situation: do you love best your father-in-law to be, your mother-in-law to be, or your bridegroom to be? (in the ballad: the sun, the moon, or the bright star?). She chooses the star, and the 'moon' takes her revenge. The expository part in version **B** is even more ambiguous: it may be that the mother-in-law tries to get the girl to love her, is rejected and so takes her revenge, or it may be that the mother-in-law merely wants to lure the girl out of the house, so that she may kill her.

Versions

A Csanádi-Vargyas, *Röpülj*, no. 24; =*Néprajzi Értesítö* (1941), p. 163 **B** Csanádi-Vargyas, *Röpülj*, no. 23; =Domokos, *Moldvai Magyarság*, no. 30; =Domokos-Rajeczky, *Csángó Népzene*, II, p. 183 **C** Faragó-Jagamas, *MCSNN*, no. 9 a **D** Faragó-Jagamas, *MCSNN*, no. 9 b **E** *MNYr*, 5, 47 **F** Domokos, *Moldvai Magyarság*, no. 31; =Domokos-Rajeczky, *Csángó Népzene*, II, p. 184 **G** Domokos-Rajeczky, *Csángó Népzene*, II, p. 181 **H** Domokos-Rajeczky, *Csángó Népzene*, II, p. 182 **I** Ortutay, *Magyar Népköltészet*, II, no. 11; =*Ethnographia*, 21, 348

Version **A**

1 'In Wallach: Merika, in Magyar: Margitka,
Which one do you love of a hundred soldiers?

2 The moon or the sun, or the bright star?'
'I like the moon, I like the sun too,

3 But I love the bright star most of all.'
In Wallach: Merika, in Magyar: Margitka:

4 The light of the sun is old Vaivode Ráduj,
The light of the moon is old Lady Ráduj.

5 The fine bright star is young Peter Ráduj,
The fine bright star is young Peter Ráduj.

6 'In Wallach: Merika, in Magyar: Margitka.
I have to go to the war, to fight,

7 To the war, to fight, to bring home good news,
To bring home good news, to lift the white flag.

8 Mother, my mother dear, take good care,
Take good care of my Merika,

9 Take good care of my Merika,
In Wallach: Merika, in Magyar: Margitka.'

10 'Will you agree to be in my woodyard, in my
          woodyard,
My block for cutting wood?'

11 'To that I cannot agree, my soul, my mother dear,
To be a block for cutting wood.'
'In Wallach: Merika, in Magyar: Margitka.

12 Will you agree to my thrusting you on a spit,
Thrusting you on a spit, browning you on the fire?'

13 'To that I cannot agree, my soul, my mother dear.'
'In Wallach: Merika, in Magyar: Margitka.

14 Will you agree to my wrapping you
In oiled cloth, in oiled cloth?'

15 'To that I can agree, my soul, my mother.'
'Where shall I begin to wrap you? At your feet or
          at your head?'

16 'Begin at my head, wrap me to my feet.'
'In Wallach: Merika, in Magyar: Margitka.

17 Shall I light it at the bottom?' 'Light it at my head,
Light it at my head, burn it to the soles of my feet.

18 Mother, mother dear, I wonder, is it dawning?'
'It is not dawning, it is not dawning, it is only midnight.

19 In Wallach: Merika, in Magyar: Margitka.'
'Mother, mother dear, I wonder is it dawning?'

20 'It is not dawning, it is not dawning, it is still
          only two o'clock.'
At this point her heart broke.

21 She burnt her as if she were a brand in the fire,
She took her away, took her out to the flower garden.

22 'In Wallach: Merika, in Magyar: Margitka,
Open your gate, open your gate!'

23 His mother rushed out, she opened the gate.
'I do not need you, mother, to open the gate!

24 Mother, mother dear, where is my Merika?'
'She has gone, she has gone to the rose meadow,

25 To the rose meadow, to pick roses,
She has just gone to the rose meadow.'

26 He looked for her, he did not find her, he returned.
'In Wallach: Merika, in Magyar: Margitka,

27 Open your gate, open your gate!'
His mother rushed out, his mother rushed out.

28 'I do not need you, mother, to open the gate!
Where is my Merika? Where is my Merika?'

29 'She has just gone, she has just gone to the cornfield,
To the cornfield, to take a turn at the reaping.'

30 He looked for her. He found her not, she had not
            spoken for a long time past.
And he returned, he returned.

31 'In Wallach: Merika, in Magyar: Margitka,
Open my gate, open my gate!'

32 His mother rushed out. 'I do not need you, mother,
I do not need you, mother, to open the gate.'

33 'She is out there, in the flower garden,
The white rose bush is flowering in red,

34 The red rose bush is flowering in white—'
He just went into the flower garden,

35 He just went into the flower garden,
There she is, his Merika, like a scorched brand.

36 'Mother, mother, bring out for me
My golden-hafted knife, my golden-hafted knife,

37 Mother, mother, have me buried
In front of the altar, in front of the altar,

38 Mother, mother, dear, have my Merika buried
At the side of this altar, at the side of this altar.'

39 There there grew—a fair little flower,
There there grew—how fair a little flower.

40 They intertwined, they intertwined,
She went there too that cursed enemy,

41 She tore them off, she made them wither in her hands,
Both the little flowers, both the little flowers.

Version **B** opens differently: *Young Peter Ráduj, young Peter Ráduj; | In Wallach: Merika, in Magyar: Margitka.* || *'Come out, my daughter-in-law, come out, I have brought you a silken veil' | 'I need it not, mother, I need it not, I have one already.'* || *'Come out, my daughter-in-law, come out, I have brought you a silken shift.' | 'I need it not, mother, I need it not, I have one already.'* || *'Come out, my daughter-in-law, come out, I have brought you a silken skirt.'*[1] *| 'I need it not, mother, I need it not, I have one already.'* || *'Will you agree to be my block for cutting wood'* . . . etc.

Versions **C, E,** and **H** run like **A**; version **D** is fragmentary and contains only the dialogue between mother and son, followed by his suicide; versions **F, G** and **I** are also fragmentary. The riddling reference to the sun, moon, and the stars appears in **A, C, E, G, H**; the boy's request that his mother take care of Merika in his absence occurs in **A** and **C** only. The first choice of death is to be a block for cutting wood in **A–C, E, G**; the second choice is missing from **B, E, G**; **C** agrees with **A**. The first two choices are **F**—to be shot in the eye, to be hit on the head; **H**—to be burnt, to be crashed. The third choice is death expressed by the riddle known from 'Barcsai' (to hold a candle, be a candlestick) in **B, C, E–H**. The dialogue between mother-in-law and Merika figures in **A** only. In **F** young Ráduj meets three soldiers on his way home, and questions them about Merika, but they have not seen her (this version does not have the dialogue between mother and son), and in **B** and **F** he learns the truth from his horse, which speaks to him. **G** ends with Merika's death. The reference to the changing colour of the roses in **A**, stanzas 33–4, is repeated in **H**.

In **H**, after her son's suicide, the mother wraps both him and her daughter-in-law once more in oiled cloth, burns them, and takes their ashes to the church, where she has them buried in front of the altar and behind the altar. The sympathetic plants are lilies here, which embrace on top of the altar.

E has red and pink marble coffins, the burial on the two sides of the altar. Lilies grow from the grave and when the boy's parents visit them the lilies droop; when the parents leave them, they straighten up: 'If you did not pity us when we were alive, do not pity us in our death.'

I is also fragmentary. This is the only version which does not come from Moldavia. Here the girl is called Durica, and the conflict begins when she, in reply to the questioning of Lady Nagy, admits that her skirt was bought for her by Anton Nagy. Anton leaves home for a

---

[1] 'Silken *skirt*' in Hungarian *fota*. This is the traditional dress of *Csángó* women: a silken skirt worn wrapped around the body, not unlike a sari.

fair; on his return he cannot find Durica. A dialogue follows with the mother's evasive answers. Finally, she admits that she has shot Durica. The version ends with the 'blood to blood' formula from 'The Dishonoured Maiden', and with reference to the sympathetic plants, as in 'Kate Kádár'.

In Vargyas's opinion the ballad has derived from 'Pocheronne' (cf. *Ethnographia*, **71**, 196–201; references to international parallels to 'Pocheronne', *loc. cit.*).[1]

'POISONED JOHN'

This ballad was recorded in Transylvania in one version and two fragments, one of which has preserved three lines only. F. Child refers to it in the discussion of 'Lord Randal' (Child, no. 12).

Text: Csanádi-Vargyas, *Röpülj*, no. 120 = Ortutay,
Magyar Népköltészet, II, no. 29 = MNGY, III, p. 7
= Kriza (1956), no. 34

1 'And where have you been, my heart, my soul, my John?'
'Alas, I have been at my sister-in-law,[2] my lady mother,
Alas, my heart aches, it aches, make my bed ready!'

2 'And what did they give you to eat there, my heart,
  my soul, my John?'
'[They gave me] a toad[3] there, my lady mother,
Alas, my heart aches, it aches, make my bed ready!'

3 'And on what did they serve it, my heart, my soul,
  my John?'
'They served it on a fine plate, my lady mother,
Alas, my heart aches, it aches, make my bed ready!'

4 'Maybe that made you sick, my heart, my soul, my John?'
'That will put me under the ground, my lady mother!
Alas, my heart aches, it aches, make my bed ready!'

---

[1] In a recent article concerning the connection between the Rumanian and Hungarian versions of 'Merika' L. Vargyas published a text recorded in Transdanubia, which he considers to be a version of our ballad. This text, however, seems to me a contamination of 'Kate Kádár' and the sharp questions–evasive answers sequence of 'The Dishonoured Maiden' rather than a version of 'Merika'. (*Acta Ethnographica*, **14**, 191–202; for further versions of the same text cf. *Ethnographia*, **76**, 446–55.)

[2] In Hungarian *ángyoméknitt*; *ángy*—its original meaning was 'sister-in-law, wife of the elder brother' or 'wife of any elder male relative'. Nowadays *ángy* means simply 'sister-in-law'; *ángyoméknitt*—'with the family of my sister-in-law'.

[3] 'Toad'—lit. 'a crayfish with four legs', a popular term for poisonous toad.

5 'And what will you leave to your father, my heart,
    my soul, my John?'
'My good iron-barred cart, my lady mother!
Alas, my heart aches, it aches, make my bed ready!'

6 'And what will you leave to your elder brother, my heart,
    my soul, my John?'
'My four fine oxen, my lady mother!
Alas, my heart aches, it aches, make my bed ready!'

7 'And what will you leave to your younger brother, my heart,
    my soul, my John?'
'My four fine harnessed horses, my lady mother!
Alas, my heart aches, it aches, make my bed ready!'

8 'And what will you leave to your younger sister, my heart,
    my soul, my John?'
'My household goods, my lady mother!
Alas, my heart aches, it aches, make my bed ready!'

9 'And what will you leave to your sister-in-law, my heart,
    my soul, my John?'
'Eternal damnation, my lady mother!
Alas, my heart aches, it aches, make my bed ready!'

10 'And what will you leave to your mother, my heart,
    my soul, my John?'
'Sadness and grief, my lady mother!
Alas, my heart aches, it aches, make my bed ready!'

The fragment runs as follows:
'Where have you been this evening, my heart, my John?'
'I have been next door, my lady mother!
Alas, Alas, my heart aches, make the bed ready now.'

A recently published version recorded by P. Szini in 1882–9, and published by F. Schram (*Néprajzi Közlemények*, 1959, **4**, 134) has an interesting variation: '*Where have you been, where have you been, my son Hermann?*' | '*I have been next door, to my sister, ay! my mother!*' || '*What did you do, what did you do, my son Hermann?*' | '*I rocked two little boys to sleep, ay! my mother!*' || '*What did you eat there, what did you eat there, my son Hermann?*' | '*I chewed a little bone, ay! my mother!*' || '*What did you drink with it, what did you drink with it, my son Hermann?*' | '*Cold water from the jug, ay! my mother!*' || '*What did you see there, what did you see there, my son Hermann?*' | '*I saw my sister slain, ay! my mother!*' || '*And what do you wish for your sister, my son Hermann?*' | '*Peace and salvation, ay! my mother!*' || '*And what do you wish for your mother, my son Hermann?*' | '*For you [damnation in] Hell, ay! my mother!*' ||

8

CONSIDERATIONS BY WAY OF
CONCLUSION

An analytical survey of this nature does not lend itself to the drawing
of general conclusions. The points of interest which emerge relate for
the most part to individual ballads. These have been already noted in
their proper place, and there would be little purpose in repeating them
here.

The collation of our Hungarian themes and motifs with international
balladry has revealed that none of the international ballads originated
in Hungary. But if the country was not important as a source, it had
its place—and a place of some significance—in the chain of transmission
of certain ballad groups, and the Hungarian evidence may be used in
deciding about the provenance of particular motifs. Thus 'Clement
Mason' belongs to the Balkan tradition, and here the Hungarian
ballad creates a bridge between South Slavonia and Rumania. 'The
Miraculous Dead' and 'The Dishonoured Maiden' seem to have
reached Hungary from a Spanish-Portuguese-Italian source. 'Kate
Kádár' and 'Anna Molnár' seem to have come from Germany, though
they underwent certain modifications. The same is true of 'The Two
Royal Children'. Certain motifs in 'The Three Orphans' betray the
influence of pagan Magyar beliefs and together with 'The Fair Maid
Julia' shed light on the process by which pagan symbols were christianised. 'Anna Betlen', 'Bátori', 'Ilona Budai', 'Lady Albert Nagy-Bihal'
appear to be of Hungarian origin, but they have not spread to other
countries. And the reason why Hungary failed to hand on her native
products while successfully transmitting material she had borrowed
has still to be discovered.

There remains, however, another problem: the connection between
Scottish-English and Hungarian ballads. The idea that there exists a
particular connection between Scottish and Hungarian ballads was first
voiced by A. Greguss in his book, *A balladáról* (Budapest, 1865): 'Our
Székely ballads resemble the Scottish ones most of all, in subject matter,
atmosphere, and narrative technique.'

A. Szerb, in his *Magyar Irodalomtörténet* (Budapest, 2nd edn., 1935,

319

p. 155), wrote: 'The kinship between the Hungarian and Scottish ballads is a mystery.'

Gy. Ortutay, in his *Székely Népballadák* (Budapest, 1935), was more careful about voicing this opinion, but when he discussed the common occurrence of certain motifs in Hungarian and international ballads, he referred to the Scottish connections:

There are times when we are inclined to believe that the similarities which exist between the central motifs of *Székely* and Scottish ballads ought to be attributed to those parallel ways of thinking which seem to link all primitive and peasant cultures. This seems a better explanation than the clumsy one of postulating a *de facto* connection. Nevertheless the original reason for these similarities cannot be attributed to the first of these suggested explanations.

Later Csanádi-Vargyas (*Röpülj*, 1954) wrote: 'Our ballads sometimes have a relationship with Scottish and French ballads.'

The concept of Scottish-Hungarian kinship where ballads are concerned, though somewhat tempered since Vargyas' own work on the French-Hungarian connections (cf. pp. 350, 352), had become a commonplace in Hungary both among critics and the general public. (Cf. also I. Hermann, *Arany János Esztétikája*, Budapest, 1956, pp.165–7). The existence of this common belief was the reason that prompted me to investigate this matter and to put a particular emphasis on the themes and motifs common to English-Scottish and Hungarian ballads when analysing our material. The result of my investigations must be described as negative, as far as this connection is concerned. Some general positive statements may, however, bemade.

Themes

1. There are certain ballad groups prominent in Scottish and English balladry, which are altogether missing from Hungarian balladry: The Hungarians have no battle ballads, no sea ballads, no ballads of shape-shifting, and relatively few magic ballads. Except for one piece which was found in Moldavia only recently, they have no riddle ballads.

Love ballads form the central body of both Scottish-English and Hungarian ballads, but there are certain themes which do not occur in Hungarian ballads: There are no bride-stealing ballads, no ballads dealing with a false accusation of adultery, no ballads dealing with a wager on someone's chastity. Lovers never forsake each other for the sake of a wealthier bride or groom. Family ballads are also relatively rare in Hungary, and those which we have are mostly unparalleled in international balladry.

2. Common themes are relatively rare, and the agreements which have been noted derive from the fact that both the English-Scottish and the Hungarian ballads drew their material from a common stock of international tales:

'Riddles Wisely Expounded' and
'King John and the Bishop' (Child, nos. 1–2, 45)—'Young King Matthias'.
'Lady Isabel and the Elf Knight' (Child, no. 4)—'Anna Molnár'.
'Willie's Lyke Wake' (Child, no. 25)—'The Miraculous Dead'.
'Lord Randal' (Child, no. 12)—'Poisoned John'.
'Lady Maisry' (Child, no. 65)—'The Dishonoured Maiden'.
'Lady Diamond' (Child, no. 269)—'The Daughter of the Cruel King'.

Other common themes are also found, but with no particular connection in the development of the narrative:

'Little Musgrave and Lady Barnard' (Child, no. 81)—'Barcsai'.
'Prince Heathen' (Child, no. 269)—'The Maid who was Sold' class 1.
'The Fair Flower of Northumberland' (Child, no. 9)—'Szilágyi and Hagymási'.
'The Cruel Mother' (Child, no. 20)—'Ilona Budai'.
'The Mother's Malison or Clyde's Water' (Child, no. 216)—'The Maid who was Cursed'.
'The Maid Freed from the Gallows' (Child, no. 95)—'The Asp'.

It is notable that some of these common ballads fall into different ballad groups in Hungarian balladry than in English-Scottish; e.g.

'Anna Molnár' is a love ballad in Hungarian, while it is a magic ballad in international balladry.
'The Miraculous Dead', on the other hand, is a love ballad in international balladry but it is a magic ballad in Hungarian.

Motifs

Most of the motifs which occur in Hungarian as well as in English-Scottish ballads are found in other international ballads. Examples are: sympathetic plants; a nightmare as an ill omen; messages sent by birds; recognition by a ring; bells tolling by themselves; dialogue between lovers through a prison wall; death from sorrow; dead mother who speaks; motifs connected with ballads dealing with the lady's death—her strength gradually failing, her thirst, and the knight's questions as to the reason for her sickness or tears.

Formulas

The formulas shared by Hungarian and Scottish and English ballads are, again, 'stock-phrases' of international balladry:

Introductory formulas:

'Lady...sat in her bower, sewing at her silken seam';
'...sat drinking at the wine';
'O, sleep you, wake you...';
'O narrow, narrow is my gown';
'O saddle me the black';
'You have died for me, I will die for you';
'O make my bed...'; etc.

Paraphrases for 'never' are also found in Hungarian ballads, but they are more prominent in folksongs.

Symbolic utterance

Here, on the other hand, Hungarian balladry provides unforeseen variations on known examples of symbolic utterances in balladry, especially when the name of a terrible idea is ritually avoided: for example, the pearly headdress in 'The Two Royal Children' and the candle in 'Barcsai'.

Common beliefs

Common beliefs are also of a very general nature: life-tokens; ominous signs; intimate objects that break, become faded, fall to the ground; flowers that wither when their owner is in danger; green regarded as an unlucky colour; and a belief in the power of the spoken word are shared by people all over the world.

Although the comparison of the Hungarian with English and Scottish balladry has offered only negative conclusions with respect to the particular connection between the two groups, the investigation has revealed certain special characteristics of both English-Scottish and Hungarian ballads which would not have come to light without placing the two bodies of ballad material side by side.

1. Although both English-Scottish and Hungarian ballads relate individual tragedies or adventures in the English-Scottish ballads, these are much more 'public' or family affairs than in the Hungarian ballads.

When the lady is burnt in 'Lady Maisry' the whole family, brothers and sisters, father and mother prepare the fire together. When the lady is pregnant 'word has gone to the kitchen, word has gone to the ha''. When the lady elopes, strangers inform her parents of the event. When the lady's lover has to be killed, all her seven brothers take part in the action. False servants, 'kitchie boys', nurses, stewards, have a wide field of action and opportunity to interfere with the events. Even when they are not taking part in the action, they are there as spectators when the lady stabs her lover to death, when she appears at her lover's wedding, when she refuses to dance with them or with her old bridegroom and prefers her lover only. In Hungarian ballads there are no outsiders who interfere, no false servants or the like, and no spectators either. The conflict is a strictly personal affair. It concerns the mother and the daughter, the mother and the daughter's lover, always only two persons at a time. Other family members are not introduced. The only exceptions to this are found in those ballads which have taken their material from sources in which the interfering outsiders played an important role in the action (e.g. the false servant in 'Clement Mason' or the presence of the other masons there; the brother and sister in 'The Dishonoured Maiden') but even in these ballads the outsiders figure in a few versions only.

This difference surely indicates a difference in cultural and social background at the time when the ballads were composed. They reflect a difference in social structure. Scottish ballads seem to reflect a much more unified society. Hungarian ballads were composed at a time when personal affairs had ceased to be of public interest, when the community life of large households or clans had disappeared.

2. In English and Scottish ballads the tragedy often lies not in the characters but in Fate or in a particular situation (e.g. the death of the lady in 'Leesome Brand', 'Sir Patrick Spens', the incest in 'Lizie Wan' and in 'The King's Dochter Lady Jean', etc.), and often when a cruel deed is committed it is done not only by personal malice, but in accordance with the standards of the community which has set laws for the punishment of certain offences (e.g. 'The Cruel Brother', 'Clerk Saunders', 'Earl Brand', etc.).

Among the Hungarian ballads only 'Clement Mason' would fall in this class. In the rest of the ballads personal malice or avarice plays the most important part.

This difference would indicate again that Hungarian ballads are of a later origin than the English and Scottish ballads.

3. Another interesting detail which points to this fact is that in Scottish ballads nature is antagonistic (cp. especially the cruel sea in 'Sir Patrick Spens', 'Bonnie Annie', analogously 'Clyde's Water'; 'The Lass of Roch Royal'), while in Hungarian ballads it is always sympathetic to the hero or heroine.

4. We have already drawn attention to the fact that suicide is relatively rare in English and Scottish ballads (cf. 'The Daughter of the

Cruel King'). I have attempted to explain this circumstance by pointing out that in English and Scottish ballads it is usually the hero who dies first, and the lady then dies of sorrow, while in Hungarian ballads it is usually the hero who follows his beloved into the grave, and suicide seems to be a more 'manly' way of dying than death from sorrow. A comparison with the English and Scottish ballads draws attention to another feature of Hungarian ballads. The central character is almost always a woman. This suggests that ballad-singing was practised much more by women in Hungary than it was in England, and it would corroborate our hypothesis that ballad-singing was very much connected with the weaving in the spinning-room (cf. chapter on 'The Bards').

5. Certain special characteristics of Hungarian ballads and some characteristics of English and Scottish ballads with respect to the narrative technique are also revealed by comparison.

(*a*) English and Scottish ballads open usually with an introductory stanza, in which the personages of the drama are introduced, or which gives us the scene of the action. In Scottish and English ballads subsidiary aspects blend with the central situation, parallel actions are described, and the dramatic effect is often achieved by the portrayal of the various attitudes of the characters placed side by side, and contrasting one with the other (e.g. 'Little Musgrave and Lady Barnard', 'Child Maurice', 'Earl Brand', 'Fair Annie', 'Fair Janet', etc.). Hungarian ballads, on the other hand, burst into speech at the denouement, without introducing the characters. The actions are given in strict chronological order, and the ballad is told from the point of view of one person only.

(*b*) In the Scottish and English ballads the proportion of the descriptive and narrative parts on the one hand and the dialogue on the other is about half and half. In the Hungarian ballads the revelatory quality of dramatic speech is far more important than description or the narration of events, and may occupy as much as eighty per cent of the whole.

(*c*) This difference in technique may be the reason for the interesting fact which comes to light when we examine the employment of incremental repetition in the two bodies of material. This is a ballad device equally prominent in English and Scottish and Hungarian balladry, but while in Hungarian ballads it is significantly used in the dialogue part (cp. 'The Dishonoured Maiden', 'The Maid who was Sold' especially), in English and Scottish ballads it appears usually in the narrative (see, for example, our comparison of the threefold incremental repetition in describing the lady's death in the Scottish ballads and in 'Clement Mason'.

(*d*) Lyric elements are rare in English and Scottish ballads, in accordance with their impersonal (i.e. impartial) way of telling the story. In Hungarian ballads lyric elements are introduced usually in two ways into the ballad: (1) in formulas (cp. the stereotype complaint of orphans); or (2) in curses, which usually form the conclusion of the ballad.

The absence of curses from the English and Scottish ballad material is again an indication of the later origin of Hungarian ballads. False servants, cruel parents, seducers, are all punished with death, and blood-feuds are frequent occurrences in English and Scottish ballads. In the Hungarian ballads the curses uttered by the sympathetic plants, or by the maid who was seduced and deceived serve as substitutes for punishments. The curse at the end of the ballad also expresses the ballad singer's view on the event and on the characters, which we are not allowed to perceive in English and Scottish ballads.

6. Finally we must observe a considerable difference between English–Scottish and Hungarian ballads with respect to the relationship between the various versions of individual ballads to each other.

There is very seldom any extensive difference between the different versions of a single ballad in the English and Scottish material. With certain additional details, and certain omissions they tell the same story, without altering the concept. This may be due in part to the stabilising effect of early printing. On the other hand, in Hungarian balladry where early printing is very rare, there is a considerable difference between the various tellings of a ballad. The different versions emphasise different aspects of the story. The elaboration of a certain motif, the omission of another, result in what is almost a new narrative (e.g. 'Clement Mason', 'The Maid who was Sold', the ending of 'Barcsai'). These differences concern the psychological aspect of the story, which again reflect the singer's point of view. The great variety of psychological aspects in the different versions of a single ballad seems to compensate for the relatively few classical ballads in Hungary, and for the fact that most of these Hungarian ballads draw their material from international stories.

APPENDIX I

In this Appendix we shall give a short account of ballads which have been recorded in fragmentary versions or are embedded in folk tales, together with two recently recorded pieces from Moldavia.

(a) Magic ballads

'THE DEAD BRIDEGROOM'

This piece is fragmentary as a ballad. It is always embedded in a ghost story: the Hungarian representative of the Lenore-legend (AT 365).

Versions

A *Magyar Népköltési Gyüjtemény*, I, p. 207 B *Magyar Népköltési Gyüjtemény*, I, p. 569
C *Ethnographia* (1927/28), p. 96 D *Ethnographia* (1908), p. 297

Versions **A–C** contain the stanzas which appear in most international tales of this group:

A 'Fair shines the moon,
Every soul is sleeping now,
Are you not frightened, my sweet rose?'
'Why should I be frightened, my sweet rose?
The true God is with me,
You, my sweet rose, are with me.'

'Fair shines the moon,
Every soul is sleeping now,
Are you not frightened, my sweet rose?'
'Why should I be frightened, my sweet rose?
God the Son is with me,
You, my sweet rose, are with me.'

'Fair shines the moon,
Every soul is sleeping now,
Are you not frightened, my sweet rose?'
'Why should I be frightened, my sweet rose?
The Holy Ghost is with me,
You, my sweet rose, are with me.'

The prose parts of the stories display certain differences.

A has the dead bridegroom, dressed in a white sheet, coming to fetch the girl and take her to 'his own country' (to the churchyard). The girl realises that her bridegroom is Death himself who wants to entice her into the grave. So she flees into the mortuary, where the corpses are laid out. Her pursuer nearly follows her even there. He urges the corpse that is lying on the bier: *Corpse, open the door, corpse!* but the cock crows and the girl escapes. **B** has a young widow, who wants to see her husband once more. An old woman advises her to boil human bones for nine days. The man arrives on horseback and carries her away with him. *Fair shines the moon, | The dead is galloping with the living,* etc. When the man tells her to descend into the grave, she answers that the man should go first. She throws into the grave a towel which she had taken with her, and escapes into the chapel. *You are lucky that you went there, because one must not disturb the dead,* says the man. **C** runs similarly. Instead of bones, the girl must boil a cross from a grave. The bridegroom arrives on a bier, asks her to escort him to the cemetery. The same incident with the towel occurs. The dialogue with the corpse follows. It ends: *You are lucky that my time is up, otherwise you would lie by my side now.* **D** has the Devil who disguises himself as the girl's lover. 'The lover of a young girl, a soldier, fell in the war. The girl wished to see her lover once again. So she went to a witch to ask for advice. The witch told her: "On the night of Good-Friday, go, my girl, to the churchyard, to the grave of your lover, take a piece from his cross and at night about eleven o'clock cook it in porridge. When the porridge bubbles, then your lover will come too." The girl did so. As the porridge bubbled, somebody began to rap on the door: *Let me in now, my Helen, | My Helen, my fair rose! | —I will not let you in, not I, | You are not my rose! | Nevertheless she let him in. || Cook some supper, my Helen, | My Helen, my fair rose! | —I will not cook supper, not I, | You are not my rose! | Nevertheless she cooked some supper. || Lay the table now, my Helen, | My Helen, my fair rose! | —I will not lay the table, not I, | You are not my rose! | Nevertheless she laid the table. || Give me something to eat, my Helen, | My Helen, my fair rose! | —I will not give you to eat, not I, | You are not my rose! | Nevertheless she gave him to eat. || Sit down by me, my Helen, | My Helen, my fair rose! | —I will not sit by you, not I, | You are not my rose! | Nevertheless she sat down by him. || Kiss me now, my Helen, | My Helen, my fair rose! | —I will not kiss you, not I, | You are not my rose! | Nevertheless she kissed him. || Come with me, my Helen, | My Helen, my fair rose! | —I will not come, not I, | You are not my rose! | Nevertheless she set out with him. ||* But as they were going out, Helen looked at her lover's feet, and noticed that they were horse's hoofs. Thereupon she became terribly frightened and started to sing: *Oh, cocks, crow, | Angels, sound your trumpets, | For I am sick, | Maybe I am even going to die! ||* Thereupon the devil said: *You are lucky that you called the angels, otherwise I would have torn you to pieces straight-away.* Because it was the devil who had assumed the figure of her lover.'

The devil in a disguise is a favourite motif in Hungarian tales. He can be recognised by his feet, which are horse's hoofs. (For the devil with horse's hoofs, cf. L. Arany, *Erdélyi népmesék*, Budapest, 1862, pp. 153–62; *Magyar Nyelvőr*, **2**, 421–2; **8**, 328–30; **15**, 182; **22**, 475–8; **24**, 332–4; *Magyar Népköltési Gyüjtemény*, XIII, pp. 248–52; *Ethnographia*, **6**, 105.)

His appearance in the ballad relates it to another type: 'the demon lover' (cf. Child, no. 243) who similarly appears in the guise of the dead lover.

Child considers the devil's appearance in the Lenore-type ballads as a Christian rationalisation of the original form of the story, in which the lover returns after his death to seek the fulfilment of old vows.

Though the fragmentary Hungarian versions of the theme cannot be taken as the basis for any positive statement, they seem to support Child's above-quoted theory in a negative way: whenever the devil is mentioned in the Hungarian versions, he never appears in the verse-part of the tale, but always in the prose supplementation. If the original form of the story was verse, it is possible that the devil was not mentioned there at all.

(b) *Christian legendary ballads*

'THE VIRGIN MARY SETS OUT'

This fragmentary piece has survived in only one version, which was recorded in the Lowland (Csanádi-Vargyas, *Röpülj*, no. 105 = Bartók-Kodály, *MNT*, II, no. 25).

1 The Virgin Mary sets out
Crying heavily aloud

2 To search for her holy Son.
She meets a Jewish maiden.

3 'Good day, Jewish maiden.'
'Good fortune, Virgin Mary.'

4 'Have you not seen my holy Son?'
'No, I do not know [where he is], I have
not seen him.'

5 The Virgin Mary sets out again,
She arrives at Bethlehem.

6 'Good day, man of Bethlehem.'
'Good fortune, Virgin Mary.'

7 'Have you not seen my holy Son?'
'What is your holy son like?'
[Lit., 'Of what colour is your holy Son?']

8 'What is my holy Son like?
He has golden teeth, auburn hair.'

9 'Go along, go along Virgin Mary,
Go along, go along, quickly:

10 Now they are crowning his holy head,
Now they are nailing his holy hands.

11 Now they are desecrating with hatchets
his holy sides,
They are letting his red blood run.'

Most probably this Hungarian ballad originated before the sixteenth century. Its text agrees with the words of the spells used in the sixteenth century by wise-women in Hungarian villages. Example:

The Virgin Mary set out carrying the little Jesus in her lap to go to a lovely field by the Jordan. There she met a Jewish maiden. This Jewish maiden unveiled the white veil that covered Jesus the lovely child of Mary, she saw him, she charmed him to death. The Virgin Mary went to the river Jordan, threw some water on Jesus, washed him and cured him. May my magic action of throwing water cure you in just the way the Virgin Mary cured the little Jesus. (*Nyelvőr*, 1908, p. 83.)

In a similar spell (published by L. Kálmány, *Szeged Népe*, I, p. 115) the Virgin Mary meets three Jewish maidens, who are amazed by the beauty of Jesus:

The Virgin Mary met three Jewish maidens. One of them said: 'Oh, how beautiful the blessed Jesus is, like the fair rosy dawn!' The second maiden said: 'Oh, how beautiful the blessed Jesus is, like the fair bright sun!' The third maiden said: 'Oh, how beautiful the blessed Jesus is, like the fair full moon!'...

(Similar accounts are to be found in Péter Bornemissza's *Az ördögi kísértetekről* [1578]. He quotes eight texts of this kind, which he took down in 1577 from the chant of an old woman who had learned them from her grandmother.)

These spells share with our ballad the motif of the Virgin Mary's meeting the Jewish maiden and the description of Jesus' beauty. In place of the 'charmed to death' formulae in the spells we have the description of Jesus' sufferings in the ballad. Other spells (Kálmány, *Szeged Népe*, III, nos. 4–6) have the search and crucifixion.

Here we have to draw attention to the Danish ballad, 'Jesus and the Virgin Mary' (S. Grundtvig, *DGF*, II, no. 97 B), which has the motif of the Virgin Mary's searching for her child. In this version the Virgin Mary awakens from her slumber and cannot find the little Jesus. She sets out to search for him, and meets Hallelujah:

> Hør du, Halleluja, kjaere Vennen min:
> saae du intet Jesus, kjaere Sønnen min?
> —Igaar var jeg i Jerusalem:
> der var Jesus, kjaer Sønnen din.
> Jeg ham hørte, og jeg ham saae:
> en Tornekrone havde han paa.
> De sloge ham med Svøber:
> de flettede hvasse Remmer.

It is not impossible that our ballad is connected with this Danish piece, especially if we take into account its similarity with another Danish ballad (Grundtvig, *DGF*, II, no. 99). This ballad has the subject of the well-known magic cure of Longinus, the story of which was first mentioned by Jacobus Voragine in the thirteenth century (cf. *The Golden Legend*, trans. by G. Ryan and H. Ripperger, New York-Toronto-London, 1948, 2nd edn., p. 191). In *DGF*, no. 99, Jesus tells his mother of his dream: he will be doomed and martyred (sts. 3–7):

> Saa ledde de Jesus ad Gaderne frem,
> saa mangen Mand tilsyne:
> saa ledte de op baade Tidsel og Torn
> deraf gjorde Jesus en Krone.
>
> Saa ledde de Jesus ad Korset op,
> de sloge hannem til med Spiger:
> 'Ak, skal jeg nu lide den haarde Død
> alt baade for onde og gode!'
>
> Saa ledde de Jesus ad Korset op,
> de sloge hannem til med Spiger:
> 'Ak, skal jeg nu lide den haarde Død
> alt baade for fattig' og rige!'
>
> Saa ledde de op den blinde Mand,
> de fik hannem Spyd i Haender:
> han stak Jesus i Siden ind,
> det hellige Blod udrender.
>
> Saa toge de af det hellige Blod
> og strøge paa blinde Mands Øen:
> den blinde Mand fik sit Syn igjen
> og saae paa Jesu hans Pine.

Csanádi-Vargyas (*Röpülj*, p. 508) suggest that the Hungarian ballad originated from the first narrative part of the spell-texts. This suggestion was made, however, without the knowledge of the Danish parallel. Considering the evidence of the resemblance between the Danish and the Hungarian ballad, it is more likely, I believe, that a ballad similar to the Danish 97, 99 existed in Hungary; the last part of this sank into oblivion and only the spell-texts have preserved the primary motif of the magic cure, since these spells were used as formulae for such cures.

The ballad is told in rhymeless octosyllabic lines.

'WHEN THE VIRGIN MARY WAS WALKING'

This fragment deserves mention because of its charming simplicity.

Text: Csanádi-Vargyas, *Röpülj*, pp. 509–10 = Bartók-Kodály, *MNT*, II, no. 513

> 1 When the Virgin Mary was walking in this world,
>   She walked about throughout the city;

2 Where can she give birth to her holy Son?
She went into the shadow of poplar-trees:

3 'Poplar-trees, may you be cursed
That you rustle all the time.'

4 She went to the crib of horses,
They were having wheat for supper.

5 'Horses, may you be cursed
That you grunt all the time!'

6 She went to the crib of oxen,
They were having hay for supper.

7 'Oxen, may you be always happy,
May you draw a furrow into the soil,
May you raise pure wheat!'

This song is recited at Christmas time. Its construction, worked up by repetition, its partly rhymeless, partly tag-rhymed octosyllabic lines suggest a sixteenth–seventeenth century origin.

'GOOD EVENING, YOU RICH INNKEEPER'

This is another Christmas song of the narrative kind. Its versions were recorded in the Lowland and in Transylvania. (See AT Type 791.)

Text: Csanádi-Vargyas, *Röpülj*, no. 19 = Berze Nagy, *BMNh*, I, p. 334

1 'Good evening to you, wealthy innkeeper!
Would you give lodging to Jesus Christ,
To Jesus Christ, for his merits?'

2 'I cannot give lodging to Jesus Christ,
For today I am expecting some very rich guests,
They would make great mock of him.'

3 'Go, Peter, go to the end of the town,
There dwells and has her being a poor widow,
There dwells and has her being a poor widow.

4 'God give you good evening, Mistress Veronica,
Would you give lodging to Jesus Christ?
Would you give lodging to Jesus Christ?'

5 'Why should I not give lodging to Jesus Christ,
To Jesus Christ, for his merits,
To Jesus Christ for his merits.

6 I have a small house, I have three beds made—
He may lie down on whichever he likes,
He may lie down on whichever he likes!'

7 Jesus lay down on one of the fine beds,
  Saint Peter waited till Jesus fell asleep,
  Saint Peter waited till Jesus fell asleep.

8 At his head rose the bright sunlight,
  At his feet rose the sparkling moonlight,
  At this feet rose the sparkling moonlight.

Other versions: Berze Nagy, *BMNh*, I, pp. 331–3 (two versions); *MNGY*, VIII, p. 226; *Ethnographia* (1901), 370–1; (1902), 87–8. Other versions circulated on broadsheets (cf. Berze Nagy, *op. cit.* notes, p. 335).

L. Vargyas (*Ethnographia*, **71**, 185) draws attention to a group of similar French ballads, in which Jesus in the guise of a beggar pleads for charity. The rich man does not take pity on him, but his wife feeds him and allows him to rest in her room. She finds the room being brilliantly illuminated, and Jesus reveals himself to her.

The mentioning of the sun and the moon may be compared to the image of the magic lamb in 'Fair Maid Julia'. Berze Nagy draws attention to parallel motifs in Radloff.

(c) Ballads of love and intrigue

'THE MAID UNDER THE APPLE TREE'

The following piece is related to 'The Fair Maid Julia' by its introductory stanzas. It has been recorded in two incomplete versions, one from Transylvania, the other from Moldavia.

Text: Kriza [1956], no. 44 = *MNGY*, III, p. 15 = Domokos-Rajeczky, *Csángó Népzene*, I, no. 54, with ample notes.

> Behold, a golden apple-tree has grown here,
> Gentle edelweiss has overgrown its roots,
> A poor orphan maid is sitting under it,
> She is binding her wreath, she is lamenting:
> 'I have neither father, nor mother, and nobody to
>   take care of me!'
> A proud soldier is listening through the door:
> 'Do not cry, do not lament, poor orphan maid,
> I shall be your father and your mother to take
>   care of you!'
> 'Indeed you shall not be that, you proud soldier,
> For I have a bridegroom, a betrothed,
> For whom I have been waiting for seven fair years,
> For seven fair years and for three full days.

But I shall wait for him for another seven fair years,
For another seven fair years, and for three full days,
And if he will not return, I shall leave,
I shall go to the nuns, to the land of the nuns.
There I shall serve God as long as I live,
And I shall stand before God when I die!'

The other fragment (Csanádi-Vargyas, *Röpülj*, no. 104 = Erdélyi, *Népdalok és Mondák*, I, no. 421) has even closer agreement with the beginning of 'The Fair Maid Julia', and it does not have the passage about the nuns.

Yonder there a sweet apple-tree grew,
And yellow edelweis grew under it.
A poor orphan girl sat under it,
She bound her wreath,
And where the edelweiss was not enough
She finished it with white pearls, and
    tied them with gold.
She was singing her learned songs,
She was wiping her bitter tears.

In Vargyas's opinion it is the fragmentary beginning of the widely spread ballad type in which a lover returns in disguise and puts his beloved's consistency to trial (*Ethnographia*, **71**, 240–9). The maid's refusal to be consoled by another suitor links it to 'The Turtle-dove that has Lost its Mate'.

'THE TURTLE-DOVE THAT HAS LOST ITS MATE'

This beautiful lyrical piece was very popular in the eighteenth century and probably before, since it appears in several eighteenth-century MS Song Books. Its *leitmotif*, as pointed out by S. Horváth and S. Eckhardt, is based on the belief widely held in the Middle Ages, that the turtle-dove mates only once, and if it loses its mate it will not perch on green leaves any more, but seeks out dried branches, thus mourning in isolation. Later on this concept was elaborated: the turtle-dove will not drink of clear water after the loss of its mate. (For bibliography and summary of studies on the subject, cf. Gy. Ortutay, *Székely Népballadák*, pp. 286–8.)

All versions come from Transylvania and Moldavia (cf. Ortutay, *op. cit.*, and Faragó-Jagamas, *MCSNN*, nos. 31 *a* and 31 *b*; also Domokos-Rajeczky, *Csángó Népzene*, I, nos. 35 and 74).

Text: Ortutay, *Magyar Népköltészet*, II, no. 45*a*
= Csanádi-Vargyas, *Röpülj*, no. 107 = *MNYr*, **10**, 479

1 In the middle of the pebbly water
  Two turtle-doves are bathing.

2 A big bird flew thither,
  It pounced upon them like a Tartar.

3 It tolerated one of them,
  It chased the other away.

4 It flew up from there,
  It flew into a green wood.

5 There it did not fly to some fine green branch
  But it flew to a dried branch.

6 It keeps on pecking at the dried branch,
  It keeps on calling its little mate.

7 'My mate, my mate, my sweet mate,
  Can you hear my great sighing?

8 I keep on watching for you, but I cannot see you,
  I keep on sighing for you, but I cannot hear you.'

9 Thereupon it flew up from there,
  It flew into the green reeds.

10 There it did not fly to some fine green reed,
  But it flew to a dried reed.

11 It keeps on hammering at the dried reed,
  It shrieks for its little mate.

12 'My mate, my mate, my sweet mate,
  Can you hear my many shrieks?

13 If I were to get hold of your bones
  I would pile them gently into a little pile.

14 If I were to find your little blood
  I would colour [the little pile] with it gently.'

15 Thereupon it flew up from there
  And it flew to a far-away country.

16 There is its dear mate grieving,
  Not believing that it would see the other again.

17 It had called to the other, the other had not replied,
  Thereupon it had nearly died.

18 Thereupon it flew up,
  It flew to a green meadow.

19 It did not fly to a green blade of grass there,
But to a dried flower.

20 It put its yellow foot into the mud,
It let itself lose heart.

21 It spread out its wings widely,
It let itself die.

22 A nightingale flew thither.
'What are you grieving at?'—it asks.

23 'Why are you crying, why are you crying, little
turtle-dove,
Fair creature of God?'

24 'Of course I am crying, nightingale,
My good little mate has gone away,

25 A big bird has chased it away,
Perhaps it has frightened it to death.'

26 'Do not cry, do not cry, little turtle-dove,
Fair creature of God,

27 I will be your mate in your mate's stead,
I will be your spouse in your spouse's stead.'

28 'I do not want anybody's mate,
Anybody's mate, anybody's curse.

29 I want my true mate only,
As far as I am concerned you may live with whom
you please.

30 My heart can rest only with him,
My faint body can fall asleep only with him.'

Another version runs as follows:

Text: Ortutay, *Magyar Népköltészet,* II, no. 45*b*
= Csanádi-Vargyas, *Röpülj,* no. 106 = *MNGY,* I, p. 179

The sadly cooing sad turtle-dove
Had lost its dear mate.
It flew away into a green wood,
It did not fly to a green branch,
But it flew to a dried branch.
It keeps on pecking at the dried branch,
It keeps on crying for its dear mate:
'My mate, my mate, my sweet mate!
I shall never have such a mate
As you have been, my sweet mate!'

The sadly cooing sad turtle-dove
Flew away to a far-away country,
To a far-away country, to the green wheat.
It did not fly into the green wheat,
But it flew to a blade of darnel.
It keeps on pecking at the blade of darnel,
And it keeps on crying for its dear mate:
'My mate, my mate, my sweet mate!
I shall never have such a mate
As you have been, my sweet mate!'

The sadly cooing turtle-dove
Flew away to a far-away country,
To a far-away country, to river water.
It does not drink clear water,
If ever it drinks, it stirs up the water.
And it keeps on crying for its dear mate:
'My mate, my mate, my sweet mate!
I shall never have such a mate
As you have been, my sweet mate!'

SUPPLEMENTS TO 'THE MAID WHO WAS SOLD'

1. *'Bey, Pasha of Buda'*

Text: Csanádi-Vargyas, *Röpülj*, p. 454 = Berze Nagy,
BMNh, I, pp. 147–9

A man went out ploughing and the devil approached him:
'Give to me, my man, that which is in your house without your knowledge, for it will earn you a great sum of money!'
The man pondered over the contents of his household and ultimately promised to grant the devil his request. He received a large payment. When he returned home he disclosed the happenings to his wife, who beat her hands together and said:
'Did you not know that I am pregnant? What have you done!'
A girl was born. When she had grown up the devil arrived to take her away in a four-horse coach. She was unwilling to go, but had to go since she had been bought. The devil fastened the girl to the tail of one of the horses, and had the coach driven through thorns and bushes and the like. At last the girl said:
'Go more slowly, more gently, Bey, pasha of Buda! My white scarf will remain on the thorns and bushes!'
Thereupon the devil said:
'Drive on, coachman! The horse it is mine, the whip it is yours!'
Then the girl said again:
'Drive more slowly, more gently, Bey, pasha of Buda! My red shoes will remain on the thorns and bushes!'
The devil said again:
'Drive on, coachman, the horse it is mine, the whip it is yours!'

Soon the girl said again:
  'Go more slowly, more gently, Bey, pasha of Buda! My red skirt will remain on the thorns and bushes!'
The devil gave the same answer:
  'Drive on, coachman, the horse it is mine, the whip it is yours!'
On they went. After a long time the girl said again:
  'Go more slowly, more gently, Bey, pasha of Buda! My tender body will remain on the thorns and bushes!'
Yet the devil urged the coachman:
  'Drive on, coachman, the horse it is mine, the whip it is yours!'
Once more the girl spoke:
  'Go more slowly, more gently, my dear, sweet husband! My tender body has been covered with blood!'
Thereupon the devil brought the horses to a stop, unfastened the girl from the tail of the horse and carried her into the coach and took her home. The girl became very ill. She longed for turtledove-liver. The devil brought her even that from the forest.

2. 'Anna'

Gy. Ortutay, *Magyar Népköltészet*, no. 7*f* = Csanádi-Vargyas, *Röpülj*, pp. 455–6 = Kálmány, *Szeged Népe*, III, p. 1

The 'Anna'-ballad is related to this group of ballads through several motifs.

1 'Make ready yourself now, make ready yourself now,
      Anna, you fair maiden,
  Your father had given you to us when you were in
      your mother's womb!'
'I am making myself ready, I am making myself ready,
      my sweet suitors,
  Wait a little, my water for washing is not ready yet!'

2 Out she runs, out she runs under where the cocks
      perched:
  'My cocks, my cocks, my black cocks,
  My sweet cocks, crow!
  For they are taking me away, God knows where!'

3 The white replies: 'Let the black crow!'
  The black replies: 'There is still time for it!'

4 'Make ready yourself now, make ready yourself now,
      Anna, you fair maiden,
  Your father had given you to us when you were in
      your mother's womb!'
'Wait, wait, my sweet suitors
  So that I may put on my red skirt!
  My skirts, my skirts, my fine red skirts,
  Fall down from the nails, go into mourning!'

5 Thereupon she runs out under where the cocks perched:
'My cocks, my cocks, my black cocks,
My sweet cocks, crow!
For they are taking me away, God knows where!'

6 The white replies: 'Let the black crow!'
The black replies: 'There is still time for it!'

7 'Hurry now, hurry now, the clock will soon strike;
Your father had given you to us when you were in
    your mother's womb!'

8 'Wait, wait, my sweet suitors,
So that I may say good-bye to my flowers!
My flowers, my flowers, my fine red flowers,
Turn to dry stalks, go into mourning!'

9 Thereupon she runs out under where the cocks perched:
'My cocks, my cocks, my fine white cocks,
My fine white cocks, crow!
For they are taking me away, God knows where!'

10 'We will not crow, for you gave us no food,
You fed the others, us you chased away.'
(The white cocks were orphan-children.)

Although the identity of the suitors is not explicit in the ballad, the fact that she had been promised to them when she was in her mother's womb (a motif which occurs in the tales where a girl was sold to the devil, cf. Thompson, S 411; Berze-Nagy, Types 811, 313; also Appendix, p. 336, 'Bey, Pasha of Buda'), and the asking for the cock-crows (which are supposed to chase away the devil and evil spirits as well as ghosts, Thompson, G 303.17) suggest that the suitor was the devil here.

3. 'Gabriel Bátori and Clara Bátori'

Text: Ortutay, Magyar Népköltészet, II, no. 7 c = Csanádi-Vargyas, Röpülj, pp. 461–3 = Ethnographia, **49**, 373

There were a brother and a sister: Gabriel and Clara Bátori. The girl did not want to get married; her brother married her off into Turkey, for three bushels of silver, for three bushels of gold. And when the king of Turkey set out from his country, he sent two white pigeons and two golden rings as a sign. The girl was sitting in the window, she was sewing some white embroidery. Two white pigeons flew on to her shoulders, two golden rings clinked into her apron.

The girl went down and told her brother:
'Brother, brother dear, whatever does this mean:
I was sitting in my window, I was sewing
    some white embroidery—
Two lovely pigeons flew upon my shoulders,
Two lovely golden rings clinked into my apron.

—Sister, sister dear, stand up on the stone bench,
Look to your left, what can you see there?'

The girl stood up on the stone bench, looked to her left and saw approaching from
Turkey with great joy and merriment three white coaches, three red flags. She
stepped down from the stone bench and said to her brother:

'Brother, brother dear! I see that they are coming from Turkey with great pleasure,
with great joy...three white coaches, three red flags.'

Her brother said:

'Sister, sister dear, now I have to confess it: I have sold you into Turkey for two
helms of silver, for two helms of gold.'

And the girl said:

'Brother, brother dear, why have you given me away
Into Turkey, into the hands of the pagans?
It would have been better if you had given me to
my smallest servant,
Or to my messenger.'

(Here the ballad singer comments in prose that the smallest servant was
a swineherd.)

She went into the little garden, where she fainted straightaway.

'My flowers, my flowers, wither from your roots,
Cast yourselves onto the ground,
So that my brother may see that you are mourning
over me!'

She went into the palace, she died there straightaway.

Her eyes are shut, her lips are closed,
Her two beautiful arms are laid upon her breast,
Her many fair bridesmaids are all the time crying
over her.

And the Turkish king arrived; he said to her brother:

'My brother-in-law, my brother-in-law, my chance-
brother-in-law,
Open your iron gate, hand over my fair bride,
My betrothed, to whom I have given my ring:
Clara Bátori!'

The girl's brother answered:

'Your bride is no more alive, your bride has died!
Her eyes are shut, her lips are closed,
Her two beautiful arms are laid upon her breast,
Her many fair bridesmaids are crying over her all
the time!'

The Turkish king answered:

'I will not believe it, I will not believe it until I myself have seen it.'

He kicked in the castle gate, it shattered to pieces. He went into the palace: he fainted there straightaway.

> 'My coachman, my servant, my dear foot-pages,
> Go and have a mourning dress cut out for everybody.
> The coach it is for the road, the horses, they are for
> the fire,
> All the things inside, they belong to me, the lord!'

They put her dead body [on the coach] and carried it away. When they got near to the palace of the king of Turkey and the king's mother spied them, [she said:]

> 'They went in red and they are coming in black.
> Son, my dear son, what does it mean?
> You went in red, you are coming in black?'

And the son answered:

> 'Mother, mother dear, we brought a daughter-in-law
> to your honour,
> [But] she will need neither food nor drink any more.'

The mother thought that [her daughter-in-law] had perhaps only fainted:

> 'Bring her here, my son, bring her here, I will cheer her up!'

When she realised that the girl was dead, she said:

> 'Carry her, my son, carry her into the dining-room,
> Whenever you turn around, you will kiss her,
> Whenever you turn back, you will kiss her,
> We will have a coffin of gold made for her,
> Its cross will be of diamonds, its top will be of silver,
> We will have sixty bells tolled for her,
> We will sixty-six of us bury her.'

SUPPLEMENTS TO 'FAIR ANNA BÍRÓ' (ROBBERY AND MURDER)

1. *'The Three Robber-lads'*

'The Three Robber-lads' seems to be an outgrowth of 'Fair Anna Bíró', while it shares the lament with 'The Great Mountain Robber'.

Text: Csanádi-Vargyas, *Röpülj*, no. 52 = Kriza (1956), no. 29 = *MNGY*, III, p. 32

> 1 On they go, on they go, three robber-lads,
> On they go, on they go through a vast forest,
> They came upon a Greek in the vast forest,
> They killed the Greek, they robbed his cart.

2 On they go, on they go, three robber-lads,
They found an inn, there they went in.
They asked straightaway,
'Hey, hostess, do you have some good wine?'
'My wine is good, my daughter is fair too,
I myself am also gay!'

3 So they eat, so they drink, three robber-lads,
But the youngest of them does not eat, does
    not drink,
He does not eat, he does not drink, he continues
    to grieve.

4 'Would that God had given that my rocking cradle
Had rather been my coffin,
That my swaddling clothes had rather been my
    shroud,
That my swaddling band—the rope that lowers me
    into my grave.'

2. ' The Bonny White Shepherd'

Violence and murder is the subject of the following ballad which is a version of the Rumanian 'Miorita'. All versions were recorded in Moldavia, and they are of obvious Rumanian origin (cf. Entwistle, *European Balladry*, pp. 347, 349).

Text: Ortutay, *Magyar Népköltészet*, II, no. 32
= *Ethnographia*, **42**, 137

The thousand lambs of the bonny white shepherd,
His thousand lambs, his countless sheep.
On they go, on they go three swineherds.
'Good morning, good morning, bonny white shepherd!'

'Welcome to you, three swineherds,
I know well, I know well that you will cut my head off.
If you cut my head off, bury me,
Bury me by the gate of my fold,

Place the bigger of my pipes at my head.
When the wind blows it, when it blows it, when it
    blows it gently,
Whoever will hear it will say straightaway,
The bonny white shepherd is lamenting about himself.

Place the smaller of my pipes at my feet,
When the wind blows it, when it blows, when it
    blows it gently,
Whoever will hear it will say straightaway,
The bonny white shepherd is lamenting about himself.

Where you will pass a small, smoky house farther down,
I have there, I do, an old mother.
She is washing the grey wool, she is mourning for me
    quietly.
I know well, I know well that she will ask straightaway,

Where you will pass a flower garden farther down,
I have there, I do, two maiden sisters,
They are planting flowers, they are mourning for me,
I know well, I know well that they will ask straightaway,

That they will ask straightaway whether I have married.
You can tell them then that I have married
The fat of this soil, the younger sister of this sun,
The fat of this soil, the younger sister of this sun.'

Other versions: Csanádi–Vargyas, *Röpülj*, no. 54 = Domokos, *Moldvai Magyarság*, no. 25; Csanádi–Vargyas, *Röpülj*, no. 55 = Utunk (1954), 23; Domokos–Rajeczky, *Csángó Népzene*, I, no. 34.

(d) Ballads of family conflict

'THE LITTLE MAPLE-TREE'

This is apparently a fragmentary version of the popular 'Singing bones' ballad (cf. also Child, no. 10; AT 720). The fragment which we quote was found in Transylvania.

Text: Gy. Ortutay, *Magyar Népköltészet*, II, no. 25

1   Three orphans set out
     With three little pots
     To the forest, to gather strawberries,
     To the forest, to gather strawberries.

2   Their dear mother
     Had left to them many costly pearls
     Which they were dividing, going on their way,
     Which they were dividing, going on their way.

3   The three orphans agreed to this—
     That she, who would be the first to fill,
     To fill her little pot,
     Would get the pearls.

4   Little Bencsóka filled hers [first],
     Whereupon her two elder sisters killed her.
     They put her into the hollow of a tree,
     And hastily went home.

5 Their dear father asks them,
Where his little daughter has been left,
His little daughter, little Bencsóka.

6 'Three of them went out, two of them returned,
Where has my little daughter been left?
Alas, my God, where shall I go,
Where shall I go, what shall I do?
Where shall I look for her, where shall I go?'

7 He went [lit. travelled] to the forest
To search for his little orphan,
Behold, there is a little pipe there!
Behold, there is a little pipe there!

8 He examines it, he even takes it out,
He is thinking what to do.
How can he play it in his sorrow?
Still, he starts to play it,
It has a pleasant air.

9 'Play the tune, play the tune, my royal father,
My dear nurse who brought me up,
My sisters have killed me,
They have put me into the hollow of a tree.'

10 They went home and played the tune
And played the tune upon the pipe:
'Play the tune, play the tune, my sister dear,
My murderer dear, who has killed me!

11 I was once a princess too,
A princess, the little Pendzsóka, [sic!]
A princess, the little Pendzsóka,
Now I am a little pipe.

12 My sisters have killed me,
They have put me into the hollow of a tree,
They have put me into the hollow of a tree.'

Anna Lochendorf has published two versions of the same story, consisting of verse and tunes, embedded in a prose tale, collected in Buják, a little village of the Lowland. (*Ethnographia*, 1937: 346–60.) As it is known that the original form of such tales consisted of verses with a tune, which later degenerated into prose, Lochendorf's publication suggests that long ago this ballad might have been popular in a widespread area of the country. Her version **A** was related to her by a sixty-year-old woman, who had learned it from her father. Version **B** was obtained from a twenty-year-old girl who had heard it from her grandfather. The two versions of the tale run as follows:

I. Three princesses go out to pick strawberries.

II. The mother has promised a beautiful dress to the one who succeeds in filling her basket first (**B** has no incident II).

III. The youngest sister wins and is killed by her elder sisters. (**A** they cover her with brushwood; **B** they cut off her head and throw her into a well.)

IV. **A** a little maple-tree springs up from the brushwood and a shepherd fashions a pipe from it; **B** does not give any details, only that the shepherd fashions a pipe.

V. At this point of the story the verse and tune begin: *Play the tune, play the tune, little shepherd, | Once I too was a princess, | But now I am a little maple-tree, | And from the little maple-tree a little pipe.*

VI. (In prose) The shepherd goes to the King. He plays the pipe and the King, the Queen, and the sisters try it in turn. Thereupon the pipe plays (verse and tune): *Play the tune, play the tune, my father dear, | Once I was your little daughter, | But now I am a little maple-tree, | And from the little maple-tree a little pipe. | ...Play the tune, play the tune, my mother dear, | Once I was your little daughter, | But now I am a little maple-tree... | Play the tune, play the tune, my murderer, | Once I was your little sister...etc.*

VII. **A** the sisters confess their deed. They are not killed, but suffer torture as a punishment. **B** the two sisters are thrown down from a high cliff. The father cuts open the pipe, and the smallest daughter emerges from it.

S. Solymossy has made an extensive analysis of this tale-type and points out that the strawberry and the pipe motifs occur only in the Eastern treatment of this tale/ballad group. For comparative studies of this tale-type, cf. S. Solymossy, 'A jávorfácska', *Ethnographia*, **31**, 14; L. Mackensen, 'Der singende Knochen', *FF* 49 (Helsinki, 1923); P. G. Brewster, 'The Two Sisters', *FF* 147 (Helsinki, 1953).

(e) Two ballads from Moldavia

'THE SOLDIER-GIRL'

This ballad was found only in Moldavia. One version and a fragment have been recorded, both of them quite recently. The fragment was first published in Faragó-Jagamas, *MCSNN*, no. 18 (1954). Our text: L. Vargyas, *Ethnographia*, **71**, 223; bibliographical references and a comparative study of the ballad-type, *loc. cit.*

> The aged Dancia is lamenting about himself:
> 'My God, my God, I have nine daughters,
> Nine daughters, but not a single son.
> My God, my God, who would redeem me from
>   soldiering-captivity?'
> His youngest daughter was listening at the door.
> 'Father, my father,
> Let us have my hair cut the way knights wear it,

344

Let us have my mantle cut the way hussars wear it.'
Indeed, she swung herself onto a grey steed.
When she reached the shore of the Danube
She set off for her soldiering-captivity.
'My God, my God, what can this be?
A knight or a lady?
Its bearing would suggest a knight,
Its person would suggest a lady.
Let us arrange fine little distaffs,
Fine little distaffs, fine little guns,
For if it is a knight, he will take a gun,
But if it is a lady she will choose a distaff.'
She did not cast a glance at the distaff, she took a gun.
Still they did not know whether it was a knight or a lady.
'Let us arrange here fine stooks,
Fine sprigs of rosemary into fine stooks,
For if it is a knight he will take from its top,
But if it is a lady she will take from the bottom.'
She did not even glance at the bottom, she took some
        from the top.
They still did not know whether it was a knight or a lady.
'Let us arrange fine stables here,
Warm baths in the fine stables,
For there we shall learn whether this is a knight or
        a lady.'
'My servants, my servants, when I will be taking
        my boots off,
Begin to cry "Flee, our master, flee, the emperor Francis
        Joseph,
Your country is being set on fire, your people are
        being robbed!"'
Still they did not learn whether it was a knight or
        a lady.
'I am, I am the daughter of the aged Dancia,
The daughter, the youngest daughter of the aged Dancia.
He had nine daughters, but not a single son
To redeem him from soldiering-captivity.'

The reference to the emperor Francis Joseph is obviously a later adaptation, since the story was known in Hungary in the sixteenth century. A *belle histoire* entitled 'King Béla and Bankó's Daughter' was preserved in the Farkas Széll codex of 1570. The author of this romance acknowledges that his work was a translation from South Slavonic. In South Slavonia the story is still popular. All the essential details of the Moldavian ballad agree with the *belle histoire*, though in the latter the father is called Bankó. In both pieces the father has nine daughters but no sons who could wage war for him, in both tellings the heroine is the youngest daughter, both have the cutting of her hair and her mantle in a manner becoming to knights, and she takes servants and a horse with herself. Both have the distaff-gun and the bath trials. Instead of the second trial in Dancia, 'The Daughter of Bankó' has shooting, running, stone-throwing, and drinking contests. For test of sex, to discover person masking as of other sex cf. Thompson, H 1578.

'YOUNG KING MATTHIAS'

This ballad was also recorded recently in one version and in a fragment, both from Moldavia. It belongs to the 'Riddles Wisely Expounded' type ballads (Child, nos. 1–2) and shares certain characteristics with 'The Clever Peasant Girl' tale-type AT 875 as well as with 'King John and the Bishop of Canterbury' (Child, no. 45, AT 922) in which there is a forfeit, or the penalty of death for the failure to solve the riddles (Thompson, H 512, H 541). In Hungarian anecdotes and tales it is the father who usually finds himself unable to solve some riddle and the clever daughter who ingeniously saves her father and secures the king for her husband by her clever replies. In the fragmentary record it is the youngest daughter in fact who solves the dream for her father (Faragó-Jagamas, *MCSNN*, no. 14). The hero of this type of folk tale and anecdote is invariably King Matthias Corvinus. For the riddle cf. riddles of the year, Thompson, H 721; for the impossible task and countertask, Thompson, H 1021.22.

Text: Néprajzi Közlemények (1958), pp. 52–3

1 Young King Matthias had a dream:
Under a glass window there was a big tall apple-tree,
The big tall apple-tree had twelve branches,
It had three hundred leaves, sixty-six flowers.

2 Up and spoke young King Matthias,
'I shall have you beheaded unless you explain this.'
She turned aside, began to cry.
'Why are you crying, why are you lamenting, my soul,
my sweet daughter?'

3 'How should I not cry, how should I not lament:
Young King Matthias had a dream:
There was a huge tall apple-tree under the glass window,
The huge tall apple[-tree] had twelve branches,

346

4 It had three hundred leaves, sixty six-flowers,
He will have me beheaded if I will not explain it.'
'Do not cry, do not lament, my soul, my sweet daughter,
My soul, my sweet daughter, go to him and tell him:

5 The big tall apple-tree is a great long year,
Its twelve branches are the twelve fair months,
Its three hundred leaves are three hundred working days,
Its sixty-six flowers are sixty-six Sundays.'

6 Up and spoke young King Matthias,
'Weave, my girl, for me with three heads of hemp,
With three heads of hemp a towel,
A tent-cover and a tablecloth.'

7 Now she turned away, she began to cry.
'Why are you crying, why are you crying to yourself,
        my soul, my sweet daughter?'
'How should I not cry, how should I not lament?
Hear what young King Matthias has told me:

8 Young King Matthias laid down the law
That I should weave out of three heads of hemp,
Out of three heads of hemp a towel,
A tent-cover and a tablecloth.'

9 'This is nothing, this is nothing, my soul, my sweet daughter!
Go to him yourself, tell him
That out of two bunches of shavings
He should have a loom and a warping reel made for you,

10 And he should tell in one word what you will need for the
        weaving.
Go, my daughter, go, go and tell him this!'
Young King Matthias could not find an answer,
Up and spoke young King Matthias,

11 Up and spoke young King Matthias:
'I do not want, I do not want this towel,
This towel, this tent-cover,
Nor this tablecloth, only you I want.'

APPENDIX II

In this Appendix I shall discuss certain possible hypotheses about the 'Lamkin' ballad (Child, no. 93).

We have seen that 'Clement Mason' has no counterpart in British balladry. But the superstitious beliefs in connection with building operations, and the practice of performing magic rites similar to that related in 'Clement Mason' prevailed in Scotland and England, and were widely held in Wales, according to Nennius and Robert Holkot (cf. quotations in the discussion of 'Clement Mason' under *Folklore and Custom* in chapter 3).

In view of these beliefs it is perhaps possible to shed some light on some hitherto unexplained aspects of the 'Lamkin' ballad.

In its present form, 'Lamkin' tells the story of a mason who did not receive his 'fee' for building a castle, and who takes brutal revenge on the lord who deceived him. With the help of the 'false nurse' he obtains access to the well-locked house, and in the lord's absence kills his wife and baby son.

In versions **A**, **C**, **D**, **F**, **G**, **I**, **N**, **O**, **R**, **T** and **V**, Lamkin mason, having cruelly murdered the mistress of the house, carefully collects his victim's blood in a (silver, golden, or clean) basin. This delicate attention is somewhat unintelligible in the context, and it is not surprising that his accomplice, the false nurse, cannot see the point of his action:

A *O scour the bason, nourice,* | *And mak it fair and clean,* | *For to keep this lady's heart's blood,* | *For she's come o noble kin!* || —*There need nae bason, Lamkin,* | *Lat it run through the floor,* | *What better is the heart's blood* | *O the rich than o the poor?* || **I** *Gae wash a bason, nourice,* | *An ye wash it clean,* | *To cape this ladie's blood,* | *She is come o high kine!* || —*I winna wash a bason,* | *Nor will I wash it clean,* | *To cape this ladie's blood,* | *Tho she's come o high kine.*

In the other versions the trait is not fully preserved:

C *O Jeany, O Jeany,* | *O scour the bason clean,* | *That your lady's noble blood* | *May be kepped clean.* || **F** *Where is your daughter Betsy,* | *She may do some good;* | *She can hold the silver basin* | *To catch your heart's blood.* || **N** *Ere the basin was washen,* | *Or haf made clean,* | *The ladie's heart bleed* | *Was rinnin in the reem.* || **R** *Now scour the bason, Jenny,* | *And scour't very clean,* | *To haad this ladi's blood,* | *For she's of noble kin.* || **T** *Saying,—where is your friend,* | *Or where is your foe,* | *That will hold the gold basin* | *Your heart's blood to flow?* || **D** *Go scour the bason, nursy,* | *Both outside and in,* | *To hold your lady's heart's blood* | *Sprung from a noble kin.* || —*To hold my lady's heart's blood* | *Would make my heart full glad,* | *Ram in the knife, bold Rankin,* | *And gar the blood to shed.* || **G** *Hold the gold basin* | *For your heart's blood to run in.* || **O** *Go scour the silver basin,* | *Go scour*

348

*it fine, | For our lady's heart blude | Is gentle to tine. || Go scour the silver skewer | Oh scour it richt fine... etc. || **V** I wuld be very sorry | To wash a basin clean, | To haud my mither's heart's blude | That's comin, an I ken.*

If we consider that there was a peculiar value attributed to human blood in the Middle Ages (cf. Holkot, *op. cit.*), and that it was especially important for buildings and builders, we may surmise that a latent relic of this tradition has slipped into the ballad, probably by reason of the fact that its hero is a mason.

It is not impossible, that there may be a deeper motivation for the murder story of Lamkin than is related in the present form of the ballad.

Why should the 'unpaid' mason exact such a fearful revenge? Is it because 'he was wicked', or is it that there has been a bond ('my fee') that was not honoured? Hitherto 'money' has been the interpretation of 'my fee'. But there could be a more terrible implication if we take into account that 'the fee' might have some relation to the sacrifice which, according to superstitious belief, was exacted so that the building might stand firm (cf. 'Clement Mason'). If this was so, then either the life devoted as sacrifice for the building was a life dear to the lord (his wife, his baby son) which he was not prepared to offer, and this is now exacted with justification by the mason, or the life devoted as sacrifice for the building *was* provided by the mason (his wife or child) and a terrible revenge-killing is now taking place.

The first alternative would justify the lord's exaggerated warnings against the mason, the wife's utmost precautions in locking the doors and windows of the castle (**B-H, K, P, R, U**) and would explain the mason's refusal to accept gold in place of the lady's life (**B-E, H, I, M, O, U**), also his refusal to accept the offers to take somebody else's life instead. The second alternative, on the other hand, would explain versions **F, T**, in which the lady—'very unnaturally' according to F. J. Child— offers her own daughter as a wife to the mason (i.e. 'wife for a wife'?).

The magic motif of blood let into a ritual basin, as an expression of *hatred*, has 'wandered' into other ballads (e.g. Child, no. 81—'Little Musgrave and Lady Barnard'):

G *Repeat these words my fair ladie, | Repeat them ower agane, | And into a basin of pure silver | I'll gar your heart's bluid rin. || ...Lord Birnes wiffe giuue that I be | He is not nou at home, | He is gone to the good grein wood | Lord let him not come home. || He gois no more into my heart | Nor de dois in my heil | To se so much of his heart blud | As wald goe in a skil. ||* (Robert Edwards' *Music Book*, Panmure Music Library, no. 11. Unpublished. I gained access to this copy through the kindness of Mrs H. M. Shire.)

It may be significant that in both these examples the words are addressed to a lady, and that there is an innocent child involved.

SELECTED BIBLIOGRAPHY

I. For international ballad collections, and for works dealing with general problems of balladry, see the comprehensive bibliographies of:

Bronson, B. H. *The Traditional Tunes of the Child Ballads*, I–II, Princeton-London. 1959– .

Child, F. J. *The English and Scottish Popular Ballads*. I–V, New York, 1957 ed. Bibl. in vol. v.

Entwistle, W. J. *European Balladry*. 2nd ed. Oxford, 1951.

Hodgart, M. J. C. *The Ballad*. London, 1950.

Lord, A. B. *The Singer of Tales*. London, 1960. This deals with some general aspects of the composition of traditional heroic epics.

Vargyas, L. 'Kutatások a Népballada Középkori Történetében', *Ethnographia*, **71**, 163–276, 479–523 (for the latter in German see 'Das Weiterleben der landnahme-zeitlichen Heldenepic in den ungarischen Balladen', *Acta Ethnographica*, **10**, 241–94); *Néprajzi Értesítő*, **41**, 5–73 (in German: 'Forschungen zur Geschichte der Volksballade im Mittelalter—Die Herkunft der ungarischen Ballade von der eingemauerten Frau', *Acta Ethnographica*, **9**, 1–88); *Ethnographia*, **73**, 206–59.

Wilgus, D. K. *Anglo-American Folksong Scholarship since 1898*. New Brunswick, 1959.

II. Hungarian material:

Acta Ethnographica. Published from 1950.

Bartók, B. *A Magyar Népdal (Hungarian Folkmusic*, transl. by M. D. Calvocoressi, London, 1931). Budapest, 1924.

Bartók, B.-Kodály, Z. *SZNd = Erdélyi Magyarság*. Budapest, 1923. A collection of folksongs and ballads collected in Transylvania. This work is often referred to as *SZNd*, i.e. Bartók's own abbreviation for 'Székely Népdalok'.

Berze-Nagy, J. *BMNh = Baranyai Magyar Néphagyományok*, I–III. Pécs, 1940– . Vol. I contains the ballad material.

Csanádi, I.-Vargyas, L. *Röpülj páva, röpülj*. Budapest, 1954. An excellent 'popular edition', authentic versions and notes, and good general introduction. Ballads of old and new style, some of them in several versions, and fifty tunes.

Dános, E. *A Magyar Népballada*, Néprajzi Füzetek no. 7. Budapest, 1938. An introduction to Hungarian balladry, with an additional catalogue of Hungarian ballads. A very useful handbook, but has to be handled with care, for many of the references are incorrect and out of date, e.g. identical versions republished in different books, periodicals, etc., are referred to as being different versions altogether.

Domokos, P. P. *MM = A Moldvai Magyarság*, 3rd edn. Kolozsvár, 1941. Contains material published in his previous collections: *Mert akkor az idő napkeletre fordul* (1940); and *A Moldvai Magyarság* (1931). Folksongs and tunes recorded in Moldavia.

Domokos, P. P.-Rajeczky, B. *Csángó Népzene*, I–II. Budapest, 1956–61. Encompasses most of the material collected in Moldavia, with tunes.

Ethnographia. The periodical of the Magyar Néprajzi Társaság, published from 1890.

Faragó, J.-Jagamas, J. *MCSNN = Moldvai Csángó Népdalok és Népballadák*. Budapest, n.d. [1954?]. Contains thirty ballads, with tunes, collected in Moldavia among the Hungarian population. Good introduction to the historical background of the 'Csángó-s'.

Gragger, R. *A Magyar népballada*. Budapest, 1927; i.e. *Ungarische Balladen*. Berlin, 1926. A study with ballad material and translations.

Greguss, A. *A balladáról*. Budapest, 1865. The first Hungarian 'theoretical' work on balladry.

Kálmány, L. *Hagyaték*, II = *Kálmány Lajos Népköltési Hagyatéka*, II, *Alföldi Népballadák*. Budapest, 1954. This is the second volume of the Kálmány-Bequest. This volume was edited by Gy. Ortutay, who added several notes and bibliographical references to the material collected by Kálmány.

Kálmány, L. *Koszorúk* = *Koszorúk az Alföld Vadvirágaiból*, I–II. Arad, 1877–8. Mostly new-style ballads collected in the Lowland.

Kálmány, L. *Szeged Népe*, I–III. Arad, 1881–91. Vols. II–III are especially rich in ballad material. The volumes contain the ballads recorded in the Lowland, at Szeged and Temesköz. Interesting notes on local customs and beliefs, mostly ballads of new style.

Kodály, Z. *Folk Music in Hungary*. London, 1960. Translation of study originally published in *A Magyarság Néprajza*, II (ed. K. Viski, Budapest, n.d.).

Kodály, Z. *MNT*, I–V = *A Magyar Népzene Tára, Corpus Musicae Popularis Hungaricae*. Eds. B. Bartók and Z. Kodály. Budapest, 1951.—The great critical edition of the entire Hungarian traditional music repertoire; further volumes in progress.

Kodály, Z.-Vargyas, L. *MNpt* = *A Magyar Népzene*, példatárt szerkesztette L. Vargyas. Budapest, 1952.

Kriza, J. *Vadrózsák*. Kolozsvár, 1863.

Kriza, J. (1956) = *Székely Népköltési Gyüjtemény*, I. Budapest, 1956. Critical edition of the first main Hungarian ballad collection, published first in 1863. Vol. I contains the ballad material; vol. II contains folk tales.

Magyar Népköltési Gyüjtemény = *MNGY*, I–XIV. Budapest, 1872–1924. Ballad material in vols. I–III, VI–VII, XI–XII contains J. Kriza's *Vadrózsák*; XIV, Z. Kodály's collection from the Lowland. Vols. IV–V contain Gy. Sebestyén's *Regös*-song collection; vols. IX, X, XII, XIII contain folk tales.

MNYr = *Magyar Nyelvőr*, a periodical which contains mostly linguistic material and several ballads. Published from 1872.

Néprajzi Értesítő. Issued by Nemzeti Múzeum, Néprajzi Múzeum. Published from 1900.

Néprajzi Közlemények. Issued by Nemzeti Múzeum, Néprajzi Múzeum. Published from 1956.

Ortutay, Gy. *Magyar Népköltészet*, I–III. Budapest, 1955. Vol. I contains a general introduction to Hungarian ballad scholarship. Vol. I contains folksongs, vol. II ballads, and vol. III folk tales. Short notes are added to each volume.

Ortutay, Gy. *Székely Népballadák*. Budapest, 1935 (2nd ed. 1948). A collection of Transylvanian ballads, with exhaustive notes and references to international parallels. This volume is illuminated with the delightful woodcuts of Gy. Budai.

Schram, F. *Magyar Népballadák*. Budapest, 1955.

Solymossy, S. Chapter on Hungarian ballads in *A Magyarság Néprajza*, III. Budapest, 1935. Ed. by K. Viski.

Vargyas, I   Kutatások a Népballada Középkori Történetében' (cf. above). This extensi   nd stimulating study investigates the connections between Siberian heroic epic, French balladry, and Hungarian ballads. For a summary of conclusions in French cf. L. Vargyas, 'Rapports internationaux de la ballade populaire hongroise' in *Littérature Hongroise—Littérature Européenne*, ed. I. Sőtér. Budapest, 1964, pp. 69–104.

MOTIF INDEX

(f) denotes formula

abandoning
> children abandoned, aided by animals, 299–300; devoured by animals, 301–2
> mother a. children, 296–300
> wife a. husband and child, 107–12, 300–2

abduction, 111–12

adultery, 230–48
> betrayed by child, 230–2, 235, 238

angel, in shape of a bird, 59, 187

animals *(see also* beasts, *individual animals)*
> and abandoned child, *see* abandoning
> curse of a., 192
> hatched out on lovers' graves, 192, 214
> speaking, 23–4, 27, 35, 38, 42, 56–60, 62–4, 72, 113, 188, 192, 214, 299–300, 316, 333–8

answer, riddling, 99–100, 102–5

apple
> golden, 31–2, 255, 332
> symbol of love, 77–8, 154, 173, 185, 255, 267
> symbol of the Virgin, 76–9

apple-tree
> in ballad opening *(f)*, 57, 76, 332–3
> in riddle, 346

avarice
> abandonment of children for a., 296–7
> maid sold for a., 149–51, 154–5, 160, 336, 338
> murder for a., 25, 33, 43

Bátori-motif, 243, 247

beasts, to mourn over the dead *(f)*, 269

bells
> 'are tolling, but not for midday-meal time' *(f)*, 191, 259
> 'For whom are the b. tolling?' *(f)*, 47–8, 144, 153, 190, 193, 195, 197, 209, 295
> heavenly, toll by themselves *(f)*, 56, 59, 80, 321
> toll for the dead, 24–5, 36, 47–8, 100–1, 144, 153, 156–7, 159, 162, 174, 190, 209, 240, 244, 259, 261, 279, 295, 306, 340
> toll three times, for the dead *(f)*, 24–5, 36, 240, 244, 279, 306
> 'Will you have b. tolled for me?' *(f)*, 156–7, 159, 162, 174, 340

bird *(see also* pigeon, turtle-dove)
> angel in form of b., 59, 187
> b. mother makes human mother ashamed, 301
> choice between b. as best messenger (raven, magpie, crow, swallow) *(f)*, 187, 196, 202, 221
> instructions given to b. messenger *(f)*, 182, 186–8, 196, 198, 221–2

reincarnated soul as b., 27, 35, 38, 113, 214
> takes a message or carries a letter *(f)*, 29, 161, 186–8, 193, 196, 198, 201–2, 279, 321
> to mourn over b., to sing in choir for the dead *(f)*, 267, 269, 270
> warns maid of danger, 23–4, 35, 42, 113

blessing of oxen by the Virgin, 331

blood *(see also* life-token)
> appearance of b. signifying mortal danger or death, 23, 33–4
> clothes, shoes, wreath swimming in b., 150, 152, 165, 293–4
> dreaming of b., ill omen, 23, 33–4
> letter written with b., 187, 193–4, 196, 203–4
> mixed with lime makes building firm, 22, 27, 39–40, 348–9
> in suicide formula, *see* suicide formulas
> value of in pagan rituals, 22, 27, 39–40, 348–9
> of victim collected, 22, 25, 190, 348–9
> water to turn into b. (curse), 86, 129, 191, 290
> well, brooklet of b., 23, 33–4

boots
> red, in dream, 186, 206
> swimming in blood *(f)*, *see* blood

bread, in curse, 129

bride
> casts curse upon herself, 153–7, 166, 170–8
> of Christ, 55–82
> dies on her way to wedding, 153–7, 166–8, 171–2, 258–63, 265, 336–7
> dying, asks for part of bird to eat, 163, 165–6, 337
> found dead by bridegroom, 158–62, 169–78, 338–40
> gives birth to baby on her way to wedding, 263–5
> murdered because she refuses to address bridegroom as such, 149–53, 163–6, 170–8, 336–7
> old b. chosen, 27, 31
> sold into marriage against her will, 148–78, 276, 336–40
> sold to Turk, 154–62, 175–7, 336–40
> taken back to parents, 263–5
> thirst before dying, 153, 155–6, 167, 265
> trailed at a horse's tail, 150–3, 163–5, 336–7

bridegroom
> attempt to break bride's will ends in her death, 149–53, 163–6, 170–8, 336–7

bridegroom (*cont.*)
 dead, returns to take his bride to his grave,
  326–8
 face unusually white, 153–4, 175–6
 finds bride dead, 126, 128, 141, 158–62,
  169–78, 180–3, 190–1, 206–23, 338–40
 takes bride back to parents, 263–5
bridge (*see also* magic objects)
 beheading-b., 186, 189, 215–16
 footb., to burn (curse), 129
brook
 of blood, *see* blood
 speaks, 159, 170
brother
 imprisoned while sister well treated in
  foreign captivity, 310–11
 kills sister for unchastity, 223–30
 love weaker than lover's, 252–3
 sells sister in marriage, 160, 338
 sympathetic, visits sister in prison, 94, 181–2,
  187, 196, 203
buffalo, puts human mother to shame, 297
building, built during night collapses by day,
  etc., 19, 22, 28, 39–41
building-sacrifice, 19–44, 348–9
burial
 request to be buried: child, b. on top of
  altar (*f*), 191, 213, 221; in front of the
  altar, behind the altar (*f*), 126, 128, 135–6,
  144, 183, 213–14, 221, 315–16; in front of
  small altar, in front of big altar, 192; in
  front of church, 128, 191; at right or left
  side of altar (*f*), 128; in the same grave as
  lover (*f*), 153, 180, 190–1, 211, 213, 221;
  60 men to bury dead bride, 340
 washing corpse before b. (*f*), 86, 97, 224,
  226–7, 274
burning
 castle to burn down (curse), 307
 to death, of daughter-in-law, 313–17; as
  punishment of false servants, 27, 34–5; for
  sacrificial reasons, 20–22, 40; of unfaithful
  wife, 231, 233–4, 236, 238
 footbridge to burn (curse), 129

candles
 in choice of death, symbolises burning
  to death (*f*), 231, 233, 238, 279, 316,
  322
 heavenly, carried by magic lamb or stag, 56,
  58, 72, 80, 82
 magic, unlit c. flares up, unextinguished c.
  goes out, 72, 80
captivity, for seven years, 257, 307–12
castles, palaces
 cursed, 26, 29, 38, 307
 promised to lady, 110–11
charms, 93, 329–30

child
 abandoned c. and animals, *see* abandoning
 refuses to return to mother, who had
  abandoned her, 298, 300
 goes to seek dead mother, 21, 26–7, 29–31,
  37–8, 82–97
 inquires about dead mother, 21, 26, 30–1, 37,
  42–3, 276–7
 promised to devil in mother's womb, unwittingly, 336–7
 recognizes mother in disguise, 116–17
 to be taken care of by wind, rain, birds (*f*),
  25–6, 29, 32, 36, 301
 to die in mother's womb (curse), 86
 warns father of his mother's adultery, 230,
  232, 235, 238
childbirth, on way to the wedding, 263–5
choice of deaths, 114, 118, 120, 231, 233, 238,
  279, 313–17, 322
 riddling, *see* candle
Christ
 compared to sun and moon, 329
 as creator of flowers, 60–2
 his beauty, 329
 looking for accommodation, 331–2
 maid taken to heaven as a bride to Jesus,
  55–82
 permits orphans' mother to rise from her
  grave, 88–90
clothes
 in dream, 186, 204–6
 fall on the ground signifying owner's death,
  267
 swimming in blood, *see* blood
 to fall down from their nails in mourning
  for their owner (*f*), 155–6, 161, 170, 174–5,
  188, 209, 267, 271–2, 337
coach (*see also* horses)
 glass, 154–5, 160, 185, 188, 190
 golden, 154–5, 185, 292
 mourning, 185, 188, 279, 282
 promised as reward (*f*), 126, 128, 190, 209
 to rust (curse), 307
coat, in dream, 186, 206
cock
 asked to crow to save maid from being
  carried away by devil, 327, 337–8
 orphan children as c.—if you do not help
  them they won't help you, 337–8
cock-crow(s)
 death of maid, brother, etc., located within
  three c., 57, 66–8, 309, 312
 revenant must return to grave at c., 327
 save from devil, 327, 337–8
coffin
 covered with black veil, 159–162
 gold, placed into c. of glass, placed in a tree,
  156

coffin (*cont.*)
  made of gold and silver, with diamond
    (cross), 159, 174, 340
  marble, 128, 156–7, 162; pink, 316; red, 100,
    128, 144, 316; white, 100, 128, 144;
    yellow, 128
  stone, cement, 100, 128
  studded with gold and silver nails, 157, 159,
    162, 174
  walnut wood, 26, 38, 153, 156–7, 174
competition
  between sisters: who can fill basket with
    strawberries first, 342–4
  winner killed, 342–4
complaint (*see also* lament)
  of imprisoned mother, 303–7
  of maid for beloved, 332–3
  of orphans, 83–90, 95–7, 325
  overheard, 241–4, 247, 273–6, 279–80, 304–7,
    309–12
  in prison-songs, 257, 272
  of robber's wife, 273–81
  of turtle-dove, 333–6
  of unrecognised brother/sister in parents'
    house, 307–12
cord, red, in dream, 186, 205
crowd, 'What c. is there?' (*f*), 190, 209–10
crucifixion, 327–30
curse(s), 26, 29, 38, 86, 126, 129, 135, 137, 140,
    153, 155, 166, 191–2, 197, 214, 259–63,
    271, 290, 305, 307, 310, 325, 329, 331
  against self, 152–7, 166, 178, 261
  animals hatched out on lovers' grave c. cruel
    parents, 192, 214
  cursing of building, 26, 29, 38, 191, 307
  daughter/son c. mother, 155, 271, 310
  dead mother c. stepmother of her children,
    86
  mother c. daughter who marries against her
    will, 259–63
  plants grown on lovers' grave c. cruel parents,
    126, 129, 135, 137, 140, 191–2, 214
  suitor c. maid's mother, 153, 191
  Virgin c. horses and poplars, 331

dancing
  offended lover makes maid dance till her
    boots are filled with blood, etc., 292–5;
    till she dies, 292–5
  with devil, 176, 292–5
Danube, as coffin and shroud (*f*), 267
daughter
  imprisons her mother who wears beggar's
    disguise, 303–7
  orders mother in disguise to be beheaded, 306
  sold d. falls in love with bridegroom, 155,
    166
  sold into marriage against her will, *see* bride

solves riddle for her father, 346
  unrecognized, 307–12
daughter-in-law, burnt to death by mother-in-
  law, 313–17
dead
  bells ring three times for the d., *see* bells
  d. lover returns from grave, 326–8
  d. lovers embrace each other, 126, 128, 140
  d. mother rises from grave to take care of
    children, 87–8, 90–7
  parts of d. body to be displayed on town
    walls, gates, etc. (*f*), 86, 96, 226–7, 272,
    274, 280
  speaks (*see also* plants), 'Are you alive, or are
    you dead?' (*f*), 128 (*see* prison); d. lover
    speaks to beloved, 126, 128, 134, 136, 162;
    d. mother speaks to her children, 21, 26,
    37, 83, 85–91, 321
  state of the d., 85, 187–90
  d. to be covered in fine crimson and washed
    in wine (*f*), 86, 97, 115, 124, 224, 226–7,
    229–30, 274, 280
death
  choice, from among three kinds of d., *see*
    choice; riddling, *see* candles
  dressing splendidly before d., 25, 36
  feigned, 44–54
  from sorrow, 21, 26, 100, 105, 143–4, 147,
    162, 303, 323–4
  wish to be left alone at the point of d.,
    165–6, 337
  wish to have died at birth (*f*), 184, 275,
    280–1, 340
delousing, 107, 112–13, 118–22, 301
demon lover, 151, 175–6, 292–3, 326–8, 336–8
devil
  child sold to d. in mother's womb, 336–8
  has horse's hooves, 151, 327
  takes the form of a lover, 326–8
  to be carried away by d. (curse), 129
  Turks' cruelty confused with d., 176, 336–7
disguise
  lover in d., 193, 219, 333
  mother in beggar's d. to test daughter's
    charity, 303–7
  wife returns to husband after abandonment
    in d., 108–9, 116–17, 124
  woman d. as soldier, 344–6
disinheritance, mother disinherits son who
  wants to marry against her will, 125, 127
door
  delay in opening d. (*f*), 156–8, 162, 224, 230,
    232, 235, 239–41, 243–4, 273, 279–80, 339
  words overheard through d. (*f*), 240–1,
    243–4, 273, 279–80, 309, 332
dreams
  of blood: ill omen, 23, 33–4
  human sacrifice suggested by d., 22, 28

dreams (*cont.*)
 interpretation of d., 186, 204–6, 221
 misinterpretation of ominous d., 23, 43–4
 ominous, 20, 23, 186, 321
 riddle in d., 346
 warning in d., 20, 23, 33–4, 186; fulfilled, 20, 23, 33–4, 186; inattention to, 20, 23
dressing
 as excuse for delay, *see* door; 337
 with splendour before death, 25, 36
drowned bodies, modes of discovering, 267
drowning (*see also* shavings), 98–107, 125–6, 128, 130–2, 139–41, 267
duel, between friends, for lady, 255–8
dying man, directs that mother/sister/beloved be kept in ignorance of his death, 342

eating, drinking together (*f*), 222–3, 227
elopement, 107, 110–11, 255–8, 300–1
example, 'Let it be an e.' (*f*), 86, 224, 226, 230, 272, 274

farewell
 from animals, 161, 170
 from clothes, 155–6, 161, 170, 175, 188, 209
 from flowers, 151, 155–6, 161, 170, 175, 188, 204, 338
father
 has daughter's lover imprisoned, 142–8; killed, 142–8
 kicks daughter to death, 144, 148
 kills son for asking for his mother whom he had killed, 277
 love weaker than lover's, 251–4
 orders daughter's execution, 194
 sells daughter in marriage, 157, 336
 solves riddle and saves daughter's life, 346–7
fear, mother abandons children for f. of the enemy, 296–300
fields, not to be green (curse), 129
fight
 one person left alive to carry the tidings home after f., 257–8, 308, 312
 with pursuers of eloping couple, 255–7, 307–8, 311–12
fish
 to be gravediggers (*f*), 270
 to be nails on coffin (*f*), 267
 to mourn over the dead (*f*), 267, 269
flames (*see also* burning)
 footbridge to go up in f. (curse), 129
 shirt, to go up in f. (curse), 129, 310
 towel, to go up in f. (curse), 129, 191, 290
flowers
 on grave (curse), 153
 to wither on their stalk in mourning for owner, 127, 133, 155–6, 159, 161, 174, 188, 209, 322, 338–9

folktale elements in ballads, 23–7, 31, 34, 41–2, 50, 52, 82, 114, 132–3, 156, 158, 169–70, 172, 202, 214, 242–3, 291–2, 267, 278–80, 296, 298–312, 326–8, 336, 340, 342–7
foundation sacrifice, *see* building-sacrifice
funeral, *see* burial

garden, speaks, 159, 161, 170
gates, of heaven
 open by themselves, 57, 59, 64, 78–80, 82, 92
 to be opened (*f*), 150, 166, 295, 322
glasses
 of heaven, get filled by themselves, 59, 68, 78–80, 82
 of wine to be spilt (curse), 305
gloves, red, yellow, in dreams, 186, 206
goose, lost, allusion to lost virginity, 255
gown, red, yellow, in dreams, 186, 206
grapes, imprisonment for stealing g., 257
grass, not to grow on grave (curse), 153
grave
 flowers, grass not to grow on g. (curse), 153
 lover's g., *see* animals, plants
green, unlucky colour, 154, 173, 322
greetings, not returned, 24, 35–6, 43

head
 cut off, request that it be washed in wine, covered in crimson, placed in casket and sent to father/mother, placed on town walls (*f*), 115, 124, 226–7, 229–30, 272, 274, 280; cut off, speaks, 115, 124, 226
 in suicide formula, 242
headdress, symbol of virginity (loss of), 99–100, 102–6, 322
heart
 and/or liver to be cut out and sent to lover, 143–8; or to be placed on town wall, gate (*f*), 86, 96, 147, 271
 in suicide formula, 211
heaven (*see also* gates, glasses, key, table)
 maid taken to h. as a bride of Christ, 55–82
 visit to h., 61–2
help
 from animals, *see* abandoning
 from dead mother, 82–97
 from the Virgin, 82–4, 90–7
hemp, to turn into hackle (curse), 129
Hero and Leander, 98–107
hiding
 adulterous wife hides lover in a chest, 230, 232–4, 236–7
 h.-place betrayed, 271–2
 mother hides daughter from the Turks, 267, 271
horse
 at a bound jumps to lover's gate, 127
 cursed by the Virgin, 331

horse (*contd.*)
  imprisonment for stealing h., 289
  order to prepare h. (*f*), 20, 23, 125, 127, 185,
    188, 240, 242, 244, 259–61, 274, 282, 289,
    303, 322
  plague to kill h. (curse), 307
  and precious gear as reward (*f*), 126, 128,
    188, 190, 209, 286, 292
  silver h., 291
  speaks, 316
  stolen by eloping couple, 256
  to be fastened to h.'s tail and dragged to
    death, 150–3, 163–5, 280, 336–7
house, to burn down (curse), 191
husband
  kicks wife to death for no apparent reason,
    281–4
  kills wife and her paramour, 230–9, 242; to
    break her will, 149–53, 163–5, 336–7
  mason h. kills wife for ritual reasons, 21,
    25–6, 28–9
  overhears wife's lullaby about her adultery,
    239–44, 247
  robber, kills wife for complaining, 274, 276,
    279–80
  tests wife's fidelity, 242, 246–7
  unexpected return surprises adulteress, 230–9

identity, undisclosed (*see also* disguise):
  children in parents' house, 307–12
  mother in daughter's house, 303–7
  wife in husband's house, 108, 116–17
immuring, wife, for ritual reasons, *see* building-
  sacrifice
imprisonment
  brother, for stealing horse, 288–91
  brother and sister (by Turks), 307–12
  daughter for unchastity (by mother), 180–1,
    185–6, 193, 196, 198–206, 221
  daughter's lover (by father), 142–6
  knights, for stealing grapes (by Turks), 257
  maid (by ravishers), 272, 307, 310
  mother (by daughter), 303–7
incest, 36, 103–5

journey, distressful, 20, 23–4, 112–13, 153–8,
  166–7, 258–60, 265–7, 284–8, 321
judge, dishonest, 288–91

key
  of chest, declared to be lost in evasive answer,
    225–6, 231, 233
  of heaven, given to pure maid, 56–9, 67, 80
  of prison, stolen to release prisoner, 256–7,
    310
knife
  in curses, 129, 137, 191
  symbolic, 103–5

lake, bottomless, 126, 128
lamb
  magic, 56, 58, 62, 70–2, 81–2
  of God, 56, 58, 62, 72, 74–5, 81–2
lamenting (*see* complaint), 57–9, 63–4, 68–70,
  78–82, 184, 275, 280–1, 340
land of milk and honey, 107, 110–11, 122–3
Leda, 72, 82
Lenore-motif, 175, 326–8
letter
  sent by bird, *see* bird; by bird who is angel
    of God, 187
  sent from prison, *see* bird
  written with fingers instead of pen, with
    tears or in blood instead of ink, etc., 187,
    193–4, 196, 203–4
life-token, 321
  flowers wither, *see* flowers
  ring changes colour or breaks, 132, 134, 136
  scarf, colour turns into red or bloody, to
    signify mortal danger or death of donor,
    125–8, 132–3, 136, 138
  see also liver, heart, wine
Longinus legend, 330
love
  forbidden, 125–48, 179–251, 258–63
  of betrothed stronger than l. of blood
    relatives, 251–4
lover
  animals on l.s' grave, *see* animals
  dead, speaks to beloved, *see* dead
  hidden in chest, *see* hiding
  killed by husband, 230–9, 242
  plants grown on l.s' grave, *see* plants
  recognizes clothes of murdered sweetheart,
    286–7
  separated by water, 98–107
  tests beloved's love, 193, 333
loyalty, toward paramour, declared by wife,
  241–2, 244
lullaby, disclosing adultery, overheard, *see*
  Bátori
lyric elements in balladry, 202, 325

magic objects
  mill, 44, 46, 49–51, 53
  saliva, 300–2
  tower, 44, 46, 49, 53
  wands, 83–4, 90–7
maid
  dragged to death at horse's tail, *see* horse
  goes to war instead of father, in man's guise,
    344–6
  sold in marriage against her will, 148–78
  taken to heaven, as a bride to Christ, 55–82
  wounded to prove her unchastity, 223–30
marriage
  compulsory, 148–79, 272–81, 336–40

marriage (*cont.*)
  forbidden, 125–48, 258–63, 292–5
  loveless, 239–51, 272–84
mason
  collects victims' blood in silver, golden, etc.,
    basin, *see* blood
  sacrifices wife to make building firm, *see*
    building-sacrifice
message (*see also* letter), 144
  deceptive, 23
  sent from prison, 180–1, 186–8, 193, 196,
    198, 201–2, 279, 321
  wrong, delivered, 23, 29
messenger
  choice of, *see* bird
  heavenly, 56–8, 60–4, 72, 81
metempsychosis (*see also* reincarnation, sym-
    pathetic plants), 100, 136, 183, 191, 214–
    15, 342–4
milk
  brooklet of m., springs from immured
    mother's breast, 27–9, 31
  to indicate safety and health, 133
mill, magic, *see* magic
miraculous appearances (*see also* messenger,
    heavenly, resuscitation)
  God places child in cradle in front of mother,
    25
  God splits wall open to liberate immured
    mother, 31
  miraculous obstacles, *see* obstacles
  prayers for miracles, 25, 35
moon
  Christ's beauty compared to m., 329
  lamb or stag, magic, carries m., 56–8, 72, 81–2
  mother-in-law referred to as m., 313
  on prince's chest, 291
  prisoner had not seen m. for 7 years, 257, 307
  rises at Christ's feet, 332
mother
  abandons children: for avarice, 296–7; for
    fear, 298; for lust, 107, 110–11, 300–1
  betrays daughter's hiding place to Turks,
    271–2
  casts curse upon cruel step-mother, 86
  casts curse upon daughter who is uncharit-
    able, 305, 307
  casts curse upon daughter who wants to get
    married without her consent, 258–63
  causes death of daughter/son, 125–42, 148–
    223, 258–63, 272, 300–3, 318
  comes to aid of child after death (takes care
    of her children), washes, combs their hair,
    etc., *see* dead
  denies having a daughter, 154, 267, 271
  disowns son, 125, 127
  has daughter executed, 152, 182, 186, 189–
    90, 318

has son executed, 127
imprisoned by daughter unwittingly, 303–7
imprisons her daughter for unchastity,
    180–1, 185–6
love weaker than lover's, 251–5
magic, performed by m., 44–7, 49–54
'May God repay you, my mother dear...'
    (*f*), 58, 69
murders her son's lover, 125–30, 316–17
orders daughter's execution for unchastity,
    182, 186, 194
plucks sympathetic plants, 126, 129, 135,
    183, 191–2, 214–15, 315
put to shame by animal's care of its young,
    297, 299, 301
refuses accommodation, etc., to her own
    children, 307–13
sells daughter in marriage, 148–79
suckles her child after death, *see* dead;
    milk
tests daughter's charity in beggar's guise,
    303–7
threatens step-mother, 87
mother-in-law, murders daughter-in-law, 313–
    17
mud, in curse, 129
murder (how?)
  beheading, 23, 108, 115, 124, 186, 189–90,
    226, 231–3, 242, 272, 274, 292, 341
  burning, *see* burning
  dancing to death, 292–5
  dragging at horse's tail, *see* horse
  drowning, 126–8, 130–1, 138, 141
  immuring, *see* building-sacrifice
  kicking, 144, 282
  poison, 317–18
  shooting, 24, 317
  slitting throat, 190, 276–7
  strangulation, 288–91
  unspecified, 143–4, 182, 285–7, 340, 342
murder (who/whom?)
  bridegroom—bride, *see* bride
  brother—sister, 223–30
  enticed wife—her enticer, 108, 115, 124
  father—son, daughter, daughter's lover, *see*
    father
  husband—wife, wife's paramour, *see* husband
  mother—daughter, son, son's lover, *see*
    mother
  mother-in-law—daughter-in-law, 313–17
  robbers—prince and princess, 291–2
  sheriff—prisoner, 288–91
  sisters—youngest sister, 342–3
  soldiers—maid, 284–8
  soldiers—merchant, 340
  suitor—girl, 292–5
  swineherds—shepherd, 341–2
  villain—enticed girl, 107, 113

murder (why?)
  for adultery, 230–51
  for avarice, 25, 33, 43
  for complaining about husband, *see* husband
  for forbidden love, 125–42, 142–8, 223–30
  for jealousy, 292–6
  for not addressing betrothed as such, 149–53, 164–5, 336–7
  for opposed marriage, 125–42, 179–223, 258–63, 292–6, 313–17
  for ritual reasons, *see* building-sacrifice
  for robbery, 284–8, 340–2
  in self-defence, 107–25
  without motive, 281–4, 317–18
musicians, to play till woman dies, 231, 238, 293–5

never, circumlocutions for never, 156, 160, 169–70, 261, 322
numbers, favourite
  three: bells toll 3 times, *see* bell; child cries 3 times to dead mother, 21, 26; choice of death: 3 ways, *see* choice; drops of tears shed upon the dead, 100; glass/gold/white coaches, 3 red flags, in wedding procession, 154, 160, 168, 339; maid sold to 3 suitors, 158–60; 1 year and 3 days, 116; orphans crying for dead mother, *see* orphans; 7 years and 3 days, 281, 305, 332; son crying for mother for 3 days, 3 days and 3 weeks, 116; tree with 3 branches, 3, *see* trees in ballad opening; 3 wolves bring up abandoned child, *see* wolf
  six: birds—reincarnated souls, 112; horses in front of coaches, 23, 157–8, 188, 240, 242, 274; horses in wedding procession, 157–8; maids killed by villain, 107, 112; tree with 6 branches, 112
  seven: bride has waited for betrothed for 7 years and 3 days, 332; candle for 7 tablefuls of guests, in death-riddle, 231, 233, 316; castles promised to lady, 110–11; husband and wife have not eaten or drunk together for 7 years and 3 days, 281; imprisonment for 7 years and 3 days, 305; 'seventh seven land' (*f*), 279; suitor rejected 7 times, 185, 294; villain has killed maids, 7th maid kills villain, 107–9, 113–15; years in prison, 257, 312; years of mourning, 332
  nine: father has 9 daughters, no sons, 344–5; flags in wedding procession, 155, 160, 168
  twelve: candles for 12 tablefuls of guests, in death-riddle, 233; flags in wedding procession, and 12 young men, 160; masons choose sacrificial victim, 19–22; men to help burning wife to death, 233; musicians play while victim dies, 294; queen, mother has 12 daughters, 184

thirteen: in curse, 290; days of imprisonment (without food or drink), 180, 186; victim is 13th daughter, 183
fifteen days of imprisonment, 181, 184
sixteen, bells toll for the dead, 156, 159, 162
sixty: bells toll for the dead, 340; dead bride, mourned over by 60 soldiers, 162; soldiers at wedding, 157–8
nuns, 193
  false, 101
  land of n., 333
nunnery, 130

objects
  speak, *see* garden, brook, plant, saliva
  upon death of or danger to owner, become bloody, 127, 133, 136; become red, 125; become withered, 127, 133, 136; break/tear, 132, 134, 136, 287; fall down, *see* clothes
obstacles
  magic, raised by God, 24, 29, 35
  overcome (beasts, hail, rain of fire, rain of stone, storm, wood), 24, 29
offer, dishonest, made by judge or sheriff, 288
omen (*see also* dreams, life-token, signs), tearing of apron, without wind, without it being caught in anything, 287
orphan(s)
  complaint of o., 83–90, 95–7, 332
  sight of o., in evasive answer, 114
  youngest o. killed by sisters, 342–4
oxen, blessed by the Virgin, 331

paramour, entertained while husband is occupied elsewhere, 230–9
pigeons
  fly on bride's shoulder to announce engagement, 158, 160, 338
  hatched out on lovers' grave curse mother, *see* animals
  reincarnated soul, 25, 27, 35, 113
  warning by p., 23, 35, 113
  white p. sent to maid as engagement present, 158, 160, 338
pipe, grown out of murdered sister's body
  cut open, sister emerges, 344
  denounces murderers, 342–4
plants, sympathetic
  acacia tree, 192, 214–15; chapel flowers, 126, 129; geranium-rosemary, 128; ivy-black grapes, 192; red-white gillyflower, 129; rosemary, two sprigs, 129, 182, 191–2; rosemary and tulip, 129; without any leaves, 129; rosemary without leaves, carnation without stem, 129; tulip with white stripes—tulip with scarlet stripes

plants, sympathetic (*cont.*)
(planted), 100; white lilies, 129 316; white rosemary, 129; white-red marble lily, 129, 144

blood spurts out when someone wants to pluck them, 183, 191, 214

cast curse upon mother who caused their deaths, 126, 129, 191–2, 197, 209, 214, 315

droop when the murderer visits them, straighten up after she has left them, 316

grow on lovers' grave, 100, 126, 128, 129, 134–5, 140, 144, 182, 191–3, 197, 209, 214, 221, 315–16, 321

plucking of, 126, 129, 135, 140, 144, 183, 191–2, 209, 214, 221, 315

speak, 126, 129, 135, 144, 183, 191–2, 316

poor, intermediators to God, 153–4, 173–4

poplars, cursed by the Virgin, 331

prayer, miraculous power of, 24–5, 29, 35, 152–7, 166, 178

pregnancy, with illegitimate child, 179–85, 192–6, 198–201, 263–6

prince, has sun on forehead, moon on chest, 291

prison, dialogue through p. wall, 144–5, 181–2, 186–8, 193–4, 196, 203–6, 257, 290–1, 321; 'Are you alive, or are you dead?' (*f*), 181, 186, 290–1, 322; 'Are you eating, or are you drinking?' (*f*), 180, 186

prisoner
escapes from captivity, 257–8
had not seen the sun and moon for seven years, 257, 307
'I am neither alive, nor dead' (*f*), 180–1, 186, 290–1, 322
state of, 142–4, 305–6

prison-songs, 204–6, 269–70

punishment, 218; for own cruel deed, by fate, 36, 43, 304–7; *see also* murder (how?)

rain, *see* child, obstacles

ransom
sister can r. brother if she spends night with judge, 288–91
wife can r. husband if she sleeps with captain of soldiers, 291–2

raven, 155
r. in dream, 205

ravishment, maid ravished by Turk, 266–72

recognition
by ring, 27, 42
lack of, *see* disguise, identity

regös lays, 70–2, 80–1

reincarnation
as animal, *see* animals
as musical instrument, *see* pipe
as plant, *see* plant

repentance, after cruel deed, 26–7, 192, 234, 259–61, 295, 297, 300, 301–3, 340

rescue, from captivity, 255–8, 307–12

rescuers, joint, quarrel over rescued lady, 255–8

resuscitation, *see* magic wand, pipe
ritual of r., 327

revenant, *see under* dead

riddle
in dream, 346
husband secured by solving r., 346
penalty of death for unsolved r., 346
solved by daughter or father, 346

riddling
choice of death, *see* candle
inquiry, 313

ring
dropped into glass at wedding, 27
recognition by old wedding r., 27, 31, 42
sign of engagement, 158, 160, 338
used as ruse, 28, 30, 32

ritual magic (*see* building-sacrifice), 327

road, in curse, 129

robber bridegroom, 160, 272–81

rose
and death, 215–17, 240, 287, 315
in evasive answers, 189, 207–8, 222, 224–5
murdered daughter-in-law buried in r. garden, 315
r.-decked footbridge—place for execution, 186, 189–90, 207
white r. bush flowers red, red r. bush flowers white, 315

ruse
to capture murderer, 277–8
to detain pursuer, *see* saliva
to immure wife, 25, 28, 30–2
to kill villain, 108, 114–15, 118–22
to win maid, 44–54

sacrifice
animal s. as substitute for humans, 40–1
human s. for appeasing local spirits in building operations, *see* building-sacrifice

St Eustache and St Hubert, stag of, 71, 81

saliva, answers for fugitive, 300, 302

sea
as coffin (*f*), 269–70
roaring—funeral choir (*f*), 269–70
surf—winding sheet (*f*), 269–70

secret
overheard, 240–3, 273–4, 279, 304, 309–12
revealed in lullaby, see Bátori-motif

servant
faithful, 20, 23
false, 23, 24, 27, 34
more charitable than mother, 310–11

Semele-story, 166

sewing, in ballad opening formula, 157, 160, 169, 241–2, 286, 297, 322, 328 shavings, burning, stuck in a piece of bread come to rest in water above drowned body, 267

shepherd, killed, 341–2

shirt
to be blown away by wind (curse), 307
to go up in flames (curse), 310

shoes
red, yellow, in dream, 186, 206
swimming in blood, *see* blood

sign, ominous, 33–4, 133–4, 174; *see also* life-token, omen

sister
elder ss. kill youngest s., 342–4
killed by brother for unchastity, 223–30
love weaker than lover's, 253
sleeps with judge in order to effect release of imprisoned brother, is betrayed, 288–91
sympathetic s. visits s. in prison, 187, 196, 203

skirt, becomes longer at the back, shorter in the front, designating pregnancy (*f*), 179–80, 184, 195, 199–200

sleeping-draught, 267

snake
to be taken out of girl's bosom, often a test of love for blood relatives and lover, 251–4
transformed into a bag of gold, 254

soldier
entices woman, 110, 117, 122
maid goes to war as s., 344–6
overhears maid's complaint, 332

son
blames mother for slaying of sister, 318
dies in mother's home without being recognized, 307–12
poisoned by sister-in-law, or wife of elder male relative, 317–18

song, robbers attracted by s. of maid in the wood, 311

speaking (*see* animals, dead, objects, plants)
'Up and speaks' (*f*), 56–7, 108, 223–4, 257, 264, 269, 282, 285–7, 308–9, 346

speed, formulas for demanding s., 20, 23–4, 29, 35, 126–7, 283, 336–7, 340

spell, *see* charms

stag, *see* regös lays

star
bright star: the beloved, 313
carried by heavenly lamb, 56, 58, 72, 81–2
carried by magic stag of *regös* lays, 71–2, 81–2
carried on forehead, 56, 58, 72, 81–2

stepmother, cruel, 83, 85–90, 97

stone, in curse, 129

strawberry, competition, *see* competition

suicide, 146–7, 210, 245–7, 323–4

suicide formulas
'He drew his sword/dagger, he let himself fall on it', 242, 245, 286–7

'He encircled her for the first time...', 190–1, 221, 246

'He snatches up his big knife, points it at his heart: Let my blood and your blood...', 50, 153, 162, 180, 190–1, 209–14, 218–19, 221–3, 242, 246, 317

'You have died for me, I will die for you', 144, 242, 245–6, 286

sun
beauty of Christ compared to s., 329
carried by magic lamb, 56, 58, 72, 81–2
carried by magic stag, 72, 81
on prince's forehead, 291
prisoner had not seen s. for seven years, 257, 307
reference to father-in-law, 313
rises at Christ's head, 332

survival under impossible circumstances, 27, 31

swineherd/turkey-herd
informs of news in the village, 126, 128, 134
kills shepherd, 341–2
preferred to Turk, as betrothed, 158, 160, 339

symbolism, *see* apple, candle, headdress, knife, rose, Virgin

table
heavenly, set by itself, 59, 68, 78–80, 82
to break, in curse, 129

tailor (dressmaker), blamed for spoiled skirt of pregnant maid, 179–80, 185, 193, 196, 199–200, 219, 221

Tannhäuser motif, 192, 214–15

task, impossible, given to maid—offset by requiring others, preliminary, equally difficult, 346–7

tears
'Are you weeping for...' (*f*), 264–5, 321
awaken villain, 107, 113–14, 117–22
raise the dead, 88, 95
on receiving letter from beloved, 188, 193, 197
in suicide formula, 211
to be concealed, 107, 113–14, 117–22, 273–4, 276–7, 279–80, 301
'Why are you crying?...How should I not cry...' (*f*), 157, 346–7

test of sex, to discover person masquerading as other sex, 344–6

testament, 152, 318, 341–2

thirst, of bride before dying, *see* bride

toad (a crayfish with four legs), as poison, 317

towel, to go up in flames (curse), 129, 290–1

tower, *see* magic

tree
at ballad beginning (*see also* apple-tree), 84, 86, 278
bower in t., 278

tree (*cont.*)
    cursed by the Virgin, *see* poplar
    dead acacia t. thrust into lover's grave comes to leaf, 192, 214–15
    mother leaves abandoned children in t., 301
    murderer's t., 107–8, 113–21
    top of t., as place for coffin, 156
trial, *see* test
truth admitted 'Why do I struggle to deny it?' (*f*), 159, 160, 179–81, 190
turkeys, request to t. to fling themselves on the ground in mourning for owner, 161, 170
turtle doves
    hatched on lovers' grave, 192, 214
    will not perch on green leaves and will not drink of clear water after loss of mate, 333–6

uncharitableness tested, 303–12

victim, intended, kills villain, 107–25
Virgin
    blesses oxen, 331
    as a bride to God or Jesus, 72–5, 78, 80–2
    casts curse upon poplars, etc., 331
    magic wand, 83–4, 90–4, 96–7
    protects orphans, 91–2, 94, 96–7
    resuscitates dead mother, 87, 90–4, 96–7
    seeking shelter to give birth to Jesus, 330–1
    symbols of, 76–82

walking, 'On they go...' (*f*), 20, 23, 47, 285–7, 297–8, 301, 340–1
wands
    golden, 84
    magic, resuscitate the dead, *see* magic
warning, *see* bird, dreams, pigeon, sign
    misinterpreted, *see* dream
water
    clean, becomes turgid or bloody, *see* blood
    drinking of magic stream results in pregnancy, 200–1
    drinking of w. gives appearance of pregnancy, in evasive answer, 179, 184–5, 200–1, 219

to swell (in curse), 129
to turn into blood, *see* blood
wedding
    customs, 67–9, 172–3, 254, 261, 280–1
    interrupted by old bride, 27
    procession, 150–1, 154–5, 157–8, 160, 168, 339
well, of blood, *see* blood
wheat, not to produce (curse), 129
whip, in curse, 186, 206
white, extraordinary w. complexion of suitor, 153–4, 175–6
wife
    adulterous, burned to death, wrapped in linen, covered with pitch, *see* burning
    denies self-compromising words, *see* Bátori-motif
    enticed, *see* elopement
    murdered, *see* husband
    not recognized by husband, *see* disguise
wind
    in curse, 305, 307
    to take care of child, *see* child
window, in ballad opening, 157, 160, 241–2, 286, 297, 338
wine
    corpse (head/heart/liver of) washed in w. (*f*), 86, 96–7, 147, 224, 227, 229–30, 271, 274, 280
    in curse, 129, 305
witch trials, 40
witchcraft, *see* obstacles
wolf, brings up abandoned child, 299–300
woman, disguised as man, *see* disguise
words, magic power of spoken w., 137, 154–7, 166, 258–63, 322
worms, to be eaten up by w. (curse), 271
wound, into which the sun has shone (*f*), 282, 284
wreath
    of virgins (*see also* headdress), 56–7, 59
    swimming in blood, 150, 152, 165, 293–4

youngest
    robber shows pity, 284–7, 340
    wolf shows mercy, 299–300

INDEX OF BALLAD TITLES

Numbers in brackets refer to Child ballads, Hungarian ballads
are shown in italics

Adam Bell (116), 34
Agnes Bernauer, 130–1, 139–40
Alison and Willie (256), 147
Andrew Lammie (233), 132, 169
Anna, 175, 337–8
Anna Betlen, 86, 97–8, 124, 147, 215, 223–30, 247, 319
Anna Molnár, 1–2, 106–25, 235, 280, 300, 319, 321
Les anneaux de Marianson, 163, 165
The Asp, 98, 251–4, 321

Babylon (14), 36, 284
Bagolyasszonyka, 105
Balthasar Bátori, 174, 215–16, 235, 239–48, 319
Barcsai, 1–2, 103, 227, 230–9, 244, 246–8, 280, 313, 316, 321–2, 325
The Baron of Brackley (203), 291
The Battle of Otterburn (161), 33–4
Beautiful Kate Bán, 6, 122–3, 300, 312
La belle se siet au piet de la tour, 146
The Bent sae Brown (71), 291
Bey, Pasha of Buda, 176, 336–7
Den blinde Mand ved Jesu Kors, 330
Bonnie Annie (24), 323
Bonny Baby Livingston (222), 199, 245
Bonny Barbara Allan (84), 147, 166, 209, 245
Bonny Bee Hom (92), 132
The Bonny White Shepherd, 341–2
The Boy who was Murdered, 91, 136, 168, 174
The Braes of Yarrow (214), 33–4, 147, 226–7
The Bridge of Arta, 28
The Brother and the Sister, 296, 307–12
Brown Robin (97), 34, 227
Burd Ellen and Young Tamlane (28), 164, 242

Captain Car (178), 33–4, 147
The Captain's Daughter, 61–7, 79
Child Maurice (83), 147, 243, 324
Child Waters (63), 171
Clement Mason, 1–2, 19–44, 103, 106, 174, 177, 190, 230, 237, 240, 244, 264, 280, 319, 323, 325, 348–9
Clerk Colvill (42), 166, 281
Clerk Saunders (69), 33, 174, 226, 291, 323
The Clerk's Twa Sons (72), 38, 132, 146–7, 199, 227
Conde Claros de Montalvan, 192, 193–204, 209–10, 217–23
The Cruel Brother (11), 38, 166–7, 172, 262, 265, 323

The Cruel Mother (20), 300, 321
The Daughter of the Cruel King, 96, 98, 105, 142–8, 210, 321, 324
The Dead Boy, see The Boy who was Murdered
The Dead Bridegroom, 19, 326–8
The Dishonoured Maiden, 6, 33, 35, 37, 98, 103, 105, 136–7, 152, 161–2, 170, 179–223, 244–6, 248, 261, 280, 291, 317, 319, 321, 323–4
Donna Aldonca, 200–1
Donna Ausenda, 200
The Duke of Athole's Nurse (212), 38

Earl Brand (7), 135, 147, 166, 214, 226, 291, 323–4
Earl Crawford (229), 38
The Earl of Aboyne (235), 147
Edward (13), 37, 200
The Elfin Knight (2), 321, 346
Elvehøj, 215
Elveskud, 281, 293
Engelens Budskab, 59–67
Eppie Morrie (223), 178
Erlinton (8), 257, 291, 311

Fæstemanden i' Graven, 95
Fair Anna Bíró, 37, 215, 245, 284–7, 340
Fair Annie (62), 243, 324
The Fair Flower of Northumberland (9), 145, 257, 321
Fair Janet (64), 132, 174, 178, 226, 245, 324
Fair Maid Julia, 2, 55–82, 105–6, 173, 217, 237, 280, 319, 332–3
Fair Margaret and Sweet William (74), 33, 34, 135, 147
Fair Mary of Wallington (91), 168, 199
La fille du Roi Loys, 145–6
The Founding of Skutari or Skadar, 28
Frændehæven, 291

Gabriel Bátori and Claire Bátori, 105, 176, 246, 338–40
The Gay Goshawk (96), 37, 146, 174
The Girl who was Danced to Death, 1, 6, 98, 136, 165–6, 176, 292–5
The Girl who was Ravished by the Turks I–II, 266–72, 312
Glasgerion (67), 34, 134
'Good Evening, you Rich Innkeeper', 55, 331–2
Graf Friedrich, 162, 166–7, 170–2, 261–2

The Great Mountain Robber, 37, 86, 97, 184, 215–16, 227, 230, 233, 235–9, 243–4, 248, 272–81, 340

Halewijn, 109–25, 227, 235, 243

Herr Karl paa Ligbaare, 49

Herr Medelvold, 215

Herr Tønne af Alsø, 215

Herr Truels' Døttre, 284

Hildebrand og Hille, 163, 165

Hind Etin (41), 242

Hind Horn (17), 31, 132–4, 141

Hustru og Mands Moder, 215

Ilona Budai, or The Cruel Mother, 1, 7, 19, 122, 217, 240, 242, 296–300, 319, 321

Iver Lang, 215

James Harris (243), 167, 175, 327

Jamie Douglas (204), 175

Jellon Grame (90), 291

Jesus og Jomfru Maria, 329–30

Jock o the Side (187), 291

Johnie Cock (114), 35

Johnie Scot (99), 37, 199

Joli Tambour, 51

Kate Kádár, 35, 91, 98, 104–5, 124–42, 147–8, 174, 207, 209–10, 214, 217, 219, 291, 317, 319

Katharina Jaffray (221), 199

King Arthur and King Cornwall (30), 291

King Estmere (60), 227

King John and the Bishop (45), 321, 346

The King's Dochter Lady Jean (52), 36, 164, 166, 227, 242, 323

Kinmont Willie (186), 291

Klosterranet No. 5, 281

Der König von Mailand, 192–9, 202–4, 209–10, 214, 217, 220, 222

Ladislav Fehér, 1, 6, 148, 288–92

Lady Albert Nagy-Bihal, or The Mother of the Rich Woman, 7, 217, 243, 296, 303–7, 310–12, 319

Lady Alice (85), 147, 209

Lady Diamond (269), 132, 144–8, 321

Lady Isabel and the Elf-Knight (4), 36–7, 107, 111–25, 242, 321

Lady Maisry (65), 34, 37, 132, 134, 178, 192, 199, 209–10, 226, 244, 321–2

The Lady of Arngosk (224), 178

The Laily Worm (36), 37, 243

The Laird of Wariston (194), 36

Lamkin (93), 34–5, 133, 348–9

The Lass of Roch Royal (76), 33–4, 36, 134, 209, 245, 263, 323

Leesome Brand (15), 103–5, 163, 165–72, 257, 265, 323

Lenore, 175, 327–8

Liden Kirstins Dans, 293

The Little Maple Tree, 342

Little Musgrave and Lady Barnard (81), 134, 235, 238–9, 244, 321, 324, 349

Little Sophie Kálnoki, 35, 281–4

Lizzie Wan (51), 36–7, 169, 323

Lord Derwentwater (208), 37, 133

Lord Ingram and Chiel Wyet (66), 132, 134, 168, 178, 199

Lord Livingston (262), 33, 43, 147

Lord Lovel (75), 134, 147, 199, 209, 245

The Lord of Lorn (271), 34–5, 243

Lord Randal (12), 87, 166, 169, 221, 296, 317, 321

Lord Saltoun and Auchanachie (239), 132

Lord Thomas and Fair Annet (73), 35, 173, 245, 291

Lord Thomas Stuart (259), 33

Lord William (254), 37, 134, 199

Die Losgekaufte, 251

The Maid and Her Goose, 255

The Maid Freed from the Gallows (95), 98, 251, 321

The Maid under the Apple Tree, 332–3

The Maid who was Cursed, 217, 258–63, 265, 321

The Maid who was Danced to Death, see The Girl who . . .

The Maid who was Sold I–IV, 6, 37–8, 91, 103, 105–6, 148–78, 183, 188, 206–9, 217–19, 222–3, 235, 239, 242, 246, 248, 262–3, 265–7, 270–1, 312, 321, 324–5

Mary Hamilton (173), 36–7, 280–1

Merika, or The Daughter-in-law who was Burnt to Death, 37, 215, 217, 296, 313–17

Miorita, 341

The Miraculous dead, 19, 44–54, 217, 319, 321

Moderen under Mulde, 87, 94

The Mother's Malison (216), 34, 43, 132, 262, 321, 323

Den myrdede Hustru, 281

Old Robin of Portingale (80), 235

Our Goodman (274), 234, 237

La Pernette, 146

Pocheronne, 317

Poisoned John, 217, 221, 296, 317–18, 321

La Povera Cecilia, 289

The Prince and the Princess, 291–2, 311

Prince Heathen (104), 163–5, 170–2, 242, 321

Prince Robert (87), 132, 147, 199

Queen Eleanor's Confession (156), 243

The Rantin Laddie (240), 37, 199

Rare William Drowned in Yarrow (215), 33–4, 132

INDEX OF BALLAD TITLES

Redesdale and Wise William (246), 227
Ridderen i Fugleham, 63
Riddles wisely expounded (1-2), 321, 346
The Ring and the Veil, 130
Ritter und Magd, 192, 195-9, 210
Rob Roy (225), 178

Schlangenköchin, 221
Sheath and Knife (16), 103-5
Sir Cawline (61), 34, 146
Sir Hugh, or The Jew's Daughter (155), 37, 80
Sir John Butler (165), 33-4
Sir Patrick Spens (58), 2, 37, 43, 125, 227, 323
The Soldier Girl, 344-6
The Sultan's Daughter, 60-7, 79
Sweet William's Ghost (77), 164, 242, 291
Szilágyi and Hagymási, 13, 145, 255-8, 307, 312, 321

Tam Lin (39), 242
Thomas Magyarósi, 263-5
The Three Orphans, 19, 37, 55, 82-97, 227, 230, 280, 319
The Three Ravens (26), 147
The Three Robber Lads, 340-1

Les Tristes Noces, 293
The Turtle-Dove, 333-6
The Twa Brothers, (49) 37, 169, 200
The Twa Knights (268), 163, 227
The Twa Sisters (10), 135, 342, 344
The Two Royal Children, 98-107, 319, 322

The Unquiet Grave (78), 133-4

The Virgin Mary Set Out, 55, 328-30

Walter Lesly (296), 178
When the Virgin Mary was Walking, 55, 330-1
Willie and Earl Richard's Daughter (102), 33
Willie and Lady Maisry (70), 147, 291
Willie o Douglas Dale (101), 199
Willie o Winsbury (100), 144
Willie's Lyke Wake (25), 44, 48, 51-2, 174, 209, 321

Young Beicham (53), 31, 145, 257
Young Hunting (68), 37
Young Johnstone (88), 33, 134, 227, 245
Young King Matthias, 321, 346-7
Young Peggy (298), 244

INDEX OF AUTHORS

Abafi, L., 2
Afzélius, A. A., *see* Geijer, E. G.
Alecsandri, V., 130
Andree, A., 39
Anonymous, 8, 9, 10, 72
Arany, J., 2
Arany, L., 327
Arnim, L.-Brentano, C., 61, 66, 101

Backman, E. L., 216
Balassi, B., 138
Balla, P., 4
Bandello, M., 130, 132
Baring-Gould, S., 39
Bartalus, A., 3, 100, 127, 273
Bartók, B., 3–4, 109, 183–4, 254
Bartók, B.-Kodály, Z., 22, 46, 83–4, 109, 127, 143, 231, 241, 254, 263, 273, 284, 303, 328, 331
Bartsch, K., 15
Benedek, E., 3
Benkő, K., 101, 104
Benkő, L., 178
Berze Nagy, J., 34, 84, 114, 133, 183–4, 210, 259, 332, 336, 338
Bethlen, J., 228
Boccaccio, G., 130, 132, 144–5, 147–8
Bonaventura, St, 73
Bonfini, A., 11
Bornemissza, P., 289, 329
Brand, J., 174
Brewster, P. G., 344
Briz, F. P., 193

Child, F. J. (see ballad titles), 48, 52, 120, 146, 170, 327–8
Cossio, J. M.-Solano, T. M., 235
Crawley, A. E., 39
Crooke, W., 39
Csanádi, I.-Vargyas, L., 7, 22, 33–4, 38, 42–3, 46, 57, 62, 83–4, 100, 105, 109, 127, 143, 149, 162–3, 171, 183, 201, 205, 225, 231–2, 241, 254–5, 257, 259, 261–2, 266, 269–70, 272–3, 284, 289, 296, 300, 303, 307, 313, 317, 320, 328, 330–7, 340, 342
Csáth, D., 13
Csoma codex, 256

D'Ancona, M. L., 76, 79
Dános, E., 21, 59, 64, 192, 199, 237
Deák, F., 40–1
Demkó, K., 218
Domokos, P. P., 3, 22, 46, 57, 59, 61–7, 70, 76, 83–4, 109, 149, 184, 254, 273, 281, 300, 313, 342

Domokos, P. P.-Rajeczky, B., 69, 83, 109, 184, 273, 300, 313, 333, 342
Dömötör, T., 71
Doncieux, G., 269
Dronke, P., 74–5

Eckhardt, S., 333
Elek, O., 133
Elliot, K., 243
Entwistle, W. J., 27, 29, 42, 87, 92, 95, 135–6, 146, 221, 341
Enyedi, Gy., 147–8
Erdélyi, J., 1, 22, 333
Erk, L.-Böhme, F. M., 60–1, 79, 87, 131, 162, 194–5

Fabó, B., 106
Faragó, J.-Jagamas, J., 3, 22, 46, 57, 83–4, 109, 127, 254, 271–3, 300, 307, 312–13, 333, 344, 346

Galeotto, M., 11
Garrett, A., 193
Geibel, E.-Schack, A. F., 235
Geijer, E. G.-Afzélius, A. A., 60
von Gennep, A., 93
Geoffrey of Monmouth, 39
Gerard of Wales, 71
Gerold, Th., 145–6
Gesta Romanorum, 234
Goldziher, I., 39
Gomme, G. L., 39, 133
Gragger, R., 59, 256
Greguss, A., 3, 245, 319
Greig, G., 167
Grozescu, J., 2
Grundtvig, S., 49, 59, 63, 87, 94–5, 121, 163, 165, 215, 281, 291, 329
Gyulai, P., 228, 245

Hardung, V. E., 193, 200
Haupt, L.-Schmaler, J. E., 89
Hermann, I., 320
Hirn, Y., 73, 78, 80
Hodgart, M. J. C., 80
Hofmann, C., *see* Wolf, F.
Holkot, R., 40
Hondorff, A., 138
Honti, J., 256
Horváth, J., 70
Horváth, S., 333
Hrvatska, M., 31

Illéssy, J., 288
Ilosvai Selymes, P., 228

Jagamas, J., *see* Faragó, J.

Kalevala, 49, 137
Kallós, Z., 4
Kálmány, L., 3, 21, 50, 83–4, 87, 92, 137, 149, 175, 183–4, 205, 214, 222, 251, 254–5, 259, 266–8, 291, 293, 300, 307, 329, 337
Kanyaró, F., 228
Katona, L., 62
Kerényi, Gy., 22, 311
Kertész, M., 215
Kézai, S., 9
Király, Gy., 130, 138
Kiss, A., 173
Kodály, Z., 3–4, 7, 50, 69, 71, 77, 83–4, 173, 261, 270; *see also* Bartók, B.-Kodály, Z.
Kodály, Z.-Vargyas, L., 22, 46, 83–4, 109, 127, 143, 149, 183, 231, 241, 254, 257, 263, 273
Köhler, R., 50
Komáromy, A., 40, 218
Korompay, B., 256–7
Kriza, J., 1–3, 19, 21–2, 57, 84, 100, 109, 127, 143, 149, 183, 225, 231–2, 241, 255, 257, 263, 273, 286, 296, 305, 307, 317, 333, 340
Kropf, L., 288
Küchenthal, P., 73

Lajtha, L., 3
Larned, M. D., 256
Liebrecht, F., 49
Lochendorf, A., 334
Lorca, F. G., 217
Lord, A. B., 239
Lübke, H., 29
Lükő, G., 4

Mackensen, L., 344
Male, E., 73, 79
Master, P., *see* Anonymous
Meiss, M., 79
Meyer, G., 50

Nennius, 40
Nygard, H. O., 109, 111–12, 117, 119–21, 123, 243, 280

Orbán, B., 3
Ortutay, Gy., vii, 4, 21–2, 27, 33, 46, 57, 59, 78, 83–4, 86–7, 92, 100, 109, 127, 143, 149, 169, 171, 183, 188, 192, 201–2, 205, 225, 231–2, 241, 251, 254–5, 259, 261, 263, 269, 273, 281, 284, 291, 296, 298, 300, 303, 305, 307, 313, 317, 320, 333–5, 337, 340–42
Ovid, 101, 166

Pais, D., vii, 11
Pálóczy-Horváth, A., 251, 254
Pap, Gy, 149, 293
Pohl, E., 251

Raby, F. J. E., 74, 77
Radloff, W., 210, 332
Rajeczky, B., *see* Domokos, P. P.-Rajeczky, B., 3
Reguly, A., 9
Rosenmüller, E., 101, 105

Sallustius, *see* Bethlen, J.
Sartori, P., 39
Schack, F., *see* Geibel, E.
Schimurski, V., 193–4, 204
Schmaler, J. E., *see* Haupt
Schram, F., 22, 46, 83, 127, 183, 232, 318
Schuller, J. K., 40
Sebesi, J., 3
Sebestyén, Gy., 70
Shire, H. M., 104, 165, 243, 349
Sidney, Sir Philip, 12–14
Simrock, K., 65
Solano, T. M., *see* Cossio, J. M.
Solymossy, S., vii, 2, 27, 29–32, 57, 344
Straparola, 130, 132
Stutz, E., 194
Sunnenburg, Meister Friedrich, 73–4
Széll, F., 131, 345

Thury, J., 256
Tímár, K., 40
Tinódi, S., 228

Varga, J., 256
Vargyas, L., *see also* Csanádi, I.-Vargyas, L. and Kodály, Z.-Vargyas, L., 3–4, 13, 27–8, 30–2, 41, 48, 50–1, 87, 95, 121, 163, 213–14, 236–7, 257, 266, 268, 284, 293, 298, 311, 317, 320, 332–3, 344
Vasady codex, 256
Veress, S., 4
Vikár, B., 3, 57
Vloberg, M., 76, 80
Voragine, J., 39, 330

Waldau, A., 50
Waley, A., 202, 214
Wenzel codex, 96
Werbőczi, I., 237
Westermarck, E. A., 39
Widter, F. G.-Wolf, A., 289
Wolf, F., 288
Wolf, F.-Hofmann, C., 193